Beneath the Ivory Tower

UNIVERSITY PRESS OF FLORIDA

Florida A&M University, Tallahassee
Florida Atlantic University, Boca Raton
Florida Gulf Coast University, Ft. Myers
Florida International University, Miami
Florida State University, Tallahassee
New College of Florida, Sarasota
University of Central Florida, Orlando
University of Florida, Gainesville
University of North Florida, Jacksonville
University of South Florida, Tampa
University of West Florida, Pensacola

Beneath the Ivory Tower

The Archaeology of Academia

EDITED BY

RUSSELL K. SKOWRONEK AND KENNETH E. LEWIS

Foreword by Lou Anna K. Simon

University Press of Florida

Gainesville/Tallahassee/Tampa/Boca Raton

Pensacola/Orlando/Miami/Jacksonville/Ft. Myers/Sarasota

Printed in the United States of America on acid-free paper

21 20 19 18 17 16 6 5 4 3 2 1

First cloth printing, 2010
First paperback printing, 2016

Library of Congress Cataloging-in-Publication Data
Beneath the ivory tower: the archaeology of academia/edited by Russell K. Skowronek and Kenneth E. Lewis; foreword by Lou Anna K. Simon.
p. cm.
Includes bibliographical references and index.
ISBN 978-0-8130-3422-5 (cloth: alk. paper)
ISBN 978-0-8130-6216-7 (pbk.)
1. Universities and colleges—United States—History. 2. College environment—United States—History. 3. Excavations (Archaeology)—United States. I. Skowronek, Russell K. II. Lewis, Kenneth E.
LA226.B435 2010
378.73099–dc22 2009038762

The University Press of Florida is the scholarly publishing agency for the State University System of Florida, comprising Florida A&M University, Florida Atlantic University, Florida Gulf Coast University, Florida International University, Florida State University, New College of Florida, University of Central Florida, University of Florida, University of North Florida, University of South Florida, and University of West Florida.

University Press of Florida
15 Northwest 15th Street
Gainesville, FL 32611-2079
http://www.upf.com

To the memory of Delton L. Scudder, former chair of the Department of Religion at the University of Florida, an educator whose wit, understanding, and tireless devotion provided guidance for the institution he served as well as for those fortunate enough to have crossed paths with him.

For Major McCollough of the Tennessee Valley Authority, for planting the seed for this book at the 1999 Heritage Resource Management in the College and University Environment Conference.

For Helen Wyszpolski Skowronek (January 29, 1921 – June 14, 2012)—New York University Class of 1942; malaria researcher at Goldwater Memorial Hospital, 1942–46; soil analyst at North Carolina State University, 1946–47; hematology researcher at Memorial Sloan-Kettering Cancer Institute, 1947–49; and teacher in New Jersey, Colorado, California, and Illinois and for the United States Information Service in Medan, Indonesia—who instilled a love for learning. For her, education was a lifelong endeavor.

And for Melissa K. Johnson, who helped make this book a reality. She is the future of archaeology.

Contents

Illustrations

Figures

Tables

Foreword

The Importance of the Past in the University of the Future

As president of Michigan State University (MSU), I saw the excavation of Saints' Rest, MSU's first dormitory, as a wonderful opportunity to connect with the past in a scholarly way. It was not until the completion of the dig, however, that I fully realized its importance. The archaeological dig combined the social and hard sciences; engaged students, faculty, staff, and the community; brought history to life; and formed a connection between the present and the past. I hope other campuses are fortunate enough to have a similar experience.

Learning about history through the remains helped to form associations with the past and created a sense of heritage in the modern campus and community. The excavation made it possible for us to hold a piece of history in our hands and reflect on its significance. Archaeology is the tangible link to those who came before us. The findings provided insights into years gone by and allowed the university to anticipate the challenges that it might face in the coming years.

Because the site fell victim to a fire in 1876 and was immediately leveled, we had no clear idea of what we would find. The information recovered added archaeological research to archival material, however, offering a more complete portrait of early student life on MSU's campus.

Benjamin Franklin once said: "Tell me and I forget. Teach me and I remember. Involve me and I learn." The Saints' Rest project accomplished just that. The enthusiasm of the dig was contagious and entertaining. I regularly visited the site and found it exciting to view the dig and learn about our history; I especially enjoyed engaging with the students and watching their quest for answers about the past. The community involvement through active learning reinforced the value of archaeology. The university and community also gained a real appreciation for the methodology involved in the project from observing the dig firsthand. Through Saints' Rest, the precise and time-consuming nature of fieldwork became evident to those of us not familiar with the process. Our diligence proved, or in some cases disproved, prior theories about campus life.

From a campus planning standpoint, we became aware that there is a university above and below the ground. As a university, we need to act more purposefully in terms of how we preserve our areas of archaeological importance. Because of this realization, a designated representative will be invited to participate on the planning teams of future projects that may have archaeological significance. The representative will ensure that archaeologically sensitive areas can be identified early in the planning process and protected from a disturbance when appropriate.

This experience reinforced our university's rich heritage, which requires more than reading books and manuscripts to understand. Saints' Rest has taught us that archaeology can enhance or call into question what we have learned from documents. As with archaeology involving ancient civilizations, campus archaeology reveals valuable information. The insights gained from this dig will help us to understand our place in the past as we look ahead to our place in the future.

Lou Anna K. Simon
President, Michigan State University

Preface

At noon the sun's rays slant through the canopy formed by the trees. Leaves are drying and rapidly changing to hues of red and gold. Still warm days evaporate the frost that has begun to coat the landscape. Anticipation of new beginnings hangs ripe in the air alongside the smell of new shoes and notebooks and freshly sharpened pencils. On Friday nights and Saturday afternoons thousands of voices create rumbling roars that echo across campuses and neighborhoods. Loudspeakers and radio and television announcers extol the heritage and tradition of the venerable teams and institutions that have come to do battle. In the United States the annual autumn migration back to school has begun.

For nearly three and a half centuries before Rod Stewart crooned in his 1971 song "Maggie May" that it was time to return to school in the early days of autumn, the youth of English-speaking America repeated this ritual. In so doing they created an idealized picture of education not simply as a process but as a place or a backdrop for examining commonly shared experiences.

Libraries are replete with campus histories. Most were written at the time of significant anniversaries, like those of our own institutions (Beal 1915; Giacomini and McKevitt 2000; Kuhn 1955; McKevitt 1979; Skowronek 2002; Widder 2005) and largely represent institutional histories. That is, they are meant to celebrate the development of larger institutions and focus on its broader scale. By necessity, they are less concerned with the daily lives of the students and faculty who lived and interacted on the campus. Institutional histories also rely heavily on documents, whose contents tend to be biased toward "accepted" behaviors and activities rather than all behaviors. Because they lack other sources, they often omit significant information about the past.

This book is the first of its kind in the field of archaeology. While many archaeologists have excavated both prehistoric and historic sites that are buried beneath campuses, very few have examined the material evidence of earlier lifeways associated with the schools themselves. The contributors to this volume have recognized that such investigations are an opportunity not only to examine the changing face of their home institution and so understand both legal and illicit behavior but at the same time to train students in the nuances of archaeology and celebrate campus history. What can we learn from studying the tangible remains of the world of academia? Can we discern patterns in the material record? Will they confirm old stereotypes or contradict popularly and institutionally created "stories" about campus life?

Recognizing Educational Stereotypes

When we consider how "school" has been depicted in novels, plays, television, and film we can see certain trends that resonate across generations. One-room schoolhouses described by Mark Twain, Lucy Maud Montgomery, and Laura Ingalls Wilder instill in the reader a sense of how, in the rudest of settings, the antipathy of some students was countered by others in their successful quest for knowledge.

Since the 1940s secondary schools have been a staple setting for examining the many issues associated with teenagers coming of age and the changing American moral, social, and technological landscape. From the light comedy of *Our Miss Brooks* and *The Many Loves of Dobie Gillis* in the 1950s and 1960s to the gritty high schools of New York, Los Angeles, and Portland, we find teachers in *Up the Down Staircase* (1967), *Room 222* (1969–74), *Mr. Holland's Opus* (1995), and *The Bill Cosby Show* (1969–71) sharing their passion for their respective subject areas. Their audience consists of seemingly uninspired and unmotivated students who seem more akin to the Sweathogs of *Welcome Back, Kotter* (1975–79) than to the imaginative Anne Shirley (*Anne of Green Gables*) of an earlier generation.

Colleges are depicted very differently in popular media. Sports are a favorite topic. Films like *Knute Rockne, All American* (1940) and *Rudy* (1993) helped shape the image of Notre Dame football. Similarly, *Glory Road* (2006) captured the excitement of a basketball team overcoming racism to win the National Collegiate Athletic Association championship.

Life in the academy is often shown as petty and dysfunctional, as a place where the adage "Never have so many fought so hard for so little" rings all too true. From Kingsley Amis' novel *Lucky Jim* (1954) to Edward Albee's play *Who's Afraid of Virginia Woolf?* (1962), Richard Russo's book *Straight Man* (1997), or the short-lived television program *The Education of Max Bickford* (2001–2) we find disillusioned university professors who are trying to negotiate their way through the arbitrary and capricious world of academe, only to find that they have lost touch with their families, students, colleagues, and research. And who can forget the memorable Oxford dons with whom Inspector Morse must cross paths and match wits as he and Sergeant Lewis delve into the arcane, twisted, and often dark side of academic politics and practices?

From the perspective of those outside academia higher education is filled with out-of-touch administrators and "egg-headed" faculty members. And how are students portrayed? In their short *Violent Is the Word for Curly* (1938) the Three Stooges are mistaken for visiting professors at "Mildew College." They not only teach the all-female student body the song "Swingin' the Alphabet" but also show the administration that sports should be part of campus life. In *Sweetheart of the Campus* (1941) Ozzie Nelson, Ruby Keeler, and Harriet Hilliard save "Lambert Technical College" from closing through a combination of winning football and a swinging nightclub. Befuddled professors wearing pince-nez are made fools of in class, and female students say they will take any class that would leave their evenings free.

Since then films like *National Lampoon's Animal House* (1978) and Rodney Dangerfield and Greg Fields' *Back to School* (1986) and books like Tom Wolfe's *I Am Charlotte Simmons* (2004) have focused on the drinking and sexual escapades of the student body. Faculty members are often oblivious to these activities and yet may be the focus of infatuations, as was Professor Henry "Indiana" Jones, Jr., in *Raiders of the Lost Ark* (1981). The public image of academia and those who inhabit it is distorted and leaves a great deal to be desired. But the printed word, film, and digital recording are not the only chronicles of higher education.

Beyond Stereotypes

In this book we examine the material record of the academic past to explore its form and address its meaning. The authors go beyond broad stereotypes to tell some of the rediscovered stories of life on some of America's most venerable colleges. The book also asks tough questions about balancing the past with present needs and the conflict that arises when a school embraces idealized concepts about "tradition" and "history" while actively destroying the evidence of that history. This is a book that honors enlightened alumni, faculty, administrators, and community members who recognize the value of celebrating campus and thus local history and who see education taking place not only in the classroom but across the landscape of the campus.

The bell is ringing. Time to go to class.

Russell K. Skowronek
Edinburg, Texas
Kenneth E. Lewis
East Lansing, Michigan

Acknowledgments

We must thank many individuals for bringing this volume together. First, we wish to thank President Lou Anna K. Simon of Michigan State University for providing the thoughtful foreword for the volume. Presidents like Dr. Simon who recognize the value of the traditions and heritage of their campuses have a special place in the hearts of their alumni, students, faculty, and larger community.

We are also indebted to our colleagues who shared their insights into the archaeology and history of their respective campuses. Many are old friends and treasured senior colleagues. All have laid a precedent-setting foundation in this volume. We hope its publication will support not only their ongoing work but that of future researchers on college and school campuses throughout the world.

Within our programs we are indebted to our colleagues in our academic home departments at Michigan State and Santa Clara Universities. We specifically thank Dr. Lynne Goldstein of Michigan State for her active support of this work and Christopher Valvano for the care and skill that went into the production of the line drawings in Chapter 2. At Santa Clara University we gratefully acknowledge the support of the Archaeology Research Lab and the offices of the president, the provost, and the dean of arts and sciences. Gail Gradowski, the librarian in Santa Clara's Orradre Library, helped with the initial research on American education and has always been a big supporter. At the eleventh hour Elwood Mills of Santa Clara University Media Services finalized many of the figures that appear in this book. God bless him.

Thanks are due acquisitions editor Eli Bortz and editor John Byram of the University Press of Florida for their encouragement and enthusiasm for this project. Thanks also to the individuals who reviewed the original manuscript. Their insights made it all the better. We gratefully acknowledge the excellent copyediting of the book by Kathy Burford Lewis.

Last, we reserve our greatest thanks for Melissa K. Johnson, a double-major in anthropology and history at Santa Clara University, whose eye for detail brought this volume together. We could never have done it without her.

1

Introduction

The Archaeology of Academia

KENNETH E. LEWIS

Some years ago, when I was an undergraduate at the University of Florida, an article appeared in the campus newspaper, the *Alligator*, announcing the discovery of two large anchors lying beneath the shrubbery surrounding one of the older buildings. Apparently no one had known of their existence at the time, and the appearance of these large and rather conspicuous artifacts seemed as unexpected as the unearthing of an Egyptian tomb. Within a day's time an explanation arose. The anchors had been placed there in association with the building's former use, and, perhaps because their size made them too difficult to move, they disappeared beneath the fast-growing subtropical vegetation. And that was that: consultation with knowledgeable authorities had revealed a logical explanation for a misplaced assemblage belonging to the recent archaeological record. But the mystery surrounding this accidental discovery has a significance beyond this minor lapse of memory. Its occurrence speaks to a larger phenomenon that is far from unique to this time or place: the absent, or at least the unconsciously suppressed, collective memory of institutional histories and the resulting ignorance of their past.

I suspect that those of us who have attended large institutions of higher learning since the 1960s have at one time or another felt ourselves swallowed up by the enormity of an organization that seems not only anonymous but timeless as well: a place with no past, no future—only an uncertain and sometimes anxious present that revolves around courses and activities in the here and now. Each class is different; each term is separate; people come and go. Only after we have been there a while do we find formal and informal groups with whom we share interests and among whom we feel comfortable. Devoted to service, social activities, or discipline-based interests, these organizations form the basis of our social networks during our residence and often afterward. As satisfying as these associations may be, they do not seem to bring about a similar connection with the larger academic institution; nor do they provoke a knowledge of its history. When we acknowledge that such a collegiate past exists, it is usually portrayed in vague, distorted terms: as a false, almost Disney-like reality, populated by peculiar objects and quaint people associated with events that are far removed from our own experience with which we find it difficult if not impossible to identify.

Why does this perception prevail? What is it about a university that isolates its residents from their institutional past? Perhaps this derives from the transiency of our presence and the perception that we are here only as a step on the way to a future somewhere else. Or maybe the rapid expansion and diversification of university programs and the growth of their physical infrastructure in the last half of the twentieth century made their earlier existence and the material things associated with it irrelevant to those who had no connection with them. It seems that the past of the university is often only the past that we remember, not the past belonging to those who came before us.

Our reticence to inquire into the pasts of large academic institutions may also be derived from the manner in which they are represented in popular culture. Colleges, universities, and secondary schools have long been the setting for popular fiction, and images from novels, movies, and television programs have shaped our notions about academic life and the people, activities, and traditions associated with them. We are all familiar with portrayals as varied as *Tom Brown's Schooldays*, *The Many Loves of Dobie Gillis*, *The Paper Chase*, and *National Lampoon's Animal House*. As comforting or unsatisfying as we may find them, these stories, like our own experiences, are set in time. They are tales of people, not of places; the institution more often than not provides a static and sometime stereotyped setting, a backdrop for more important actors. In themselves, schools do not seem to be that interesting.

Despite the general lack of awareness of institutional history, the collection of information about the academy's past has not been neglected by scholars and other writers of nonfiction. Most colleges and universities have been the subject of one or more official histories detailing their progressive growth, celebrated events, the development of programs and policies, and the influence and accomplishments of notable people associated with the institution. Often they are handsomely published volumes, released with a great fanfare; yet they seldom become best-sellers. Perhaps their lack of wide popularity lies partly in the nature of the phenomenon they set out to examine. Institutional histories are not accounts of attempts to achieve simple, straightforward, clearly defined goals, such as winning an athletic contest. Instead, they offer an encyclopedic account of the unfolding of many concurrent and intertwined efforts whose course is difficult to follow; consequently they fail to capture and maintain the attention of readers. These efforts directed at multiple goals lack the excitement of sport, and their successes are often difficult to recognize. Therefore the achievements of institutional endeavors frequently go unnoticed; the results derived from them are taken for granted and remain unappreciated. Although unsung, these achievements are worthy of note. Identifying them and explaining their significance, however, requires that their stories be told in a manner that will allow us to recognize and showcase the elements that shaped the course of academic institutions within the anonymous complexity of the organizations. Such an approach should attempt to construct integrated topical analyses that focus on the roles of key institutional elements relative to issues whose importance extends beyond their boundaries.

Investigating academia's past requires more than an account of policies, personalities, and places. If we are to understand an institution's development, we cannot examine these elements by themselves. They can be approached only as components of larger phenomena that serve as topics that evoke questions. Exploring such questions requires that we recognize the place of the research topic within the broader institutional milieu and be aware of those processes that affect it. In addition, it is also imperative that we acknowledge the physical structure in which all the activities of the institution take place. It forms a larger spatial context that is more than just the place where events occurred. It is also a record of the activities that took place and their chronological arrangement, as well as a reflection of the motives and ideas that led people to engage in them. The histories of colleges and universities are recorded in the arrangement and composition of the artifact assemblages, buildings, thoroughfares, monuments, and decorative plantings as well as the spaces between them. Collectively these elements form a landscape that constitutes a physical record of the institution's past and the influences that shaped its evolution.

The elements of academic landscapes provide an unwritten record of activities associated with the populations that resided on colleges and universities or used their facilities. If we assume that these activities reflected the functions of the settlements that encompassed them and that their patterning shaped the larger landscape, then we may anticipate that the form, layout, and composition of the landscapes of an academic institution will not only identify its function but provide a record of the processes that affected it over time. The elements of landscape are, of course, easily discernible on the surface, in the presence and arrangement of dormitories, classroom buildings, laboratories, gymnasiums, offices and service structures, sports complexes, sidewalks, and gardens. Their architecture and arrangement identify the nature of the institution as well as the activities they house. Their size, prominence, and state of repair reflect factors such as their relative order of construction, their roles, and their importance. The landscape also reveals change in response to the continuous modernization of campuses. Much of the evidence of this landscape is no longer visible above ground and may be accessed only through excavation. Consequently, an examination of the archaeological record is an important part of reconstructing and analyzing landscape history.

When we observe the landscapes of academic institutions, we are immediately struck by their size and the need to adopt the scale of our inquiry to the elements of the landscape appropriate to our questions. As archaeologists, we are limited in how we can carry out our work. We cannot dig anywhere or everywhere. The nature and cost of archaeology place further limits on the extent to which excavations can be conducted. As a result, almost all archaeological investigations are a compromise between what we would like to do and what we can. But lack of access to the entire site of a building or insufficient time or funding to examine it completely does not mean that these features cannot be investigated or that we cannot ask meaningful questions about the past on the basis of material evidence. Rather, it obliges us to frame our questions on a scale suitable to the data at hand. The authors of the following chapters were faced with the need to tailor their work in response to constraints imposed by outside factors, yet all overcame these obstacles by identifying research questions and constructing research designs that could be implemented under the existing conditions.

The chapters in this volume do not attempt to construct the histories of institutions; these questions are too broad and perhaps more suitable to other forms of inquiry. Instead, the authors have chosen to focus on problems related to more specific issues, such as the nature of student life and accommodations, architectural form and function, medical ethics, sanitary reforms, social control, "forbidden" activities, the construction of sport facilities, and the power of images of the past in constructing present reality. Answering these questions will not replace traditional institutional histories, but it will oblige us to see them in a new light. The scale of the inquiry does not equate with the significance of its results.

The studies presented in this book explore different aspects of the academic past through an examination of the sites of structures and activities associated with academic institutions across the United States. The projects from which these works emerged resulted from different circumstances. Some were carried out as a result of research or to preserve or interpret campus features, while others assessed the impact of construction or other modern acts of disturbance. These chapters are diverse in their geographical distribution as well as their scope. We have organized them according to three general themes that encompass the broad range of topics approachable through an analysis of the material record. The first group examines the nature of the archaeological record of sites occupied by literate societies. The studies included here ask basic questions about what the record consists of, how it is configured, what condition it is in, and how it can identify the components of academic settlements. But they address larger questions about how analyses of that record can inform us about past events and lifeways and the processes that link them to its creation. They also introduce the topic of archaeology in a campus setting and speak to the larger issue of the university's role in historic preservation.

The second group contains studies of past life at academic institutions. Employing archaeological research, the authors of these chapters examine material evidence of life on college campuses in times past. Ranging from seventeenth-century Harvard to twentieth-century William and Mary, material remains and their arrangement in space are shown to be a key element in shedding light on aspects of student life of which we are otherwise only vaguely aware.

The final group explores the role of archaeology on campus and how it relates to the university as an evolving institution. The authors also address the role of archaeology in defining the university's position in the larger community. Archaeology has many products and can serve numerous constituencies. The discipline fulfills its normal research function on campus; but because the past of its parent institution is the subject of investigation, archaeology also takes on a wider responsibility of interpreting that past within the context of existing traditions and practical demands dictated by present circumstances and future needs.

The contents of this volume make it clear that the archaeology of academia is hardly a coherent research topic with a fixed research agenda and a single theoretical stance. This was not our intent. Rather, we hope to present it as an additional arena in which to explore the kinds of questions that archaeologists have begun to ask about the recent American past. Since the colonial period, academic institutions have been an integral part of life in what became the United States and reflected the evolution of the larger society that gave rise to them. Examining their material remains has the potential to let us observe the broader, rapidly changing, increasingly complex, and often unstable milieu in microcosm and examine how it manifested itself through its institutional organization and structure. These studies illustrate directions for such research and provide examples of its potential.

I

The Process of Identifying the "Educational World" in the Archaeological Record

When archaeology is mentioned in connection with historical research, we often think of its role as discovering ruins, objects, and other tangible remains that are linked to events of the past. A traditional task of archaeology has always been to find material evidence of previous human behavior. Its results allow us to identify such events in space but also to understand them in the context of larger processes and explore them on different scales of inquiry. Archaeology involves much more than simply identifying and describing old things, and the authors of the initial chapters in this book address questions that reach far beyond these limited goals. Their investigations at four university campuses examined the nature of the archaeological record and how it was formed as well as how its nature and composition reflect the activities that produced it and the broader milieu in which they were carried out. All of the historical contexts studied were dynamic in the sense that they represented institutional responses to wider changes in American society. College campuses and their inhabitants adapted to the evolving role of higher education and to the uncertainties that accompanied its development, yet these changes are only poorly documented in the written record. Unconscious and deliberate omission of information has left a less than complete account of the history of academic institutions. These chapters demonstrate that much of this untold story lies buried with the material record it generated. Their results argue that archaeology has value as a tool for conducting basic historical research on campus and must have a continuing role in examining our academic past.

2

Function, Circumstance, and the Archaeological Record

The Elusive Past at Saints' Rest

KENNETH E. LEWIS

One hot summer day a field school student looked up from her work and observed in frustration that the site we were excavating was not yielding the kind of evidence she expected to find. Here we were, exploring the innards of Saints' Rest, Michigan State University's first boarding hall (constructed in the mid-nineteenth century), and finding it difficult to relate the items recovered to daily life in a building that once served as the residence and dining facility for the early inhabitants of Michigan Agricultural College. How could this be? On a winter's night in 1876 it burned to the ground; its collapsed remains entrapped everything inside the building in its cellar. The college never reused the site of Saints' Rest, and the buried contents that filled its cellar lay undisturbed for nearly 130 years. Since the room and board of the institution's students was the structure's *raison d'être*, we might expect that material objects associated with these activities were in the building at the time of its destruction. Many of those items that were durable enough to have survived the conflagration should have accumulated with other debris and been preserved in the dormitory's rubble. Why, she asked, weren't they more obvious?

The prospect of discovering interesting material objects that inform us about people and events of the past has always been one of the chief attractions of archaeology. Artifacts constitute a direct tie to those who lived in another time, and the contexts that contain them reflect their behavior. Archaeologists assume that patterning observable in this record is linked to past behavior and that recognizing the meaning of such patterns holds the key to drawing meaningful conclusions about the societies we study. It has always been tempting to draw quick parallels between particular artifacts and behavioral phenomena; because the function of artifacts reflects meaning as well as use, however, simple one-to-one equivalents frequently bear a closer resemblance to our desires than to past reality. The available written, oral, and graphic evidence combines to inform historical archaeologists about objects and their contexts, producing a more nuanced material record of the past. The relationship between the archaeological record and past reality is not always straightforward, and we must employ careful bridging arguments to link behavior and its material byproducts. Clearly the solution to the student's dilemma at Saints' Rest would require further thought.

One of the principal goals of the Saints' Rest archaeological work, conducted as a field school by the Department of Anthropology at Michigan State University in the summer of 2005, was to investigate the building's function. This task seemed relatively unambiguous. This past residence hall had modern counterparts that could surely provide analogies useful in interpreting the past lifeways. But we had to be careful in making comparisons over a century in which many things had changed. Before pursuing such questions, we had to examine the building at the scale of both the larger community of which it was a part and the members of this institutional household. This would help us draw analogies to discern the nature and distribution of boarding-hall activities in the archaeological record. How did Saints' Rest fit in the historical milieu of nineteenth-century academia?

The College in the Wilderness

An interest in agricultural education reflected the larger agricultural improvement in the antebellum United States. This period witnessed the growth of national food markets and increasing interregional competition to supply the expanding demand for agricultural products. In an effort to improve the efficiency of production and increase yields, farmers sought to acquire and implement the new methods and technologies emerging from private and publicly sponsored research (Danhof 1969: 50–51; Gates 1960: 295). Their needs led to the formation of state boards of agriculture and agricultural societies that disseminated information and encouraged systematic improvement through legislation, fairs, publications, and education (Bidwell and Falconer 1941: 318–20; Gray 1958: 805; True 1925: 297–304).

Michigan's agricultural college grew out of this perceived need for agricultural education and the concomitant expansion of higher education in the antebellum United States. Funded largely by private sources, church-related liberal arts colleges arose to train ministers, while new specialized institutions concentrating on scientific, technical, and engineering education also came into being and normal schools and female seminaries provided education for teachers (Berger and Calkins 2002: 1035–36). Inspired by the success of agricultural schools in Europe, American colleges established programs devoted to scientific agricultural research and training (Gray 1958: 789–92; Danhof 1969: 52–53).

The Agricultural College of the State of Michigan came into existence in 1855, five years after its authorization in the state's new constitution. The state legislature situated the new Agricultural College near Lansing and appropriated land for its financial support (MAL/A 1850/130). In 1857 it provided $40,000 to erect buildings and begin operations (MAL/A 1855/142). The college was unique in that it incorporated a "model farm" as an integral element of the campus. Its presence provided an alternative curriculum to that typically found in contemporary higher education. As an adjunct to their classroom studies, the model farm afforded students the opportunity to learn to operate and manage a farm under the supervision of their professors. This "novel plan," involving regular student participation in farming activity, was essential to the college's success (M/SPI 1858: 315). The faculty also carried out agricultural research at the farm, and the students' participation in these experiments became an integral part of their educational process. When it opened its doors in 1857, the Agricultural College became the first institution of higher learning in the United States devoted to this specialty (Widder 2005: 26–28).

The early years brought growing pains to the Agricultural College but strengthened its central role. Continued controversy over the curriculum and program brought formal recognition of a course guaranteeing the importance of liberal arts, science, and a central role for research and practical experience in agriculture. Placing the college under the auspices of a Board of Agriculture that oversaw its operation guaranteed its academic independence and tied it more closely with agricultural interests in the state (Widder 2005: 42–43). Support for the Agricultural College improved with the passage of the 1862 federal Morrill Act, which provided funds to establish state land-grant colleges devoted to agriculture and the mechanical arts (Cochrane 1979: 241–42). Despite continuing debates, the Agricultural College persevered and maintained its central role in the service of agriculture (Kirkendall 1986: 7–8; cf. Nassaney et al. 1996: 67–69; Widder 2005: 57–65).

Apart from the political battles, the Agricultural College also faced more practical challenges in its early years. Located away from older settled regions with easy access to the outside world, the campus and farm lay on an uncleared 677-acre site three and one-half miles east of Michigan's new capital at Lansing and had to be built literally from the ground up. Established as the seat of government only a decade earlier, Lansing was chosen for its central location in that portion of the state then in agricultural development (Goodrich 1886: 124). Nevertheless, it lay in a heavily forested area described by one observer as a "howling wilderness" that was only just being settled in the 1840s (Lewis 2002: 191, 2004: 129). Although the state completed its capitol building in the winter of 1848, Lansing had yet to acquire a railroad connection and had only recently begun to take on the semblance of a nucleated settlement (Bishop 1877: 515; Dart 1897: 174–77; Michigan Railroad Commission 1919: 88).

Situated on undeveloped land still largely in its natural state, the college had to be built from the ground up. Constructing buildings and clearing land for the college farm absorbed the attention of college administrators in the institution's early years. A shortage of provisions, the high cost of supplies, and bad weather hampered construction, but much was accomplished during its first year of operations (M/SPI 1858: 314–15). At the time of its dedication on May 13, 1857, the college's first permanent buildings rose on a half-acre of cleared land "in the midst of the woods." They included four brick faculty houses, a wooden frame dwelling, and College Hall, an academic building containing classrooms, laboratories, a library, and a museum. The college also erected a boarding hall, named "Saints' Rest" by its student residents, after a contemporary devotional (M/SPI 1858: 318; Inventory of College Property 1860, Box 1142, Folder 27, MKC/MSUAHC; James Gunnison, Essay, n.d., Box 1140, Folder 8, MKC/MSUAHC; Michigan Agricultural College 1857; Widder 2005: 31–32).

Saints' Rest remained the sole boarding hall at the Agricultural College for thirteen years. Williams Hall opened in 1870 to accommodate increasing enrollment, but Saints' Rest continued to serve as a residence hall for nearly seven more years. Its destruction by fire in December 1876 marked the end of nearly two decades of use, a period that witnessed institutional changes that affected the students' activities and their way of life (Widder 2005: 57). This historical context helped frame our expectations for the archaeological record at Saints' Rest.

Student Life at the Agricultural College

Saints' Rest initially housed multiple activities that mirrored its role at the agricultural college. When the institution opened in 1857, the boarding hall accommodated all of the activities necessary to house, feed, supervise, and

Figure 2.1. Saints' Rest at the time of its construction in 1857. This view, from the east, reveals the recently cleared campus on which the boarding hall was constructed. A portion of College Hall, the first classroom building, is visible behind the tree to the right behind Saints' Rest. (Courtesy of Campus Buildings Photographs, Michigan State University Archives and Historical Collections)

support its student residents, all of whom were male. Saints' Rest was a large, unadorned three-story brick structure resting on a semisubterranean stone basement (Figure 2.1). It consisted of a northern section 46 × 50 feet and a southern portion measuring 36 × 40 feet (Inventory of College Property, 1860, Box 1142, Folder 27, MKC/MSUAHC). The cellar housed the kitchen, the laundry, and a "dressing and washing room." The first floor contained the dining room, the parlor, and the living quarters for the steward, whose wife served as the cook. Fourteen student rooms, housing up to four students each, filled the remaining two floors (J. F. Johnstone to J. M. Gregory, Oct. 27, 1859, Box 1141, Folder 66, MKC/MSUAHC; Widder 2005: 286).

Although there was no plan showing the layout of activities at Saints' Rest, we made several assumptions about their spatial arrangement. Certainly the functional segregation of space by floors reflected a vertical organization of activities. The students' living areas were confined to the upper floors, while the floor directly below them was divided into the manager's private quarters and common space for the students. The basement contained a number of specialized work areas used by different groups, including the students, the steward's family, and other college employees. Multiple specialized activities

Figure 2.2. The Michigan Agricultural College in the 1870s. This photograph, taken from the north, shows Saints' Rest on the left. The newly constructed boarding hall, Williams Hall, is in the center and College Hall is to its right. (Courtesy of Campus Buildings Photographs, Michigan State University Archives and Historical Collections)

on the lower two floors should have produced discrete areas characterized by assemblages of objects that mirror distinct past activities. The student rooms occupying the entire two upper floors all served a similar function and represented an activity that was distributed evenly across the whole interior of the structure. As long as Saints' Rest remained the principal boarding hall, it is likely to have housed all of these activities and their spatial arrangement. But in a growing institution change was inevitable.

The opening of Williams Hall in 1870 dramatically altered the composition of the campus at the State Agricultural College (Figure 2.2). This large new brick structure, measuring 116 × 166 feet, dominated the landscape. Resting on a stone basement, Williams Hall contained three and a half stories and an attic. Designed in the then-fashionable second empire style, it featured a mansard roof and tower and exhibited external decorative elements that Saints' Rest lacked. Of greater relevance, Williams Hall took on many of the activities formerly found in the older boarding hall, including those associated with a dining hall, kitchen, and laundry in the basement and the steward's room and a public parlor on the first floor. Eighty students were accommodated on the upper two floors, and a "society room" occupied the mansard (Michigan Agricultural College 1876: 47, 1878: 45).

Documentary sources implied that Saints' Rest took on the narrower role of a dormitory after the erection of Williams Hall. The economy of eliminating redundant activities would have appealed to an administration on a perennially tight budget, and it may have taken advantage of this opportunity. Inventories of college properties clearly spelled out activities carried out in the two buildings from 1872 to 1875, the period when both buildings were in use. These records carefully distinguished between students' rooms situated in the "old hall" and those in the "new hall." They also referred to "cellars" and "help's rooms" and "spare rooms" in the plural, implying the presence of residential and vacant spaces in both structures. The term "private rooms" presumably meant the space devoted to the steward's quarters. All other spaces (including the "public parlor," "office," "kitchen," "dining room," "wash room," "ironing room," and "store room") are referred to in the singular, suggesting that they were present in only one of the buildings. These functions are known to have been housed in Williams Hall, so Saints' Rest would have accommodated only students and possibly some college employees (Michigan Agricultural College, Inventories of College Property, 1872–77, JRWP/MSUAHC). Its limited role was supported by a statement in the newspaper account revealing that, "since the completion of the new boarding hall, it [Saints' Rest] has been occupied as a dormitory" (*Lansing Republican*, Dec. 12, 1876). The use of the term "dormitory" as opposed to "boarding hall," which supplied meals and other services as well as a place to live (Rubczynski 1986), documented the absence of specialized functions originally contained in the older building. At the time of its destruction Saints' Rest appears to have served solely a domestic function. The only other activities underway at the time of the fire were related to repair work on the foundations (*Lansing Republican*, Dec. 12, 1876). Because Saints' Rest functioned as a dormitory during the final stage of its existence, the material remains probably reflect activities related to this limited role. This had powerful implications for the archaeological record and might help supply an answer to the student excavator's dilemma.

The Material Byproducts of Student Life

Archaeologists have long recognized that the materials they study bear a relationship to the activities carried out by a settlement's past occupants, but they are also aware that the transition from a state of use to the static condition in which we find them is shaped by processes related to the circumstances of their deposition. A site does not represent simply an inventory of items summing up all previous behavior by a cultural system (Binford 1981: 201). Rather, an archaeological assemblage is a product of the manner in which items associated with particular types of behavior accumulate. Consequently, analyses of its composition, condition, and arrangement must consider the nature and organization of past activities, the conditions under which they terminated, and the manner in which sequential uses of the site affected earlier contexts. Understanding these variables allowed us systematically to derive links between material patterning and the past behavior responsible for it, a key to explaining the assemblages at Saints' Rest and linking them to our knowledge of its documented past.

Certainly the archaeological record at Saints' Rest represented the building's function within the Agricultural College, but it was also a byproduct of the manner in which that system organized its activities, how they changed over time, and how they were terminated, in this case abruptly. Documentary sources provided information helpful in understanding this specific building's functions by identifying the kinds of activities usually associated with them. Comparative historical records supplied analogies specifying both the artifacts used in a particular activity and how they were incorporated in its archaeological contexts. Written sources were also helpful in distinguishing the two functions of the antebellum building; however, we did not know if evidence for all these activities, even those associated with its last use, would be contained in the archaeological record. Although Saints' Rest was destroyed cataclysmically, we had to be careful in assuming that it represented a little Pompeii, capturing the past intact. Other processes intervened to affect the composition of its material record and had to be considered when interpreting its archaeological remains (Schiffer 1985: 38).

Several decades ago archaeologists concerned with the relationship between the content of the archaeological record and the activities that produced it emphasized the impact of processes associated with deposition. Despite disagreements about whether or not *formation processes* were the end product of past behavior or separate processes that acted on the nature of its deposition (Schiffer 1977: 16; Binford 1981: 201), most agreed that: (1) the content of an archaeological assemblage differed from that of the activity that generated it, and (2) the variation between the two had to be explained by considering how people employed artifacts and how they disposed of them. The archaeological record at Saints' Rest accumulated as its occupants discarded and lost objects as part of their regular activities between 1856 and 1876 and abandoned them following the building's destruction. *Discard* is the deposition of waste material and usually occurs when objects break, wear out, or become obsolete. *Loss*, in contrast, involves the inadvertent or unintentional deposition of usable objects. Both occurred throughout the building's history and were probably responsible for a long-term accumulation generated by a number of separate activities. We had to be aware of how people at Saints' Rest discarded and lost items but not neglect the effects of subsequent activities on those that preceded them. *Abandonment* deposits consist of usable artifacts left behind after an area is no longer in use (Schiffer 1976: 32–34, 1977: 19–24). This process may be rapid or prolonged.

At Saints' Rest, where the site was buried quickly and subsequently left undisturbed, abandonment assemblages included all the surviving artifacts associated with the activities current at the time of deposition. These are referred to as *in situ de facto refuse* (South 1977: 297). An awareness of the circumstances under which the archaeological record at Saints' Rest accumulated provided the key to understanding how the activities there were likely to be represented in the material remains of this building. Investigating the site's contents as an accumulation of assemblages formed under distinctive conditions allowed us to address the earlier question of its contents.

Predicting the Nature of Assemblages at Saints' Rest

The archaeological record at Saints' Rest represented the material generated over a twenty-year occupation, during which the building served two functions: as a boarding hall and later as a dormitory. In its earliest role the structure provided food-service facilities, housed students and nonstudent college staff, and accommodated a number of specialized activities related to the support and subsistence of the students. We assumed that this function, curtailed by the removal of support activities to Williams Hall in 1870, would have removed all material evidence relating to the specialized boarding-hall activities. Evidence for these activities was likely to take the form of subterranean assemblages formed as a result of discard and loss of items that remained undisturbed in the cellar. Living area assemblages were likely to have accumulated as discard and loss throughout the existence of Saints' Rest; the persistent cleaning of the upper floors continuously disturbed earlier deposits, however, leaving only those present at the time of the last occupation.

The nature of specialized activity assemblages is related to the manner in which artifacts were deposited. Several *disposal modes* describe the material patterning produced by discard and loss, and each is characterized by the kinds of artifacts as well as their size, condition, and spatial distribution. *Dropping* involves discarding small items of waste at the location of use or losing items in the course of activities. *Tossing* produces a wider spatial distribution of refuse deliberately discarded after the completion of some action, removing objects from their place of use. *Dumping* may take place in pits or on the surface as sheet midden scattered over a wider area. *Maintenance activities*, which displace and redeposit previously discarded items, may also affect the composition of artifact assemblages on continuously occupied sites (South 1977: 297–98, 1979: 221; Binford 1978: 344–47).

The nature of these disposal modes was especially important in considering evidence for the boarding-hall period. These activities had ceased six years before the building's destruction, but activities associated with its continued residential use worked to remove evidence of their presence. Thus, we assumed that intact deposits representing the residue of cooking, dining, food storage, laundering, and other services would be absent. Instead of representing abandonment assemblages, they were far more likely to be the results of dropping, tossing, or dumping or modified subsequent maintenance activities, such as cleaning or architectural modification.

But what about the residential activities that continued until the time of the building's destruction? The removal of the specialized activities, along with all their associated artifacts, to Williams Hall narrowed the range of activities at Saints' Rest. The material remains generated by the students living there were not likely to have been substantially different from those of the earlier residential occupation or to be distinguishable from it. Students probably used the structure as intensively as before and continued to discard and lose items on and around the premises. Ongoing maintenance activities intended to keep the building clean, and repair work would have limited the size and extent of such deposits throughout the time of its use.

The fire that consumed Saints' Rest in December 1876 interrupted these processes and created a very different deposit. The swiftness and completeness of its destruction prevented the removal of anything when the dormitory burned. A contemporary account described a fire that spread quickly from an upper-floor room to turn the interior into "an immense mass of flame." The exterior walls then collapsed into the building, trapping all of the contents inside (*Lansing Republican*, Dec. 12, 1876). Although the conflagration that destroyed Saints' Rest at first seems to have ensured that the remains of ongoing activities were captured intact, one factor complicated the formation of the archaeological record. Classes at the Agricultural College were suspended during a winter break following commencement in late November and did not resume until late February (Michigan Agricultural College 1878: 49; M/SPI 1877: 108). Alas, Saints' Rest may not have been

Pompeii after all. The empty building contained only what the students had left between terms.

Past Activities at Saints' Rest and Archaeological Expectations

The physical remains of two distinct yet functionally overlapping occupations occurred at Saints' Rest over the twenty-year course of its existence. The longest and most persistent forms of deposition at Saints' Rest were discard and loss of items within the building. These processes continued to generate a material record throughout the building's existence but differed in the boarding-hall and dormitory phases. Both are likely to have been influenced by the activities they represented, their distribution in the structure, and the practices associated with the generation and deposition of byproducts. How did these factors affect the disposal modes that produced and modified these two formation processes? Let us examine the activities that took place at Saints' Rest over the duration of its occupation.

Activities in the Cellar

During the decade when Saints' Rest served as a boarding hall, the cellar housed the kitchen, laundry, and wash room; however, their horizontal placement remained unclear. Because the assemblages they generated accumulated at the building's lowest level, their patterning was likely to reflect the activities' original distribution (compare South 1977: 297). The specialized activities at Saints' Rest involved a host of articles that people used to accomplish the tasks at hand. Many of those were situated in the basement. Deposition generated by the kitchen and laundry would have accumulated directly on the ground and stood the greatest likelihood of remaining undisturbed. The kitchen employed three women, who prepared, cooked, and cleaned up after meals. Their work equipment included ceramic crocks and jars, bread tins, a meat safe, glass jars, bushel baskets, a hand cart, and a flour shovel to collect and store food; coffee and pepper mills, a set of scales, quart and bushel measures, milk pans, cleavers, meat saws, a meat pounder, and tables to process and prepare food; copper boilers, baking pans, and two ranges and their associated furniture for cooking; and an oven scraper, ash pans, and swill barrels to handle the waste. The two women who worked in the laundry were responsible for washing and ironing the students' clothes and for making soap. They accomplished their work with a water pump, pails, washtubs, washboards, wash barrels, a pounder, clothing racks, an ironing table, and clothes baskets as well as a work bench and mops (Michigan Agricultural College, Inventory of College Property, 1860, Box 1142, Folder 27, MKC/MSUAHC; R. F. Johnstone to J. M. Gregory, Oct. 27, 1859, Box 1141, Folder 66, MKC/MSUAHC).

Although both of these activities involved the use of multiple distinctive artifacts, these portable items were shifted to other locations when the function of the building changed. The ranges, pumps, tables, benches, and other substantial or specialized equipment were probably valuable enough to be reused and moved with the kitchen and laundry to Williams Hall. None remained in Saints' Rest in 1876.

Small pieces of broken artifacts might also be lost or dropped in the work areas devoted to each activity in the cellar at Saints' Rest. Accumulating on or in the floor, smaller artifacts would be trapped in the ground or on open pavement. Thus the artifacts most likely to be found in either kitchen or laundry work areas were not the tools and equipment used there but rather the smaller objects being processed. Bone and other nonbiodegradable byproducts of food preparation and buttons and other small items removed, loosened, or broken in the course of washing, ironing, or repair of clothing might be dropped or lost where these activities occurred. In addition, broken or unusable equipment items or their parts as well as food waste could be dumped, presumably at the periphery of the work areas.

Activities on the First Floor

The dining hall apparently occupied a portion of the first floor and included an eating area that could accommodate half the students at a sitting (E. G. Grainger, Diary, Dec. 10, 1858, EGGP/MSUAHC). Storage areas for serving and eating utensils contained an array of dishes, bowls, cups, saucers, tumblers, teacups, forks, knives, and spoons for individual use as well as serving utensils, sauce dishes, molasses cans, milk and water pitchers, pickle dishes, sugar tins, gravy boats, tin urns, teapots, tureens, serving dishes, waiting trays, and dishpans for use at the table (Inventory of College Property, 1860, Box 1142, Folder 27, MKC/MSUAHC).

Dining-room activities undoubtedly generated debris in the form of broken ceramics and glass as well as nonbiodegradable food remains, but regular cleaning would have minimized their accumulation on the wooden floor. Presumably the accumulation of small fragments was confined to a distinct portion of the building. With the shift of the dining area to Williams Hall, the furniture, equipment, and supplies stored in these rooms were removed from Saints' Rest and could not have contributed to the in situ de facto refuse deposit created by the 1876 fire.

The steward's quarters occupied the remainder of the first floor. Because no inventory of its contents was included in the college records, it was probably furnished with the occupant's personal household goods, which were removed when his family left the employ of the college. In 1870 the steward relocated his family and took their belongings to the new steward's residence in Williams Hall, removing material evidence of his stay at the older building. Consequently, the stewards are likely to have left little evidence at Saints' Rest, beyond small objects lost or misplaced.

The Student Rooms

Students occupied the top two floors during the boarding-hall period and perhaps the upper three floors when the building was used as a dormitory. As living quarters, they were the site of most student activities apart from dining, classroom work, and labor on the college farm. Each room contained clothing, books, classroom supplies, and the personal possessions of as many as four students as well as a standard set of furniture, equipment, and appliances. These included two bedsteads (students slept two to a bed), a clothing cupboard, a small wood stove and fire irons, a slop pail, and a spittoon. In addition, students rented mattresses, bedspreads, woollen blankets, pillows, bed sheets, white spreads, wash stands and pitchers, soap dishes, mirrors, light stands and chimney lamps, cane seat and wood bottom chairs, center tables, small tables, and oil carpets from the college (Inventory of College Property, 1860, Box 1142, Folder 27, MKC/MSUAHC; Student Receipts for Furniture, 1861, Box 1142, Folder 81, MKC/MSUAHC; Miscellaneous University Bills and Accounts, 1872, Box 1141, Folder 95, MKC/MSUAHC; Gunnison n.d., Box 1140, Folder 8, MKC/MSUAHC: 8–9; Charles A. Jewell to Parents, Box 861, Folder 8, TCAP/MSUAHC; James Satterlee, MAC Farm Labor Record, 1866, Box 1141, Folder 49, MKC/MSUAHC). Continuous use and regular cleaning mitigated against the accumulation of material deposits. Only personal items small enough to be lost or overlooked or trapped in corners or between floorboards or fragments of larger objects similarly neglected are likely to have remained. Unlike the remains of specialized activities on the lower floors, these not only extended throughout the entire building but also lasted until Saints' Rest was destroyed.

The 1876 Fire and Its Material Consequences

The burning of Saints' Rest is likely to have created two types of archaeological assemblages. The first encompassed the accumulated loss and discard of a number of discrete activities over its fourteen-year use as a boarding hall and six years as a dormitory. The second type of assemblage, deriving solely from the building's post-1870 occupation, consisted of in situ de facto refuse buried in the ruins of the building. This conflagration deposit differed substantially, because it included complete assemblages generated by all the building's last activities and preserved their spatial integrity. Such assemblages might reflect the contexts of their use and can be useful in identifying and describing the nature of past activities.

Unfortunately the thorough destruction wrought by the fire mixed the contexts of assemblages on the upper floors. Progressive but uneven burning from the roof down destroyed the vertical separation of deposits on each of the three upper floors. As the floors gave way and the walls collapsed, a mixed layer of ash and debris accumulated in the basement. Although it was not possible to distinguish the content of individual student rooms from one another, their common function implied similar content and made it possible to analyze their contents collectively for evidence of domestic activity at Saints' Rest.

Only activities that took place directly on the cellar floor are likely to have left an array of artifacts arranged in their original context. The collapsing building buried these assemblages in the debris of the overlying floors and trapped them as in situ de facto refuse. Although they were burned and crushed, their nature, association, and distribution made it possible to isolate basement activities from those represented in the collapsed debris and identify the activities with which they were associated.

Examining the Remains of Saints' Rest

The 2005 archaeological project investigated portions of the northern part of Saints' Rest, an area that encompassed at least fourteen of the twenty-eight student rooms as well as half of the first floor and cellar (Figure 2.3). The excavation units exposed the walls of the building and sampled the contents of most of its interior. An examination of unit profiles revealed that the remains of the upper three floors were contained in a compacted, mixed deposit in which it was impossible to identify and separate assemblages from

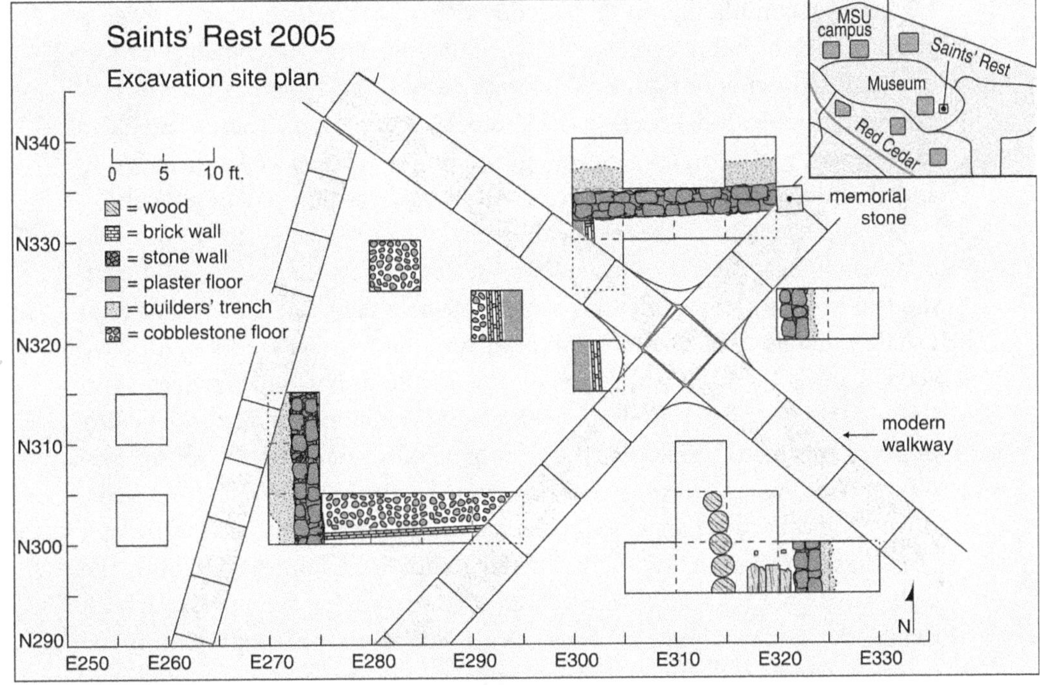

Figure 2.3. Plan of excavation units at Saints' Rest. Modern sidewalks restricted access to the site.

the individual floors (Quates et al. 2006). Nevertheless, this layer remained undisturbed and contained everything that survived the fire.

Despite the cataclysmic nature of the fire, it did not disturb the archaeological contexts and architectural features on the cellar floor (Mustonen 2007: 59–60, 87–90). The presence of in situ de facto refuse assemblages could help us identify the last activities carried out in the cellar of Saints' Rest. The cellar floor deposits also held the potential to yield evidence of materials discarded or lost as a result of previous activities in the cellar. An examination of deposits here could identify not only the building's later function as a dormitory but its earlier role as a boarding hall as well.

We anticipated that the only evidence for the specialized activities of the boardinghouse period would consist of items that accumulated as loss or discard and were not removed by regular cleaning and maintenance over time. Because the nature of the surfaces on which these activities were carried out also influenced the extent to which their deposits were modified or removed, the presence of such evidence at Saints' Rest probably varied.

Materials accumulating on the wooden floors of the upper stories stood a good chance of being removed by periodic cleaning. Assemblages of lost or discarded items in the cellar were more likely to have been preserved, however, trapped in its packed dirt and cobblestone floor. These were likely to represent food storage, processing, and preparation as well as laundering and clothing-repair activities carried out in the boarding-hall basement.

We expected the archaeological evidence to reflect the dormitory role that Saints' Rest played in its later years. Because the fire occurred during the winter recess, the students' rooms probably contained fewer items than usual. Valuable objects and those used on a daily basis are likely to have accompanied their student owners home, while heavy, bulky artifacts and those associated with schoolwork might have remained in their rooms during their absence. The latter group probably also included the rented furniture, bedding, ceramics, and other room furnishings as well as the beds, stoves, and other appliances with which the rooms were equipped. Although all of these items were originally situated in individual contexts by room, the collapse of the upper floors mixed and scattered their contents throughout the debris layer overlying the floor. As a single assemblage representing the students' rooms collectively, the artifacts could be examined as a deposit of de facto refuse no longer in situ. This assemblage would be characterized by personal items associated with day-to-day living but not those associated with cooking and other household activities.

The specialized activities may have been removed from the cellar during Saints' Rest's last six years of existence, but the cellar may not have remained unoccupied during this time. The newspaper account of the fire mentioned that carpenters were employed in the cellar and other workmen were grouting and repairing its walls. The circumstances of the building's destruction would certainly have trapped artifacts associated with these activities where they were left at the end of the previous workday. We anticipated that these recent cellar activities would have generated in situ de facto refuse assemblages.

The Search for Boardinghouse Deposits

We expected that evidence of boardinghouse activities associated with the initial occupation Saints' Rest would be found in the cellar deposits. The floor of the cellar yielded no direct surface evidence of the equipment or appliances related to the kitchen or laundry; however, it revealed that the cellar interior contained three large rooms and a central hallway (Figure 2.4). The

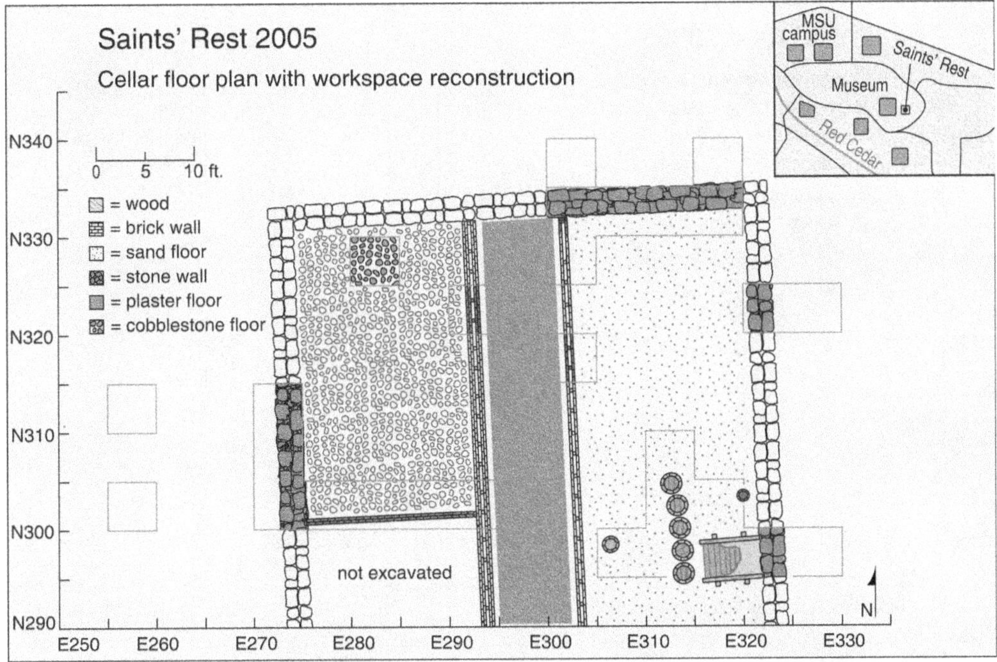

Figure 2.4. Plan of the cellar floor at Saints' Rest, showing the locations of architecture and other features as well as revealed workspaces.

presence of a cobblestone pavement in the northwestern quadrant of the building suggested the laundry. As a surface designed to remain dry in a wet environment, cobblestones were certainly appropriate for a room devoted to this purpose. This room was separated by an interior wall from another room with a dirt floor immediately to the south. A wide, raised, plastered hallway, with walls on either side, opened into both rooms and separated them from the cellar's unpaved eastern half.

The distribution of kitchen deposits identified another specialized activity associated with the boarding hall. Items lost or discarded in the course of kitchen activities are likely to have accumulated close to the place of their most frequent use. The distribution of these artifacts indicates that these activities were mainly carried out at or adjacent to the wall dividing the two western rooms. Food preparation and consumption artifacts included utility wares, glass container fragments, and bottle fragments as well as a few sherds of dining ceramics. Their absence in the remaining part of the cobbled room implies that kitchen activities did not extend farther into this room (Figure 2.5). Indeed, they may have spilled over from the unexcavated room immediately to the south.

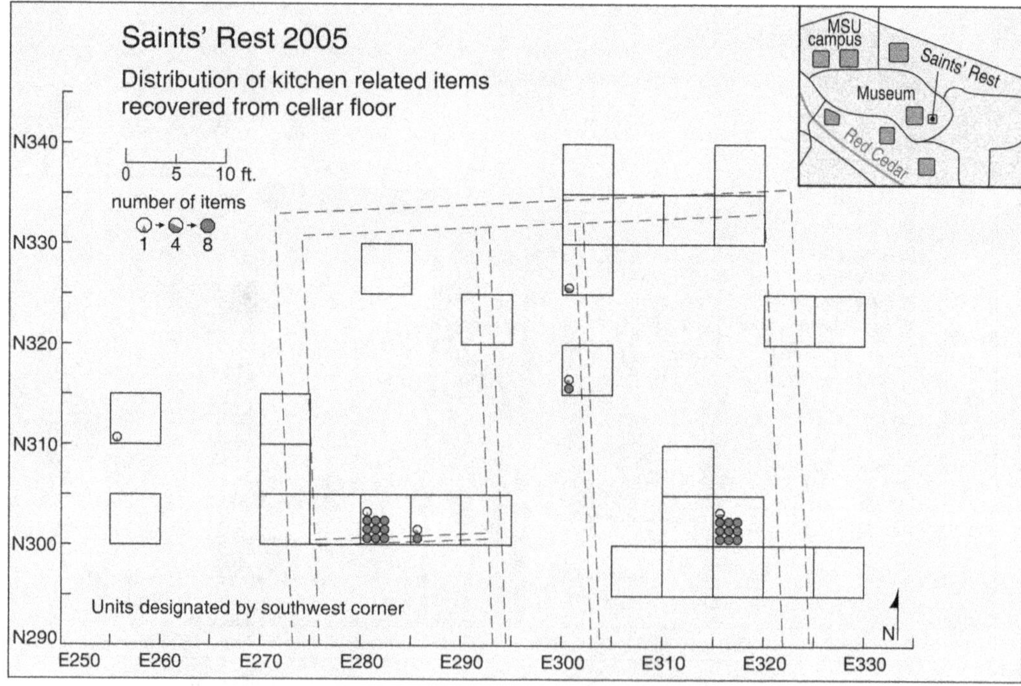

Figure 2.5. Distribution of kitchen-related items recovered from the cellar floor at Saints' Rest.

A second assemblage of artifacts, consisting of buttons, further identified the function of the cobbled room as the laundry. These clothing fasteners were a ubiquitous and necessary element of the nineteenth-century male wardrobe and accompanied their owners wherever they went. Because of their small size, however, they were also easily lost. Students dressing and disrobing in the cellar wash room increased the likelihood of button loss, and the handling involved in laundering clothes undoubtedly contributed to their loss as well. Although buttons are found scattered in several locations throughout the excavated portion of the cellar, the largest number of them came from the room with the cobbled floor, further implying its use as a laundry and wash room (Figure 2.6).

Identifying the Dormitory Deposits

We knew that the layer of building fill contained material evidence of the six-year existence of Saint's Rest as a dormitory, but the degree to which archaeological deposits from the three occupied floors had been mixed by

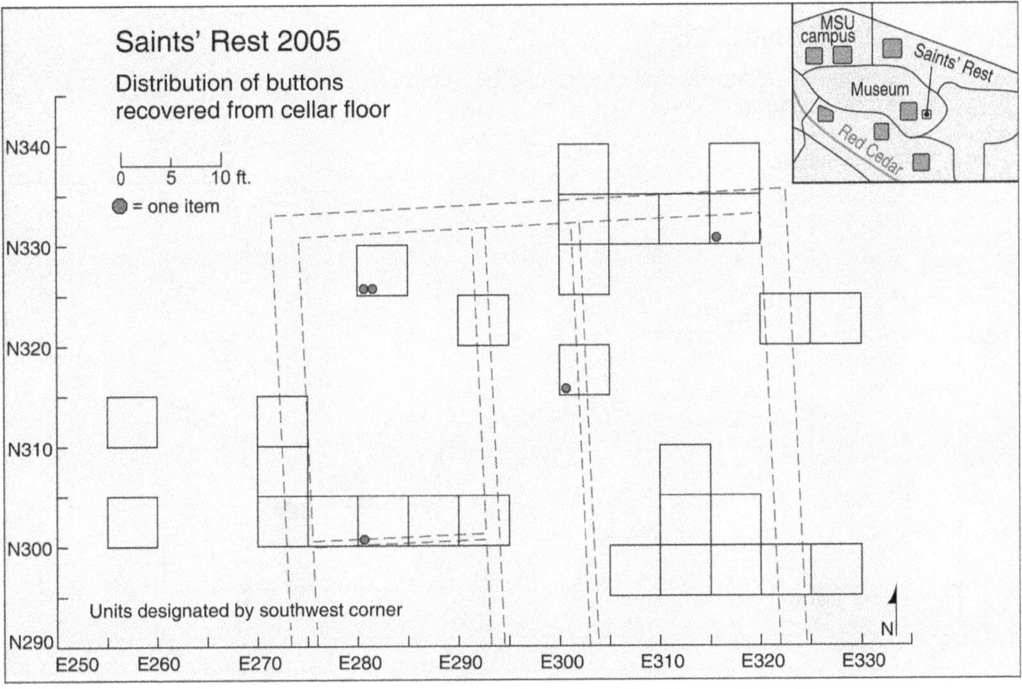

Figure 2.6. Distribution of buttons recovered from the cellar floor at Saints' Rest.

their collapse remained uncertain. How did the intense fire that totally gutted the interior of Saints' Rest actually affect the distribution of the students' room furnishings and personal belongings? If the fire burned downward from the roof, collapsing the building vertically, it certainly mixed the artifacts contained on each floor but may not have altered their horizontal provenience substantially.

We examined this assumption by plotting the horizontal distribution of a nonportable artifact whose original locations could be surmised. The placement of heating stoves was dictated by their proximity to central chimneys, shown in the photograph of Saints' Rest (Figure 2.1). The building's configuration implied that rows of three rooms were situated on either side of the two upper floors and a seventh room was situated between them at the front of the building. The two chimneys were placed near the center of the east and west walls. If the stoves were placed so as to minimize the length of the stovepipe from each to the nearest chimney, they would have been grouped near the walls closest to the chimneys. Falling directly downward when the floors beneath them collapsed, the stoves on both floors would have accumulated

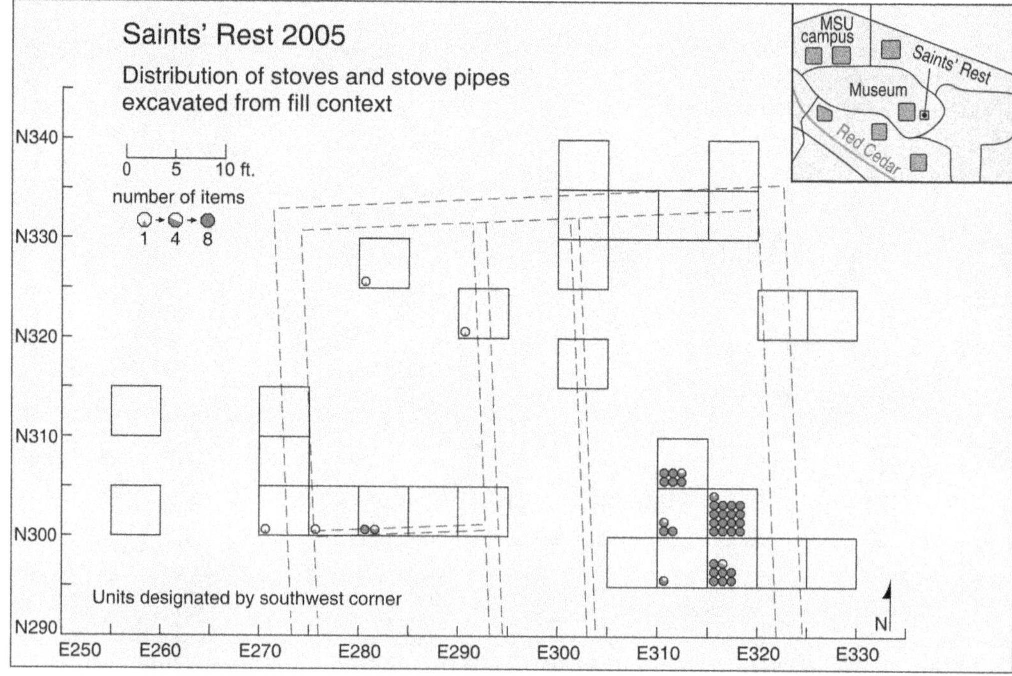

Figure 2.7. Distribution of stoves and stovepipes from the fill context at Saints' Rest.

in clusters toward the center of the building (Figure 2.7). This pattern was clearly observable in the distribution of stove fragments and stovepipes in the debris layer. Nearly absent elsewhere in the interior, these artifacts were present in substantial numbers about midway along the east and west exterior walls. Fragments also recovered from the northern end of the building indicate another stove situated in the end room. The concentrated patterning of stove-related artifacts supported our assumption that there had been little horizontal displacement of artifacts from the upper floors of Saints' Rest.

Based on the distribution of stove fragments, we anticipated that the spatial patterning of other items from the upper floors would provide clues to the arrangement of specific activities in the student rooms. Specific classes of artifacts recovered in the excavations could be linked to particular kinds of domestic activity. Personal hygiene, which included washing and shaving, required the use of a number of ceramics, such as soap dishes, basins, pitchers, bowls, and other vessels (Figure 2.8). Our assumption that utilitarian ceramics were used in all of the dormitory rooms was borne out by the substantial number of diagnostic ceramic fragments recovered and their widespread distribution throughout the interior. Early photographs of dor-

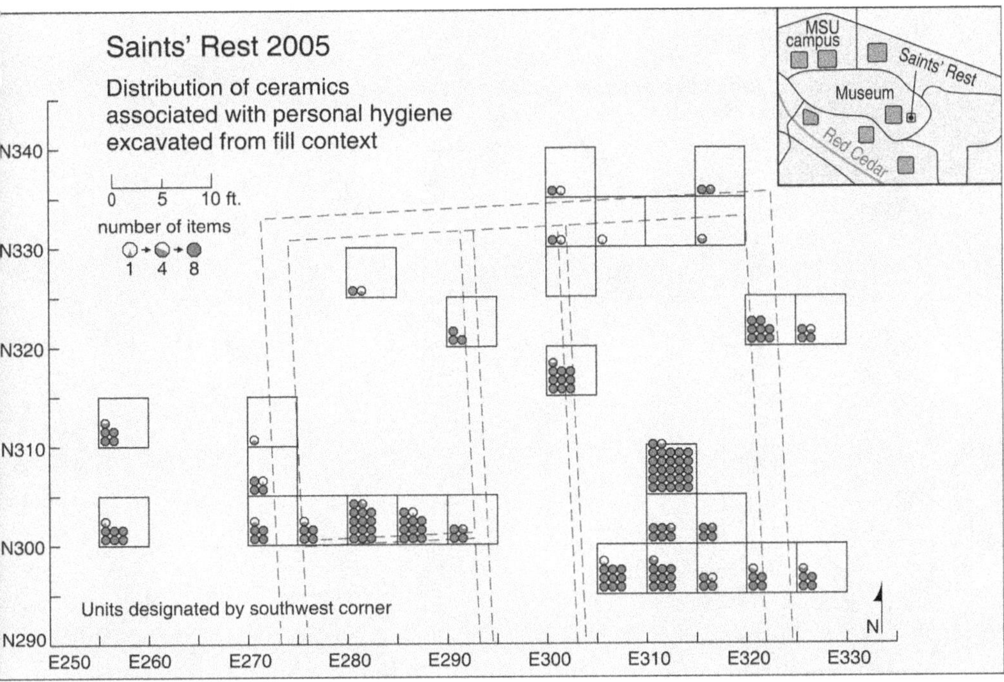

Figure 2.8. Distribution of ceramics associated with personal hygiene from the fill context at Saints' Rest.

mitory room interiors (Widder 2005: 290) showed the tables, chairs, beds, bookcases, and other pieces furniture placed throughout the rooms, and we expected their remains to be uniformly distributed throughout the building. Although furniture remains (represented by casters, legs, furniture tacks, and other hardware) were not numerous, their occurrence in most of the excavation units indicated the widespread presence of furniture on the upper floors of Saints' Rest (Figure 2.9).

The presence and distribution of clothing items at Saints' Rest revealed discrete patterns of storage. Clothing was probably kept in closets or cabinets, and its remains were likely to be concentrated in the locations of these fixtures. Of the durable clothing items recovered, buttons were the most common. Most of them were plain ceramic and metal buttons normally found on work clothes, but shell buttons used on finer clothing also appeared. Their presence mirrored the variety of clothes required by students, whose daily experience included work in the fields as well as attending classes and participating in social activities associated with their preparation for a professional career. Buttons were recovered from most of the excavation units but tended to cluster in several locations, implying that most garments were stored in

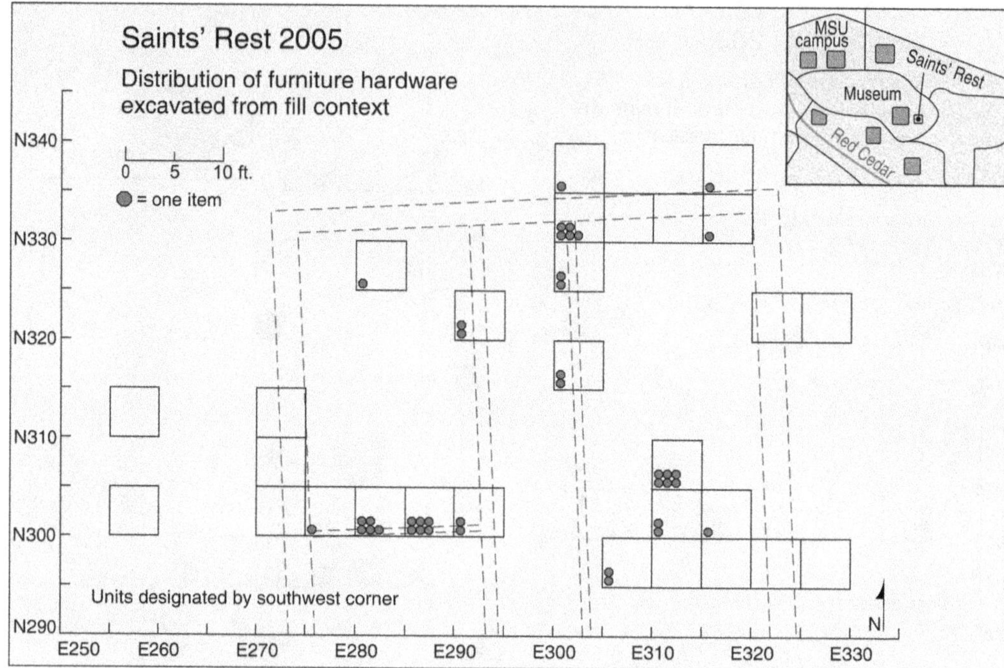

Figure 2.9. Distribution of furniture hardware from the fill context at Saints' Rest.

specific places (Figure 2.10). The occurrence of a smaller number of buckles in the same areas further implied that these were storage areas. Pins (used in tailoring and mending rather than being worn on clothing) were also present in the highest numbers in places where buttons and buckles clustered.

Personal items used by students in their studies were also highly patterned. Stored in rooms pending the beginning of the new term, pen nibs, pencils, rulers, paper fasteners, compasses, inkwells, writing slates, and other small but durable items formed clusters in the building's interior. Writing implements were by far the most common of these artifacts; their distribution suggested distinct storage areas, which also contained inkwells and instrument parts (Figure 2.11). These concentrations generally corresponded to those of clothing items, suggesting that supplies may have been stored close by. All of these data represented ongoing activities directly related to the dormitory function of the structure at the time of its destruction and are consistent with Saints' Rest's last role.

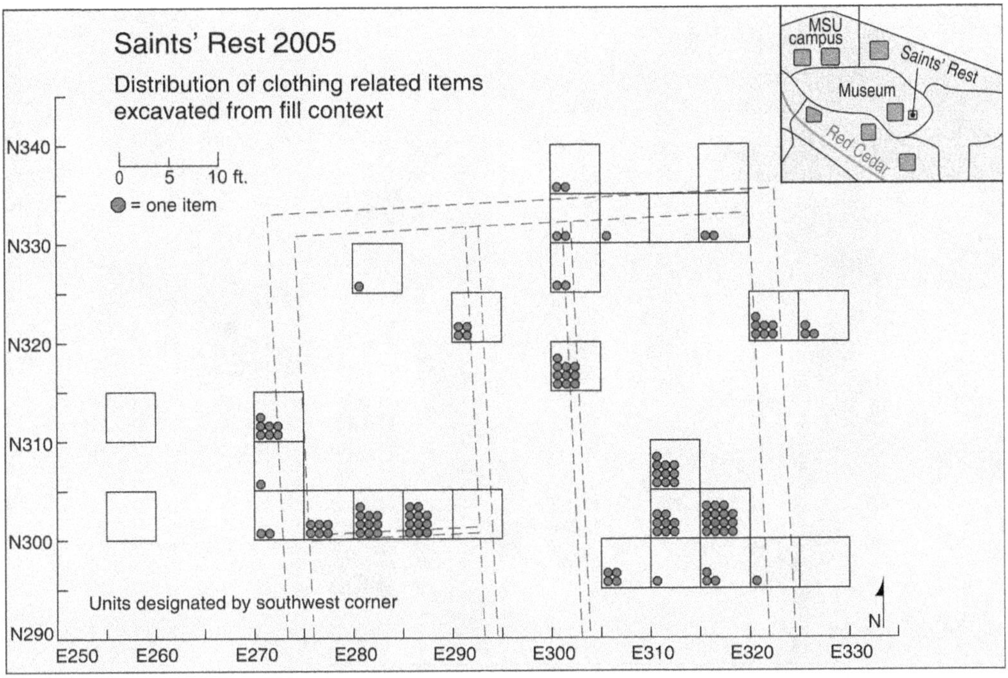

Figure 2.10. Distribution of clothing-related items from the fill context at Saints' Rest.

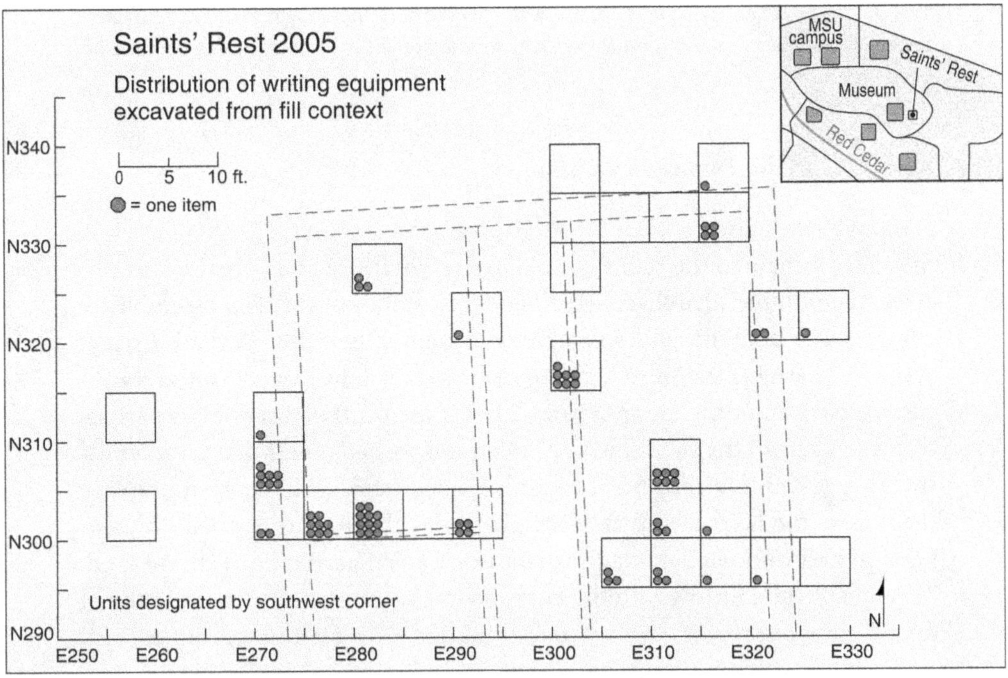

Figure 2.11. Distribution of writing equipment from the fill context at Saints' Rest.

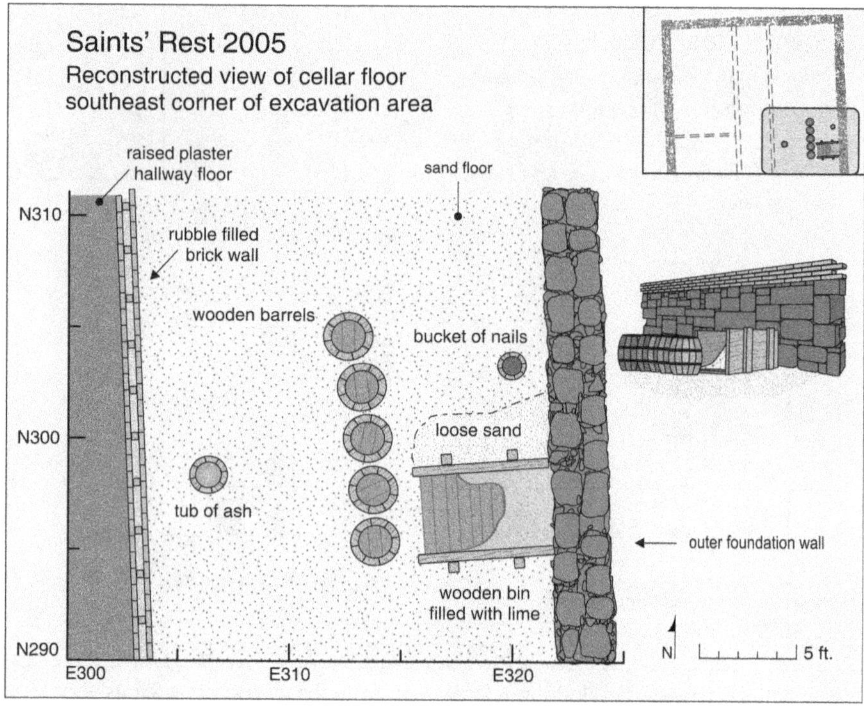

Figure 2.12. Reconstructed plan of the southeastern corner of the excavation portion of the cellar floor at Saints' Rest. The features uncovered here show the remains of artifacts and materials associated with repair work being carried out in the building at the time of its destruction by fire.

Activities in the Dormitory Cellar

Although the living floors of Saints' Rest were vacant on the night of the fire, the cellar remained the scene of ongoing activity. The 2005 excavations uncovered a number of archaeological features containing artifact assemblages whose form, content, and spatial arrangements identified several distinct activities. Perhaps the most striking of these was a work area in the southeastern portion of the cellar (Figure 2.12). It included of a set of five barrels, burned nearly to the sand floor on which they rested. Their preserved lower sides suggested that they had been filled with water, which helped preserve them from the holocaust that descended from above. Directly behind them lay a floored wooden bin filled with lime and an adjacent pile of coarse sand. Together these elements are the components of mortar, a material integral for carrying out repairs in a masonry building. This feature was almost cer-

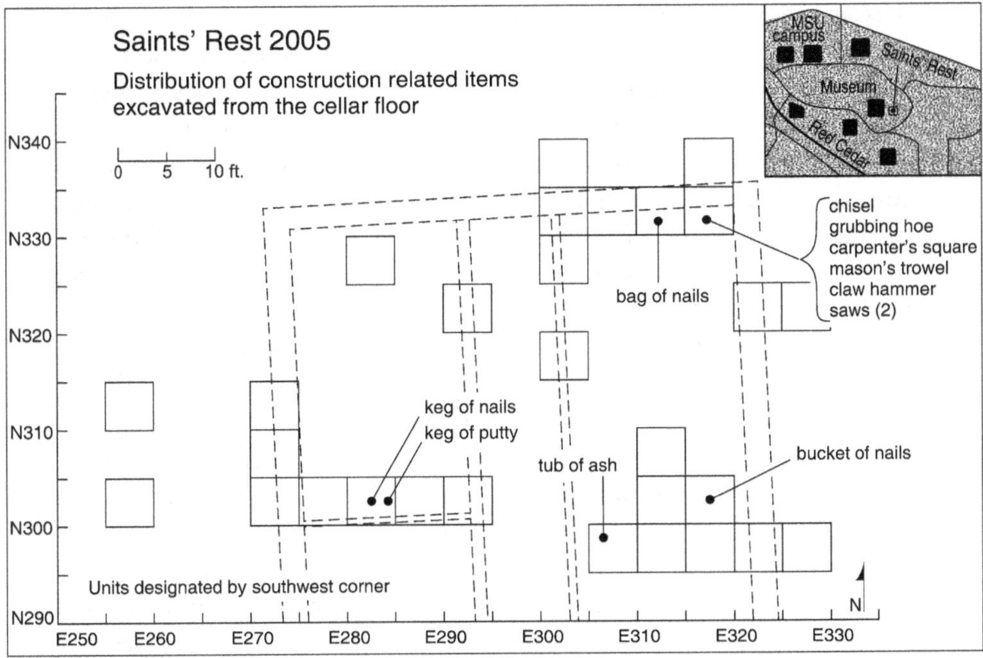

Figure 2.13. Distribution of construction materials in the cellar floor at Saints' Rest.

tainly evidence of the grouting to repair the cellar and center walls reported in the newspaper account of the fire.

Additional artifacts attested to the ongoing repair work in the cellar of Saints' Rest. They included a wooden tub containing ash and a bucket filled with nails in the southeastern part of the cellar, a keg of nails and a keg of putty in its southwestern quadrant, and a bag of nails and a cache of hand tools found near the northern wall (Figure 2.13). All of these constituted a larger assemblage of tools and supplies associated with building maintenance. The absence of assemblages related to other activities implied that the cellar of Saints' Rest was largely unused in 1876.

What It All Means

After struggling through a turgid discussion of historic-period artifact assemblages and activity areas, it is tempting to ask, so what? What has material evidence told us about the documented settlement that we did not already know? Was the archaeological work worth all the trouble? To answer these questions we must return to the original inquiry made by the student at the beginning of this chapter: why wasn't evidence of student life more obvious in the archaeological remains it helped create? At first glance, recognizing the presence of students did not seem difficult. Artifacts used by students should be readily discernible, but can we be sure these items represented students? Given that the clothing, implements, furniture, and other items used by the occupants of Saints' Rest were mass produced by an industrial society and were widely available, the artifacts alone would not identify the presence of students.

Observing the student presence at Saints' Rest required an understanding of context. The content and spatial arrangement of an assemblage reflects the behavior that produced it, but links between the two can only be recognized if we understand how the archaeological record formed. As much as we might prefer otherwise, past activities cannot be observed directly, because the record they leave is static (Binford 2005: 25). Only by constructing bridging arguments linking activities to their byproduct can we breach this gap. Analogies, aided by knowledge supplied by historical texts, allowed us to formulate arguments linking student residence activities to the archaeological record. The manner in which past people used and disposed of artifacts, however, told us only how that record was formed. On a site with multiple occupations, we also had to consider how later activities affected earlier assemblages. The student presence was the most readily identifiable because it represented the most recent occupation, the remains of which had passed into the archaeological record in a rapid, cataclysmic event that preserved objects and their spatial context. It was not Pompeii but came close.

Historical sources also provided analogs useful in recognizing material evidence of the building's earlier boarding-hall occupation. This knowledge served as a basis for defining the nature of its initial function. Bridging arguments helped identify the material remains of these activities, based not on the presence of intact in situ deposits but rather on assemblages of lost or discarded objects overlooked when the activities that produced them were removed to another location. Although lacking the "completeness" of the dormitory deposits, those left by the people engaged in the kitchen, dining room, and laundry were sufficient to document the existence of the boarding-hall activities and the presence of those engaged in them.

The Saints' Rest project opened the door to the archaeological study of Michigan State University's academic past. Our examination of the site demonstrated that physical remains had much to tell us about the early institution and those who lived there. Although the artifacts we recovered were in themselves mundane and mute, when examined in their larger behavioral contexts their presence and patterning revealed information not otherwise available. The material record has much to tell us. Archaeological methodology is capable of investigating topics ranging from architecture to the semiotics of campus design to students' behavior. Examining these and other anthropological questions requires only the foresight to ask them and the imagination to explore their archaeological implications. This work has only begun to explore this potential.

3

Exploring the Foundations of Notre Dame

Archaeology at Old College

MARK R. SCHURR

The Old College site consists of the Old College building (the first brick building constructed on campus) and the Log Chapel (a reproduction of the original log chapel that stood at this location in 1842). The site (as defined here) consists of these two buildings and the surrounding lawn, creating a parklike setting bounded by roads and walkways. Figure 3.1 shows the Old College (the brick building on the left) and the Log Chapel (nearly hidden by pine trees on the right).

The general location of the Notre Dame campus was once the site of a Jesuit mission named Ste. Marie des Lacs, established by Father Claude-Jean Allouez in 1686 (Anonymous 1895; Schlereth 1976: 3–4). Almost nothing is known about this mission, so it was probably a satellite to the St. Joseph's Mission at what is now Niles, Michigan, that was established by Father Allouez in 1680. The precise location of the mission, which may have been little more than a bark hut or even just a convenient place to meet, is unknown. St. Joseph's Mission and Ste. Marie des Lacs were no longer maintained when the British suppressed Catholic missionary activity after seizing the region in 1759 during the French and Indian War. The Catholic mission at Ste. Marie des Lacs was reestablished with the opening of the Northwest Territory to Euro-American settlement in 1830, when a log chapel was erected near what is now Old College by Father Stephen Badin, the first priest ordained in the United States. This chapel, one small frame house attached to it, a few sheds, and a clearing of about ten acres were located on the site when Father Edward Sorin arrived on November 26, 1842, to found Notre Dame du Lac (Anonymous 1895: 46). Local tradition holds that this had been the location of the earlier mission of Ste. Marie des Lacs.

The Old College building was constructed in 1843 and is the only structure that survives from the first decade of Notre Dame's history. It was con-

Figure 3.1. Old College and the Log Chapel today.

structed of yellow bricks made from marly clay found on the banks of the campus lakes; yellow "Notre Dame" brick has been a signature theme of campus architecture ever since. Through the years the Old College building served many purposes. At various times it was a community house, convent, bakery, farmhouse, house of studies, band headquarters, student dormitory, and retreat house. It is now used as the undergraduate seminary for the Indiana Province of Holy Cross Priests. Archaeological evidence from any or all of these activities can be expected at the site.

The log chapel built by Badin burned in 1856 (Anonymous 1895: 53). Its location was commemorated and preserved by the erection of an earthen mound topped by an iron cross. During the nineteenth century the University of Notre Dame expanded and prospered, and the Old College became the heart of the university farm. A Sanborn Company fire insurance map from 1885 shows that the Old College building (then in use as a farmhouse), a privy, a second farmhouse, and two stables stood on the site at that time (Figure 3.2). A photo of the site dating to 1888 (Figure 3.3) shows a rather unattractive farmyard scene where livestock had easy access to St. Mary's Lake. Old College is the nearest brick building. The wooden building in the foreground is the icehouse, and the small wooden building on the extreme right is the pig shed. The 1888 scene is a shocking contrast from today, where

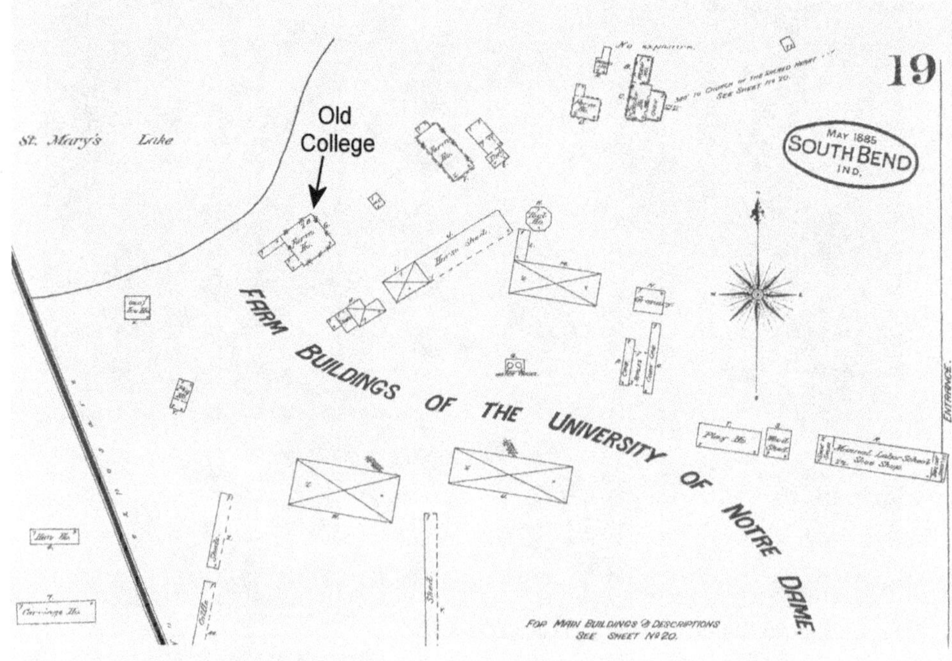

Figure 3.2. Sanborn Company map of the Old College site in 1885.

Figure 3.3. Notre Dame farms with hog lot near Old College in 1888. (Courtesy of Notre Dame University Archives)

a scenic pathway along the lake is frequented by strollers and joggers instead of hogs.

The farm operation at Old College was discontinued around 1900, when the university farm moved to another portion of campus and then farther away as the university continued to expand (Schlereth 1976: 149). Most of the farm buildings were razed except for Old College, which was converted to the headquarters of the Mission Band. A reproduction of the log chapel was reconstructed on the site of the original in late 1905 or early 1906, and the Old College site then took on its modern function as a part of the academic campus commemorating the founding and early years of the university.

Archaeology at Old College

A very limited test excavation was conducted at the Old College site in 1985 by Professor James O. Bellis (now emeritus). The test excavation was conducted because utility work had produced a large number of historic artifacts. Professor Bellis took this opportunity to add an actual field component to a class on archaeological method and theory by conducting the test excavation. A single one-meter-square unit located 6 meters west of the southwest corner of the Old College building was excavated in arbitrary 10 cm levels to a depth of 65 cm below surface. Profile maps of the unit walls show that a stratified deposit of abundant historic remains approximately 40 cm thick lay over a buried soil surface that produced prehistoric artifacts. The excavation of this single unit indicated that historic and prehistoric archaeological deposits existed at the site in the area between the Old College building and the Log Chapel.

The 1991 excavations at the Old College site were inspired by the rich and well-preserved deposits found in 1985 and had several purposes. The first was to gather archaeological data that can be used to increase our understanding of the historical events associated with the founding of the University of Notre Dame. Careful investigations of intact archaeological deposits at the site were conducted to provide information about events in the early Notre Dame community that were not documented in historic records.

A secondary goal was the assessment of the historic significance of archaeological deposits at the site to determine whether the characteristics of these deposits were such that the site would merit further investigation, preservation, or nomination to the National Register of Historic Places or the Indiana Register of Historic Sites and Structures.

The third goal was to provide excavation experience for students in the

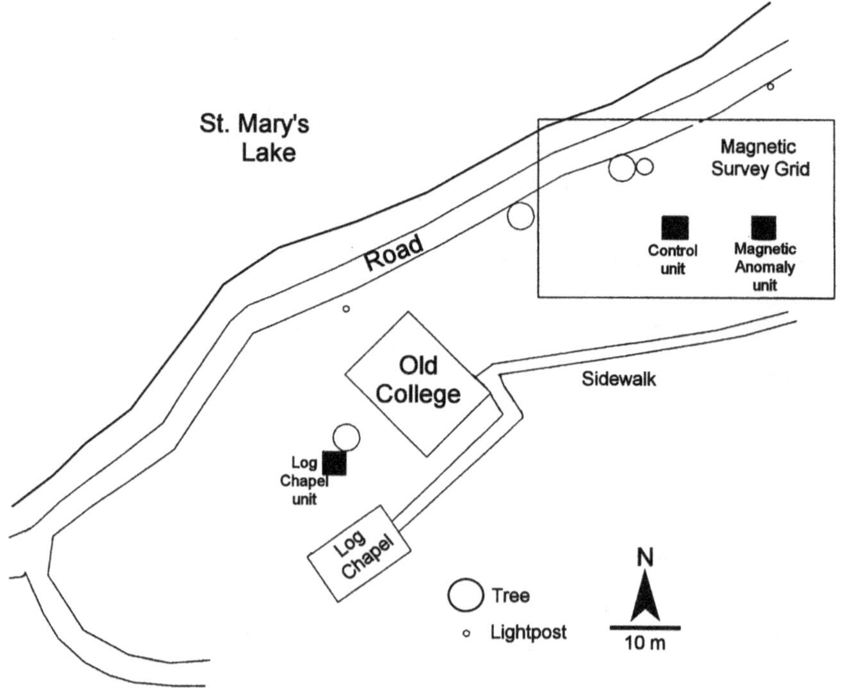

Figure 3.4. Locations of the magnetic survey grid and excavation units.

1991 Notre Dame Field School in Archaeology. The course carried six hours of credit and introduced students to the theories, methods, techniques, aims, and ethics of professional archaeological fieldwork.

The Magnetic Survey

The fieldwork at Old College began with a magnetic geophysical survey. A Geoscan FM36 fluxgate gradiometer was used to survey of an area of 240 m^2 on the lawn east of Old College. The location of the magnetometer survey grid within the modern site is shown in Figure 3.4. The sidewalk along the southern edge of this portion of the site and several trees along the northern and eastern edges of the site complicated the collection of the magnetic data, so the magnetometer survey grid had the shape of a parallelogram rather than the rectangular shape that is usually employed in magnetic surveys. Individual magnetic readings were taken at 0.25 m intervals within the grid. The magnetic survey was further complicated by the need to stop traffic on the road north of the site whenever magnetometer readings were being taken.

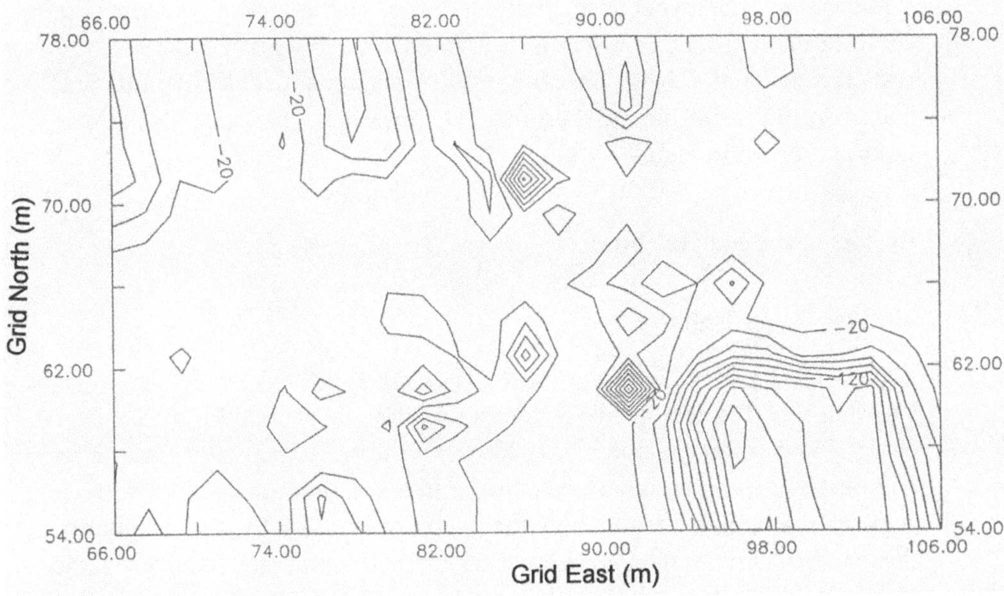

Figure 3.5. Contour map of the magnetic data.

Field maps of the magnetic data were prepared on the day of the survey. These crude maps (not shown) indicated that a very intense negative magnetic anomaly was present in the southeastern corner of the grid. After the field season, an improved magnetic contour map (Figure 3.5) was prepared from the survey data. This map shows that the large negative anomaly in the southeast corner of the magnetic survey grid represents a rectangular area of low magnetic intensity surrounded by an uneven margin of higher-intensity magnetic peaks and valleys. The rectangular structure so clearly visible in the magnetic contours suggested that a large buried feature was present at the site.

Locations of the Excavation Units and Excavation Procedures

Based on the results of the magnetic survey and the 1985 excavation, three test units were placed to sample three different areas. One unit (called the Log Chapel unit) was placed between the Log Chapel and Old College north of the location tested in 1985 in order to investigate the extent and characteristics of the stratified deposits previously identified between the Log Chapel and the Old College. Two excavation units were located within the area surveyed by the gradiometer. These units were placed to evaluate the significance of the magnetic anomalies revealed by the survey. One unit (the control unit) was located just outside and to the northwest of the area of the scattered magnetic highs. The other unit (the magnetic anomaly unit) was placed within the area of greatest magnetic intensity. The locations of these units are shown in Figure 3.4.

Results of the Excavations

The Log Chapel Unit

Eight arbitrary levels and one feature (Feature 1) were defined during the excavation of this one-meter-square unit. Feature 1 was apparently a portion of a shallow, roughly semicircular intrusive pit that extended to the north and west of the unit boundaries. A thin band of sand at the base of the feature suggests that a hole was dug here that stood open for at least several hours during a brief rain or deliberate watering and perhaps longer, but not so long that a thick band of water-laid sand could form in the base of the feature. The feature was refilled very soon after its excavation. It was probably a pit that was dug in the course of landscaping activities at the site.

The rest of the unit uncovered a complex sequence of stratified historic and prehistoric deposits. The complexity of the deposits is exemplified by the differing appearance of all four profile walls in the one-meter-square unit, representing a large amount of archaeological variation in a very small area.

The overall stratigraphy of this unit was best depicted in the eastern profile wall (Figure 3.6), as the layers in this wall are closest in appearance to the "layer cake" stratigraphy that all archaeologists love to see. As this profile shows, the deposits in this part of the Old College site can be divided into six archaeological strata. These revealed that the original ground surface lay at the interface between archaeological Strata 4 and 5, at approximately 55 cm below the present ground surface. Stratified deposits of historic debris were dumped on this surface to form archaeological Strata 3 and 4. Fresh subsoil was then deposited on top of these levels to reach the present elevation of the ground surface. These events probably occurred in 1905/1906 when the crypt below the existing Log Chapel was excavated. The years that have passed since then have allowed a fresh topsoil horizon to develop so that Stratum 1 (the present topsoil) is now differentiated from Stratum 2. Sometime after 1906 a pit (Feature 1) was quickly excavated and refilled in this location. This pit extends to the north and west of the unit. Many of the artifacts in Strata

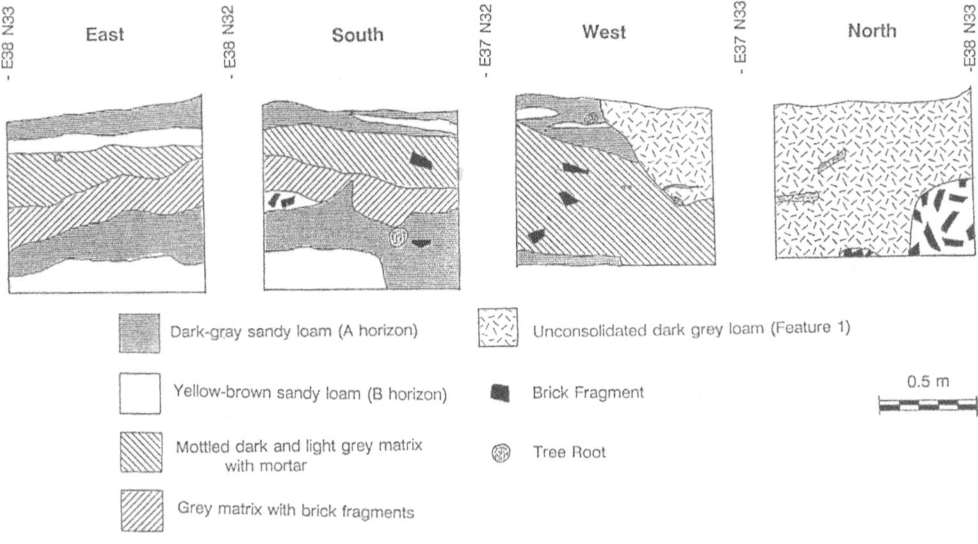

Figure 3.6. Profile maps of the Log Chapel unit.

3 and 4 are likely to represent the remains of the original log chapel, which was destroyed by fire in 1856.

The artifacts in Stratum 5 (the original ground surface in 1842) represent activities at the site dating from the prehistoric period until at least 1906. Strata 1 and 2 contain artifactual evidence of activities at the site from 1906 to the present. Indications of present activities at the site include buried telephone lines and water pipes, amenities that were obviously not present during the early years of Notre Dame (which is just as well, because they would have been uprooted by the hogs).

Excavations to Evaluate the Magnetic Survey

The control unit, located northwest of the area of high-intensity magnetic anomalies, was excavated in four levels. No artifact concentrations or other features were identified in this unit except for several small concentrations of square iron nails on the floor of Level 3. One of these nail concentrations was in the southeast corner of the unit and may be related to a magnetic dipole located just to the southeast of the unit (Figure 3.7). This unit reflects the natural undisturbed stratigraphy of the sandy loam soil on the site and did not contain intact archaeological deposits.

Figure 3.7. Locations of control and magnetic anomaly units within the magnetic survey grid.

The magnetic anomaly unit was placed within the area of high-intensity magnetic anomalies to evaluate their significance. It was excavated in four archaeological levels that followed the existing stratigraphy. Level 1 was virtually identical in appearance and thickness to Level 1 in the control unit. In contrast to the control unit, however, the floor of Level 1 in this unit showed several zones with marked differences in soil color and also contained abundant historic debris, especially fragments of brick and mortar. Simply stripping off the sod and topsoil was enough to show that there was a good correlation between the magnetic survey and the archaeology.

The excavation ultimately determined that five different strata were present in this location. Stratum 1 was the topsoil. Stratum 2 was a mottled mixture of very dark gray and pale brown sandy loam. It was only present in the northern portion of the unit and apparently represents a thin layer of poorly developed subsoil. Stratum 3 consisted of densely packed historic debris in a matrix of mottled black and dark reddish brown sandy loam. The dense artifacts of this stratum formed a virtual pavement of architectural debris that was responsible for the high-intensity magnetic anomalies detected in this location. Stratum 4 was a thin lens of very light, reddish yellow sandy soil approximately 4 cm thick. It lay between the artifact-rich Stratum 3 and the relatively culturally sterile Stratum 5, a yellowish-brown sandy soil whose clay content increased with increasing depth below surface. Very few artifacts were found in this stratum, which seems to correspond to the natural subsoil in this portion of the site.

Summary of the Excavations to Evaluate the Magnetic Survey

The high-intensity magnetic anomalies mapped by the magnetic survey are the products of a dense stratum of historic debris located 9–20 cm below the surface. According to the magnetometer maps, the maximum northern extent of this scatter extends at least 3 m north of the magnetic anomaly unit. The southern extent of the scatter extends beyond the southern limits of the magnetometer grid and is therefore undefined at this time. Archaeological Stratum 3 was probably formed when debris from a structure was scattered across the hillside in this portion of the site. This is likely to have occurred when the structure was demolished. The structure that produced the debris probably stood to the south and east of the unit. The contours of the magnetometer map suggest that at least a portion of the foundation of this structure may be largely intact in the southeast corner of the magnetometer grid. The pronounced negative magnetic anomaly could also be a product of buried historic debris. The absence of a layer of topsoil below the debris of Stratum 3 and the presence of topsoil and subsoil (Strata 1 and 2) above the debris-rich Stratum 3 suggest that the original ground surface contours were significantly modified when this archaeological deposit was created. A photograph of the Old College site taken shortly after the Log Chapel was completed (see Schlereth 1976: 76, Figure 1–27) indicates that these activities occurred before 1906.

Most of the debris within this unit was apparently derived from a structure with a concrete and brick exterior. The interior was finished with lath and plaster walls painted white, and portions of the interior were tiled with characteristic porcelain tiles (see below). The structure probably dated to the second half of the nineteenth century. According to Sanborn Company maps of the campus from 1885 to 1899, this structure was probably a farmhouse that stood east of Old College. The location of this structure relative to the magnetic survey grid and the excavation units is shown in Figure 3.8.

Photograph 65/16 (University Archives) depicts a two-story brick building seen from the east, which is described on the back of the photograph as the first college building (Figure 3.9). However, this building cannot be the Old College for several reasons. First, the building in photograph 65/16 is a

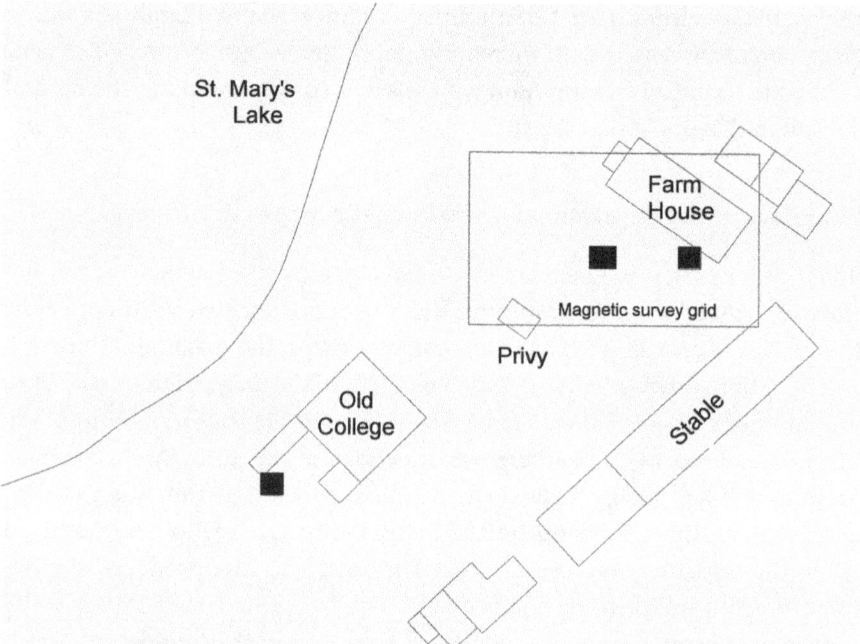

Figure 3.8. Map of structures at the Old College site in 1885 along with the magnetic survey grid and excavation units.

rectangular structure with two stories of windows visible along its eastern wall. The Old College building has always been a square two-story structure, and the Sanborn Company maps dated 1891 and 1893 (Box 11, University Archives) indicate that windows should be visible at the northern end of the east wall of Old College. Second, a structure with a conical roof is visible to the west of the brick building shown in photograph 65/16 and is clearly separated from the brick building. Sanborn maps from 1885 through 1899 indicate that the Old College building had a rectangular structure attached to its southwest corner throughout this period. Furthermore, the Sanborn Company map for 1899 depicts an octagonal structure to the west of the farmhouse that once stood east of Old College. The brick structure depicted in photograph 65/16 is therefore the farmhouse that once stood to the east of Old College and not the Old College itself. A small wooden shed at the left edge of the photograph is probably the privy that stood between the Old College and the farmhouse. This privy was demolished between 1893 and 1899 (according to Sanborn Company maps curated at the University Archives) and photograph 65/16 must therefore have been taken sometime between 1893 and 1899.

Figure 3.9. Farmhouse that produced the architectural debris located by the magnetic survey. (Courtesy of Notre Dame University Archives, no. 65/16)

Artifacts

A diverse array of artifacts was recovered during the excavations. These include numerous bone fragments from both domesticated and wild animals; abundant architectural debris; religious artifacts, including two crucifixes and a votive candle holder; and domestic artifacts, such as crockery, tableware, a pearlware chamber pot, and bottles for wine and spirits. Other artifacts testify to the use of this area as a farm that nourished the university during the later nineteenth century.

The most abundant types of artifacts recovered by the excavations were architectural debris, including fragments of brick, mortar, plaster, nails, and porcelain floor tiles. Over 114 kg of whole and broken bricks were catalogued. These bricks and fragments are primarily yellow and were undoubtedly made of marl from the campus lakes. The farmhouse depicted in photograph 65/16 was made of light-colored brick and is the likely source for the archaeological bricks. The vast majority of the more than five thousand nails collected are machine-cut nails that were probably manufactured before 1880. They confirm the nineteenth-century dates for the structures that supplied the architectural debris of the Old College deposits. Square and hexagonal porcelain mosaic floor tiles were recovered only from the magnetic anomaly unit. The tiles are colored white, pink, or olive green and provide evidence of the distinctive flooring in the structure that produced the archaeological deposits identified by the magnetic survey. Similar tiles in different colors can be found today in the second floor of the Main Building (constructed in 1879), which suggests a late nineteenth-century date for the vanished farmhouse.

Domestic artifacts include both fine and coarse earthenware. Most of these artifacts were recovered from the Log Chapel unit. Fine earthenware vessels are represented by fragments of a pearlware mug and a chamber pot rim, both of which were probably manufactured prior to 1850. The pottery sample from the Old College excavations is rather small (a total of 217 sherds), but a preliminary examination of the catalogued sherds suggests that most of the assemblage dates to the later half of the nineteenth century (Sutliff 1992), because it largely consists of undecorated ironstone, which was in vogue then (Branstner 1989). Glass artifacts include the base of a wine bottle, fragments of a bottle decorated with an eagle that probably held spirits, fragments of lamp chimneys, and a votive candle holder. Two bottle necks in the assemblage have lips that were manufactured using technologies in common use between 1850 and 1870.

Personal items include several varieties of white glass buttons, a fragment of a pearl button, and one bone button. Brass clips for clothing and suspenders were also found. Other personal items include one small crucifix (probably from a rosary), fragments of what may have been a jet crucifix, and many fragments of white clay smoking pipes. Two coins were also found. An 1882 Indian head penny was found in Feature 1. This artifact shows that Feature 1 could not have been created before 1882, although the feature is probably much later than that and the penny was probably incorporated into it by accident. The second coin, a 1966 dime, was found in Level 1 of the control unit, showing that recent material has been incorporated only into the upper levels of the site and that artifacts found below the level of the topsoil are likely to predate the twentieth century.

Bone was extremely well preserved at the site, and over six hundred bones and bone fragments were collected during the excavation (most of these came from the Log Chapel unit). A preliminary analysis of this bone assemblage from the site (Schirtzinger 1991) concluded that it represented the remains of meals consumed between 1860 and 1880. The faunal assemblage included the remains of domesticated mammals (predominately cows and pigs), birds (including goose or turkey bones and fragments of eggshell), and wild animals such as reptiles (probably turtles), rodents (such as squirrels), and fish (tentatively identified as catfish, probably from the campus lakes). A close examination of Figure 3.3 reveals a fisherman with pole on the lakeshore. Erin Schirtzinger's (1991) preliminary analysis of the faunal assemblage was accompanied by archival research, and her work has laid the foundation for future studies that will compare written descriptions of university diets with the remains found at Old College. For example, the residents of the Old College site consumed both domesticated and wild animals. The consumption of wild animals obtained through fishing or hunting is not listed in historical records of university menus, which were apparently bountiful and nourishing but monotonous. Further research will be needed to determine whether wild animals were consumed for economic reasons or simply to provide dietary variety.

Prehistoric artifacts from Old College primarily consist of lithic debitage (flint chips produced when stone tools were manufactured or refurbished at the site). One complete biface (a knife or spear point) recovered during the 1985 test excavation apparently dates to the Terminal Archaic period (dated 2000–1000 B.C.).

The large collection of artifacts from the 1991 excavations at Old College was catalogued and entered into a simple database. The Old College collection provides a significant resource for studies of material culture at the University of Notre Dame and has been incorporated into several laboratory courses in archaeological data analysis. Through the years following the excavations, the data from Old College have been used in many different types of research projects conducted by undergraduates, ranging from dating historic ceramics (Sutliff 1992) to determining what kinds of animals were consumed (Schirtzinger 1991), preparing digital maps (Downey 2002), and studying the best ways to preserve historic metals (Kern 2004), to name just a few examples. The excavations at Old College continue to provide inspiration for future additional laboratory studies such as those that will more precisely date the Old College deposits and reconstruct activities that occurred at the site during the nineteenth century.

Conclusion

The 1985 and 1991 excavations provide clear evidence for significant intact archaeological deposits in the area between the Old College and the Log

Chapel. A stratified historic deposit circa 55 cm thick was found to lie over a paleosol that contains prehistoric artifacts. The prehistoric occupation associated with the paleosol appears to date to the Terminal Archaic period (2000–1000 B.C.). The historic deposits probably span most of the nineteenth century, but most of the deposits probably postdate 1856, when the original log chapel was destroyed by fire. However, early nineteenth-century artifacts found at the level of the original ground surface in the Old College unit suggest that a sealed archaeological record of the university's earliest years may be preserved there.

A magnetic survey and excavations east of the Old College uncovered a previously unsuspected deposit of historic debris. The source of this debris was a farmhouse that once stood in this location and was demolished between 1899 and 1906 (Figure 3.9).

The 1991 field school at the Old College site demonstrated that this location contains intact archaeological deposits that provide a record of the growth of the university throughout its first century and a half. The archaeological deposits at Old College are very complex. This complexity, which would hardly be anticipated by someone walking over the well-manicured lawn, is a product of the changes that have occurred at Notre Dame throughout its history. During the nineteenth century Notre Dame participated in the overall transition of American society from a pioneer society to an urban one. These changes are reflected in the archaeological deposits at Old College, which are the products of a dynamic institution in a dynamic society. The archaeological investigations at Old College provide a unique record of these changes. The continuing analysis of these materials and future excavations will allow the discipline of archaeology to provide its own distinctive contribution to our understanding of Notre Dame's history.

Acknowledgments

Any successful archaeological excavation is a product of the efforts of many people. I am especially grateful to Professor James Bellis, at that time chair of the Department of Anthropology, for inviting me to teach a field school at Notre Dame. His enthusiasm and support for this project made it possible for me to conduct the Old College excavations, and I will always cherish the memory of the summer when we worked at the Old College during the year of Notre Dame's sesquicentennial. My task was simplified by the efforts of Lori Butchko-Curran, the departmental secretary, who helped a newcomer to the campus arrange all the details associated with teaching an archaeological field school. I would also like to thank Roger Schmitz, vice president and associate provost, for the administrative authorization to conduct our excavations.

A field crew is the one absolutely essential element of any field project. My students in Anthropology 490, who actually conducted the excavations, learned the methods of field archaeology with enthusiasm and speed. The quality of their work was such that their efforts have provided a first-rate and very professional example of how meaningful archaeological research can be conducted in a field school setting. My thanks to Jodie Bellis, Rita Deranek, Therese Gales, Paul Gimber, Bill Nichols, Erin Schirtzinger, Luke Shattuk, Jeff Sutliff (all undergraduate students of the University of Notre Dame), Ed Nolan (graduate student in American Studies), Elizabeth Graner (St. Mary's College), and Melissa Windler (Holy Cross Junior College). Jodie Bellis took most of the photographs that provide an important part of documentation of the 1991 excavations. A special thank-you is owed to Jeff Sutliff, who diligently completed what initially appeared to be the overwhelming task of cataloguing the majority of the Old College artifacts.

Stephen Ball (Glenn Black Laboratory of Archaeology, Indiana University) conducted the magnetometer survey at the site. We also thank Christopher Peebles, director of the Glenn Black Laboratory, for use of the magnetometer, and Jessica Marks for assisting with the magnetic survey. Thomas Schlereth, professor of American Studies, shared his wealth of knowledge about the architectural history of Notre Dame. His book *The University of Notre Dame: A Portrait of Its History and Campus* has proven to be an invaluable resource for interpreting the archaeology of the 1991 excavations. Charles Lamb, Peter Lysy, Wendy Schlereth, and Elizabeth Hogan of the University Archives were extremely helpful in providing access to the materials in their care and provided permission to use the image in Figure 3.3. We are also grateful to Cynthia Scott for preparing the press releases and other notices that have informed the community of our activities and to the groundskeepers under the direction of David Woods for putting up with our flags and excavation units and for doing an excellent job of repairing the scars left by our work.

Finally, we thank the faculty, staff, students, alumni, and curious passersby of the Notre Dame community, who stopped to talk with us, check on our progress, and share their knowledge of Notre Dame's history and who gave us the opportunity to explain what we were doing and why.

4

Campus Archaeology on the University of South Carolina's Horseshoe

STANLEY SOUTH

More than three and a half decades have passed since the field aspect of the "Horseshoe" project on the oldest area of the University of South Carolina campus was initiated in June 1973. The name of this campus area comes from the shape of the current road in front of the original buildings flanking the common leading to the current McKissick Museum, in front of which the original home of the university president was located (Figure 4.1).

Time often provides perspective on the significance of what seemed at the time to be a short, small project of little consequence. While many of the people who figured prominently in this project have moved on to other careers, retired, or died, the research stands as a testament to the value of historical archaeology as a way of retrieving the landscapes and lifeways of yesterday not only for academicians but for administrators who seek to cloak their university in the context of "greatness" as dictated by age of their institution. Historical archaeology demonstrates that greatness is neither inherent nor preordained but rather is a product of evolution within the context of hard work, luck, and administrators who understand that today's universities were built on the shoulders of those who came before.

It often behooves an institution to remember its past when planning for the future. In 2005 the University of South Carolina marked its bicentennial. In reflecting on the creation of a world-class university the focus becomes even clearer when the results of a pioneering archaeological study of the college campus are added to the picture of the nascent days of American academe.

Situating the Horseshoe Project in Historical Archaeology

In 1973 historical archaeology was in its nascent stages. For students just entering the field in the twenty-first century it may be difficult to imagine a

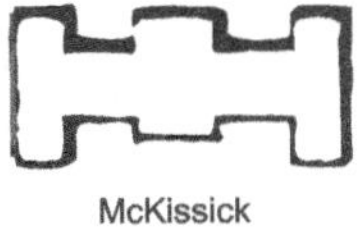

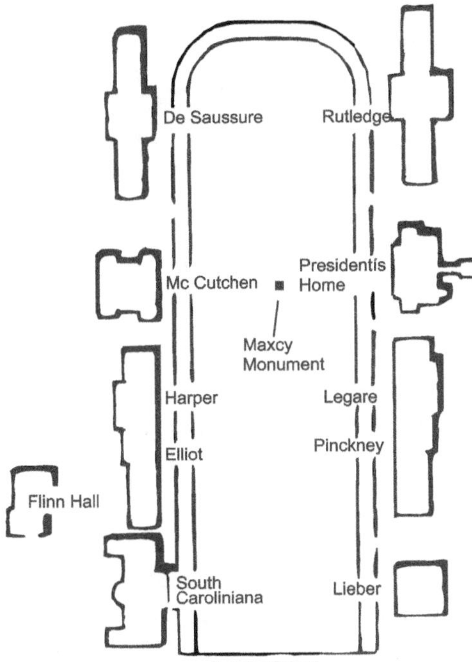

Figure 4.1. Current layout of the Horseshoe on the campus of the University of South Carolina in Columbia. (Hollis 1968)

time when there was no "historical archaeology" as we see it today. But the Conference on Historic Sites Archaeology that I founded was only a gangly teenager, some thirteen years old, and the Society for Historical Archaeology was only six years old in 1973. It would be four more years until the publication of my book *Method and Theory in Historical Archaeology* (1977).

The Horseshoe Project was also a transition from my work on seventeenth- and eighteenth-century English colonial America in the Carolinas and Maryland (South 2005: 107–210, 2008) to my second "career" studying the sixteenth-century French and Spanish efforts on Parris Island, the site of the Spanish capital of La Florida at Santa Elena (South 1997).

Today it is still difficult in many arenas to justify costly archaeological endeavors on sites from the recent past. It is up to the archaeologist and sponsors to recognize the value of such sites and act accordingly. Thirty-five years ago, fresh from work conducted as part of the observation of the tricentennial of the founding of Charleston, South Carolina, I was called upon to work

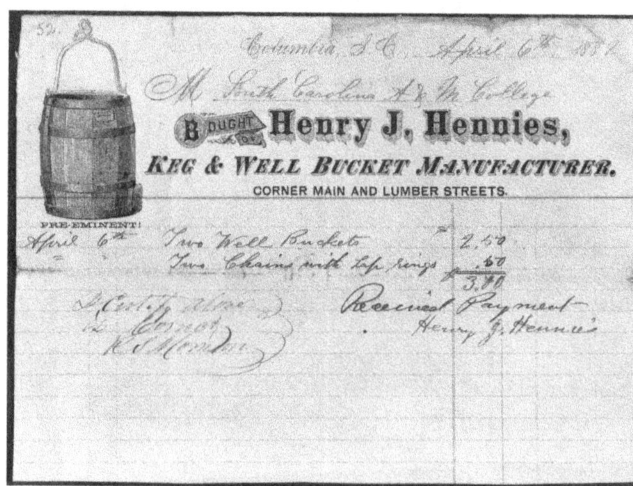
Columbia, S.C. April 6th 188
M South Carolina A & M College
Bought of Henry J. Hennies,
KEG & WELL BUCKET MANUFACTURER.
CORNER MAIN AND LUMBER STREETS.
PRE-EMINENT!

April 6th	Two Well Buckets	2.50
	Two Chains with lap rings	.60
		3.10

Received Payment
Henry J. Hennies

Figure 4.2. An invoice for well buckets and chains for two wells on the Horseshoe in 1882, when the college was known as the South Carolina College of Agriculture and Mechanic Arts. (Hollis 1982: xix)

in the virtual backyard of the South Carolina Institute of Archaeology and Anthropology—in the front yard of the University of South Carolina.

The Project

In the spring of 1973 archaeological investigations were conducted on the Horseshoe common, the oldest part of the campus. These excavations were directed toward the exposure of evidence of early wells and other features in support of a broader proposed renovation plan for the buildings and grounds.

The historical archaeology process involves research into the documentary record as well as excavated material evidence, and the text that follows relies on both types of information. Discovered in the documentary research is an invoice for "two well buckets" and "two chains with lap rings" (Figure 4.2).

The initial research effort was prompted by concerns over proposed campus renovations and may be considered by some to be a form of cultural resource management (CRM). Often CRM archaeology is thought by administrators to be an unwanted but necessary precursor to development or renovations. Universities accepted large amounts of federal funding and so are morally, and sometimes legally, obliged to meet federal guidelines regarding historic preservation when dealing with properties that meet the minimal criteria for significance as defined in the National Register. That includes the age of a structure, which today can be as little as fifty years. Across

Figure 4.3. A close-up view of the Elliott/Harper well house, with Legare and Pinckney Colleges in the background. (Meriwether 1889)

the country, colleges are filled with classrooms and residence halls that are even older, and the University of South Carolina is no exception.

Why Do Campus Archaeology?

Early in 1973 plans were underway for renovation and restoration of the original buildings on the University of South Carolina around the tree- and grass-covered common known as the Horseshoe. In addition to architectural improvements, enhancements to the common were also suggested. One idea proposed by an architect was that a series of classic Greek-style statues appropriate to the period of the early nineteenth century could be attractively arrayed around the Horseshoe. I objected to the Greek invasion.

Counter to this suggestion was the view held by John Califf, architect for the university, who had learned from a lithograph of around 1850 (Green 1916: 50) and from engravings (Meriwether 1889; *Garnet and Black* 1899) that well houses were once located on the Horseshoe. He wisely suggested that restoring the original well houses as reminders of the history of the Horseshoe would be more appropriate than Greek statues (which had never been there), if their original locations could be determined.

One of the original well houses is shown in Figure 4.3.

For nearly a century after its founding in 1805 the primary water sources for structures built on the Horseshoe or main quad of the University of South Carolina were the wells. When plumbing was brought into the buildings on the Horseshoe common in 1900, the well houses were torn down and the well shafts filled.

In order to explore the reconstruction of the well houses idea and learn more about the Horseshoe area, Hal Brunton, vice president for business affairs at the University of South Carolina, contacted the university's Institute of Archaeology and Anthropology. Russell Wright, the architectural consultant, had heard of my archaeological work at the Paca House (South 1967) in Annapolis, Maryland, and informed Brunton, who expressed an interest in locating evidence of the original road and the wells (Brunton to Stephenson, March 29, 1973, South Carolina Institute of Archaeology and Anthropology, Columbia).

On April 25 Robert L. Stephenson, the director of the institute, asked me to meet him in Brunton's office. The three of us met with Richard Webel, landscape consultant; John Califf, university architect; and Russell Wright, historic preservation architect, to discuss the Horseshoe Archaeological Project goals (Stephenson memo, 1973, South Carolina Institute of Archaeology and Anthropology, Columbia). It was decided that the goals would be to locate remains of wells and the central pathway to the original house of the college president at the curve of the Horseshoe.

In May 1973 I used a steel probe and located the brick footings for some of the well houses that once stood in the college green. I then wrote a proposal in which I outlined the fieldwork to be performed (South 1973a). To locate details of the wells, I would remove soil from the areas where I had probed footings. I would determine the size of the various well houses, recover any artifacts associated with them, photograph the ruins, and make profile drawings to reveal any architectural details. There was no plan to excavate the interior contents of the wells.

As I explained: "To excavate all wells would be a costly and time consuming process, the results of which might not warrant such a cost merely for the recovery of relics. The emphasis in this exploratory archaeology project is architectural in nature, designed primarily to provide data of use in the restoration of the area of the University common and the buildings facing it" (South 1973a: 3).

In addition to examining some of the well ruins, I planned to cut a trench across the central area of the Horseshoe to attempt to locate evidence for the original central roadway to the President's House, shown in a painting of South Carolina College made about 1850 (Green 1916: 50).

Of incidental interest was the area around Maxey Monument, erected in 1827 in the center of the common. John Califf wanted to see if postholes or a construction ditch dating from the early nineteenth century could be found adjacent to the monument, possibly indicating a previous structure or scaffolding used in its construction.

Field Results and Archaeological Method

The project, sponsored by the university's Institute of Archaeology and Anthropology, was carried out as planned from June 11 through July 18, 1973, using university students as the archaeological crew.

Archaeologists use a number of methods to search for evidence lying below the surface of the earth before they dig large holes to reveal ruins such as the well ruins we sought on the Horseshoe. If masonry features of brick or stone or drain pipes are sought, a sharp pointed steel probe is often pushed into the earth to strike such objects lying below the surface of the earth. When the probe strikes something, it is pulled out and carefully examined. If a white lime powder is seen on the tip of the probe that leaves a white streak when smeared with the finger, it probably struck lime mortar; if a red powder is seen on the tip, it is likely that it struck brick. If a white powder is seen that does not leave a white streak when smeared on the finger, the probe probably struck stone.

When linear features such as a ditch, a road, a moat, a foundation ditch, or a buggy lane are sought, long narrow trenches are often used in an attempt to cross the linear feature at a right angle and reveal it as a discoloration in the soil at the bottom of the trench or in the profile wall of the trench where it crosses the feature. I cut such a trench and crossed the buggy ruts that identified the location of the original road up the Horseshoe to the president's home nestled in the curve (Figure 4.4).

If the ruins of a house site or village site are sought, where occupation debris from those once living on the site is expected to be concentrated, the method often used is to dig a series of sample holes in a randomly placed pattern within a grid in order to recover artifacts. By plotting the density of the artifacts in the various holes the archaeologist is able to determine where the greatest density of objects is and, once this is determined, to excavate large

Figure 4.4. A view of the south end of the trench (facing south), revealing buggy ruts in the central Horseshoe area.

areas where most artifacts were found. This usually results in the discovery of the limits of the occupation site.

Other methods involve simply collecting artifacts from past occupation of a site from the surface in a controlled manner in order to determine the area of greatest concentration. Because of the constant maintenance of the Horseshoe since the nineteenth century, no surface artifacts from that century were seen.

In some cases geophysical procedures such as ground-penetrating radar, resistivity, and a proton magnetometer may be used. I chose to use the steel probe, however, because I was looking for brick supporting footings for the well houses, and I knew that the search process would be greatly shortened when I struck something solid. I was also using documentary information,

Figure 4.5. The trench at Rutledge College, showing the arc of the well-hole feature beneath the sidewalk, with students David Mullis (*left*) and Leonard Henry (*right*) pointing to postholes for the well house. Note the dark soil arc at the left of the photo, representing the replacement well.

including photographs and engravings, that indicated where the wells on the Horseshoe might be located.

I reasoned that if brick footings or walls for supporting the well houses were still below the surface of the Horseshoe, I might strike them using this method, and I did. One of the wells was identified from a depression in the ground surface. A below-surface hole, such as a filled well shaft, will sometimes continue to settle downward as the water table fluctuates, softening the soil in the shaft and causing it to go into solution. Settling also occurs when the shaft is filled with some biodegradable material, such as bark, sawdust, or wood.

From the archaeology, along with the documents, I was able to arrive at a summary of the wells on the Horseshoe. The first series of wells was constructed at the time of the founding of the university around 1805. Documents indicate that these were cleaned in the late 1830s. Through the century more wells were dug, old ones were back-filled or cleaned, and new well houses were built.

The archaeological evidence for the 1807 well in front of Rutledge College and a replacement well is shown in Figure 4.5. We also found evidence

Figure 4.6. Students David Mullis (*left*) and Leonard Henry (*right*) pointing to the outer edge of the large hole for the well at DeSaussure College. The four brick-bat footings for an 11 × 14 foot well house are seen just outside the well hole.

Figure 4.7. Students Wayne Roberts (*left*) and Leonard Henry (*right*) working on removing artifacts from the top few feet of the Elliott/Harper well, which was arched with bricks in 1898 and filled up in the early years of the twentieth century.

for the well in front of DeSaussure College (Figure 4.6) and the 1898 arched brick top of the earlier Elliott/Harper well (Figure 4.7).

At the end of the use-life for the wells in the late nineteenth century, they were filled with campus-generated refuse that speaks of the lives of the students.

Evidence of Student Life from the Material Record

The Elliott/Harper well contained a mass of laboratory test tubes, microscope slides, and other chemistry laboratory refuse. This deposit was carefully sampled but not excavated (Figure 4.8).

The wells also contained evidence of earlier renovations on the campus. One of the most telling of these was in the realm of lighting—parts of oil

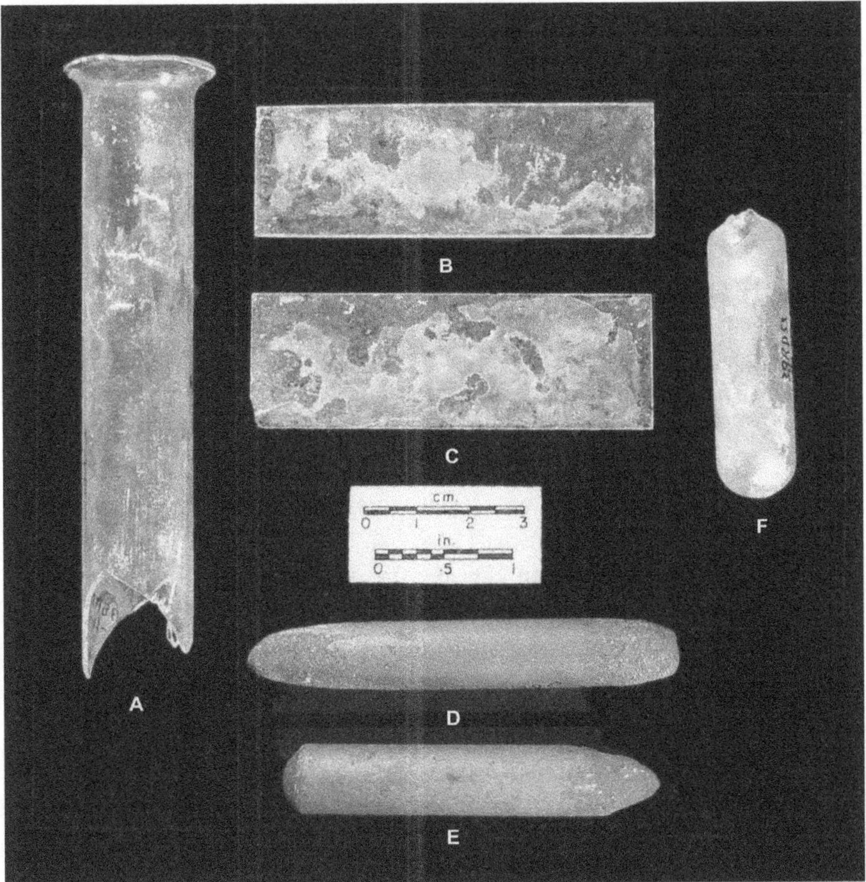

Figure 4.8. Science-related artifacts: (*A*) test tube; (*B* and *C*) microscope slides; (*D* and *E*) carbon electrodes for arc outdoor arc lamps; (*F*) snap-top ampoule.

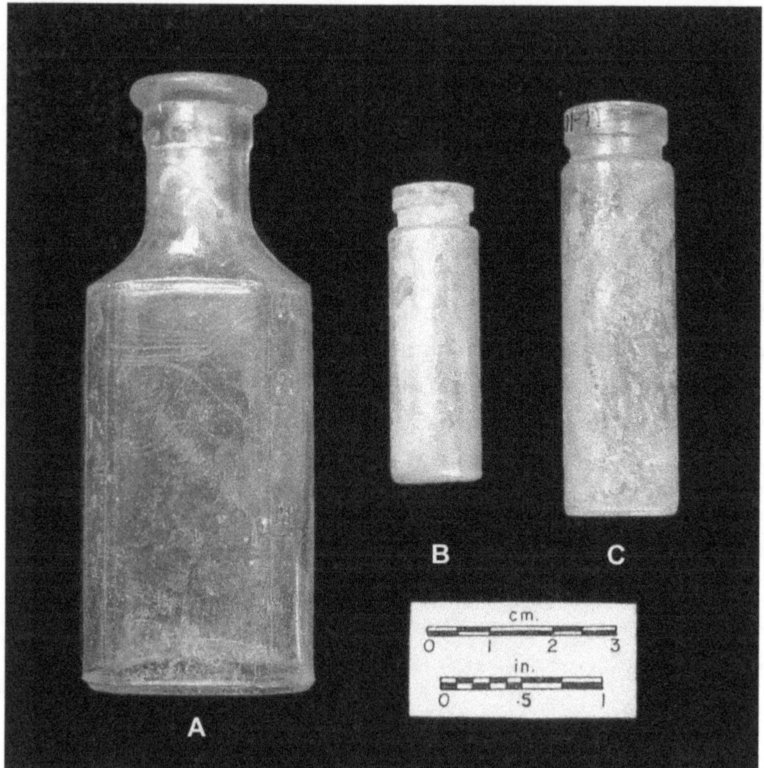

Figure 4.9. Medicine bottles from the Elliott/Harper College well: (*A*) graduated patent medicine bottle; (*B* and *C*) medicine vials.

lamps, carbon electrodes from arc lamps, and electric lightbulbs and switch plates reveal the evolutionary changes that took place in the nineteenth century on the Horseshoe common. Discarded medicine bottles reflect students' needs for medication for illnesses (Figure 4.9).

Throughout the nineteenth century the wells were periodically cleaned out, as revealed by artifacts dating from the last third of the nineteenth century through the first three decades of the twentieth. Many personal items were discarded in the wells as they were filled, such as buttons, coins, pins, thimbles, marbles, and fragments of combs and toothbrushes (Figure 4.10).

The recovery of a variety of bottle forms indicates that students were drinking wine, beer, ale, and harder spirits. Poker chips provide evidence that they gambled. We also found evidence (in the form of jewelry) that fe-

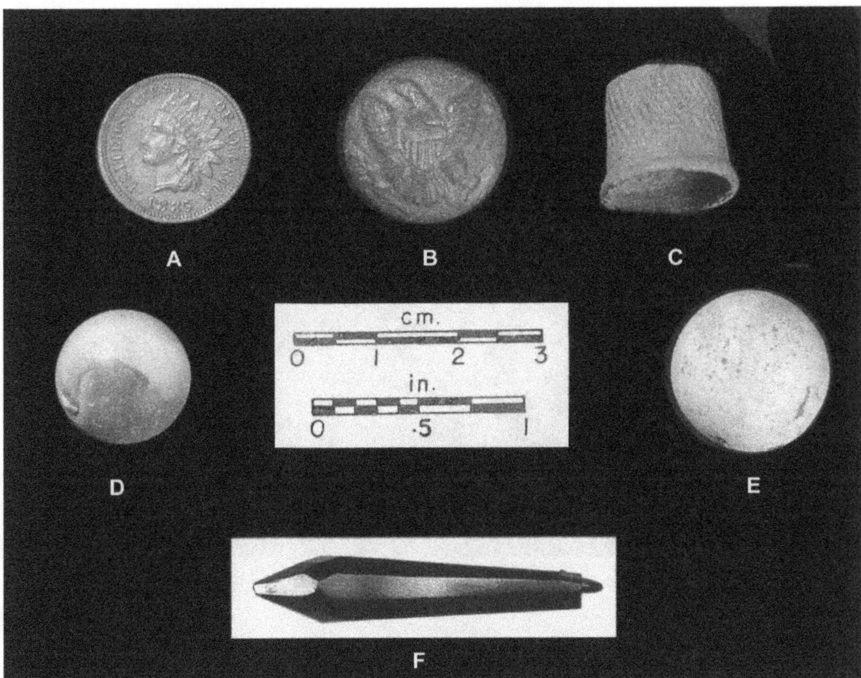

Figure 4.10. Selected artifacts from the Horseshoe: (*A*) an 1885 Indian head penny; (*B*) an enlisted man's button, possibly lost on the night Columbia burned on February 17, 1865, when thousands of refugees and federal soldiers camped on the Horseshoe; (*C*) a thimble; (*D*) a marble made of glass; (*E*) a marble made of marble; (*F*) a jet or black glass pendant or earring.

males were entertained on the all-male campus and that at least some of the students indulged in the taking of snuff.

When students came to the well to fill their pitchers with water for bathing and washing their hands in their rooms, they sometimes dropped and broke their blue transfer-printed vessels, perhaps while engaging in horseplay (Figure 4.11).

Of course, all of these artifacts simply reflect the larger society in which the campus was situated. We did find evidence of its function as a place of education, including ferrules from pencils and the laboratory supplies mentioned above.

From the exploratory archaeology on the Horseshoe we recovered much information about three types of wells once located there as well as artifacts reflecting the daily lives of students.

Figure 4.11. A blue transfer-printed whiteware pitcher from the Horseshoe excavation.

Revealing Clues to the History of Building Architecture

In the process of revealing the clues to the well in front of DeSaussure College, some ditches were discovered that proved to be a foundation ditch for that building at a different location than the place where it was later constructed.

As I puzzled over the function of these dark-colored linear features, thinking that I might have found a series of walks for a formal garden, I finally decided to cut a profile of one of the features to determine its depth. The profile revealed that the hole was eight-tenths of a foot deep below the subsoil level. With six inches of topsoil above that, this meant that the original ditches had been about eighteen inches deep—so much for the walk theory! With this information I realized that the ditches were a foundation ditch for a building.

As I pondered my plan view drawing of these ditches, I noticed that the junction of the two arms extending from the central area lined up with the junction of the wings of DeSaussure College with the larger central part of the extant building (Figure 4.12).

Suddenly a light dawned: could this series of ditches be an earlier foundation for DeSaussure College? I took my ditch drawing to the basement

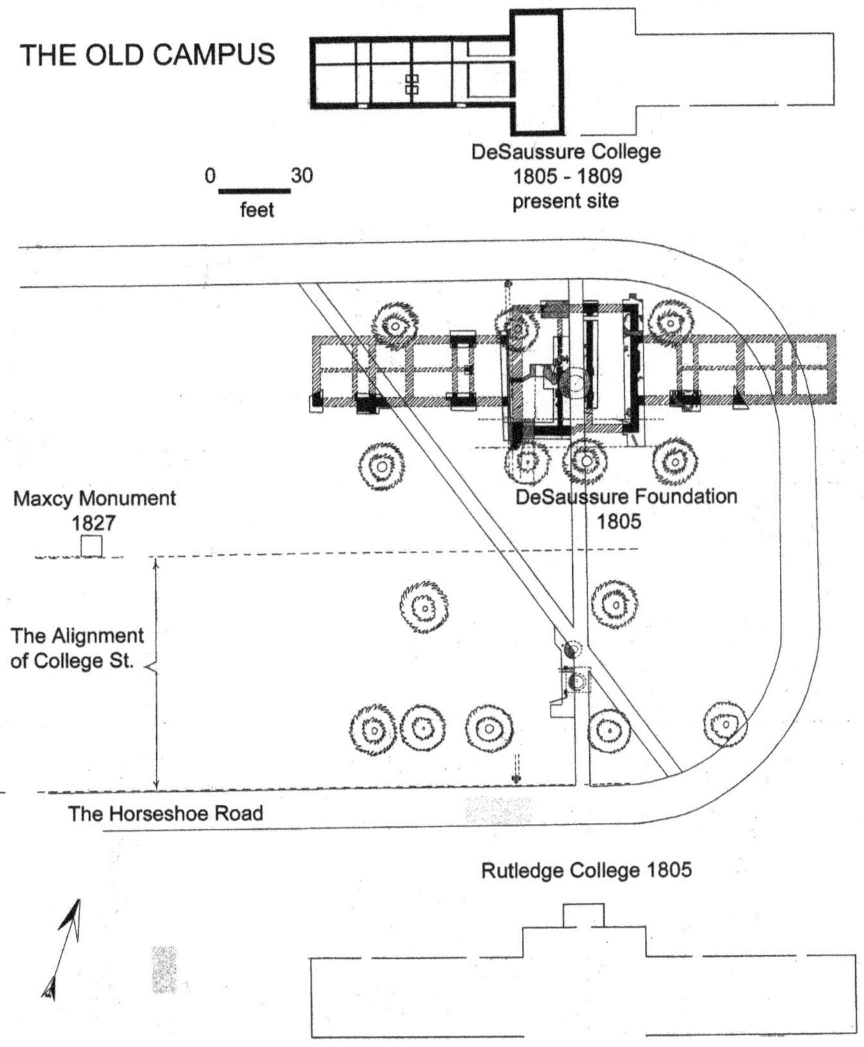

Figure 4.12. Comparison between the modern floor plan of DeSaussure College and the archaeologically revealed ditches for the originally planned location. The recommendation that the well houses be reconstructed with benches for students to enjoy the character of the original Horseshoe setting was not accepted by the university.

crawlway door of DeSaussure and went beneath the floor to see if the pattern of cross-walls lined up with ditches I had found. I took measurements and discovered that the foundation of DeSaussure matched this set of ditches. I had found the explanation for the ditches. They were the original dug foundation for DeSaussure College that had originally been laid out 100 feet farther south than the building standing there today.

The original plan had apparently called for the wings of DeSaussure College to be built 220 feet north of Rutledge College; but after the foundation ditches were dug, a decision was made to build DeSaussure College farther north, making a commons area between them 320 rather than 220 feet wide.

I wondered why this early decision had been made by the college officials, since it was a major one that determined the location of all subsequent buildings on the Horseshoe. Why had DeSaussure's foundation originally been planned and the ditches dug, before the controlling Board of Trustees realized that the commons area between the two buildings would be too narrow and that DeSaussure needed to be built 100 feet farther north?

In addressing this question I noticed that College Street at the west end of the Horseshoe is off-center from the Horseshoe, with the north edge of the street lining up with the center of the Horseshoe. I then drew a map showing Rutledge and DeSaussure Colleges and the location of the original foundation ditches for DeSaussure College in relation to the projected position of College Street.

When I did this, it became clear that DeSaussure College had originally been planned to be the same distance from College Street as Rutledge, since both Rutledge and the original foundation ditches of DeSaussure are 47 feet from the edge of the projected edge of College Street. It was apparent, therefore, that the street layout of the city of Columbia had originally influenced the positioning of DeSaussure College. I had found the reason for the original positioning of the DeSaussure building.

When the campus *Gamecock* newspaper published my map on July 19, 1973, showing the original location of DeSaussure's foundation, a history professor chastised me for suggesting that I had found the originally planned location of DeSaussure College. He said that he did not have any idea what I had found but that it could not be the ditch for the originally planned location of DeSaussure. If that were the case it would have been written down somewhere. I reminded him that about ninety percent of what we know from the past was not written down but was derived from archaeological knowledge of the material remains that have survived. He insisted, however: if it existed in the past, the written word would witness it. If a document turned up saying the board voted to move the building site 100 feet to the north he said he would believe it, but not until that happened.

Archaeologists often face skeptics who assume the written word is somehow more complete, more accurate, and more sacrosanct than material remains from the past surviving in the pages of the earth. Archaeologists know that the two disciplines work hand in hand as historical archaeology.

Later another researcher found that a building plan was to have two 160-foot-long buildings facing each other and 160 feet apart (Bryan 1976: 29). It is interesting to note that Rutledge today is 220 feet long, not 160. The original building size was also later changed.

This decision called for a comparable 220-foot separation of the two buildings, and the foundation ditch for DeSaussure was dug where I found it. Sometime after that, but before the brick masonry was laid in the ditch, another decision was made to move the location of DeSaussure College another 100 feet to the north, creating the 320-foot separation between the two buildings that we see today. If this last decision had not been made, the Horseshoe-shaped common today would be the same width as the length of Rutledge College—220 feet.

Archaeology revealed that the original foundation wing was 220 feet from the Rutledge wings, which is the same distance as its width. The historical documentation from Edward Hooker has allowed us to learn of the 160-foot stage in the planning process, which, however, was never carried out and is not reflected in the real world.

We also learn there of the board's idea that the distance between the buildings should not exceed 300 feet. I wonder what Richard Clark, the architect, thought when he had the foundation ditch for DeSaussure College dug 220 feet from Rutledge and then had to do the same thing again 100 feet farther north. We know from the archaeological record that this did indeed happen.

John Bryan tells us that Richard Clark and the Board of Trustees were in serious conflict in 1806. I suggest that one conflict may have been the decision to move DeSaussure 100 feet to the north after the foundation ditches had already been dug (Bryan 1976: 43–44), a story told in the archaeological record.

Some months after my work on the Horseshoe project was completed, minutes of the Board of Trustees were found by an alert researcher. They had been misfiled among papers in the treasurer's office. The minutes revealed the decision of the trustees to move the site of DeSaussure 100 feet to the north. Later I again happened to meet the history professor who had challenged my archaeological finding and asked him what his view on the matter was. He said he now believed what I had found.

What Was Learned

In addition to the architectural data archaeologically recovered, the artifacts from the Horseshoe excavations have told us a great deal about the daily lives of the students, providing us with evidence regarding the physical plant of the university.

We know that the wells were places where students gathered to fetch water and apparently to wash dishes—I certainly hope that they were neither dumping their chamber pots in the well nor using them to fetch water! The presence of beer, wine, and whiskey bottles tells us that students drank alcohol in the nineteenth century even as they do today. Marbles and poker chips tell us of their gambling, petty though it may be, while some artifacts such as an enlisted man's military coat button postdating 1854 suggest the presence of federal troops on the campus during the Civil War.

The use of documentary and material evidence in a recursive manner allows us to expand upon the data that can be derived from either source independently. Neither the documentary nor the archaeological records of the Horseshoe have been fully expended. Further research in the Horseshoe area of the university campus has the potential to provide considerably more details illuminating student life and the activities there, as the artifacts speak to us through archaeology.

Project Results

A few months after my project, on February 19, 1974, university president Thomas F. Jones wrote a letter to colleagues regarding the USC Horseshoe Renovation (Jones to colleagues, South Carolina Institute of Archaeology and Anthropology, Columbia). He pointed out that a faculty/staff/student planning committee had been working on possible uses of the Horseshoe, while architects, engineers, and landscape consultants studied "various aspects involved in the renovation and restoration of the famous Horseshoe" and its buildings. The reconstruction of well houses on the Horseshoe was one of the questions of interest.

President Jones reported that the University Board of Trustees had asked him "to appoint an advisory committee representing faculty, staff, students, alumni and interested local and State Historical representatives." He asked archaeologist Robert L. Stephenson, director of the Institute of Archaeology and Anthropology, to serve on the advisory committee and stated that "the Horseshoe Renovation Project is one of the most important projects undertaken in recent years." This committee was primarily interested in the restoration of the buildings on the Horseshoe, not in the well houses.

On February 26, 1974, Stephenson and I met with the Horseshoe Renovation Committee and various architects involved in the project to make a preliminary report. I showed slides of the archaeological evidence for the various wells and artifacts recovered during excavation. Also presented were the photographs taken during the project, the master plan map, profile drawings, and documentary research compiled for a final written report. The committee was not interested in restoring the well houses, which removed the urgency for preparing a final report. I set that project aside, and the report remained unfinished as other sponsor-funded projects impinged on my time.

As a result of the later interest of the vice provost, George Terry, a campus-wide committee was formed to conduct additional on-campus archaeology. Two meetings were held at the South Carolina Institute of Archaeology and Anthropology in August and September 1991, to discuss the data I had in hand from the 1973 Horseshoe Project. As a result of these meetings, Bruce Rippeteau, director of the institute, made funding available to allow the preparation of a belated report on the Horseshoe Project (South and Steen 1992).

I was appointed to a Cultural Resource Management Review Committee by George Terry to review planned ground-disturbing activity on campus resulting from construction of new buildings, but that committee, to my knowledge, never met. After I noticed several new projects digging holes on campus, I happened to meet George on campus and asked him if his committee had approved the work as complying with federal CRM guidelines. He said that he was frustrated, because those in charge of such construction simply had to check a box indicating that a university committee existed (never mind that it had never met), and that took care of the CRM requirements.

I hope that more than that is now being done to mitigate the damage to the cultural resources on campus by the many construction projects as the university continues to expand. My calls to university officials to inquire about the current procedure remain unreturned.

The Project's Significance

The primary goals of the Horseshoe Archaeological Project of 1973 were limited to locating the wells and the original road down the center of the Horseshoe to the President's House. The Horseshoe excavations should prove valuable as a background example for future campus archaeology. As the University of South Carolina grows and changes because of continuing damage to the archaeological record through construction and maintenance activities, there will be an ever increasing need to record, through archaeology, the cultural remains lying beneath the surface of the campus.

Some of the goals of historical archaeology include: (1) the discovery of architectural features such as wells, roads, paths, privies, walls, and foundations when history has failed to record their exact location and discoveries that would lead to the reconstruction of architectural features; (2) the recovery of artifacts associated with the architectural features (such as broken dishes, coins, glassware, and other discarded trash) that can help determine the function of a feature and pinpoint its use in time as well as the behavioral patterns related to it; and (3) the discovery of the processes of culture and patterns of past lifeways that prompted those behavioral patterns.

A major consideration of the 1973 project was the planned reconstruction of the well houses in the exact location of the original wells. As it turned out, this was not done, due to financial or other political or administrative considerations, but the data we recovered are presented here in case reconstruction is undertaken in the distant future.

As I have indicated, one result of the 1973 project was the accidental discovery of the original foundation ditch for DeSaussure College in a location other than its current one, providing a surprising bonus to the history of the Horseshoe and the university.

The uses to which this archaeological information is put revolve around education, training, and public awareness. Sometimes the major motivation for undertaking excavation is to recover information for exhibits to educate the public.

In the case of restored buildings, those in charge of interpreting the houses to the public sometimes are interested in furnishing it with authentic artifacts like those used by the original inhabitants. Fragments of dishes are sufficient to allow similar vessels to be purchased to furnish the restored structure. Museum exhibits explaining the Horseshoe area and the early days of South Carolina College can well be designed around archaeological fragments joined with historical documentation.

As I have demonstrated, artifacts used in exhibits are reflective of past lifeways in which those who used and discarded the objects were involved—such as life on a college campus. Scientific comparison of artifact assemblages from college campuses, public buildings, domestic households, factories, and other such architectural use areas can be carried out by archaeologists involved with comparative analyses for methodological reasons. The refining of archaeological methods is an ongoing process, with each project contributing to the accumulation of knowledge on how best to deal with the archaeological record.

Training college students in the methods and theoretical concepts and techniques of archaeology is an educational function served by the archaeological process. Archaeology conducted primarily for the purpose of training students is considered an unethical practice by the American Anthropological Association, however, since the scientific values of the site take precedence over solely educational goals. A research design must accompany any archaeology conducted as a training program for students, and a professional quality report must be written and made accessible.

The general public and media are interested in archaeology as an endeavor that captures the imagination. Some sponsors of archaeological projects have found that the public is attracted to the site to watch the archaeological process, as students and faculty were when I dug on the Horseshoe.

Town Creek Indian Mound State Historic Site in North Carolina, for instance, was investigated archaeologically for forty years, not only with scientific goals in mind but also for the education and enjoyment of the visiting public.

At the colonial capital of Spanish Florida (Santa Elena) on Parris Island, South Carolina, archaeology is being carried out for scientific as well as educational purposes. Tourists and schoolchildren are given a lecture by an archaeologist while they watch archaeology being conducted. Workshops for training teachers are also offered to familiarize them with the goals and methods of archaeology.

The political goals of generating good public relations and stimulating interest in archaeology in sponsors and the public to gain support are also a part of the archaeological process.

Archaeology is an expensive process, and proposals in keeping with the goals of the funding agencies are the ones that are funded. Because of this, archaeology is carried out on sites that are of interest to some funding agency, either for research- directed goals or for the purpose of legally mitigating some damage to the cultural resource in question. Campus archaeology carried out to mitigate damage to the buried archaeological record is a worthwhile endeavor; but it should be conducted under the direct, on-site supervision of a qualified archaeologist who has time to devote at least four months of analysis and writing for each month of fieldwork.

The 1973 Horseshoe Project involved thirty work study students and volunteers. Newspaper articles appeared in the *State*, the *Columbia Record*, and the *Gamecock*. Charlotte and Columbia television stations reported on the excavation project as it progressed. Much interest was generated by the discoveries through public relations media and through students and others passing by the excavation site as work was underway.

A future program in campus archaeology at the University of South Carolina can be successfully carried out on a continuing annual basis if a full-time archaeologist is responsible for coordinating academic and research interests, supervising digs, writing proposals for funding, coordinating public relations aspects of the dig, supervising analysis of artifacts recovered, writing an annual scientific archaeology report, planning the logistics, and making sure the CRM guidelines for mitigating damage are followed.

Such a responsibility cannot be adequately carried out by a committee alone or by an archaeologist committed to a full-time academic position or other research. A multidepartmental, multidisciplinary campus archaeology program, however, would have many benefits, not the least of which would be a continuing high public relations profile for the university resulting from the effort.

The Horseshoe Project of 1973 is best seen as a pilot effort demonstrating the results that can be forthcoming from a small-scale, two-month, part-time project. It took nineteen years for a report to be completed, which is testimony to the need for a full-time archaeologist with a budget to carry out an ongoing Campus Archaeology Program adequately on an annual basis. It would be difficult to work such a project into an already existing academic or archaeological research schedule, as was the case with the Horseshoe report. Perhaps one day the University of South Carolina and universities elsewhere will see the merit of such an undertaking.

CRM Archaeologists on American Campuses

This project demonstrates the potential of excavation on campuses under a Campus Archaeology Program. Such a program would involve students and professional archaeologists in a multidisciplinary historical archaeology effort to preserve the material culture remains surviving from the past as an integral part of the university's legacy. A Campus Archaeology Program with a full-time, year-round archaeologist could address the goals of cultural resource management.

Under such a program the cultural and historical resources lying within campus archives and the pages in the earth throughout America can be read and preserved for posterity. I hope that such a program is established on campuses nationwide in the future. When and if that ever happens, the value of conducting on-campus research to address the cultural resources waiting to be archaeologically discovered will be demonstrated as each new dig is undertaken.

Beyond Simply Salvaging Historic Tidbits from the Past

Thirty-five years have passed since some visionaries dreamed of reconstructing a series of well houses on the Horseshoe common to provide an authentic nineteenth-century atmosphere for that historic ground. In 1973 students lay on the Horseshoe grass to relax, to study, to sunbathe, or to sit around and talk and spend a leisurely afternoon. Nothing has changed since that time except that some of the buildings have been architecturally revamped. Students must still sit or lie on the grass.

The dream for some had been that the well houses in front of the college buildings could be reconstructed through the architectural and historical archaeology research carried out there, using the wealth of data available. Each well house, with benches around a central water fountain, would serve as an added respite for students from their studies as the grass continues to do today (but only when the grass is dry).

Perhaps in another fifty or one hundred years the historic preservation movement will have advanced beyond simply conducting CRM projects to salvage tidbits of information from the past before such resources are destroyed through progress. In the future, reconstruction of historic campus elements to preserve the authentic character of the past for generations still to come may yet become a reality.

5

Guns and Roses

Ritualism, Time Capsules, and the Massachusetts Agricultural College

MICHAEL S. NASSANEY, UZI BARAM, JAMES C. GARMAN, AND MICHAEL F. MILEWSKI

On a spring morning in 1991 our archaeological crew and several heavy equipment operators dug carefully around an old pine tree stump on the Amherst campus of the University of Massachusetts. Five hours later, we came upon what we were looking for. After more than a century underground, the time capsule buried by the Class of 1878 during a tree planting ceremony saw the light of day (MAC 1878a:31).[1]

Time capsules—often-mysterious collections of objects that people select to represent themselves and their cultural milieu—have great potential to inform us about the past, yet they and the circumstances surrounding their interment have received little, if any, attention in the historical or anthropological literature. Scholarly discussion of time capsules is extremely rare, and the only serious overview of the formal variation and meaning of time capsules has been offered by an anthropologist from a popular culture perspective (Ascher 1974). This lapse is unfortunate, because material remains of encapsulated time—objects deliberately set aside in the past—provide an entry point into discussions concerning relationships between past, present, and future (Leone 1981; Lowenthal 1985). The actual contents of a time capsule, however, constitute only one dimension of a broader discourse, because the burial process is often a ceremonial activity charged with meaning for the participants.

Our collective effort in the recovery of a time capsule at the University of Massachusetts galvanized our fascination with time capsule creators and their intentions. Our discovery raises a series of interesting questions about the act of encapsulating time. By "encapsulating time," we mean the intentional act of selecting representations of one's particular world for the edification of future generations, the deliberate curation of the present for the future. Some of the questions posed by our find are site-specific, pertaining to the institutional identity of what was once known as the Massachusetts Agricultural College. For example, what is the historical context of the time capsule, and how is it related to the role of a land-grant college in the post–Civil War era?

Other questions relate to anthropological and historical ideas about ritual activity and time: might the burial of time capsules be for audiences in the present as well as in the unknowable future? Similarly, the relationship of ritual to artifact becomes especially pertinent in treating time capsules as archaeological assemblages. The contents are constrained in two directions—first, by the physical limits of the actual time capsule; and second, by the aspects of material culture that the creators actively choose to commemorate for the benefit of future generations. Yet despite the efforts made in their selection—the Class of 1878 referred to the capsule as "a box containing documents of great importance to future ages" (MAC 1878a:31)—time capsule inventories are arguably of less significance than the motivations for their creation and the rituals surrounding their burial. This chapter addresses these issues by considering two University of Massachusetts time capsules—one that we recovered and one that we helped to design and bury. We begin with a description of the events surrounding the interment of the first capsule in 1877 and its recovery from a hillside overlooking the center of the campus 114 years later.

Burying the Present

On August 27, 1874, a group of twenty-six young men assembled for freshman registration at the Massachusetts Agricultural College in Amherst, Massachusetts (Figure 5.1). Many in this Class of 1878 were the sons of small-scale farmers from rural places or from Massachusetts villages such as Amherst, Bridgewater, Hadley, Franklin, Leverett, and Marlborough. Earlier classes at the college, established in 1863, also were made up for the most part of local students and young men from other places in the state. Admission to the college required the ability to pay tuition and board promptly and to show "a certificate of good moral character" from a teacher or pastor (Carpenter and Morehouse 1896: 548). On average, the students were a little older than seventeen. The majority in these classes worked for wages at the college, suggesting that most of the students were not comfortably middle class.

Nearly three years later, on April 4, 1877, the seventeen remaining stu-

Figure 5.1. The Massachusetts Agricultural College Class of 1878 on the steps of North College. (Courtesy of Special Collections and University Archives, W.E.B. Du Bois Library, University of Massachusetts, Amherst)

dents in the Class of 1878 agreed to plant a class tree during that year's commencement week and noted their decision in the class secretary's record book. They chose to place a white pine near the flagpole that stood in what was then the center of the campus (Figures 5.2 and 5.3) and also to bury "a box containing documents of great importance to future ages" (MAC 1878a: 31). The selection of the documents to be set beneath the tree was left to the discretion of a committee. At a meeting on June 12, they made final arrangements for the upcoming event. The dimensions of the box, which was to cost no more than seventy cents, were specified as ten by seven by three inches.

When commencement week finally arrived in 1877, the students were prepared for their special event. The program for the event featured a number of activities, but it does not even mention the time capsule. On June 19 "the exercises were held under the old chestnut tree. . . . A suitable platform was built under it for the accommodation of the speakers and singers. A vast concourse of spectators gathered to witness the ceremony" (MAC 1878a: 31). An oration and poem were read, interspersed with music by the glee club and followed by a seven-gun salute. In the poem he wrote for the occasion, Charles Francis Coburn pointed out to his classmates the way to "True Nobility" and drew analogies from the upright pine that would soon be planted.

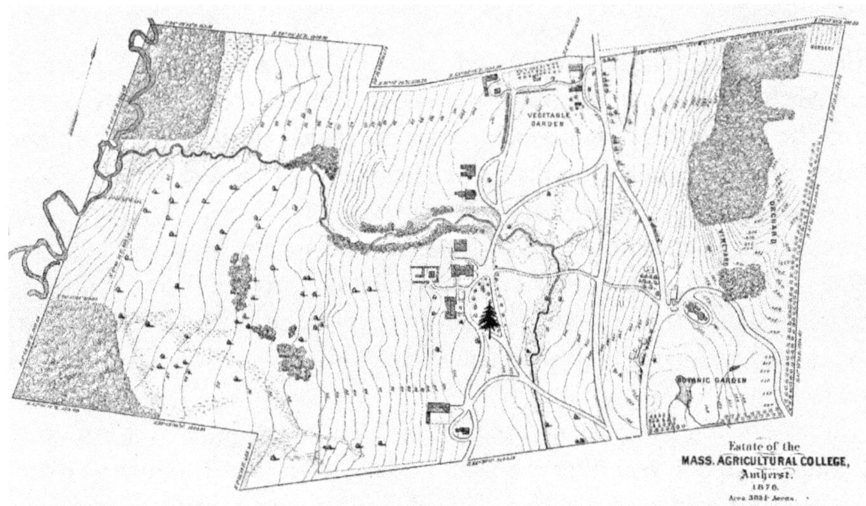

Figure 5.2. Map of the "Estate of the Massachusetts Agricultural College, Amherst," 1870, published in *Eighth Annual Report of the Massachusetts Agricultural College* (January 1871). The star shows the approximate location of the pine tree and the time capsule.

Figure 5.3. The white pine tree of the Class of 1878 stands between the flagpole and the walkway right of center in this photograph, taken between 1886 and 1892. The planting of the tree predates the campus chapel, built in 1885. The building in the background on the right is South College. (Courtesy of Special Collections and University Archives, W.E.B. Du Bois Library, University of Massachusetts, Amherst)

Members of the class carefully laid the box of papers in the ground and placed the white pine immediately above it. They then gathered around to sing the *Ode to the White Pine*, a song that valedictorian Arthur Amber Brigham had composed for the event; after they had covered the tree's roots with earth, they cast rose petals around its base (MAC 1877). After an eight-gun salute and the closing hymns, the crowd dispersed from the hillside.[2] One year later, on the eve of their own graduation, two members of the Class of 1878 examined the condition of the pine tree. These inspectors reported to the class that the tree they had planted the previous year was alive and had set new buds.

The 1878 commencement was held on Wednesday, June 19, at Amherst College Hall, one year after the time capsule ceremony. Twenty eager students were finally awarded their bachelor of science degrees. Eight of the graduates planned to follow agricultural pursuits, six were undecided, three chose business, and one each selected medicine, veterinary science, and chemistry. The class met periodically until their fifty-year reunion in 1928, when the eight surviving members sat on the commencement platform as honored guests. When the exercises were completed, the men, marking their final group activity as members of the class, gathered around the white pine tree. The last alumnus of the Class of 1878, John Franklin Hunt, died in 1943, and knowledge of the ceremony surrounding the tree's planting was lost to living memory.

Memory Awakened

In the fall of 1990, more than a century after the planting of the white pine, a severe windstorm seriously damaged the majestic tree. The university's landscape architect decided that it should be cut down. Within weeks of the storm, Michael Milewski (then university archives assistant) located and reexamined the long-ignored class records during his research to identify the historical origins of the pine tree. When members of the Office of Alumni Relations were notified of the tree's legacy, they contacted Michael Nassaney (then an anthropology graduate student at the University of Massachusetts) to develop a recovery strategy to find what became known as the "time capsule." To an anthropological archaeologist, it was a most unusual survey and excavation project. By far the majority of objects that archaeologists typically recover are haphazardly discarded, somehow lost, and not meant to be found. In this case, our predecessors had intentionally created an archaeo-

Figure 5.4. Selected objects found during the time capsule excavations: large mammal bones (*left*), ceramic fragments (*lower right*), and two shell casings (*top right*) possibly used for the seven- and eight-gun salutes fired during the June 1877 time capsule ceremony.

logical assemblage for some unknown future. By embarking on the quest for the capsule, we, in the present, became that future.

We initially examined the base of the tree using a proton magnetometer, which measures magnetic intensity below the surface of the ground. Magnetometers differ from metal detectors in their ability to measure fields of magnetic change rather than merely specific metal objects. The survey results were equivocal at best, suggesting that the box might be nonferrous, buried deeper than the instrument could detect, or situated immediately beneath the decaying tree stump, which was nearly six feet in diameter. We would need to conduct exploratory excavations.

The university supplied a backhoe and operator to cut four short trenches along the margins of the trunk and thus to sever the tree's root system and expose the underlying soils. We carefully monitored the excavations, occasionally noting and collecting historic artifacts such as construction debris (for example, brick and roof tile fragments); pieces of metal, glass, and ceramics; and a few large mammal bones (Figure 5.4). These objects were probably associated with later filling and landscaping modifications and not

Figure 5.5. The 1877 time capsule in situ, immediately after its discovery.

with the Class of 1878's activities. Two shell casings that were found in the excavations, however, deserve special notice because they might derive from the salutes fired during the tree-planting ceremony of 1877. The casings are .45–70 caliber, standard military issues for the period and conform to those dating from 1876 found at the Little Big Horn Battlefield in Montana (Scott et al. 1989). Furthermore, these casings were designed for blank cartridges, not for shooting with bullets—precisely what we might expect in ceremonial salutes (Richard Colton, personal communication to Michael Nassaney, 1991).

The tree stump presented a formidable obstacle to further excavation, so it was removed with a larger backhoe. Once it was severed from the earth, we examined the massive root system of the stump to see if the time capsule was entangled in its grip. Meanwhile, excavations continued. Remarkably, our efforts were rewarded when a slightly dented and discolored metal box was exposed about six feet below the present ground surface, just northeast of where the pine once stood (Figure 5.5).

Over the course of the day, many spectators paused to watch the excavations at the center of campus. By the time we found the box, an anxious crowd of about 150 onlookers had assembled to witness this historic event. Some began to chant "Open it! Open it!" when they saw our excitement at having located the elusive treasure. The news radiated far beyond the cam-

Figure 5.6. The copper box had somehow been forced open during its more than a century underground; moisture entering from the corner damaged the time capsule's contents.

pus: local and even national media began to report the discovery (*New York Times* 1991).[3]

The find was a copper box of the dimensions described in the class notes; its top was soldered shut, but a corner was bent open (Figures 5.5 and 5.6). There were no fresh scratches on the box to indicate recent damage; it had been forced open prior to excavation either by natural processes or by disturbances associated with landscaping activities.[4] In any case, moisture had entered the box, partially damaging its contents and rendering them unstable. Once in the laboratory, the delicate contents of the box were removed and placed in a heavy, airtight plastic bag in preparation for freezing. This process would temporarily stabilize the documents until appropriate conservation measures could be undertaken.

When the contents were finally examined in detail (Figure 5.7), they appeared to be generally mundane (Table 5.1). The box contained no rare coins, personal mementos, or popular culture icons of the 1870s. Indeed, many of the contents were duplicated by holdings in the special collections and archives of the university library.[5] Only one of the documents—an original handwritten manuscript that contains a prophecy or "future words"—has no duplicate in the university collections. Though only a portion of the ten- to

Figure 5.7. The 1877 time capsule contents after conservation (see Table 5.1).

Table 5.1. Contents of the Class of 1878 time capsule

Contents	Description
Manuscript	Poem delivered at the planting of the class tree on June 19, 1877, by Charles Francis Coburn, '78
Manuscript	Signatures of the junior class as listed in the *Index*, November 1876
Manuscript	"Future Words": 10–12 handwritten manuscript pages, mostly illegible
Program	"M. A. C. '78, Programme of Exercises at the Planting of the Class Tree, by the Class of '78, Massachusetts Agricultural College"
Business Card	J. L. Lovell (father of Charles Otto Lovell, '78), Amherst photographer, 2.5" by 4"
Report	Twelfth annual report of the Massachusetts Agricultural College, January 1875
Yearbook	The *Index* of the Massachusetts Agricultural College, vol. 8, no. 1, published by the Class of 1878, November 1876

Note: The contents are listed as they were found stratigraphically from top to bottom in the copper box.

twelve-page text is legible, that portion is worth quoting: "If we apply ourselves to this development of our agriculture, manufacture, and commerce and elevate the moral and intellectual tone of the people then we may indulge the hope that our country will ever be the abode of peace and prosperity, the seat of learning and the arts. Our nation has yet begun to work out her possibilities richly endowed by nature. The wealth of her resources remains to be harvested."

This passage is particularly interesting in light of the final examination question given to the graduating Class of 1877 on the topic of "the importance of agriculture as a producing industry and its relations to other arts and industries" (*Amherst Record* 1877). The question and the prophecy may well reflect concern over an issue that preoccupied many agriculturalists, students and nonstudents alike, during this period. In the early and mid-nineteenth century most Americans thought the United States would remain an agrarian society and the population would remain primarily rural (Kulik et al. 1982: xxxi). In the post–Civil War years, however, the burgeoning of industry in the Connecticut Valley may have impelled the Massachusetts Agricultural College and its students to reflect upon (and perhaps doubt) their role in a rapidly changing political economy.[6] Furthermore, the college was established amid controversy, and its future was in jeopardy from the start.

Institutionalizing Agriculture

The Massachusetts Agricultural College was established in 1863 by the Morrill Land Grant Act of 1862 as an agricultural institution (Cary 1962). The Commonwealth of Massachusetts placed the institution for scientific agriculture in Amherst, in the western part of the state, amid fierce competition from other towns (Figure 5.2). The purpose of the college, as an act to incorporate its trustees stated, was "to teach such branches of learning as are related to agriculture and the mechanic arts, in order to promote the liberal and practical education of the industrial classes, in the several pursuits and professions of life" (Commonwealth of Massachusetts 1863). A nationwide trend in the establishment of similar institutions signaled a shared concern "to combine the knowledge which the common farmer ought to possess in practical life, with the theory as studied in a four years' course at college" (*Amherst Record* 1877: 4; see also Lewis, this volume; O'Gorman, this volume).

By the mid-nineteenth century the landscape of western Massachusetts had begun to change as urban populations grew and as industry and transportation networks developed; the agricultural economy oriented itself more concertedly to the market (Clark 1990; Klimm 1933; Larkin 1988; Pabst 1940–41; Paynter 1982). State agricultural institutions throughout the country were established to increase farm efficiency and productivity in order to supply the growing urban areas. For western Massachusetts, the more diversified agricultural practices of the past gave way to increased specialization, particularly the large-scale production of tobacco and onions (Clark 1979; Pabst 1940–41). The expansion of commercial agriculture had both positive and negative consequences. Agricultural output rose, population increased, and the value of tobacco production more than tripled between 1860 and 1870. Land prices also rose to new heights in this expanding market. Yet economic growth was abruptly curtailed in the 1870s when demand for Connecticut Valley tobacco fell and markets became depressed. Population and land values declined over the next two decades until tobacco markets rebounded in the 1890s (Clark 1990: 327). As historian Christopher Clark (1990: 327) has suggested, farmers in the valley must have worried that "they might share the economic decline faced by their cousins in the [Berkshire] hills."

Although the positive economic trends of the 1860s were fueled by the progressive ideology of the day, the state legislature was reluctant to support the agricultural college in the early years, and administrators initially had problems attracting students. In the first decade of the college the number of matriculants and graduates varied widely. The benefits of a scientific and liberal education were not always apparent to the sons of traditional farmers, especially during the depressed economy of the 1870s. By the end of the decade the college was $32,000 in debt (Rand 1933: 46–51).

The first class consisted of 47 individuals, 8 of whom were from Amherst. The next year 56 students entered the college, 13 of whom were from Amherst; all but 2 were from other Massachusetts towns. From 1870 to 1877 the total number of matriculating students steadily declined from 123 to 67. The entering Class of 1878 included 26, less than half the number of students who had entered only a decade before; and by the junior year, just 17 students remained in the class. In 1877, when only 10 degrees were granted, the college graduated its lowest number of students.

The Amherst community regarded the role of the institution with considerable ambivalence in its early years. One local history notes that Amherst farmers voiced initial opposition to the college, while "lawyers, physicians, settled ministers and teachers, including the entire faculty of Amherst College, all merchants, mechanics, and business men" supported it (Carpenter and Morehouse 1896: 542). Farmers, some of whom did not welcome the Morrill Land Grant Act, believed that the new colleges for scientific agriculture had been designed primarily "to change farming rather than to preserve it" (Kirkendall 1986: 21). The professional, scholarly, and business community, in contrast, believed that the application of scientific principles and insights to agriculture could only strengthen the local economy and the position of the state in the national economy.

These were difficult times for the students as well. William H. Bowker (1907: 11–12), a member of the first entering class in 1867, recalled forty years later that "it certainly took courage on the part of the young student to come and remain here when the tendency of the times, and in many cases the home influence, was against it and in favor of classical education. . . . Even the agricultural press, at times, has been lukewarm; and as for the farmers, for whom the college was supposed to be established, they have contributed, until recently, less than half the students."

Similarly, support for the agricultural college was never strong in the state legislature, whose appropriations were barely adequate for the school's survival. From its inception in 1863, the college was established as an independent corporation and was expected to generate its own revenues from the land-grant fund, student tuition fees, and produce from the college farm. The first two state appropriations of $10,000 each were made as loans, with the idea that they would be repaid out of future revenues.

William S. Clark, the college's first president (1867–79), spent much of his time struggling to retain state support for the college, even at its minimal levels. He probably encouraged other advocates of the school, including the faculty, to do likewise. In an attempt to bolster the image of the institution among many of the commonwealth's farmers, Professor George Loring (1870: 177–78) compellingly presented the mission of the college to the Massachusetts Board of Agriculture in an 1869 address.

> It is not because the farming of this State has not been successful that we are establishing an agricultural college here; it is not because the farmers of the State are ignorant of certain principles upon which, heretofore, they have been successful, that this college has been established; but it is because, under the trails of modern agriculture, the

> best education is necessary in order to enable the farmers of the State to carry on their business profitably and successfully. It is the application of definite rules to the business of agriculture that we are striving for.

Loring's emphasis on the "definite rules" of agriculture was meant to convey to members of the audience the obvious economic benefits of scientific agriculture and to persuade them to view the college as indispensable. Loring (1870: 176) professed wonder about the state's priorities in funding other institutions of higher education within its borders:

> It was somewhat astonishing, that notwithstanding Massachusetts had spent upon Harvard College, from its inception and infancy, almost down to this very hour, hundreds of thousands of dollars from her own treasury, and from the private pockets of her citizens as much more; notwithstanding she had endowed every scientific institution within her limits; had bestowed upon Williams College her bounty; upon Amherst College her bounty; upon Tufts College her bounty; and upon almost every female academy, upon the School of Technology, and upon the Museum of Natural History, a liberal share of her wealth; the instant an institution was put into her own development, she not only began to pause herself, but her most enterprising and liberal citizens began to pause also. It is difficult, my friends, to account for this. An institution which is the only one . . . that Massachusetts can claim as her own . . . is met by the most formidable opposition.

Despite Loring's plea, the state legislature in its 1870 session considered a resolution to cut off funding for the college altogether. In the spring of 1871, while the pioneer class was preparing for its graduation, the state legislature again debated the policy of supporting agricultural education. Legislators ultimately agreed to meet their legal obligation to maintain the level of funding that the Morrill Act required, but they underscored the idea that the college was to become financially self-supporting or what they considered "independent." Yet by the mid-1870s internal revenues were dwindling, due to decreasing enrollments. The financial position of the college continued to disintegrate with the economic decline of the 1870s. The legislature stood adamant in its refusal to grant annual monetary support, and the Panic of 1873 moved the state to attempt to relinquish its responsibilities. Despite these serious threats to the well-being of the institution, however, it managed to weather these hard times.

The survival of the Massachusetts Agricultural College may have been due in part to its dedicated leadership. Clark in particular was an important and influential figure in its early history.[7] Like other late nineteenth-century college presidents, he was a model member of the emerging professional class (Bledstein 1976). According to historian Burton Bledstein (1976: 333), institutions of higher learning during this period sought to project "before society the image of the modern professional person, who committed himself to an ethic of service, was trained in scientific knowledge, and moved his career relentlessly upward." Clark was an administrator who managed both the campus and many aspects of town life. For example, he was a member of the Amherst Town Common Beautification Committee, the Amherst Gas Light Company, and the Amherst Water Company. Clark was away on leave in Japan for the purpose of establishing an agricultural college for the imperial government when the Class of 1878 buried its time capsule.

In all of the controversy surrounding the college in the 1870s, the students had little, if any, voice. We suspect that the students' notion to create a future memorial was a consequence of both Clark's absence and the economic uncertainty of the times. Although Clark was unavailable to address the Student Literary Society, as had been customary, another speaker could have been invited; others had previously given the address. In lieu of this presentation, the class members decided to "occupy the time usually devoted to some dry exercises in the drill hall, with exercises of a livelier nature in the open air" (MAC 1878a: 31).[8] The tree-planting ceremony that they consequently proposed and staged was, in their words, "the most interesting event of the year" (MAC 1878a: 31). Addressing the future, the Class of 1878 students straddled change as they became professionals, learned to apply scientific principles to agriculture, and equipped themselves intellectually to deal with increased specialization, the one aspect of the agricultural college's endeavors that farmers most opposed.[9]

The ceremony may also have expressed the tight bonds of fraternalism that members of the class had forged by their junior year.[10] The time capsule ceremony was a public affirmation of their shared experiences amid recognition of how jeopardized it was by declining college enrollment, the degree to which their own class had shrunk, and the ambivalence toward their enterprise at both local and state levels. Through their ritual act the Class of 1878 addressed an unknowable future and a tenuous present.

Encapsulating Time

Thousands of time capsules have been buried in the United States, and reports of their preparation and interment in modern times are numerous. Yet relatively few have been found and documented (Bergesen 1987).[11] The extreme rarity of recovered time capsules probably explains why they have been ignored in scholarly discourse. Destruction of buildings, transformations of landscapes, and oblivion have all erased the memories of most capsules from the collective consciousness. Robert Ascher (1974: 242) believes that people persuade themselves that their capsule will be recovered: "All time capsules—ancient, futuristic, and contemporary—are, by definition, deliberately designed and placed to be found at a later time." Analogies of writing and reading are appropriate here: the time capsule is a text written by human agents for an unknown audience, perhaps labeled simply "The Future." Yet if we were to conclude our analogy there with a linear equation (former culture buries time capsule for unknown later culture), we would be shortsighted. The pomp and circumstance surrounding the tree-planting ceremony and time capsule interment seems entirely incommensurate with the box's contents. The Class of 1878, it would seem, buried the time capsule as much for itself as an audience as it did for future audiences.

The description of the events that surrounded the burial of the time capsule suggested to us that it was a ritual act, a social performance that conveys information about the participants and their cultural traditions (Kottak 1987: 267). In this light, the contents became much less interesting to us than why the box was buried in the first place. For the Class of 1878, we think that issues of identity and self-affirmation were very much at stake. These students were preadolescent children when the Civil War was fought in the previous decade. The decade after the war was plagued by economic depression that led to a decline in agricultural prices. And industry had begun to challenge agriculture for predominance in the Connecticut Valley. These factors, along with an influx of immigrants into the valley, led to changes in the patterns of farm labor. "Whereas at the end of the eighteenth century the great majority of people worked on the land, by 1860 this was not true in many places, . . . in Northampton, less than one-third of the workforce owned farms or labored in agriculture. Farming remained the predominant activity in the poorer hill towns and on the rich lands along the Connecticut River, but in both places, and in differing ways, the development of markets and commercial agriculture had transformed it" (Clark 1990: 8). Enmeshed in an American culture that had recently, and self-consciously, celebrated itself at its 1876 centennial, the members of the Class of 1878 may have felt compelled to affirm their own place in history and society through a ritual act.

The centennial raised historical consciousness throughout the nation, particularly in New England, and encouraged the preparation of numerous town histories, atlases, and biographies. This event also engendered a variety of expositions dedicated to "modern" ideals, including, as several archaeologists have put it, "industriousness, technological progress and international commerce, and co-operation" (Praetzellis et al. 1989: 195). These ideals were not without contradiction, however. Although scientific agriculture was espoused as a worthy goal among progressive thinkers, state funding was slow in coming. As agricultural students facing a world in which agriculture seemed destined to play a comparatively lesser role in the New England economy, the Class of 1878 may have perceived the future as threatening, particularly as the hill towns of western Massachusetts were abandoned and industrial cities such as Holyoke, Springfield, and Turners Falls took shape (Nassaney and Abel 1993). Would agriculture follow a similar fate in the Connecticut Valley? The world beyond the academy that the Class of 1878 would have to face was in a dramatic state of change, and the burial of the time capsule was a stay against these altered conditions. As the farm threatened to become only a memory and the future of the academy lay in doubt, they did not want to be forgotten.

Thus the students asserted their modernity to themselves and to others beyond the college in time and space. In keeping with nineteenth-century ideas about time, the past and the future had become recognized as clearly disconnected from the present. Geographer David Lowenthal (1985: xvi) notes: "During most of history men scarcely differentiated past from present. . . . Up to the nineteenth century those who gave any thought to the historical past supposed it much like the present." By the 1870s members of society had begun to appreciate the idea that their present would be of interest to the future when it became past. This realization and the acts that followed set the Class of 1878 apart from other late nineteenth-century cohorts at the college.

The time capsule interment ritual also served as an affirmation of identity and fraternal solidarity for these young men who would soon become professionals. The contents of the box do not reflect the totality of American culture in 1877; nor do they compel scholars to draw sweeping conclusions about the state of that culture. Furthermore, it appears that more time was spent in planning the ceremony than in determining what should be put in the capsule. The copy of the *Index*, the handwritten manuscript, and the

Figure 5.8. Members of the University of Massachusetts Class of 1991 and the Alumni Office lower a time capsule, actually a child's coffin, into the ground during the 1991 fall homecoming weekend. (Courtesy of Special Collections and University Archives, W.E.B. Du Bois Library, University of Massachusetts, Amherst)

other printed materials reflect the internal world of the Massachusetts Agricultural College at a critical moment in its development. Despite its recovery in 1991, and despite its creators' assertion that it was "of great importance to future ages," the time capsule relates primarily to the Class of 1878, not to the future. It may have had its greatest impact on the students of the nineteenth century. That it has spoken to the future is a testimony not so much to the contents of the capsule as to their interment, an action that speaks louder than any of the words that can be deciphered in the entombed documents. As Albert Bergesen (1987: 16) states: "Somehow, the most compelling aspect of time capsules seems to be the burying of them, the marking of our spot"; when recovered, he notes, they "almost never contain items of much interest or value, or tell us anything about the past that we might actually care to know."

Not only are time capsules seldom found and generally contain little of interest, but the idea of saving a representative sample of a society or culture in a small box, as some have noted, is both senseless and impossible (Ascher 1974; Bergesen 1987: 17). Time capsule planners and builders, Bergesen (1987: 17) argues, "lack the necessary perspective to judge what is most important"

Table 5.2. Selected contents of the Class of 1991 time capsule

Contents	Description
Clothing	Class of 1991 T-shirt
Manuscript	Signatures of a subset of the class of '91 (count unknown)
Videotape	Footage showing campus life and highlights of band and basketball team activity
Programs	"M. A. C. '78, Programme of Exercises at the Planting of the Class Tree, by the Class of '78, Massachusetts Agricultural College"; 1991 time capsule ceremony; 1991 commencement; football program (autographed by the team); New World Theater program
Printed Card	Invitation prepared for the 1991 time capsule ceremony
Newspaper	Homecoming issue of the *Massachusetts Daily Collegian* and a copy of the *Massachusetts Daily Collegian* dated May 15, 1991; newspaper clippings re Class of 1878 time capsule discovery
Audiocassette	Popular hits of 1991, sounds of the UMass Marching Band
Documents	Senior committee article in *Massachusetts Magazine*; personal documents by the 1991 time capsule committee
Books	*Farmer's Almanac* (1991)
Tickets	Senior Semi-formal Dance, Senior Picnic, Senior Weekend, Homecoming Football Game
Banner	University of Massachusetts pennant
Card	Student identification card
Letter	Admissions acceptance letter
Manuscripts	Unpublished text of addresses delivered at the ceremony
Miscellaneous	Lamba Chi coffee mug; copy of the U.S. Constitution; local pub menus; various UMass publications; *The Wall* (compact disc and videotape set by Pink Floyd)

about society or what the future may want to know about the past. Thus the act of creating a time capsule seems to reveal more about the makers than the capsule's inventory itself does. Furthermore, there are some similarities in outlook among time capsule makers through the ages, as a comparison between two time capsules buried on the campus of the University of Massachusetts (in 1877 and 1991) makes clear.

After the homecoming football game in October 1991, the newly graduated Class of 1991 emulated the Class of 1878 by dedicating a young pine tree where the earlier tree once stood. They also lowered a time capsule, albeit a somewhat larger one, into the ground next to their sapling (Figure 5.8). The ceremony surrounding the burial was intentionally designed to replicate the events of 1877: speeches were read, songs sung, an ode recited, rose petals strewn, and salutes fired. Rather than invent a new tradition, they sought to associate themselves with the past by re-creating the ritual acts of some 114 years earlier. The Office of Alumni Relations and the Class of 1991 invited a large public audience to help them "make history," as the invitation put it. A child's coffin held the contents of the modern time capsule (Table 5.2), which is supposed to be opened in the year 2113 to celebrate the 250th anniversary of the institution.

Several interesting parallels can be drawn between the classes of 1878 and 1991. In the late 1980s the University of Massachusetts began to suffer drastic reductions in state funding as appropriations dropped from $167 million in 1988 to $128 million in 1991. These budget cuts had a severe impact on salaries and payroll, hiring practices, and the quality of many academic programs. The library budget was particularly hard hit: 1,650 periodicals were canceled, and the university library became one of the worst funded in the nation. In a November 20, 1989, letter to more than sixty thousand alumni (on file in the Department of Anthropology, Western Michigan University, Kalamazoo), Gordon Oakes, chair of the university's Board of Trustees, urged support for the institution in words reminiscent of the words of Professor Loring more than a century earlier. "Now is the time for all of us . . . to raise our voices in protest. . . . We *must* raise our voices against further cuts lest we become an unwilling partner in the Commonwealth's mindless march toward mediocrity." Throughout this economically turbulent period, which lasted into the early 1990s, the faculty and students staged public rallies and planned strikes; state employees were threatened with furloughs. In the fall of 1990 the campus newspaper, the *Massachusetts Daily Collegian*, reported that "the rift between the student body and the administration grows with each campus cut" (Elliot 1991: 1; see also Grabar 1991; Pratt 1990).

The Class of 1991 seemed to respond to a perceived threat to the well-being of the university, much as their predecessors reacted to the late nineteenth-century challenges to the survival of the college and of agriculture. There are notable similarities in the motivations that triggered the activities associated with the creation and interment of each time capsule. A feeling of pride and optimism as well as a sense of fear and apprehension permeated both of the ceremonies. We might suggest, therefore, that time capsules represent a response to economically, politically, and socially stressful conditions and are most likely conceived and interred when the future seems most uncertain or identity is in doubt.[12] What would become of agriculturalists and the agricultural college during the expansion of industry in the late nineteenth century? What would become of a late twentieth-century public institution of higher education as politicians seeking to privatize society forced severe financial cutbacks upon it?

The act of burying the time capsule is a ceremony of self-affirmation intended to reinforce group identity and solidarity. Thus it is not surprising that the items enclosed in them often deflect attention from political and economic uncertainties that are particularly difficult to face, let alone resolve. The unknown can be left to the future, which, through its realization, presupposes resolution. Time capsule creators usually present themselves as optimists whose choice of items to bury ignores political tensions, social conflicts, and economic stress; they strive to construct a more idyllic picture of the present to themselves and the future while simultaneously hoping for a better world. In a fictional interchange between father and his sons, the novelist E. L. Doctorow (1985: 284) noted as much of the time capsule that the Westinghouse Electric and Manufacturing Company created for the 1939 World's Fair: "He asked my brother and me why we thought there was nothing in the capsule about the great immigrations that had brought Jewish and Italian and Irish people to America or nothing to represent the point of view of the workingman. 'There is no hint from the stuff they included that America has a serious intellectual life, or Indians on reservations or Negroes who suffer from race prejudice. Why is that?' he said as we finally edged him away from the Immortal Well and into the Hall of Science."

Like the celebration of the American centennial, the burial of a time capsule is a self-conscious ritual that purposely avoids representing injustices of the day.

Whereas time capsules are unlikely to contain anything of historical interest or intellectual value, as the literature suggests, why would anyone want to dig them up? For our part, we might have been much less enthusiastic had we known initially what the box contained. In our ignorance, the time capsule undoubtedly represented an intentional voice from the past, which presumably would speak to us much more clearly than the muffled sounds we are able to pick up from lost or haphazardly discarded objects. The search for a time capsule and its discovery are means of establishing a direct connection through the ages. When the Office of Alumni Relations authorized us to find the capsule and we did everything in our power to recover it, we were collectively seeking to connect ourselves with the past and reaffirm our role as members of a long-standing institution that we hoped would persist into the future despite the embattled circumstances of public higher education in the commonwealth in both the present and the past.

Postscript

Although the Class of 1991's tree and associated stone marker were removed by the university's Physical Plant employees, the time capsule is still there, eight feet underground. Michael Milewski left three "information packets" in the Special Collections and University Archives for future generations to assist them in recovering the capsule in 2113.

Acknowledgments

This essay first appeared in *Old-Time New England* 74(262): 59–80, a publication of the Society for the Preservation of New England Antiquities (SPNEA). We thank Historic New England (formerly SPNEA) for permission to reprint it in this collection. Michael Nassaney coordinated the efforts to recover the time capsule. Uzi Baram, James Garman, Al Greene, and Michael Volmar assisted him. Michael Milewski rediscovered the records that indicated that the Class of 1878 had buried a box of documents beneath its class tree and worked to conserve the capsule's contents. We would like to thank the University of Massachusetts Office of Alumni Relations and Special Collections and Archives for involving us in the time capsule project and supporting the preparation of the figures that accompany this text. Richard Gumaer conducted the proton magnetometer survey to locate the capsule. Mitch Mulholland, director of UMass Archaeological Services, made the field equipment available to us. The crew of the UMass Grounds–Physical Plant Department cooperated by providing and operating the mechanical equipment used to find the copper box. James Clifton, James Ferreira, Edward Hood, Alan Jacobs, Kathryn Grover, Cheryl Lyon-Jenness, and an anonymous reviewer offered useful suggestions on earlier versions of this paper. Andrew Beaupré, Emily Powell, and Stephen Mrozowski provided bibliographic assistance. The documents and artifacts recovered through the time capsule project are curated in Special Collections and Archives, W.E.B. DuBois Library, University of Massachusetts, Amherst.

Notes

1. Although we use the term "time capsule" throughout our discussion, the Class of 1878 did not use the phrase. It did not come into popular usage until more than sixty years later when the Westinghouse Electric and Manufacturing Company used it for the box it buried at the 1939 World's Fair (Bergesen 1987).

2. We suspect that the seven- and eight-gun salutes, rather unconventional from a military protocol perspective, symbolized their year of graduation: 1878.

3. For example, a *New York Times* correspondent contacted Nassaney and Milewski for their reactions to the discovery, and a related article was printed in the Campus Life section (*New York Times* 1991).

4. Construction of the Campus Chapel, less than a hundred feet from the capsule, was completed in 1885. In the 1930s excavations to install steam lines may also have disturbed the copper box.

5. The members of the Class of 1878 were apparently quite adamant in their desire to ensure that a record of their four years at the college be preserved. For their ninth reunion on June 21, 1887, they voted that the secretary's book, together with a copy of the *Index '78*, the printed exercises of the class supper, and the *Class Record*, be deposited in the college library for safekeeping. These and other memorabilia relating to the class were assembled in 1921 and placed in a tin box that is kept in the library (MAC 1878b). These acts appear to be atypical for alumni, as there are no records of any other class taking this precaution.

6. For a look at the changing political economy of the region, see Clark (1990), Nassaney et al. (1989), Paynter (1982: 59–86), Taber (1955), and Thorbahn and Mrozowski (1979).

7. For biographical information on William S. Clark and a report of archaeological investigations at his campus home, see Baram (1989).

8. In essence, the students sought to distinguish themselves from previous classes and create a new tradition. For an extended discussion and examples of invented traditions, see Hobsbawm and Ranger (1983).

9. Most of the graduates became successful professionals in agriculture, industry, and medicine. Obituaries published in various issues of the *Alumni Bulletin* provide some biographical information on several prominent class members. For instance, John Hosea Washburn of Bridgewater did postgraduate work at Brown University prior to receiving his Ph.D. from the University of Göttingen, Germany, in 1889. A professor of agricultural chemistry, he became president of the Rhode Island Agricultural College (1889–1902). His father's small Bridgewater farm was valued at $2,500 in 1870 (U.S. Bureau of Census 1870). In 1884 Horace Edward Stockbridge of Hadley was also awarded his Ph.D. at Göttingen. He spent the next four years as professor of chemistry and geology at the Imperial College of Agriculture and Engineering in Japan. Upon returning to the United States, he served as president of the North Dakota Agricultural College (1890–94) and professor of agriculture at Florida Atlantic College (1894–1906). One of the founders of the *Southern Ruralist*, Stockbridge was its editor for sixteen years.

Graduates also chose to enter other fields. John Franklin Hunt became a civil engineer after graduating from the college, worked as a railroad construction superintendent in Texas, and later in his career supervised the construction of the first steel building in Boston. Josiah Newhall Hall, the son of a Chelsea farmer in eastern Massachusetts, was one of two graduates to receive a medical degree from Harvard.

A year after his 1882 graduation, he went to Denver and began practicing medicine in the small neighboring town of Sterling. Hall was mayor of Sterling in 1888–89 and later became professor of therapeutics at the University of Colorado. In addition to writing a book and more than 140 articles for national medical publications, Hall was a member of the American Medical Association and president of numerous other professional organizations, including the Colorado State Board of Medical Examiners (1891), the Colorado State Board of Health (1903–4), and the American Therapeutic Society (1916).

10. Fraternal organizations of all sorts were common in nineteenth-century America (see Carnes and Griffen 1990).

11. In a typical search to find a time capsule from 1897, workers drilled numerous holes into the cornerstone of the University of Montana's Main Hall. "The university hoped to open the capsule at its centennial celebration . . . but has been forced to abandon the search for fear of damaging the building's structure" (*Chronicle of Higher Education* 1993: A5; see also May 1991). Since the original publication of this essay in 1996 we have noted popular interest in the creation and recovery of several other time capsules, particularly as the millennium approached (e.g., Cecil 2001; Collins 1996; Mays 1997; Wilson 1999).

12. In 1996 we learned of another time capsule that was motivated by somewhat similar circumstances. In 1895 the Women's Centennial Commission was organized in Cleveland, Ohio, to discuss why the city fathers had ignored women in the planning of their centennial party. To remedy the situation the commission created a time capsule for the "Unborn Women of 1996," which was designed to document women's history and celebrate their accomplishments in the greater Cleveland area. It is interesting to note that even though the women of Cleveland were motivated by conspicuous lack of attention from the city fathers, the text of their sealed letter favorably compares the state of their world with what it had been one hundred years earlier (see King 1996).

II

Diachronic Views of College Life

Separating the Real from the Ideal

We often see the past as a mirror of the present and transpose current function and meaning onto objects of the past. Educational institutions seem particularly prone to be viewed as changeless entities whose pasts are assumed to mirror the present or are so entwined with romantic myth as to bear little semblance to reality. The following six chapters challenge us to examine the pasts of universities as well as public schools, to see how well our perceptions fit with reality. Archaeologists investigate portions of campuses, observing the material record of buildings and the features and objects associated with them, in order to gain knowledge of not only what they looked like but how they reveal the nature of the way people lived and carried out their academic activities. As a diachronic discipline, archaeology is employed to explore change on campuses through the material remains of their components. This ability has allowed the authors to trace the changing roles of buildings and the development of technologies but also to use these particular results to examine phenomena far larger than the individual contexts in which they were observed. Colleges and schools underwent substantial transformations in the past two centuries, and our understanding of them is enhanced by the information revealed by the archaeological record.

6

Campus Archaeology/Public Archaeology at Harvard University, Cambridge, Massachusetts

JOHN D. STUBBS, PATRICIA CAPONE, CHRISTINA J. HODGE, AND DIANA D. LOREN

Introduction

The beginnings of Harvard College were modest. After having been established in 1636, the college opened in 1638 with one master and nine students, all of whom lived in a house facing out on Braintree Street (now Massachusetts Avenue) just up the bank from the Charles River in Cambridge, Massachusetts. The house sat on a lot measuring about an eighth of an acre in size, which, together with the one-acre cow yard in back, made up the complete campus. Today Harvard covers some 220 acres in Cambridge and Allston and enrolls more than 18,000 degree candidates. Harvard Yard has always been the central focus of the campus. The Yard we know today is larger than it was years ago, but at its core is the original plot of land that made up the college in 1638 (Figure 6.1).

The western part of Harvard Yard, known today as the Old Yard, is a long, extended quadrangle surrounded by buildings on all four sides, including Wadsworth House and Harvard, Massachusetts, Matthews, Grays, and Weld Halls. It is dotted with stately elms and oaks and a variety of younger trees. At most hours of the day the mood is quiet and contemplative. One can often see clusters of students talking, the occasional Frisbee flying, and a range of people—students, faculty, administrators, and visitors—passing from one place to another on the walkways that crisscross the space.

The quiet mood, the age of the adjacent buildings (all constructed between 1718 and 1871), and the age of the college (some 370 years old) might lead the casual observer to conclude that Harvard Yard has always had this kind of appearance, but the place had a different look in its early years. During the seventeenth and eighteenth centuries various parts of the Old Yard

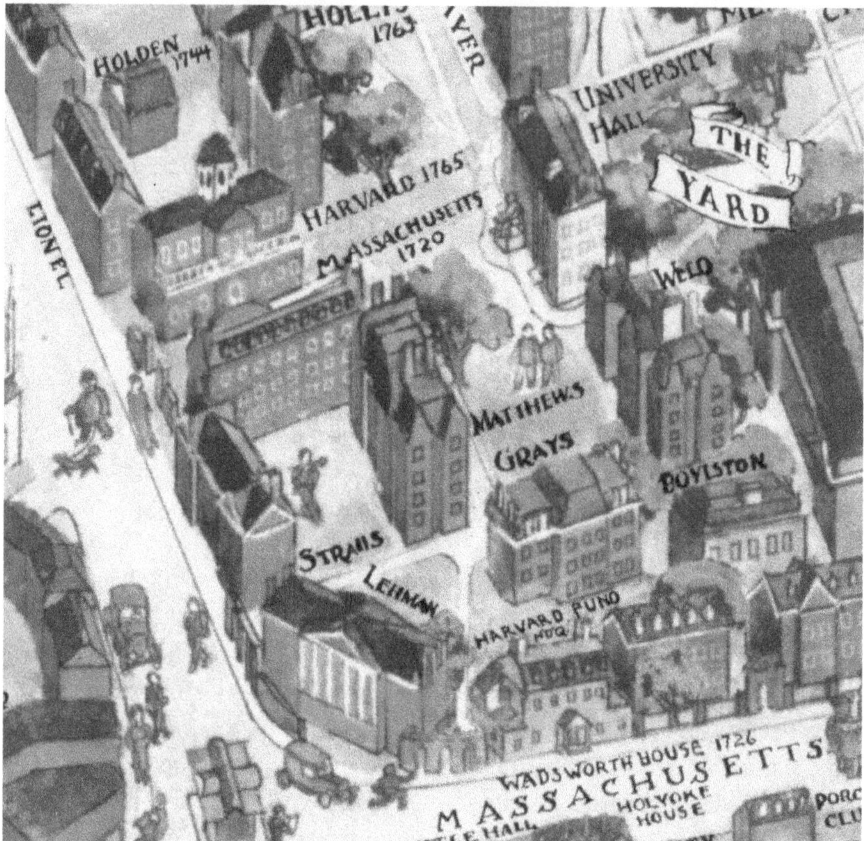

Figure 6.1. "Tercentenary Map," Harvard Yard: detail of Old Yard area, 1935. (Courtesy of Harvard University Archives, call no. HUA 632)

were devoted to cow yards, plowed fields, or planted orchards. Trash was strewn about, a variety of fences penned in livestock or otherwise segmented the space, and several outbuildings—barns, privies, sheds, and the like—were scattered across the property. Even major college buildings, now gone, occupied part of the Yard in earlier times. Historical records provide some details of this past, but the tangible evidence for these buildings and for campus life comes from underground.

Archaeology at Harvard

Hints that archaeology could be a potentially valuable source of information came as early as 1871, when bricks and stones that may have been debris from the Indian College (a brick building that stood in the Yard from 1656 to 1698) were discovered during the construction of a dormitory. Similar observations were documented during the construction of the Boston to Cambridge subway through Harvard Square in 1909, when the remains of the foundations of two houses, both acquired and used by the college early in the seventeenth century, were exposed. The location of these finds is under present-day Massachusetts Avenue, near Wadsworth House, which can be seen along with the locations of subsequent excavations and collections in Figure 6.2.

During the past thirty years archaeology has become an important contributor to our understanding of Harvard's past. Small collections obtained during construction projects have provided a glimpse into the early years

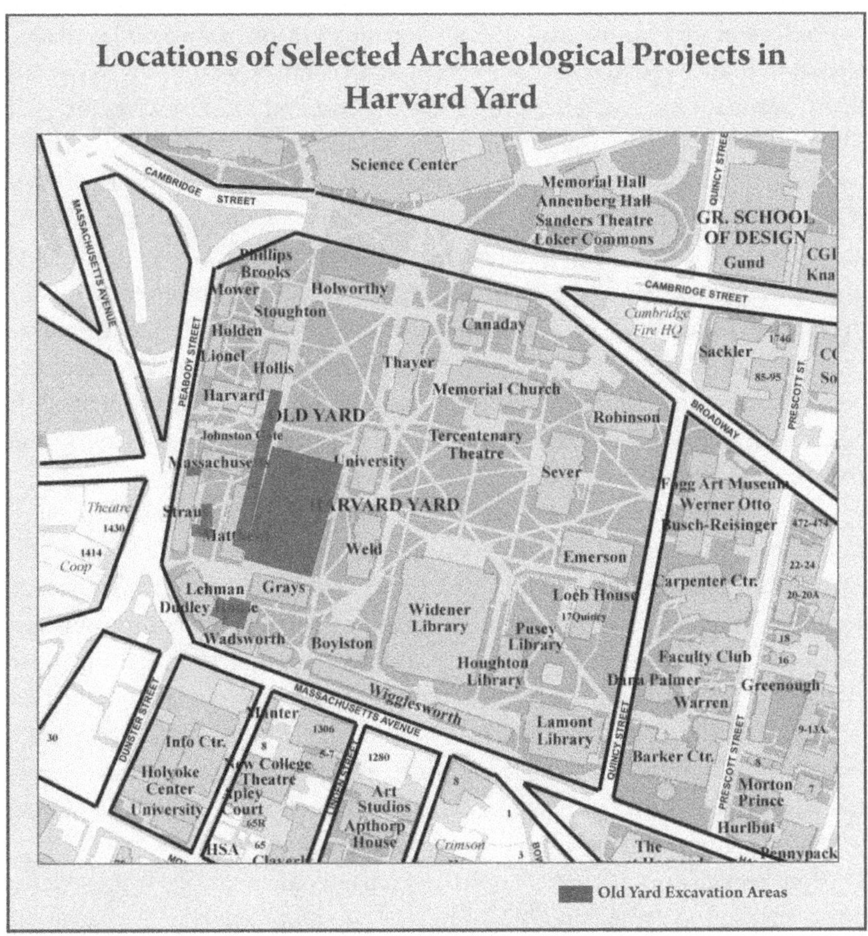

Figure 6.2. Major archaeological excavations in Harvard Yard to 2007. (Map by Kim Nichols, 2008)

of the college. Even one of the presidents of the university, Abbot Lawrence Lowell, made a collection of earthenware in 1921. Several other collections (consisting mostly of ceramics, clay tobacco pipe fragments, bottle glass, and other miscellaneous materials) made in 1969, 1973, and 1983 have added information about earlier life on campus.

Systematic excavations carried out in 1979 revealed the true potential of archaeology as a window on Harvard's past. Extensive excavations in the southwest corner of the Yard near Wadsworth Gate were carried out as a required mitigation project associated with the extension of the subway system through Harvard Square (Graffam 1981, 1982). Among the major features discovered in the excavations were the remains of a well and a trench associated with the backyard of the Olmstead-Goffe house, a residence acquired by the college in 1651 for use as a student dormitory. More than 5,500 artifacts, all dating to the second half of the seventeenth century, were recovered from those two features. A smaller project off the east end of Massachusetts Hall (the oldest building now standing in the Yard, constructed in 1719), carried out as an archaeological field school, took place during the summer of 1979 (Gerry 1988). The variety and quantity of artifacts from these excavations made it clear that much could be learned about the everyday lives of students and other members of the college community, since they often provide important details that have not survived in the historical record. As the excavations proceeded and the features and abundant artifacts were revealed, the project caught the attention of the community, which became fascinated. It became clear that more features and objects related to the early days of the college were likely preserved in other parts of Harvard Yard.

Further systematic excavations, also operated as field schools, took place in the southern part of the Old Yard during the summers of 1984 through 1987. While the work of the first two summers consisted of small test pits aimed at characterizing the archaeological potential of the entire southern part of the Yard (Gorman 1984), the last two summers focused on more extensive area excavations designed to investigate features related to the Old College, a building constructed in 1644 and finally demolished about 1679 (Stubbs 1992b). In 1985 a small excavation project was located near the western edge of the Old Yard. The objective was to find the college brew house, which is mentioned in college documents as early as 1654.

More recent work includes extensive archaeological salvage from a water line construction project in 1992 (Stubbs 1992a) and a systematic excavation in 1999 in the vicinity of Wadsworth House (constructed in 1726) on the southern edge of the Old Yard. Later that year salvage excavation of features

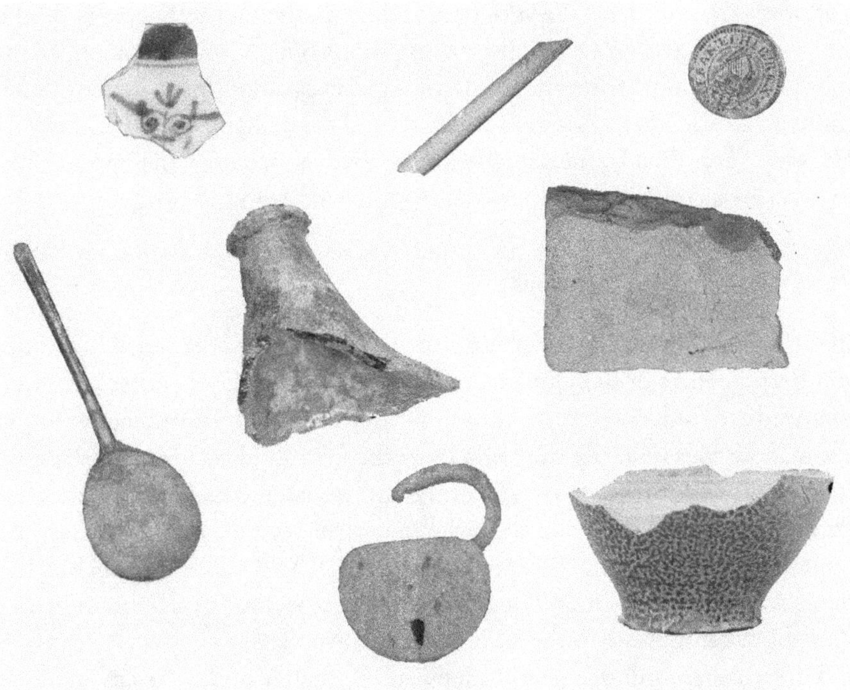

Figure 6.3. Selection of seventeenth- and eighteenth-century artifacts excavated from Harvard Yard:(*top row, left to right*) Chinese porcelain, slate pencil, button; (*middle row, left to right*) rat-tailed pewter spoon, green wine bottle neck, tile fragment; (*bottom row, left to right*) iron padlock, salt-glazed stoneware jar base.

encountered during the renovation of Holden Chapel took place. A current project, begun in 2005 and resumed in 2007, consists of excavations that focus on the southwest portion of the Old Yard in an effort to locate additional features related to the Indian College.

These collections and excavation projects have produced significant data that enhance our understanding of life at the college from its earliest years to modern times. They provide broad spatial coverage over much of the southern portion of the Old Yard and can therefore be used to guide future investigations into Harvard's past. The excavations have revealed a rich and diverse set of artifacts buried beneath the surface of Harvard Yard, including ceramics, tobacco pipes, personal items, decorative objects, food remains, and architectural materials (Figure 6.3).

We have chosen to elaborate on three projects in order to illustrate the range of archaeological research in Harvard Yard. Each excavation project tells a different story about Harvard's past and life at the school. Just as importantly, they illustrate the variety of factors motivating archaeology on the Harvard campus. The Old College excavations offer a look at student life at the college through time. The Holden Chapel excavations provide the opportunity to consider some of the academic (and particularly scientific) finds in Harvard Yard. Finally, the Indian College excavations offer the opportunity to describe a collaborative approach to archaeology in the Yard.

The Old College Excavations

In the summer of 1986 and 1987 extensive excavations were carried out in the southern portion of the Old Yard, as part of a field school course designed to introduce students to excavation techniques. The primary objective of the excavations was to locate the remains of the first building to be constructed for the express purposes of educating and housing college students. That building, originally referred to in the historical records as "the College" or "Harvard College," soon became known as the "Old College," which is the name we use here. A second objective of the project was to obtain information about campus life in the early years of the college.

Historical records are nearly silent on the matter of day-to-day living at the college. In terms of the building itself, no existing map shows the location of the Old College; nor do we have any drawing or other depiction of the structure, so it is left to archaeology to provide evidence of its location. Fleeting references to the Old College provide tantalizing information about the number and types of rooms in the building. An inventory of the college property made in 1654 briefly describes the Old College. It reads: "The building call the old Colledge, conteyning and Hall Kitchin, Buttery, Cellar, Turrett & 5 Studyes & therin 7 Chambers for Students in them. A Pantry & small cone Chamber. A library & Books therin, valued at £400" (CSM 1925, 15: 208). By 1679 the building had deteriorated to the point of falling down, and it was demolished soon after.

Harvard historian Samuel Eliot Morison used the above description, a list of student studies made around 1645, and other historical documents to present a reasonable although conjectural floor plan for the wood-framed building, which must have had two stories and a garret (Morison 1935: 271–89). Studies were small, closet-like stalls where students could do their schoolwork and, according to archival documents, were often located off the sleeping chambers in the building. Morison was able to tease out a plan for the Old College, but it remains for archaeology to place the building, to confirm its plan, and to fill in the details of its appearance and construction.

Evidence of the Old College

Throughout most of the southern half of the Old Yard, the seventeenth-century ground surface lies from 50 to 100 cm below the present ground level. Archaeological features are usually highly visible, since they contrast significantly with the light yellow-brown sandy subsoil. The most significant feature discovered was a deep and large penetration into the subsoil, full of artifacts (including substantial architectural debris), dating from the mid-seventeenth century to the late eighteenth century, which was identified as the cellar to the Old College. Though the full dimensions of the cellar have yet to be determined, we know that it must have measured more than 10 m in one dimension and from 4.5 to 6 m in the other. Parts of the cellar walls were lined with stacked slate and brick pieces, and evidence suggests that it had a brick and slate slab floor.

Excavations also located what had been the eastern boundary of the college property until 1794. The boundary was marked by a trench overlain by a concentration of rocks and several postholes along the length of the trench. This interpretation is strengthened by the exposure of plow marks to the east of the trench feature. Historical records confirm that the property to the east of the college was used both for grazing cattle and for growing corn at various times during the seventeenth and eighteenth centuries.

Together these two features allow us to reconstruct the location and layout of the college during its early days. Although we have not yet determined the full dimensions of the Old College, we know that the building stood over the cellar (and was certainly larger than the cellar area). We also know the position of the cellar relative to the property boundary, which offers further clues about the overall size of the building, which Morison estimated to be 90 feet long and 60 feet wide.

Significant architectural debris associated with the building recovered from the excavations includes bricks, lime mortar, clay roof tiles, turned lead, nails, painted plaster, and an especially high concentration of window glass. The accounts of the college steward list charges to many students for glass mending. Historical documents mention major episodes of glass breaking at the college in 1651/52 and the following year, but the reason for these events is unclear (Morison 1936a: 121). There are also references to glass breaking at quarter-days, the final day of each fiscal quarter at the college, when each student was presented with a bill that was to be paid within a month's time. Students are known to have protested their charges by breaking windows.

Archaeology reveals how the space around the Old College was used through the centuries. Excavations indicate that debris was strewn around much of the open area in the vicinity of the Old College during Harvard's early years. By 1720, with the completion of several new buildings (including Massachusetts Hall), the focus of the college shifted to the western portion of the Old Yard. The Old College became the backyard and, among other purposes, was used as a dumping ground for trash, a significant portion of which ended up in the exposed cellar hole of the Old College. The function of the space changed again in the early nineteenth century, when President John Kirkland ordered a general cleanup (Morison 1936b: 216). The thick layer of nineteenth-century fill provides evidence for that change, as the fill was brought in to cover over accumulated debris. Kirkland's cleanup efforts, along with the addition of new buildings, transformed the area formerly occupied by the Old College from a private, unkempt backyard to a more attractive public space.

Evidence of Campus Life

Just as significant as locating the cellar of the Old College was the discovery of its contents. Numerous types of ceramics were used at the college, ranging from locally produced redware to imported earthenwares from England and Spain, porcelain from China, and stonewares from Central Europe. Other foodways items include glass tableware, iron cooking vessel fragments, flatware, wine and spirit bottle glass, and a corkscrew. An array of faunal remains was also recovered, including cow, sheep, goat, pig, and deer bones.

Foodways items found in the Old College excavations are similar to those found at other sites in New England. One noticeable difference is the large quantity of wine and spirit bottle glass, which is high when compared with domestic sites. Within the late seventeenth-century assemblage from the Yard, the wine bottle glass constitutes 20 percent of the artifacts assigned to the kitchen group category, which also includes ceramics, case bottle glass, tumblers, pharmaceutical bottles, glass tableware, flatware, and general kitchenware. At two roughly contemporary domestic assemblages (one in nearby Charlestown, Massachusetts, and the other in Pemaquid, Maine), the wine bottle glass makes up 5 and 8 percent of the kitchen group, respectively (Camp 1975; Pendery 1984, 1987; Stubbs 1992b: 593). The frequency of such glass in the Yard even exceeds the frequency found at some tavern sites. For example, wine bottle glass represented 17 percent of the kitchen group artifacts at a tavern site in Pemaquid dating to about the same period (Camp

1975). Given that the College Laws clearly forbade drinking except on rare special occasions, this circumstance is surprising. Additionally, artifacts indicate that drinking on campus actually increased over time (Stubbs 1992b: 513). Smoking was similarly prohibited during the seventeenth century, yet the presence of tobacco pipe bowls and stems indicates that smoking was a common activity on campus.

Various other finds have also been recovered, including lead balls, gunflints, and lead shot as well as slate stylus fragments, book clasps, and lead printing type used on the college printing press. Coins, keys, folding knives, jewelry, an eyeglass lens, and toothbrushes are just some of the personal items recovered in the Old College excavations. Even a clay wig curler was found. The historical records of the college are nearly devoid of information about student dress, but the buckles, buttons, clasps, and straight pins recovered in the excavations provide tangible evidence of student clothing at the college as well as hinting at some of the ways in which students dressed in relation to College Laws.

The Old College Excavations in Context

The Old College excavations differed from much of the previous work done in Harvard Yard, which tended to be opportunistic and guided by construction projects. This project was planned and had defined research objectives. The excavations yielded results that were shared with the Harvard community on the occasion of the college's 350th anniversary in 1986. We not only determined the building's location but also recovered important information regarding its architectural details and construction. In addition, because of the fortunate preservation of numerous artifacts (all cushioned from disturbance by a layer of fill), we have been able to gain a better understanding of campus life through time.

The excavations have yielded tangible evidence of college life. Although the evidence must be assigned to the college community collectively, it also provides occasional glimpses of the individual. The base of a late eighteenth-century redware tankard inscribed with the initials "BP" made with a compass stylus (Figure 6.4) and a gold wedding band inscribed with the words "never to change" (also associated with eighteenth-century objects) serve as good examples of such finds. Though the owners of these objects remain anonymous, these artifacts serve as reminders of compelling stories buried underneath Harvard Yard.

Figure 6.4. "BP" tankard excavated from Harvard Yard.

The Holden Chapel Excavations

Built between 1742 and 1744, Harvard's Holden Chapel was the first free-standing space for worship at the University (Figure 6.5). While the chapel's footprint was small (only 30 by 46 feet), its mission was distinguished. Holden's donor intended the building to manifest Harvard's institutional maturity and to remain a place of "Sobriety, Righteousness, and Godliness" (Gritt 1955). Whether the structure has successfully fulfilled this mandate is dubitable. Holden served as the college chapel for only twenty-two years before it was used for an assortment of secular purposes. The building functioned as a government assembly space, army barracks, naval store, fire station, medical school, anatomical museum, and, most recently, choral classroom and rehearsal space.

The latest overhaul of Holden's fabric took place in the summer of 1999, when the interior of the building was gutted. A small bulldozer excavating beneath the floor hit the wall of a buried circular brick feature and exposed a

Figure 6.5. *1783. Holden Chapel, Cambridge*, circa 1883. (Courtesy of the Center for the History of Medicine, Francis A. Countway Library of Medicine, call no. 97.320)

mass of jumbled bone, glassware, ceramics, and other materials inside. When workers suspected that some of the finds were human skeletal remains, they contacted the appropriate officials. As the importance of the discovery was recognized, several members of the Department of Anthropology mobilized to plan and carry out a salvage excavation. The results of the excavation were written up as an undergraduate thesis (Sexton 2000).

Beneath the Georgian Gem

Holden Chapel has always been lauded for its fine proportions and classical exterior. As with so many of Harvard's places, however, a placid facade and stately name belie a convoluted history. Archaeology has confronted us with this history. The feature fill excavated in 1999 reflects one of Holden's most fascinating periods, from the 1780s to the 1880s. Holden housed the new Harvard Medical School and the Harvard Chemistry Department in 1782–1810; was divided into several medical, chemical, and general lecture rooms in 1814; and underwent a subsequent slow disintegration from an undergraduate anatomy lab and dissection hall (1810–25) to a store for specimens and half-forgotten curiosities (1825–80). In 1880 the chapel was again renovated and returned to its one-room configuration (Batchelder 1921: 415). The structure was by then largely abandoned, save for an annual anatomical

Figure 6.6. *A Midnight Foray into the Medical Room in Holden Chapel*, from "College Scenes" drawn by N. Hayward (1850). (Batchelder 1924: 26)

lecture and "midnight raids" (Figure 6.6) by generations of undergraduates in search of morbid dorm accessories (Batchelder 1921: 413, 1924).

The circular brick feature excavated in 1999 was sunk below first-floor level and had a sand bottom for drainage. The feature was apparently a temporary receptacle for the detritus of chemical and medical instruction, a certainly noxious and potentially dangerous mix of biological remains and other materials. Durable artifacts recovered from the fill date from the late eighteenth through mid-nineteenth centuries, but fragments of a yellow-ware bowl date the filling episode after about 1840. The feature was probably constructed during the 1800 or 1814 renovations and filled and capped during renovations in 1850.

The brick feature fill yielded 2,504 artifact fragments: 166 ceramic; 2,151 glass; 160 architectural; 14 "personal"; and 13 miscellaneous (Sexton 2000: 65). The feature contained a variety of materials: creamware, pearlware, and yellow-ware flat and hollow vessels; a stoneware inkwell; stoneware and porcelain crucibles; unglazed porcelain cups, bowls, and basins; glass specimen jars, jar lids, and stoppers; microscope slides; capillary tubes; test tubes (including one with hand-etched graduations); lamp globes; and several bottles. Some fragments of animal bone are marked with red pigment, as an instructional aid (Sexton 2000: 64–73). More poignant are the human skeletal remains. Three shoes and several buttons (possible remnants of cadaver clothing discarded during the dissection process) were also recovered.

We know that dissected human remains were temporarily kept in Harvard Medical School's "dissecting vault" at its second location in Boston (Harrington 1906: 327). Based on the condition of human and other skeletal remains in the Holden brick feature, it seems that the feature was the Medical School's first such receptacle. Some human skeletal portions recovered from the brick feature were still articulated. Many elements showed post-mortem cuts, probably from dissection and/or preparation as teaching specimens (Sexton 2000: 73–76). Human remains are generally recovered from burials or mortuary sites. The Holden Chapel site presents an unusual context for human remains: academic instruction.

During the eighteenth and nineteenth centuries medical lectures were heavily illustrated with prepared human and animal specimens, biological models, and drawings. Students dissected cadavers to learn practical anatomy. Public opinion did not favor this aspect of medical training, as taboos against violating corpses were strong (Sexton 2000: 33). Dissection subjects were not always obtained legally. Harvard Medical School's first head, John Warren, reluctantly accepted cadavers of dubious provenience. His son, John C. Warren, recorded how he stole a body from a new grave in 1796 for use in his father's anatomy lectures at Holden Chapel; this incident was one of many (Warren 1860: 404–9). Legal sources for corpses included poor farms, hospitals, and prisons (Ball 1928). Mores regarding the treatment of human remains in academic and other settings have changed dramatically since the early nineteenth century. Finds from Harvard's Holden Chapel reveal an early phase in this ethical trajectory.

The Holden Chapel site is unique at Harvard because it represented a wholly academic deposit. The brick feature was filled and sealed when the building was devoted to student instruction and scientific inquiry. It helps us to understand the maturation of Enlightenment ideals and the social mechanisms through which modern medical science came to be. Locally, the story of anatomy at Holden Chapel strips away any cloak of moral superiority or intellectual objectivity that medicine, science, or academia—or Harvard University—cares to assume. The truer story is more challenging and more interesting.

Larger Lessons

Holden's human anatomical specimens and nineteenth-century relic raids remind us how easily troubling histories are smoothed over in collective memories. Commemorative speeches and reminiscent volumes use Holden Chapel to illustrate a tale of rational progress, enlivened by an occasional anecdote of youthful indiscretion. People who visit Harvard now are struck by the university's quiet tranquillity, sun-dappled paths, and stately structures. The timeless public face of the institution is a crafted facade, an amalgam of centuries of conscious and unconscious manipulations. Remembering Holden Chapel only as a "little gem of Georgian architecture" (Morrison 1936b: 94) is a disservice to some of the most revealing facets of the structure's past.

The dig at Holden Chapel was salvage archaeology. Construction was in progress when the find was made. The postponement of planned renovations fostered the attitude "It's actually an interesting [archaeological] find . . . I just wish it wasn't something that stops the work" (Lonergan 1999). Beyond its value to archaeology and history, the Holden Chapel excavation served as another reminder to the Harvard community that important materials from its past exist underground and are an important and truthful reflection of the institution's past. Another important benefit was that the excavation set the stage for more proactive management of the archaeological resources of the university in the future.

Indian College Excavations

Current directions of campus archaeology in Harvard Yard are research-based and community-driven initiatives with particular focus on seventeenth-century Harvard, the involvement of Native Americans in that history, and the potential for building living Harvard history through reflexive and collaborative approaches to a shared future. Harvard's Indian College, built in 1655, was the first institution in North America committed to the education of Native American students. The 1650 charter of Harvard College dedicated the institution "to the education of the English and Indian youth of this country, in knowledge and godliness" (document on file, Harvard University Archives, 1650). The financially and operationally ailing Harvard College was revived by new leadership under President Henry Dunster and by the Society for the Propagation of the Gospel in New England (SPGNE) through the 1650 charter and a substantial infusion of funds, some of which

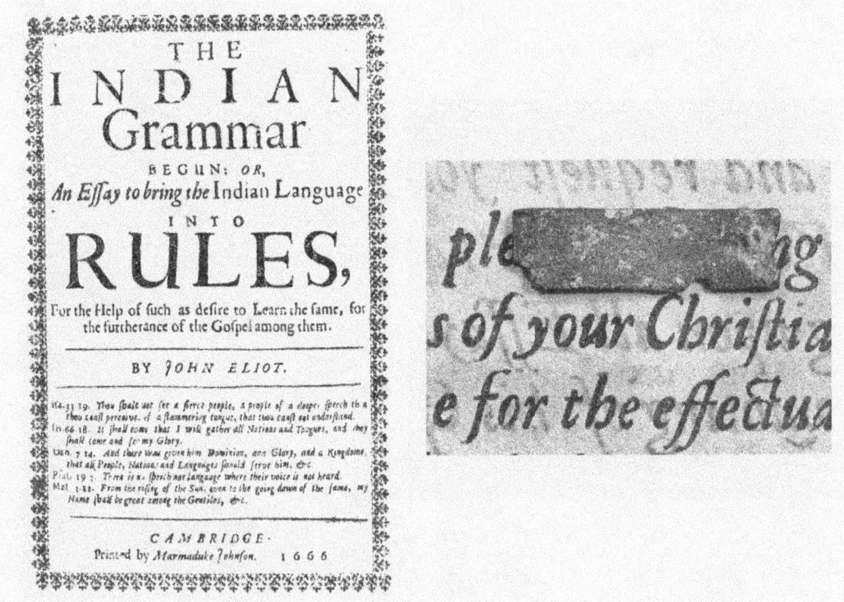
THE
INDIAN
Grammar
BEGUN: OR,
An Eſſay to bring the Indian Language
INTO
RULES,
For the Help of ſuch as deſire to Learn the ſame, for the furtherance of the Goſpel among them.

BY *JOHN ELIOT.*

Isa. 33.19. *Thou ſhalt not ſee a fierce people, a people of a deeper ſpeech than thou canſt perceive, of a ſtammering tongue, that thou canſt not underſtand.*
Isa. 66.18. *It ſhall come that I will gather all Nations and Tongues, and they ſhall come and ſee my Glory.*
Dan. 7.14. *And there was given him Dominion, and Glory, and a Kingdome, that all People, Nations and Languages ſhould ſerve him, &c.*
Pſal. 19.3. *There is no ſpeech nor language where their voice is not heard.*
Mal. 1.11. *From the riſing of the Sun, even to the going down of the ſame, my Name ſhall be great among the Gentiles, &c.*

CAMBRIDGE:
Printed by *Marmaduke Johnſon.* 1666

Figure 6.7. (*Left*) Eliot Bible, 1663; (*right*) "o" printing type excavated from Harvard Yard. (Courtesy of Harvard University Special Collections)

were used to construct the Indian College. SPGNE was concerned with the Christianization of Native peoples to facilitate their mercantile potential and their salvation. One particular educational focus was the challenge of communication across languages. While aimed at training Native American students in English, Greek, and Latin for their edification and to enhance their ministerial potential, the institution similarly aimed at exposing their English counterparts to Native languages to improve their ability to serve the proselytizing goals of the SPGNE.

Before being taken down in 1698, the Indian College at times housed students from New England Native American tribes, English students, and the first printing press in the American colonies. The first book printed in America, a translation of the Bible into the local Algonquian language to serve Christianization, was crafted there in 1663. The only verifiable archaeological presence of the Indian College today relates to another early product of the press, John Eliot's *The Indian Grammar Begun*, printed in 1666: a minute piece of type recovered through cultural resource management archaeology in advance of subway construction (Figure 6.7). The Indian College was the most robust of the college buildings at the time, since it was built of brick. Surprisingly, the landscape shows no physical remnant of the Indian Col-

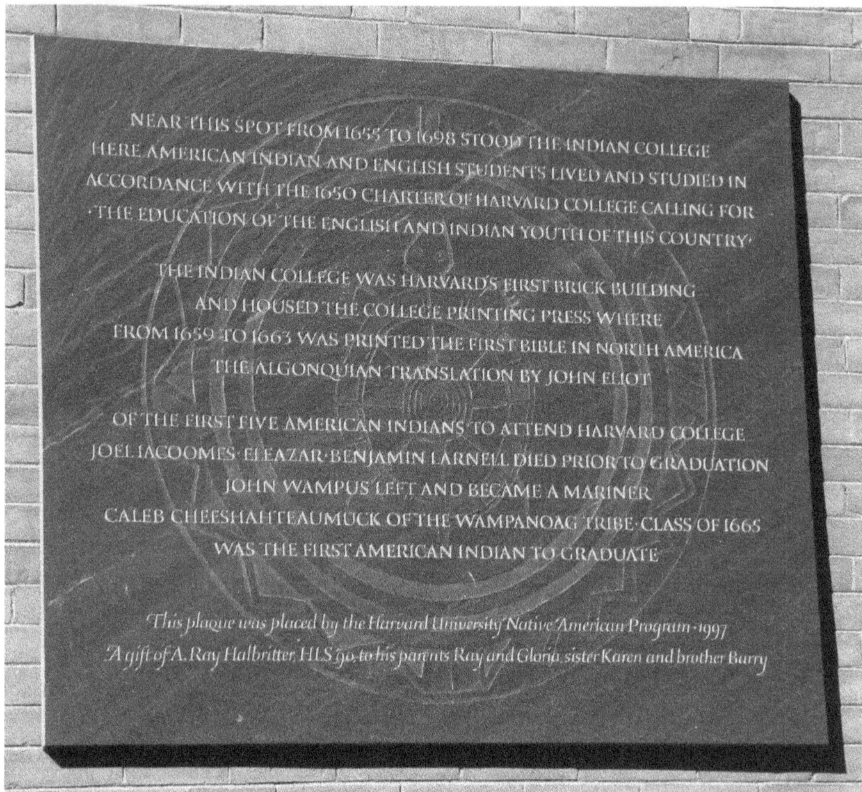

Figure 6.8. Indian College plaque, created in 1997. (Photograph by Kim Nichols, 2008)

lege, which may have measured some 70 feet in length. Nineteenth-century dormitory construction of Matthews Hall revealed brick foundation walls, which likely were remains of the Indian College. A plaque on the southwest corner of Matthews Hall created in 1997 by the Harvard University Native American Program (HUNAP) commemorates the Indian College (Figure 6.8).

Until the 2005 commemoration of the 350th anniversary of its founding through a conference by the Harvard University Committee on Ethnic Studies and the Harvard University Native American Program, the Indian College was quiet on the intellectual landscape. The timing of the 350th anniversary intersected with a time of heightened awareness of indigenous perspectives in archaeology, anthropology, and museums. Harvard, particularly through the work of the Peabody Museum of Archaeology and Ethnology, increased activity in these intellectual directions and became further energized by growth in functioning relationships with Native American groups through the Native American Graves Protection and Repatriation Act (NAGPRA) of 1990. The university was poised to engage in a collaboration of perspectives on Native American education and the Indian College.

Current campus archaeology at Harvard focuses on the seventeenth century (which includes the underrepresented story of Native American education at Harvard) as a platform for reflecting on the shape and aims of today's educational community as well as relationships to Native American neighbors and indigenous communities around the world. Toward this end, three university entities have come together in exploration and dialogue through a course: The Archaeology of Harvard Yard. In this course the Department of Anthropology, HUNAP, and the Peabody Museum of Archaeology and Ethnology aim to train students in historical public archaeology as a means to explore educational history, colonial America, and our collective future. The course emphasizes public archaeology and the relationship of study to stakeholders. Students not only explore the guiding frameworks of historical public archaeology but also are given an opportunity to engage archaeologists in dialogue through public events and creating public information.

Public events have included opening and closing ceremonies in collaboration with the local Native American communities and the Native American community at Harvard, "open houses" during which students share results and finds on site, and daily excavation docent duties (the site can be high in foot traffic). Public information includes numerous media: newspaper and magazine stories; a website with weekly installments created by the students (http://www.peabody.harvard.edu/harvardyard/); a radio show on the student-run radio station WHRB; on-campus exhibits and traveling artifacts; and exhibit-based school program opportunities. This year the course took the next step in exposing students to a means of public education by involving them, along with representatives of stakeholder communities both within and outside of the university, in the development of a Harvard Yard Archaeology exhibit at the Peabody Museum: "Digging Veritas: The Archaeology and History of the Indian College and Student Life at Colonial Harvard." Students experience archaeological resources as nonrenewable and shared, and they are exposed to the realms of cultural resource management as well as the responsibilities of museums to be ethical and effective stewards of the past.

Excavations began in the fall of 2005 as part of the course described above. The archaeological goals of the excavations were twofold: to identify archaeological remains relating to the Indian College and to mitigate a construction project associated with Massachusetts Hall, the oldest building on campus. The excavations aimed at the Indian College did not identify remains relating to it or to the seventeenth century but instead revealed significant demolition debris, likely dating to a nineteenth-century building and the widespread use of coal fires and furnaces. The 2007 edition of the course explored a potential location for remains relating to the Indian College more proximal to known seventeenth-century remains of the Old College previously described.

Contemporary stakeholders turn to the college charter's commitment to Native American education as a platform for strengthening the university's commitment: the already strong Harvard Project in American Indian Economic Development and its Honoring Nations program at the Harvard Kennedy School of Government; HUNAP and the collaborations by the Peabody Museum of Archaeology and Ethnology through NAGPRA; visiting artists; Native American community and student outreach; and revising museum exhibits and education programs relating to North America. Together with all these fora for dialogue, campus archaeology at Harvard can continue to shape the university's educational community and consider future directions for its role as an educational community and as resource and neighbor to indigenous groups worldwide.

Harvard Yard as Public Archaeology

As we have summarized, archaeological research in Harvard Yard has been initiated from a number of different venues. While salvage archaeology was no doubt one of the most common impetuses for work in the past, more recent excavations are guided by practice of archaeology as public archaeology (Potter 1994). Since the excavations in the 1980s and over the past few years have been taught as a course within the Department of Anthropology, we are poised to share with the students a number of guiding principles that are currently impacting the work of archaeology around the globe. No longer an insular process, archaeology is increasingly viewed as collaborative, seeking to embrace the needs and concerns of stakeholders (Jameson 1997; Merriman 2004). Similarly, we view our work in Harvard Yard as a way to educate the public (Harvard and beyond) on the importance of the university's unique multicultural past and preservation of this past for a variety of stakeholders (Figures 6.9 and 6.10).

We know that remnants of seventeenth-, eighteenth-, nineteenth-, and twentieth-century Harvard lie beneath the current ground surface. Our excavations of all of these pasts require the work of a community: not just

Figure 6.9. Opening ceremonies: (*top*) 2005 and (*bottom*) 2007.

Figure 6.10. Student excavators in Anthropology 1130: The Archaeology of Harvard Yard, 2007.

the team of archaeologists supported by the Peabody Museum and the Department of Anthropology but all potential stakeholders in these past, on campus and beyond. Within Harvard, our partners include a wide-ranging group, from HUNAP to University Archives to Harvard Yard Operations and Maintenance. While there are logistical issues concerning the practice of community archaeology, as many authors have recently noted (Jameson 1997; Merriman 2004; Potter 1994), our complex network of interaction need not drive us away from practicing due diligence as stewards of Harvard's past. Rather, we collaborate with our university and other partners so that they too become involved in the stewardship, to work with us in interpreting the stories found in the ground with the Harvard past that is currently known in the written record and local lore.

Community involvement outside Harvard has taken several forms. First, students engaged the public both formally and informally during the excavation itself within highly visited Harvard Yard, as described above. Interpretive signs and take-away cards at the site also offered initial information to the public throughout the duration of the excavation. Second, representatives of Native American neighbor communities and state and local history representatives joined together with HUNAP and Harvard University administrators to address the students with formal remarks and informal dialogue in the context of excavation opening and closing ceremony events. These opportunities for dialogue extended to the indoor classroom and laboratory throughout the spring semester of 2008 through lectures and seminar discussions together with the community representatives mentioned above.

The spring 2008 concluding seminar of the course in part addressed front-end evaluation of exhibit themes and community consultation plans. Students shared the results of the combined field and lab efforts, proposed themes for an exhibit, and sought advice on how to proceed with engaging these communities in the exhibit development process. The exhibit development process continued through the following summer and fall with contributions by a number of student curators (some as summer interns at the museum) as well as fall independent study students for course credit. The exhibit development (including community consultations) brought significant experience beyond the classroom and academic environment, such as honing planning skills, teamwork, community visit protocols, and refinement of roles and goals.

While drafting exhibit text, student curators brought materials and questions to these communities and interviewed representatives about broad messages as well as specifics. For example, one story garnered special enthusiasm from a variety of individuals and entities, including the Wampanoag Tribe of Gay Head (Aquinnah), Bruce Curliss, a Nipmuc Nation descendant of James Printer (an Indian College printer and pre–Indian College Harvard student), and the Cambridge Historical Commission. The story was about the students' discovery of seventeenth-century printing type, its connection to its printed counterparts, and its relationship to the power of literacy and colonization. All the representatives urged students to exhibit an Eliot Bible alongside the tiny but significant printing type. While calling attention to many aspects of seventeenth-century education at Harvard, especially those based in inequality, the printing type and Bible also inspired present-day consideration of the value of diversity within an educational environment and beyond to the ethics of world citizenship.

Perhaps the greatest educational tool we have for the students is this: an understanding of the archaeological record as the fragile remains of the past of all people. We encourage students to reflect on our responsibilities regarding the interpretation of this material for the public and descendant and other stakeholder communities. Archaeological approaches to the past are not necessarily more valid than other interpretations of that past, but all parties should be similarly interested in issues of preservation, dignity, conservation, and community access. The weighing of such topics is particularly important within museums, which are quickly becoming arenas of negotiation and resolution whose primary goal is to interpret the past for the general public while simultaneously acting as responsible stewards of collections with great importance to stakeholders of the past.

7

The Progressive Era and Sanitation Reform

Social Purity and Privies at Rural Schools in Northeastern Illinois

CATHERINE BIRD, CARRIE KOSTER, AND ROCHELLE LURIE

Introduction

Rural schools represent an easily identifiable but infrequently excavated cultural resource in Illinois (Koster-Horan, Lurie, and Bird 2007; Koster-Horan 2002, 2003, 2004). Archaeological investigations in northeastern Illinois at the circa 1862–1948 Tamarack School (11–Wi-2487) founded by immigrants from Scotland at the cross-road community of Tamarack, the circa 1868–1914 Meade School (11–Gr-257) established by Irish immigrants in rural Grundy County, and the circa 1864–1952 Lower Ridge School (11–Wi-2807) in the German farming community of Manhattan, Illinois, provide baseline data for preliminary interpretations regarding the spatial organization of rural schools (Figure 7.1).

Ambitious research questions formulated in the data recovery plan written for Lower Ridge School and testing goals at Meade School and Tamarack School met with limited success. Historical and contextual limitations hindered the use of artifacts recovered from privies to answer questions regarding gender rolls, ethnicity, and school versus nonschool activities. For example, in Will County, Illinois, 1855, 1901, and the mid-twentieth century provide incremental watershed moments in the movement of control over education away from the parent and local community. Schools that predate 1855 and the establishment of free public schools in the state are more likely to contain an ethnic/local imprint. Artifacts recovered from sanitary privies provide limited information about schoolhouse activities other than at the time of abandonment. However, site plans indicating locations of schoolhouses, wells, privies, fences, and other features can address the relationship

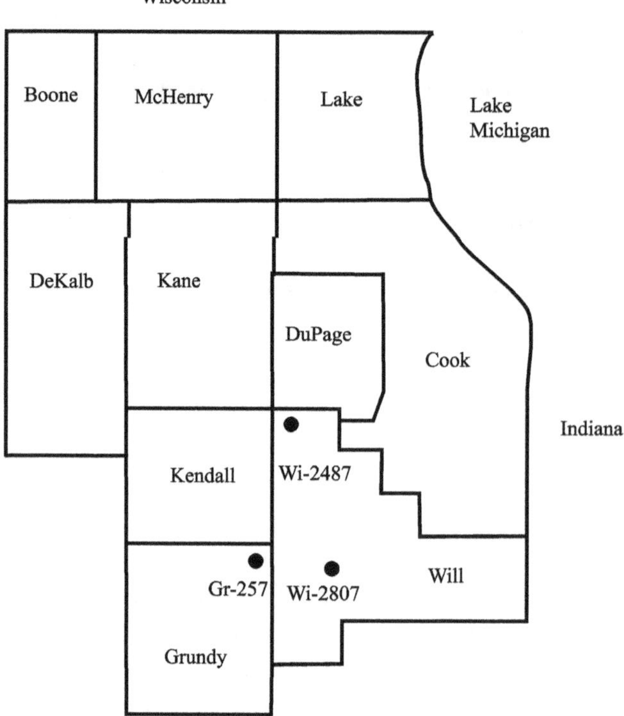

Figure 7.1. Map of northeastern Illinois, showing the location of schoolhouse sites discussed.

between changes to the physical school plant and reform movements. In particular, examination of the sanitation facilities at the three excavated rural schools illustrates reforms advocated by the Clean Living Movement of the Progressive Era (1900–17 as narrowly defined or 1895–1925 as more broadly defined).

National and Local Watershed Moments

The central theme in the history of education in the United States is the tug-of-war between local control and centralized control over all aspects of education from funding to standards for professional training, the physical plant, and the curriculum. Principles of home rule and self-government under the rural school district system gave way to centralized control and standards under the township system beginning in the early twentieth century, with an accelerated effort in Illinois in the mid-twentieth century.

Historian David Hackett Fischer in his seminal work *Albion's Seed: Four British Folkways in America* described the learning ways for each of four regions in Colonial America: Massachusetts (Fischer 1989: 130–34), Virginia (Fischer 1989: 344–49), the Delaware Valley (Fischer 1989: 530–38), and the Backcountry (Fischer 1989: 721–27). Views on education varied across the four regions and through time. Key school reform movements in the United States include the Common School Movement at the middle of the nineteenth century and various reform initiatives of the Progressive Era.

The Common School Movement may be traced to New England and economic and social changes triggered by the expansion of commerce and industry and the concomitant influx of immigrants. American leaders looked toward the common school to secure a literate workforce, to instill common values, and to provide a common language as immigrants arrived from Europe and rural residents crowded into the cities. Educator and historian Carl Kaestle (1983: 116) reported a substantial shift from private to public schooling between 1830 and 1860 throughout the United States. As Horace Mann (1796–1859) led the call for educational reform during the Common School Era, John Dewey (1859–1952) led the reform movement during the Progressive Era in the first part of the twentieth century. Key themes of the reform effort included the move toward mandatory attendance and codification of the school year, an effort to design a standardized curriculum that enhanced citizenship and provided moral training, and the passage of legislation to alleviate differences in school and teacher quality and in access to educational resources by class, gender, and/or race (Bird 2007).

Initial funding for Illinois schools came from federal public domain land sales. The Land Ordinances of 1785 and 1787 provided school funding to the states under the Articles of Confederation. Subsequent federal grants tied to land sales provided funds for Illinois schools through 1863, when sales in the state ended (Hibbard 1924).

Of the four Illinois constitutions, neither of the first two (1818 and 1848) referenced education or provided funds for schools (Cook 1912: 56). The state's January 15, 1825, Act for Providing for the Establishment of Free Schools established a tax scheme, payable in cash or "good merchantable produce," to educate every class of white citizen aged five through twenty-one (Cook 1912: 32). The next legislature (1826–27), however, cut free schools out of the law: "No person shall hereafter be taxed for the support of any free school in this state unless by his own free will and consent, first had and obtained in writing" (Illinois Secretary of State 1827: 364; Pulliam 1967: 193). Informal fireside and subscription schools scattered around the state provided educational opportunities for Illinois children until 1855 (Davis 1998: 173). Training and curriculum varied widely, while the earliest schools were often crude log buildings on poor sites. Direct control over the rural schools resided with the parents and neighborhood board.

As a candidate for the Illinois Senate in 1832 (unsuccessful, but elected in 1834, 1836, 1838, and 1840), Abraham Lincoln pleaded: "Upon the subject of education, . . . I desire to see the time when education, and, by its means, morality, sobriety, enterprise and industry, shall become much more general than at present, and I should be gratified to have in my power to contribute something to the advancement of any measure which might have a tendency to accelerate the happy period" (Lincoln 1832). As New Englanders streamed into northern Illinois after 1832, support for tax-funded public schools increased, resulting in new legislation (Pulliam 1967: 194). Illinois established a free public school system with passage of the Free School Law of 1855. Within two years (1855–57) the districts built 2,400 schoolhouses in Illinois: "many of these . . . take the place of the old, unsightly, inhospitable, log pens which once squatted about in the obscure corners of the highways" (Cook 1912: 83). All of the three schools in our sample (Meade School, Tamarack School, and Lower Ridge School) postdate 1855. After 1855 school organization and control resided with each township. Lower Ridge School was numbered School District No. 7 within the Jackson Township system. On July 1, 1901, Lower Ridge School became School District No. 74. The renumbering of school districts signaled the move toward centralized control in Will County. Control over funding, standards, the plant, and curriculum moved another step away from the parents.

As early as 1847 Will County disbursed state and federal funds to the townships and maintained statistics such as number of school-age children, number of children attending school, and number of schoolhouses. The legislature charged the secretary of state with administration of Illinois schools beginning in 1845: "to make such rules and regulations as may be necessary to carry into efficient and uniform effect the provisions of this act and of all laws for establishing and maintaining free schools in the State" (Hoffman and Booth 1912: 5). By 1907 Illinois had established a separate office of the state supervisor of rural schools serving under the state superintendent of schools (Hoffman 1908).

The Illinois School Consolidation Law of 1919 had little effect on school consolidation within the state. Not until the development of a good highway system and state funding for transporting students did rural Illinois witness the demise of one-room schools. The 1947 Common Unit District Law, which allowed the combination of high school districts and elementary school districts, accelerated school consolidation (Illinois State Board of Education [ISBOE] 2004). In one decade (1944–54) state-mandated school consolidation and reorganization reduced the number of school districts from 11,955 to 2,607 in an effort to save money through "economies of scale" (Naumer 1985: Table 1). The ISBOE currently oversees the operations of 874 school districts, numbered within a state system (Naumer 1985: Table 1). Control over schools resides with the layered bureaucracy of elected and appointed extralocal boards as well as county, state, and federal agencies. Opened in 1914, McAuley School on Roosevelt Road in West Chicago was the last one-room school in Illinois when it closed in 1991 (Rozek 2004). Fewer than four hundred one-room schools, a legacy of rural America, function as such in the twenty-first century (Ellis 2005).

Progressive Era Reforms and American Schools

The Progressive Era was a period of popular revolt and an optimistic spirit of humanitarianism that brought social as well as economic reform (Link 1954: 1). The era's Efficiency Movement and Clean Living Movement provided the impetus for a number of reforms implemented to solve or alleviate social problems. Reformers advocated scientific solutions for social problems, fairness in economic matters, and an increased role for government agencies and churches "to restore an America weakened by urbanization, immigration, government corruption, and ruthless capitalism" (Engs 2000: 7). President Theodore Roosevelt's concept of the federal government as an important force in social and economic affairs led to the establishment of the Country Life Commission in 1908. Chaired by Liberty Hyde Bailey, an agricultural scientist, the commission gathered information, made recommendations, and guided national policy regarding rural ways of living (Bailey 1911; Jones and Larson 1975; Neth 1995: 108–9). President Roosevelt's 1912 Progressive Party platform provided the basis for the future development of the reform movements, although Republican candidate William Howard Taft won the presidential election (Link 1954: 16).

The Efficiency Movement espoused the scientific study of a problem by experts to discover the best way to reduce waste and inefficiency. Highly influential in the era, Frederick Winslow Taylor (1865–1915), a business professor at Dartmouth College, applied engineering principles to time and motion studies for the scientific management of people in the workplace. School administrative experts with formal training in curriculum and pedagogy made decisions about schools and education (Tozer, Violas, and Senese 1998: 99). Critiques of public education at the time related to efficiency of scale. Reformers identified rural schools as too small and underfunded, with untrained teachers and outmoded parochial values (Tyack, James, and Benavot 1987: 109). Remedial solutions included a push toward consolidation of rural schools into graded schools, a new curriculum that included physical education, compulsory attendance, and health and sanitary requirements (Tyack, James, and Benavot 1987: 115, 125).

Advocates of the era's Clean Living Movement, including the Woman's Christian Temperance Union (WCTU), brought to the public consciousness a number of health reforms, many with moral overtones, including temperance and social purity. In addition to promoting temperance, reformers advocated sexual abstinence outside of marriage, raising the age of consent from between seven and twelve years to eighteen years, and a single moral standard of sexual conduct for men and women; reformers campaigned against obscenity, regulated prostitution (which implied acceptance of a double standard), and sexually transmitted disease, all under the aegis of social purity (Engs 2000: 13, 142; WCTU 1888).

In 1902 pressure from reformers spurred Congress to expand the role of the United States Public Health Service (PHS) by adding the words "protecting, promoting, and advancing the health care of a nation" to its mission statement. Founded in 1798 under President John Adams, the loose federal network of locally controlled hospitals created for the relief of sick and disabled seamen became the Marine Hospital Service in 1870 and the Public Health and Marine Hospital Service in 1902, with the name shortened to Public Health Service in 1912 (Parascandola 1998: 487–93). The PHS fostered preventative sanitation efforts, such as the introduction of milk and meat inspection, antispitting campaigns, paper napkins and towels, and schemes to thwart contamination by flies (screens on windows, covering excreta, etc.), in a national effort to avoid epidemic diseases such as typhoid, cholera, and dysentery (Engs 2000: 174; Rosenkrantz 1972: 98–99). Sanitation reforms and improved personal hygiene pushed during the Clean Living Movement and embraced by the populace dramatically reduced the spread of acute communicable diseases (Engs 2000:6; Winslow 1945: 194).

Health scientist Ruth Clifford Engs (2000: 3) identified three cyclical health reform or clean living movements in the United States: the Jacksonian (1830–60), the Progressive Era (1890–1920): and the Current Millennial (1970–2005±). Engs (2000: 3–5) defined four phases of agitation for change in the reform movements: moral suasion (education and social pressure), coercion (public policy), backlash (lack of compliance and enforcement), and complacency (derision of reformers and disregard or repeal of laws) until the next cycle commenced. The Civil War and World War I, respectively, led to the complacency phase during the first two movements. The Clean Living Movement of the Progressive Era included health reform crusades, popularized in the press and through public school education that at rural schools focused on improved sanitation and social purity such as gender separation of privies and elimination of obscene graffiti. Printed materials distributed by the various state departments of education and individual reformers included plans and specifications for ideal, progressive rural schools.

Publications distributed in 1908 and 1912 by the Illinois state supervisor of rural schools, Urias Hoffman, noted that even the best rural schools lacked comfortable and sanitary conditions (Hoffman 1908; Hoffman and Booth 1912: 8). Suggested remedies included the abolition of dust, the common drinking cup, and the shared towel; the establishment of a well or cistern to supply water; and the erection of two privies placed as far apart as possible, with vine-covered screens and walls free of obscene language and pictures (Hoffman and Booth 1912: 36–39). The caption under the photograph of a two-seat or double privy captures the feeling of the day in regard to social purity: "Here depravity lies in wait for the innocence of childhood. This is used by both sexes. It is a reproach upon common decency and should be prevented by law" (Hoffman and Booth 1912: 39).

Both the 1908 and 1912 reports expand upon the problems of double outhouses and include an identical paragraph: "There are yet to be found double outhouses on school grounds. It is difficult to conceive of a worse arrangement than these double-doored abominations. To build one should be a penal offense. Better expose the children to a deadly contagious disease than to subject them to the moral leprosy which lurks in these double outhouses" (Hoffman 1908: 3; Hoffman and Booth 1912: 39).

Plains educational reformer and academic Harold W. Foght published *The American Rural School* in 1910 to enlighten professionals and school board members about the changing role of schools in the community, including the "hygienic appliances demanded in this Progressive Age" (Foght 1910: 130–33). Foght, a Norwegian immigrant, advocated the use of vine-covered screens and walls free of graffiti (he suggested a coat of sand paint) as noted above but also encouraged the construction of sanitary indoor toilets for rural schools, made possible by pneumatic pressure tanks and underground sewage tanks.

The lag between improvements suggested by the reformers and implementation in the rural schools appears to have been significant. Local resistance to rural school improvements, in addition to the dissatisfaction with diminution of local control, centered on the push for higher standards of sanitation in the rural schools that in many cases eclipsed the level of home sanitation. The New York State Education Department in 1916 referred to the sanitary toilet requirements as "irksome and expensive," a symbol of the excesses and inappropriateness of the educator's agenda (Barron 1997: 69).

Historian Wayne E. Fuller (1982: 37–38) reports that by 1900 rural schools had privies where none existed before and schools with a single privy now had two. Although the New York State Education Department mandated the use of sanitary chemical toilets for rural schools in 1918, as late as 1931 the state allowed pit privies in rural schools lacking access to a piped water supply but specified indoor plumbing in new urban construction (Barron 1997: 69–70). Installation of chemical toilets (boys' and girls') in rural schools appears to date to the 1920s, although arguments presented in the mid-twentieth century by medical officer F. J. G. Lishman (1951) of Alberta, Canada, suggest that not all unsewered schools resolved health concerns with these hygienic appliances. The advantages of the "chemically-charged pail closet" or chemical toilet included a lessened offense to children, deterrence of flies, labor-saving maintenance, and safer disposal of the excreta (Lishman 1951: 151). Disadvantages were limited to possible skin irritation on contact such as splashing. The liquid chemical (initially strong alkali and coal tar but later a solution of formaldehyde and detergent) supposedly rendered the human waste innocuous, broken down, and "somewhat sterilized" (Lishman 1951: 149). Staff emptied the toilets about twice a week and poured the treated waste into narrow "soakaway" trenches or holes (Lishman 1951: 150).

During the Depression the New Deal's WPA (Works Progress Administration, later Works Projects Administration; 1935–43) replaced the remaining outhouses with indoor chemical toilets and installed windows on at least one wall of the rural schools (Boles 1998). These WPA standards remained the standards for rural schools in the United States until consolidation. Indoor plumbing in rural America, powered by electric well pumps, increased from 10 to 25 percent of rural households in the first five years after passage of the New Deal's Rural Electrification Act of 1935 (Leuchtenburg 1963: 157). In comparison, 90 percent of urban households had indoor plumbing in 1930.

Leaders of the Progressive Era reform movements engaged the rural teachers, ministers, and county agents in implementing the reform goals of the movement (Neth 1995: 108).

Archaeological Evidence for Sanitation

The water and sewer components of the sanitary systems at two of the three school sites (Tamarack School and Lower Ridge School) illustrate two of the social reforms—the spatially delimited built environment meant to encourage social purity and the health benefits of pure water and proper sewage disposal—advocated during the Progressive Era. Pipeline construction adversely impacted a significant portion of the third school site (Meade School), leaving only two possible wells as part of the sanitary system (Figures 7.2, 7.3, 7.4).

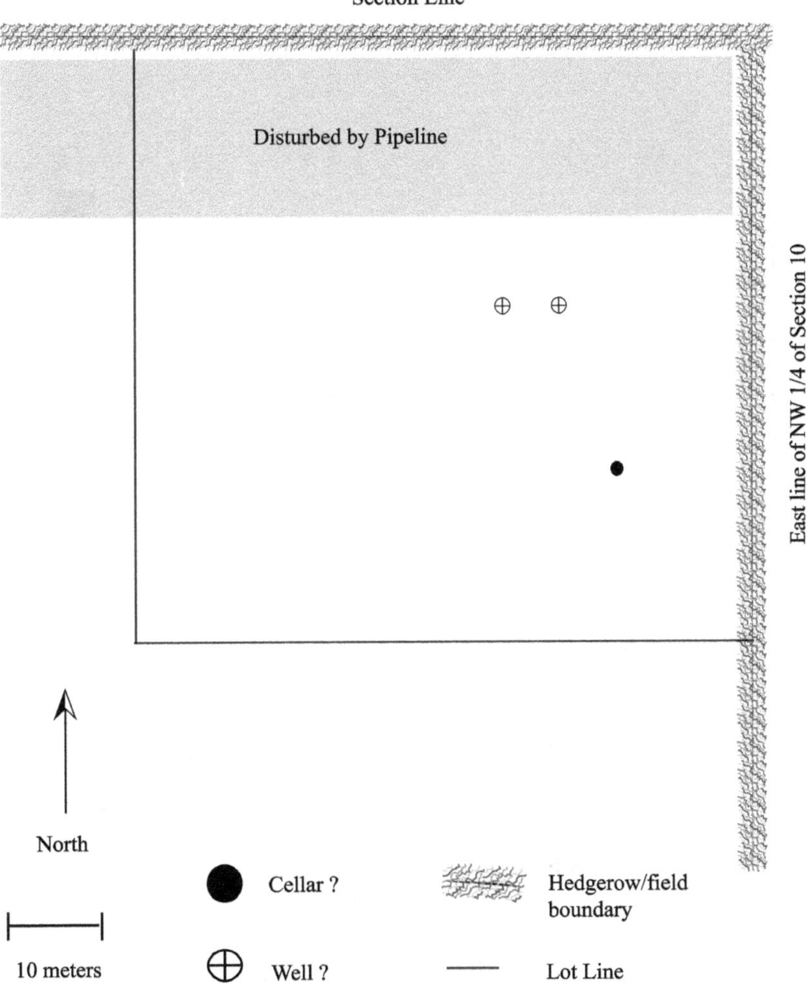

Figure 7.2. Plan of Meade School (11-Gr-257), showing the built environment and the limits of the schoolyard as noted in photographs (snapshots and aerials) and through archaeological excavation.

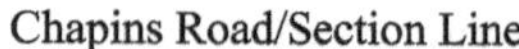

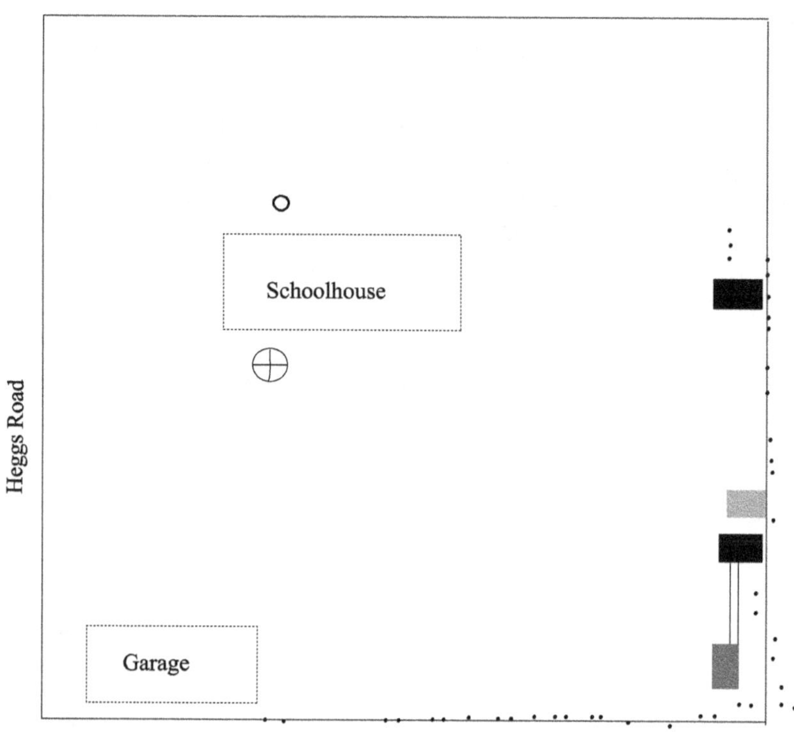

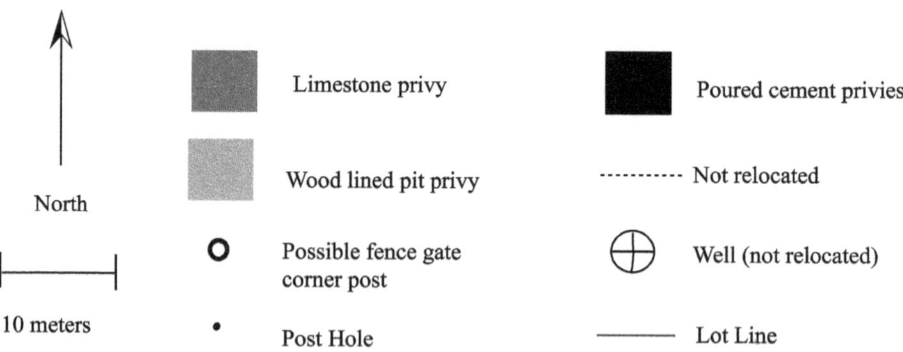

Figure 7.3. Plan of Tamarack School (11–Wi-2487), showing the built environment and the limits of the schoolyard as noted in photographs (snapshots and aerials) and through archaeological excavation.

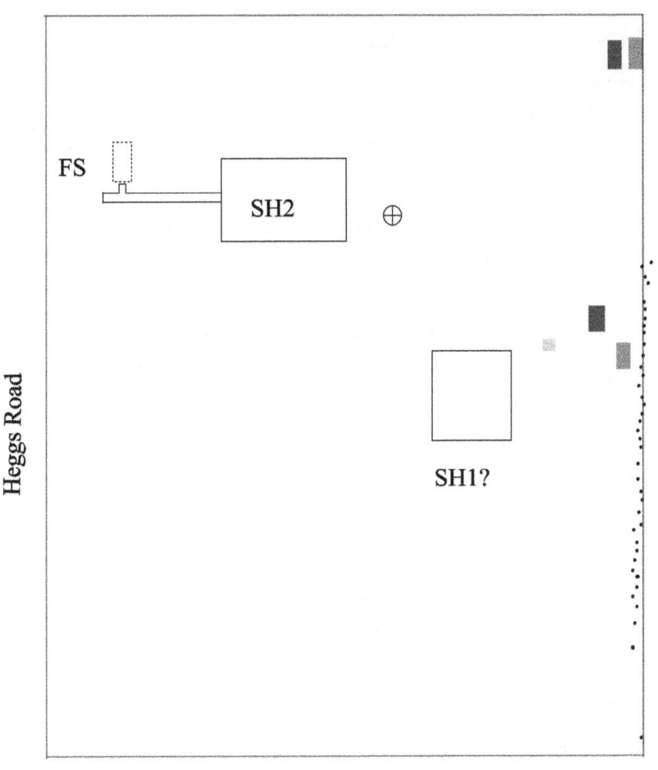

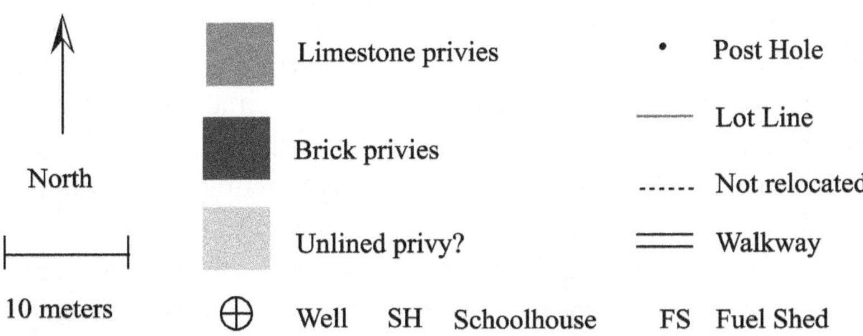

Figure 7.4. Plan of Lower Ridge School (11-Wi-2807), showing the built environment and the limits of the schoolyard as noted in photographs (snapshots and aerials) and through archaeological excavation.

Example 1

Deed transfers between the Meade family and the Aux Sable Township school trustees establish the size (1.0 acre) and temporal existence of Meade School (1868 through 1914). The school was established by Irish immigrants between the canal towns of Joliet and Morris in rural Grundy County. Irish farming communities sprang up along the Illinois and Michigan (I & M) Canal as the state accepted canal script issued to laborers by the cash-strapped I & M directors in payment for state lands (Davis 1998: 360). The I & M, under construction from 1836 through 1841 and 1845 through 1848, is about 6 miles south of Meade School in the northeast corner of Grundy County.

The three features (possible failed well, clay-capped well, and possible earthen cellar) uncovered during testing in 2003 may be associated with Meade School or the Rodney House preemption claim. Wagon-maker Rodney House of New York squatted in the vicinity of the future school as early as 1833 (Biographical Publishing Company 1900: 619–21). He purchased 160 acres from the public domain at the Chicago land office on June 13, 1835; the General Land Office issued the patent on October 1, 1839, at which time House lived in nearby Joliet with his wife and children and operated a wagon shop.

An artifact scatter that spread just beyond the deeded boundaries to 4,200 m^2 or 1.04 acres defined the site. Recovered artifacts (N = 675) include a 1909 nickel, a clay marble; window, container, and chimney glass; undecorated ceramics; brick fragments; machine-cut nails; lime-sand mortar; slate pencil and tablet fragments; coal and cinders; and iron desk parts, with at least one school-related artifact in each feature. Impacts to the site relate to school consolidation and subsequent construction activities. Upon closure of the school, Aux Sable Township auctioned the school building. The Meade family won the bid and removed the superstructure a short distance to their farmstead, initially for use as a storage shed and subsequently as a temporary residence. Fire engulfed the building in 1993, according to a descendant. Construction of a natural gas pipeline adversely impacted the northern section of the site prior to the archaeological testing, while industrial development followed these investigations and completely destroyed the remainder of the site. The rural Meade School closed during the Progressive Era, perhaps having been consolidated rather than renovated or replaced.

Example 2

Tamarack School (11–Wi-2487) first appears on the 1873 Wheatland Township plat at the corner of Heggs and Chapin roads in the cross-road community of Tamarack (post office opened in 1858, closed in 1901; Matile 2005). A victim of mid-twentieth century consolidation, the rural Will County School District No. 34 closed in 1948 (Farrington 1967: 215). Stephen Findlay (circa 1794–1864) founded Tamarack about 1844, following his emigration from Loudoun, Ayrshire, Scotland.

The artifact scatter defining the site contained household and architectural debris as well as school-related items and extended over 1.6 acres within an agricultural field. Testing in the spring of 2002 uncovered midden remnants, four privies (two cement, one limestone, and one wood-lined), a drainage trench, and numerous postmolds defining the schoolyard within a 0.32 acre parcel. The archaeologists inventoried 8,805 artifacts from surface and feature contexts. School-related artifacts (whole and fragmentary inkwells and ink and medicine bottles as well as chimney glass, cast iron desk parts, lead pencils, and slate pencil and tablet fragments) filled the cement privies. Connections to Scotland are limited to one medicine bottle recovered from the wood-lined privy, manufactured between 1907 and 1920 in Kinghorn, Fifeshire, Scotland. Photographs (snapshots and a 1939 aerial) and former students (Ernest King and Paul King) identify the locations of the schoolhouse, a garage, and a well with a hand pump (features not located during testing). Ernest King, grandson of 1852 immigrant Thomas King (1832–1911) of Ayrshire, Scotland, attended Tamarack School from 1912 to 1917; Ernest's son Paul King attended from 1932 to 1937 (*Plainfield Enterprise* 1911).

Limestone footings about 4 × 10 m supported the schoolhouse, and limestone lined the first privy (1.6 × 0.9 m). Wire nails used to construct the wood-lined pit privy (0.95 × 1.2 m) date its construction to the last quarter of the nineteenth century. The paired cement privies (1.0 × 1.7 m), built about 1920 and situated just over 11 m apart, appear to be the last privies used for the school. Postmolds perpendicular to the long axis of the northern cement privy and parallel to the schoolyard fence may indicate the use of a privacy screen. The tile-lined drain (0.7 m wide) between the southern cement privy and the limestone privy may have channeled liquid waste from a urinal. Separation of liquid waste from solid waste, which slowed the rate of excreta accumulation, was achievable in boys' privies and toilets. Postmolds (12 to 60 cm) mark the location of wood and later metal posts that define the eastern and southern limits of the schoolyard. Chapins Road and Heggs Road define the northern and western limits, respectively, of the schoolyard. Photographic evidence shows that the Tamarack School gained electricity between 1935 and 1945, following the creation of the New Deal's Rural Electrification Administration.

The schoolhouse currently functions as a private residence, situated 1 mile south on Heggs Road. The artifacts recovered from the paired cement privies relate to the final abandonment of the school.

Example 3

Settlement in Jackson Township, Will County, Illinois, began in the southwest corner in Reed's Grove (5 miles southwest of the school) about 1832, with the arrival of Charles Reed and his kin from Indiana. German farmers followed in the mid-nineteenth century; some were refugees of the 1848 revolution (Meyer 2000: 234). Built during the summer of 1864 in Jackson Township and appraised at $500, Lower Ridge School (11–Wi-2807) closed in 1952, according to the county records. New owners moved the surplus frame schoolhouse 2.5 miles southeast to Manhattan, Illinois, about 1955; it served as a carpentry shop until it was destroyed by fire.

Field investigations at Lower Ridge School began during the summer of 2003 and culminated with data recovery in the fall of 2004. Although the schoolyard, as defined by fence lines and Heggs Road, includes 0.5 acres, the surface scatter of artifacts measured 40 × 60 m or 2,400 m^2 (0.6 acres). Local lore, photographs, and archaeological investigations suggest that the schoolyard encompasses the remains of two limestone schoolhouse footings (the 1864 Schoolhouse 1 and the circa 1902 Schoolhouse 2), a limestone-lined dug well retrofitted with a driven well point, and five privies (one possible unlined privy, two privies with brick footings, and two privies with limestone footings), among other features of minor import to this discussion. Early in the interpretations of the site, Koster suggested that Schoolhouse 1 could be a teacherage (combined school and living quarters). Although the various Will County superintendent's reports and diaries, the census records, and the Lower Ridge School registers identify a number of teachers at Lower Ridge by name, none can be identified as living in a teacherage: all boarded with others or owned their own home. Additionally, a plaque on an early photograph of Schoolhouse 2 appears to read: "Dist. 74 [above] est. 1902 [below]." The $949.30 in expenses disbursed by the Lower Ridge treasurer may be for construction costs associated with the replacement school. Jackson Township built a series of schools in the nearby Village of Elwood in 1854, 1916, and 1956—upon settlement, during the reform movements of the Progressive Era, and during consolidation, when it needed to accommodate the influx of rural students (Bird 2007). Review of photographs at the Will County Regional Office of Education suggests that the county replaced other schools as well during the Progressive Era.

Testing and mitigation recovered 3,054 artifacts from Lower Ridge School (almost all within feature context), including ceramics, container glass, personal items, household items, architectural debris, hardware, miscellaneous items, and prehistoric artifacts (*N* = 13). School-related artifacts signal the presence of children and two lighting systems. Selected artifacts of import include a child's ring from one of the brick privies, a harmonica comb and reeds from one of the limestone privies, and a barrette, hair combs, slate pencils, marbles, iron desk parts, and an inkwell from Schoolhouse 2. Both of the schoolhouses and the midden contained slate pencils; lead pencil fragments came from the limestone and brick privies. The archaeologists recovered iron desk parts on the surface of the agricultural field, within Schoolhouse 2, and from a limestone privy. Liquid fuel lamps and candles lit the schools prior to the extension of electricity into the rural countryside—during the 1945–46 school year at Lower Ridge according to the county records. The archaeologists recovered chimney glass in both schoolhouses and a brick privy and a porcelain insulator in Schoolhouse 2.

Records at the Will County Regional Office of Education provide a timeline for some of the school improvements and feature sequences at Lower Ridge. A tornado destroyed some trees and the outhouses (probably the limestone-lined privies) in 1917. The well was not fit to use from September 1918 through September 1919 but was described as "good" at the end of the 1919–20 school year. Expenditures totaling $1,150 in 1918 may have provided the two new privies associated with the brick footings as well as the lift pump for the well. Driven wells replaced dug wells beginning in the last quarter of the nineteenth century and the availability of portable steam drills (PSU n.d.: 348). The acquisition of new individual drinking cups in 1919 improved health within the classroom. Water, formerly hand-drawn, poured from pneumatic hand pumps available as early as 1894 from the Montgomery Ward catalogue. Further innovation in the rural water supply followed when electricity became available. The *Inventory of School Property* reports end with the 1924–25 school year for Lower Ridge School, with privies still in use. Indoor chemical toilets (boys' and girls'), possibly installed by WPA laborers, replaced outdoor privies at Lower Ridge by 1944 (Boles 1998).

Discussion and Conclusion

School and health reform movements, with roots in the revolutionary town of Boston, affected the construction, renovation, and consolidation for rural schools in the Illinois countryside and nationally. While Thomas Jefferson promoted free education and the Continental Congress provided a mechanism for funding education, nearly seventy years (1787–1855) passed before Illinois offered tax-supported, free public school education to the children of the state, following the Common School Movement championed by Horace Mann of Massachusetts. Public health innovator Lemuel Shattuck (1793–1859), a contemporary of Mann, delivered a *Report of a General Plan for the Promotion of Public and Personal Health* to the General Court of Massachusetts on April 29, 1850, the impetus for the 1869 establishment of the Massachusetts State Board of Health (Winslow 1945: 191–92). Shattuck's pioneering statistical analysis of vital records led to exploration of the social and scientific nature of disease and a program of public health reform (Rosenkrantz 1972: 17, 98). National public health reform lagged (1890–1920), with sanitation reform in rural schools accomplished somewhat later (1920–45). Movements that are salient to the discussion of sanitation reform and social purity include the Efficiency Movement and the Clean Living Movement of the Progressive Era (1890–1920). School consolidation, suggested and encouraged during the Efficiency Movement, slowly progressed until World War II. Rural residents relinquished control only when war forced sacrifice upon the nation; rural schools were inefficient in wartime.

The water supply at the three sample schools started with dug wells at the time of construction (1862–68), with two schools (Tamarack School and Lower Ridge School) transitioning to driven wells with lift pumps about 1920. Meade School, which included two dug wells, closed in 1914. The first well probably failed, but the school board capped the second well with impervious clay when the school closed during the Progressive Era. Capping abandoned wells protects the health and safety of the public and prevents contamination of the groundwater supply. Particular county codes and the Illinois Water Well Construction Code, under the jurisdiction of the Illinois State Water Survey, protect the water supply within the state (Dalsin 2003). Founded in 1895 at Urbana within the Chemistry Department of the University of Illinois, the survey's initial mission established scientific management of the state's water resources and traced the spread of typhoid and other waterborne diseases (Winstanley et al. 2002). Although electricity reached the two schools about 1946, the school boards did not retrofit Tamarack or Lower Ridge with indoor plumbing. With consolidation looming, the renovation may have been cost prohibitive.

The hygienic appliances and their spatially delimited built environment at Tamarack School and Lower Ridge School illustrate the coercive success of the Progressive Era sanitation reforms (pure water and proper sewage disposal) and encouragement of social purity (separation by gender). The Wheatland Township and Jackson Township school boards constructed unisex privies or "double-doored abominations," according to the Illinois state supervisor of rural schools (Hoffman 1908: 32; Hoffman and Booth 1912: 32). The unisex privies in the sample include a limestone-lined privy (1862–80) followed by a wood-lined privy (circa 1880–1910) along the fence behind the schoolhouse at Tamarack and an unlined possible privy (circa 1864–1902) immediately behind Schoolhouse 1 at Lower Ridge. Paired privies, cement-lined at Tamarack (circa 1910–48) and limestone-lined (circa 1902–18) followed by brick-lined (circa 1918–40) at Lower Ridge, mark gender separation of toilet facilities at both schools. Spatial separation ranges from 11 m at the 0.32 acre Tamarack School to 22 m at the 0.5 acre Lower Ridge School. Lot size could have allowed additional spatial separation at both schools, but lot dimensions provided more space at Lower Ridge. Perhaps to compensate for the lack of adequate separation, the northernmost of the paired privies at Tamarack shows evidence of a visual screen, suggesting that the privy is the girls' toilet. The southernmost of the paired privies includes a drainage trench that articulates with the then-abandoned limestone-lined singular privy, suggesting that this privy is the boys' toilet.

Sometime between 1925 and 1944 the Will County school board approved the installation of chemical tank toilets with a capacity of about 125 gallons at Lower Ridge School and at least four other schools within Jackson Township. Ventilating pipes, which extend well above the roofline, identify the schools with indoor chemical toilets in photographs. During renovations, the laborers removed a portion of the limestone footings to accommodate the chemical toilets, as illustrated at Lower Ridge School, where the girls' tank remained in place in the southwest corner of Schoolhouse 2 (Figures 7.5 and 7.6). The chemical toilet is nearly identical to one illustrated in a United States Department of Agriculture (USDA) bulletin (Warren 1922: 21) published in the Progressive Era (Figure 7.7). The oily chemical disinfectant deterred flies, dissolved the solid waste, and did not contaminate water supplies when disposed of in soakaway trenches that required little space and infrequent locational changes (Lishman 1951: 149, 150). A narrow trench (70 × 40 cm) along the fence line could be the soakaway trench for the burial of chemical toilet effluent.

Rural schools in existence prior to the Progressive Era renovated, built new structures, or closed. The school and the teacherage, through moral suasion and example, promoted the reforms advocated during the Progressive Era. Professor of education Spencer J. Maxcy identified the first teacherage

Figure 7.5. Overview of Lower Ridge Schoolhouse 2, showing the pierced south wall and placement of the girls' chemical toilet in the southwest corner of the schoolhouse.

as a 22 × 28 foot building erected in Hall County, Nebraska, in 1894 (Maxcy 1979: 268). Initially a solution to a late nineteenth-century housing problem in the West and an alternative to "boarding around" for itinerant teachers, the teacherage with indoor plumbing also functioned as a model of "tasteful and economical domestic furnishing and decoration" for the edification of the community (Maxcy 1979: 271; Rapeer 1920: 204). Reformers displayed a model teacherage at the Pan-American Exposition, a world's fair held in 1901 at Buffalo, New York.

The rural school reflected the social issues of the day in the spatial dimensions of the schoolyard and the evolution of the hygienic appliances available to the students. Federal land grants from the sale of the public domain provided public funding for schools at the birth of the nation, while the federal programs of President Franklin D. Roosevelt near the middle of the twentieth century provided labor to implement school and other reform issues related to rural life that had been identified during the tenure of President Theodore Roosevelt a quarter of a century earlier. In Illinois parent-controlled fireside and subscription schools faded as the state passed taxed-supported school legislation in 1855. Township school boards guided construction and renovation at the rural schools from 1855 through 1901, with oversight from

Figure 7.6. Detail of the chemical toilet at Lower Ridge School, with the tube connecting the commode to the tank on the left.

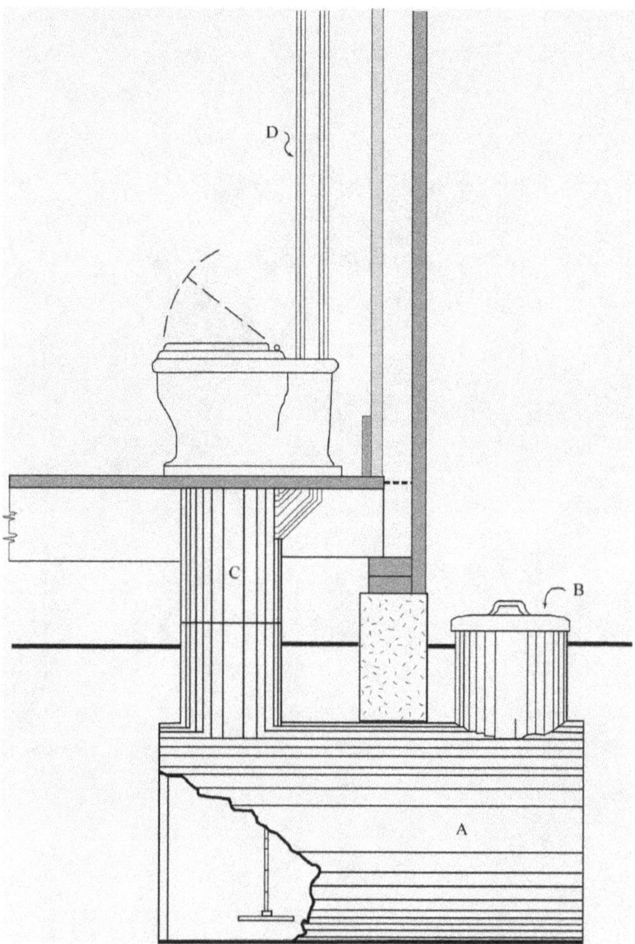

Figure 7.7. Schematic drawing of a chemical toilet from USDA Farmers' Bulletin No. 1227 (Figure 16 in Warren 1922: 21), showing (*A*) tank, (*B*) exterior maintenance opening, (*C*) tube connecting commode to tank, and (*D*) ventilating pipe.

the county and state. Will County worked to improve and consolidate the rural schools through the first half of the twentieth century. As historian Hal S. Barron suggests (1997: 77), parents in rural northeastern Illinois initially resisted reform efforts due to concern about the diminution of local self-government, financial extravagance, and animosity toward the arrogance of outside "experts." New Deal programs such as the Works Progress Administration and the Rural Electrification Administration and the advent of World War II alleviated some of these concerns and provided the tipping point for acquiescence to reform.

8

The Eagle and the Poor House

Archaeological Investigations on the University of North Carolina Campus

R. P. STEPHEN DAVIS JR., PATRICIA M. SAMFORD, AND ELIZABETH A. JONES

The University of North Carolina (UNC) at Chapel Hill is the oldest public-supported institution of higher learning in the United States. Since 1991 archaeologists at the Research Laboratories of Archaeology have conducted numerous archaeological investigations on its campus. These investigations have included archaeological surveys, site testing, monitoring of ongoing construction projects, and full-scale excavations. Most, but not all, of these studies have been undertaken at the university's request to help it fulfill its statutory obligations under North Carolina's Archaeological Resources Protection Act (ARPA), and collectively they provide a unique resource for viewing the university community during its first one hundred years. The buried architectural remains and associated artifact assemblages from several campus sites, particularly those located adjacent to downtown Chapel Hill and within the core area of the original campus, recall a quaint era of college and town life now beyond personal memory and provide tangible evidence of the university's most humble beginnings. This evidence has become increasingly important to the university community, providing connections to the past and a sense of place that cannot be wholly conveyed by the restoration of campus buildings alone. In this way, archaeology on the UNC campus has served to expand our understanding and appreciation of Chapel Hill's historical character.

In this chapter we describe the results of excavations undertaken during the 1990s at two archaeological sites on the UNC campus. The Graham Memorial site, where a tavern and hotel stood from the mid-1790s until 1921, offers a perspective on one of Chapel Hill's first businesses that catered to university visitors and also provided room and board for students. The nearby Pettigrew site was the location of two successive buildings that also served student housing needs: the Poor House (an affectionately named private dormitory) and later the Phi Delta Theta fraternity house.

Early Campus History

On October 12, 1793, a group of prominent North Carolinians gathered on a wooded hilltop—New Hope Chapel Hill—in Orange County for a ceremony that would mark the beginning of public education for the state and the new nation. The gathering was led by William Richardson Davie of Halifax, grand master of North Carolina's brotherhood of Freemasons and author of the bill (passed by the legislature in December 1789) that established the University of North Carolina. Others in attendance included the Rev. Dr. Samuel McCorkle, who delivered the sermon; university trustees; members of the building committee; numerous Masonic brethren; and several prominent local citizens. The purpose of the ceremony was to lay the cornerstone for East Building (now Old East), the first university structure to be erected. While construction had actually commenced the previous July, October 12 would thereafter mark the official beginning of the university (Connor 1953, 1: 236–40).

Immediately following the laying of the cornerstone, twenty-nine two-acre and four-acre lots adjacent to the new campus were auctioned to raise money for construction (Figure 8.1). These lots, most of which were located along newly platted Franklin and Columbia streets, became the town of Chapel Hill. The town lots and the original campus were part of a sizable tract of land, totaling more than 1,200 acres, which a dozen local citizens had offered to donate to the state if it would establish the university there. Although the legislature also had created an endowment fund out of debts owed to the state prior to 1783, this fund initially lacked the ability to support the university, which had to rely heavily on loans and the generous gifts of other private citizens (Connor 1953, 1: 39–54, 244–46).

Despite financial constraints, construction of East Building, the President's House, and the Steward's House (that is, the dining hall) was sufficiently complete for the university to open its doors to students on January 15, 1795. Within a few years a fourth building, now known as Person Hall, was built as the Chapel. At the same time, East Building proved to be too small, and an addition was constructed (Henderson 1949). In 1831 an astronomical observatory was erected a short distance east of the campus center. This structure reflected President Joseph Caldwell's strong interest in astronomy and was the first of its kind at an institution of higher learning

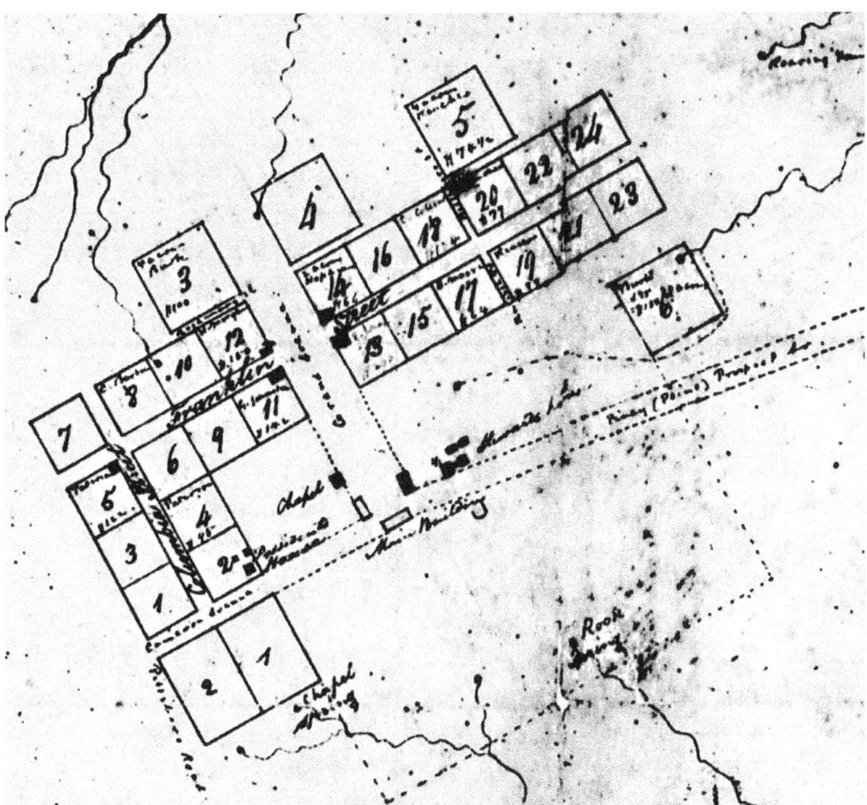

Figure 8.1. Portion of a plat of Chapel Hill and the University of North Carolina, drawn sometime after 1797. Four campus buildings are shown (from west to east): President's House, Chapel, East Building (not labeled), and Steward's House. The locations of two other planned buildings (Main Building and West Building) are also shown. The Graham Memorial and Pettigrew sites are located on town lots 11 and 13. The building depicted on Lot 13 is the Tavern House. From a plat titled "Plan of the Village at the University with the Adjoining Lands Belonging to the Institution." (Courtesy of the University Archives, Wilson Library, University of North Carolina at Chapel Hill)

in America (Powell 1979: 47). Unfortunately, it was poorly constructed and had to be abandoned just four years later. By 1840 three new buildings had been constructed and a third story had been added to East Building. Two of the new brick buildings—South Building and West Building—created a horseshoe around the university's well; the third building—Gerrard Hall—replaced Person Hall as the university chapel. During the 1850s the final episode of antebellum campus construction took place with the erection of two large dormitories flanking East Building and West Building (called New East and New West) and the construction of Smith Hall as the university's library

(Henderson 1949). With the exception of the President's House, Steward's House, and observatory, all substantial university buildings that predate 1860 are still standing (Figure 8.2).

As in its earliest years, the university continued to operate within tight financial constraints throughout the 1800s. This situation was perhaps most dramatically manifested in its continual space needs, particularly as it related to student life. As the student population grew (from seven in the first graduating class of 1798 to eighty-nine in the graduating class of 1859), more and more students had to seek off-campus room and board. Accommodations included boardinghouses, hotels, rooms in private homes, small shacks erected by townspeople in their backyards, and even camping in the nearby woods or in unfinished buildings (Battle 1907: 179, 1912: 40). In addition to dining at the Steward's House, early students could find good meals at the town's taverns (such as the Tavern House at the Graham Memorial site) and also took their meals in the homes of local townsfolk.

The university faculty and trustees, however, wanted to keep students away from the taverns and private homes because of the alcohol served there. Students on college campuses all over the country in the early nineteenth century were extremely boisterous and even violent. Fighting was a favorite pastime among friends as well as enemies. It was not considered harmful to a student's reputation to sneak up behind a classmate and hit him over the head with a club (Battle 1907: 271). Student riots, vandalism of university property, and pranks played upon faculty were fairly constant, and alcohol fed this unrest. In the beginning the university tried to force students to dine in the Steward's House, where the only beverages available were water, coffee, tea, and milk (Battle 1907: 51). Yet complaints about the food there, as revealed in students' letters describing starvation rations and maggoty meat, finally forced the university to allow students to dine off campus in 1819. Steward's House ceased operation altogether in 1844 (Battle 1907: 89). By 1855 student drinking was banned on or off campus, and the sale of alcohol was forbidden within two miles of Chapel Hill.

Similarly, the university had difficulty controlling firearms. In addition to a few duels, guns were frequently drawn on fellow students in the heat of a brawl, were fired in the buildings as part of general revelry, and were even pulled on professors. Loud explosions of gunpowder were a favorite prank throughout the early years of the university. In the 1840s a ball of gunpowder was actually ignited under a professor's chair, which catapulted him, relatively unharmed, into the center of the classroom (Battle 1907: 577–78). Some students, who could not afford to eat at Steward's House or the taverns,

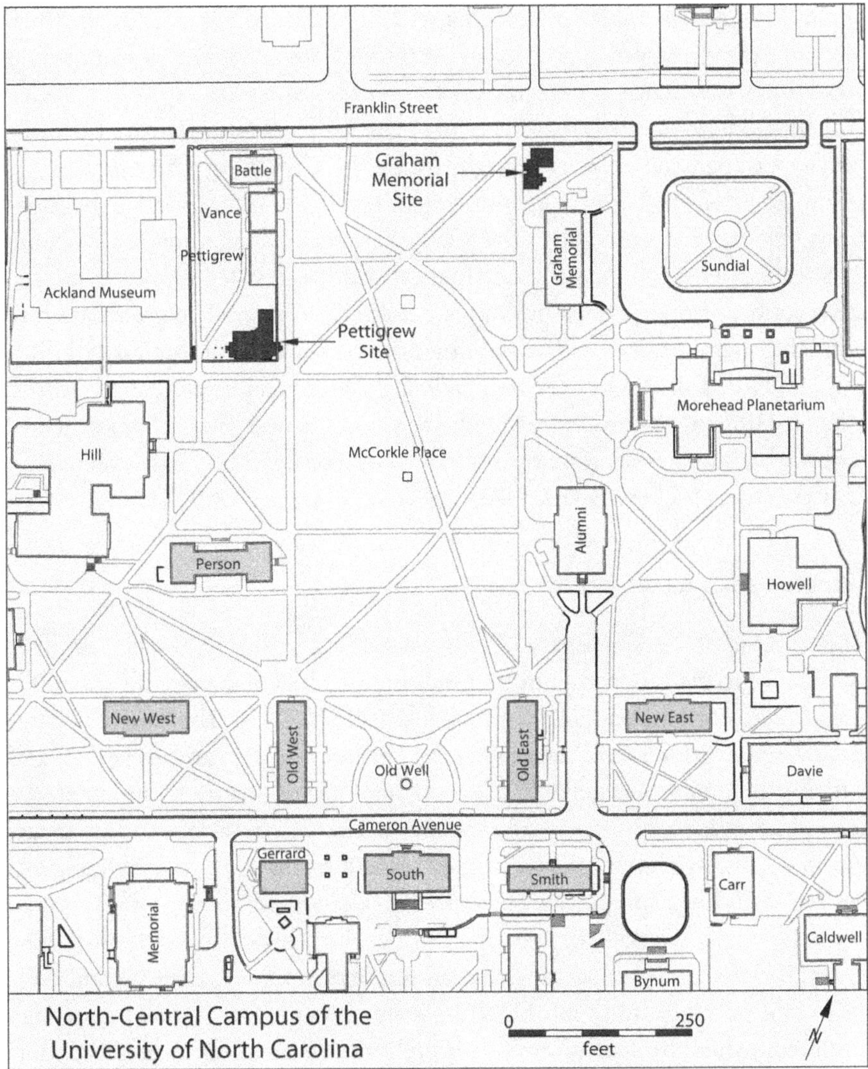

Figure 8.2. Map of the north-central campus of the University of North Carolina, showing the areas excavated at the Graham Memorial and Pettigrew sites. University buildings erected before the Civil War are shown in gray.

had to hunt down their own dinner each day in order to feed themselves, so the university did not forbid the possession of firearms or gunpowder until 1856.

Despite a steady growth in student population prior to the Civil War, the size of the faculty and the corresponding size of the town (made up largely of faculty and persons whose livelihood was directly dependent upon the university) remained small. In fact, Chapel Hill remained a small college town well into the twentieth century, and even today the university community is sometimes nostalgically, if erroneously, regarded as a village.

Unlike many southern universities, the University of North Carolina largely escaped the ravages brought on by the Civil War. The campus was occupied briefly by Union forces during the spring of 1865; however, negotiations between the university's president, David L. Swain, and Gen. William T. Sherman ensured that the occupation did not result in any substantial destruction of the campus buildings or other property. The greatest act of vandalism apparently was the stabling of horses in several university buildings, including the library (Powell 1979: 69). Far greater outrage, both within Chapel Hill and statewide, resulted when Swain's daughter, Eleanor, fell in love with and married Gen. Smith B. Atkins, commander of the occupying Union forces (Vickers 1985: 73–75).

Campus Archaeology

The campus of the University of North Carolina before 1870 bears little resemblance to the modern campus, even though most of the significant buildings of the early nineteenth century are still standing. The university has done a remarkable job in preserving the heart of the old campus center, and surrounding buildings generally complement its architectural character; the overall landscape, however, is far different. This difference is readily apparent in the rare photographs from the late 1800s, which provide glimpses of campus buildings and private structures located on adjacent properties now owned by the university. Images of buildings that are no longer standing also reveal the rich archaeological potential of the campus (Figures 8.3 and 8.4).

In 1991 staff and students of UNC's Research Laboratories of Archaeology initiated a small project to provide a preliminary assessment of the significant and potentially undisturbed archaeological remains of the campus as they related to the early years of the university (Carnes-McNaughton 1991). The reasons for undertaking this project were twofold. First, we wished to establish a systematic program for assessing the potential impact of current and future construction and facilities-improvement projects on campus archaeological resources. Although a significant portion of the campus was within the Chapel Hill Historic District, listed in the National Register of Historic Places, university managers routinely did not consider the impact of their actions upon the grounds surrounding individually listed historic structures such as Old East, Old West, and the Old Well. A preliminary ar-

Figure 8.3. View of Franklin Street about 1892, looking west. At left, along the south side of the street, are the Eagle Hotel (formerly the Tavern House), McCorkle Place, and the Central Hotel. The Poor House and the later Phi Delta Theta fraternity house stood at the rear of the Central Hotel lot. (Courtesy of the North Carolina Collection, University of North Carolina Library at Chapel Hill)

Figure 8.4. View of the Eagle Hotel and rear annex about 1892, looking east. Shortly after this photograph was taken, the north end of the hotel (at left), which was the original Tavern House and Eagle Hotel building, was demolished and a new, Victorian-style structure was erected. The entire complex burned in 1921. (Courtesy of the North Carolina Collection, University of North Carolina Library at Chapel Hill)

chaeological assessment was seen as a first step in helping administrators understand that the university's significant historic properties included more than just the old campus buildings. The message we wanted to communicate was that the heart of the original campus could reasonably be viewed as one large archaeological district, whose soils contained a rich artifactual and architectural record of university life from its beginnings in 1793 through the early years of the twentieth century.

Second, as the University of North Carolina prepared for its Bicentennial Observance in 1993, academic departments were invited to participate by undertaking special projects unique to their own interests and abilities (Tepper 1998). For the staff and students of the Research Laboratories of Archaeology, the logical project was to undertake an archaeological investigation on campus that would shed new light on the university during its earliest years. The preliminary campus archaeological assessment was the first step in determining the feasibility of such an investigation.

Evidence used to conduct this assessment included: (1) early maps and drawings of the campus from the late eighteenth and early nineteenth centuries; (2) Sanborn insurance maps from the early twentieth century; (3) photographs from the late nineteenth and early twentieth centuries that showed campus buildings and landscapes; (4) histories of the university written by Kemp P. Battle (1907, 1912), R. D. W. Connor (1953), Archibald Henderson (1949), William S. Powell (1979), and others; and (5) the results of a pedestrian survey of footpaths and other eroded surfaces within the area of the original campus (between Franklin Street and South Building).

The preliminary archaeological assessment identified four sites that could potentially yield important information about early campus life. The first of these was Steward's House, which stood from 1795 until 1847. As the university's first commons (or dining hall), this building was an important part of student life and could provide significant information about campus dietary conditions. Unfortunately, early plats are not sufficiently accurate to determine this building's location, and a preliminary field investigation using systematic soil auger testing failed to locate it. Because Steward's House stood near the current footprint of New East, it was thought that the construction of this building in the 1850s could have obliterated all evidence of it.[1] A second site, located near Old West, was identified during a pedestrian survey of McCorkle Place, a wooded quadrangle between the heart of the campus and Franklin Street. This site was defined by a concentration of mid-nineteenth-century artifacts eroding from the ground surface along a footpath and was initially interpreted as possible evidence of the occupation of the campus by

Union troops in April 1865. Testing of this site prior to sidewalk construction, however, revealed it to be no more than a trash-filled stump hole.

The remaining two sites were the Pettigrew site (adjacent to Pettigrew Hall), where maps and photographs placed the Phi Delta Theta fraternity house during early twentieth century, and the Graham Memorial site, where the Tavern House and later Eagle Hotel stood from 1796 until 1921.

The Graham Memorial Site

For our Bicentennial Observance project, we chose to begin excavation at the Graham Memorial site, since it appeared to provide the best potential for yielding preserved archaeological remains from the university's earliest years. The Pettigrew site provided "insurance" just in case we found nothing of interest at Graham Memorial. Indeed, it seemed quite possible that all evidence of the earlier buildings had been bulldozed away when nearby Graham Memorial Building was constructed in 1931. Despite this prospect, our previous research indicated that the businesses that stood here were integral to the early life of the university and might yield significant archaeological data concerning student life and town development during the late 1700s and throughout the 1800s.

In keeping with the university's tripartite mission of teaching, research, and public service, the excavation of the Graham Memorial site was conducted as an archaeological field school during the 1993–94 academic year to train undergraduate students in field and laboratory methods in historical archaeology. It also provided a highly visible example for the public and campus community of how archaeologists conduct their research and interpret what they find. Several thousand people visited the excavations during three open houses, and hundreds of visiting schoolchildren were afforded an opportunity to observe and in some instances participate in the excavation.

Historical Overview

Following the laying of the cornerstone for Old East on October 12, 1793, the UNC Board of Trustees held an auction to sell two-acre and four-acre town lots for the adjacent village that became Chapel Hill. One of the two-acre lots, Lot 13 at the southeast corner of Franklin Street and McCorkle Place, was bought by Jesse Neville, who then sold it to "Buck" Taylor, the university's first steward. Upon resigning his university position in 1797, Taylor opened a tavern there, which he and his son operated until the 1820s. Known simply as the Tavern House, it was one of Chapel Hill's first businesses. The Tavern House was a two-story wooden building; like most taverns in the late eighteenth century, it served not only as a drinking establishment but also as an inn and a place for public gatherings (Figures 8.1 and 8.2).

In 1823 the property was sold, became a hotel, and began to take in boarders, including UNC students. It also became a popular place for ceremonial gatherings such as the university's commencement ball. These balls were the culmination of the important and highly regarded commencement activities each year. Students dressed in formal attire for these events, and seniors were allowed to return home a month before commencement to procure the proper clothing, which might cost as much as six months' room and board at the Steward's House.

By the mid-1830s the hotel, now called the Eagle Hotel, began a period of relative prosperity and notoriety. The best known of the hotel's proprietors was Nancy Hilliard, who ran the Eagle from about 1838 until 1857. During Hilliard's tenure the hotel was greatly enlarged; by 1850 the number of students living there had risen to 103, representing over 40% of all students attending the university (Samford and Davis n.d.).

With the onset of the Civil War and its aftermath, the hotel fell upon hard times and never fully regained the prominence and prosperity it had achieved during the antebellum years. In 1892 extensive renovations were made to turn the property into a profitable resort hotel. The old tavern building was torn down and replaced with a large, Victorian-style structure with an expansive porch. An annex that had been built at the rear of the building and additions to the east were left intact (Figure 8.4). This business venture failed, and in 1908 the University Inn and Annex (as the hotel was now known) was acquired by the university to be used as a dormitory. During the following decade the facility was poorly maintained; in 1921 it caught fire and was completely destroyed (Samford and Davis n.d.).

Excavation

When archaeological excavations began in September 1993, we already had some idea of where we might uncover undisturbed traces of the tavern and hotel complex, based on a careful examination of historical maps and photographs as well as limited archaeological testing. After establishing a grid of 5 × 5 foot units across the suspected site area, we focused our initial excavations on an area behind the original tavern where earlier auger testing had revealed deeply stratified layers of soil containing artifacts and other debris from the building. Although we were clearly beyond the probable site of the original tavern's foundations, we hoped that the area we had selected would contain both artifact deposits in the tavern's backyard and architectural traces of a large addition that was constructed on the south side of the hotel sometime during the 1830s and 1840s.

The first 5 × 5 foot unit that the students excavated revealed the top of the shallow foundation trench from the rear addition, less than a foot beneath the ground surface. Just 10 feet west of this excavation unit, toward McCorkle Place, a second unit contained much deeper archaeological deposits, which extended almost three feet below the surface. Five soil zones were recorded, and these were excavated separately. In the uppermost zone, students found artifacts of modern campus life, including aluminum pull tabs, a beer bottle cap, and fragments of phonograph records. As we dug deeper, we found fragments of broken whiteware dishes and discarded glassware, wood charcoal, and other building debris that most likely were deposited when fire destroyed the structure in 1921. At the bottom of the excavation unit, the students found items that dated to the earliest years of the university and can be attributed to the Tavern House and the early Eagle Hotel. These included an English gunflint, a clay marble, a lead button, fragments of English white clay pipes, and numerous pearlware sherds.

After these two encouraging discoveries, the students spent the remainder of the fall excavating within a 25 × 30 foot area to expose more of the foundation trench and the much deeper deposits of late eighteenth- and nineteenth-century refuse that accumulated along the west side of the hotel. By semester's end, we had retrieved over 12,000 artifacts, had located part of the hotel's foundation, and had exposed ample evidence of the 1921 fire; however, we still did not know if any architectural traces of the early tavern remained (Figure 8.5).

Our goals for the spring semester were to complete the excavation begun in the fall and to locate the Tavern House. We extended our excavation toward Franklin Street and almost immediately found evidence of the late eighteenth-century structure. The first trace of the tavern to be uncovered was the brick base of the west chimney, buried less than half a foot below the ground surface. As we removed the topsoil just east of the chimney, we encountered several large stones at the top of a massive, dry-laid stone foundation that enclosed an 18 × 18 foot cellar (Figure 8.6). Oriented along Franklin Street, the cellar extended only about two feet below the present ground surface, and it is likely that it was a half (or English) basement with small above-grade windows letting in light. The two-foot width of the stone foun-

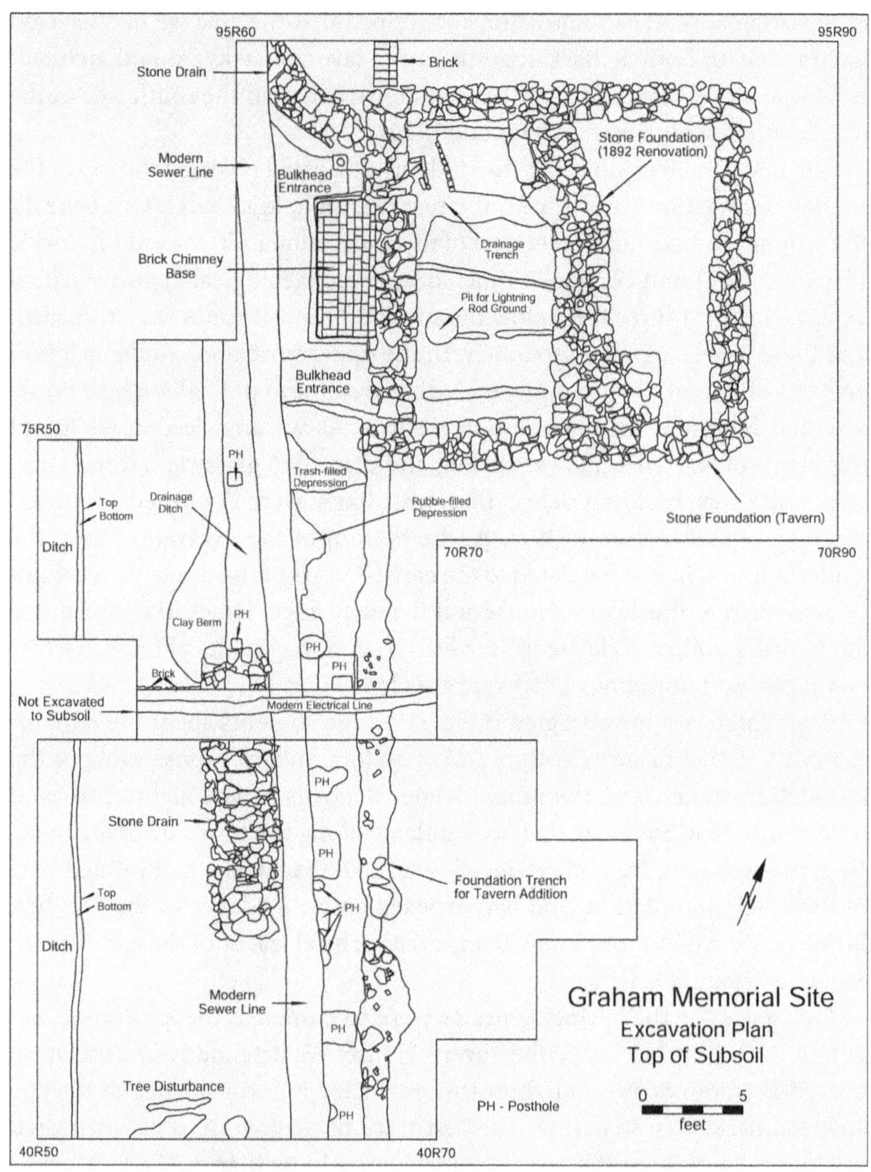

Figure 8.5. Excavation plan of the Graham Memorial site, showing architectural remains and other features associated with the Tavern House and Eagle Hotel.

Figure 8.6. View of the excavated tavern cellar and foundation at the Graham Memorial site (looking southwest). The west wall foundation for the 1892 Victorian structure, which replaced the original tavern building, crosses the center of the cellar (from left to right). Note that this foundation rests upon fill above the cellar floor.

dation suggested that it supported a two-story structure, a conclusion that is consistent with late nineteenth-century photographs showing the original tavern building (Figure 8.4). This original structure probably measured 36 feet by 18 feet. The below-ground stone walls appeared to have been laid directly abutting the sides of the hole dug for seating the cellar, since there was no builder's trench apparent along the exterior edge of the foundation.

The soil at the top of the cellar, filled in when the building was torn down in the 1890s, contained numerous artifacts and debris from the demolished tavern. Beneath this debris were three cellar floors, separated by sand that had been intentionally deposited to help alleviate moisture problems. Several broken plates and bowls, as well as a few coins, buttons, and other small broken or lost artifacts, lay on these floors (Figure 8.7).

One confusing aspect of the cellar was a large rock foundation that cut across its interior. At first, it appeared as if the tavern had two small cellars rather than a single large one. Once we had excavated the cellar to its original clay floor, however, we realized that this interior (Figure 8.6) foundation was built later to bridge the old cellar and to support the west wall of the 1892

Figure 8.7. Artifacts from the Graham Memorial site: (*top left*) an early nineteenth-century blue shell-edged plate from a deeply buried trash deposit along the west edge of the excavation; (*top right*) a stoneware pot, made by local potter Nicholas Fox (1797–1858), recovered from the drainage ditch along the west side of the structure; (*bottom left*) a mid-nineteenth-century transfer-printed whiteware plate from the cellar floor; and (*bottom right*) a late nineteenth-century stoneware ale bottle from fill deposited in 1892 atop the cellar floor.

Victorian structure. Even the curvature of the circular turret at the building's northwest corner can be seen in the later foundation.

Quite unexpectedly, we learned a great deal from our excavations about how the hotel's owners dealt with problems of moisture and drainage. Being dug into stiff piedmont clay, the building's cellar acted as a catch-basin, partially filling with water when it rained. On two separate occasions, the cellar floor was raised by depositing a half-foot-thick layer of clean river sand. Although this tactic probably worked temporarily, it did not solve the problem, since the water had nowhere to go. Following the apparent failure of the second layer of sand to keep the floor dry, a much more radical step was taken. A shallow drainage ditch was cut diagonally across the sand floor to the northwest corner, where it fed a newly constructed stone-lined drain. This drain connected to a ditch about six feet west of the tavern, which directed water to the edge of Franklin Street. A similar stone drain along this ditch also was found just southwest of the tavern, beneath an entryway to the rear addition (Figure 8.5).

The Pettigrew Site

Almost three years after the bicentennial excavation, we learned that plans were underway to construct a new building for the university's Institute for the Arts and Humanities on the nearby Pettigrew site, where our earlier surveys and archival studies had identified potentially significant buried archaeological remains. Given the success of our initial project at Graham Memorial, a research proposal was submitted and funded by UNC's Office of Facilities Planning and Design for an eight-week excavation during the summer of 1997 to evaluate the site.

Historical Overview

The Pettigrew site was originally part of Lot 11, another two-acre lot sold at auction by the university's trustees in 1793 (Figure 8.1). The lot also fronted on Franklin Street and was originally purchased by George Johnston. By the time the university reacquired the property in 1929, it had changed ownership some two dozen times. When it was first surveyed, we believed that most of the archaeological remains at the Pettigrew site probably were associated with the Phi Delta Theta fraternity house, which stood there from about 1908 until the early 1930s. This area was the backyard of a residence built on Franklin Street during the late 1790s and was also the back lot of the Roberson/Central Hotel (which stood at the site of Battle-Vance-Pettigrew Building in the late 1800s and early 1900s), so we also expected earlier archaeological remains (Figures 8.2 and 8.3). Because of this long history of activity, we had hoped to excavate the Pettigrew site during the Bicentennial, once work was completed at the nearby Graham Memorial site. This did not occur, however, due to the extent and complexity of the archaeological remains found there. What we did not know at the time was that a substantial, privately owned dormitory known as the Poor House also stood at the south edge of Lot 11 from the 1830s or 1840s until about 1880.

A reference to this dormitory, with dimensions and a method of construction that could be confirmed archaeologically, was found in an 1883 deed, which described the property: "The land whereon formerly stood a row of Brick offices called the 'Poor House' One hundred & twenty feet long & Eighteen feet wide on the Extreme Southern end of the lot" (Jones et al. 1998: 9). The university had been plagued by shortages of student housing for most of the nineteenth century, and student letters and diaries of the 1830s and 1840s indicate that housing was at a premium. To help alleviate the problem, many entrepreneurial Chapel Hillians rented rooms or constructed separate buildings in their yards to serve as student quarters.

With the onset of the Civil War, such temporary residences were no longer needed, and many fell into ruin and were removed during the subsequent Reconstruction period. Kemp Battle (1912: 40), president of the university during the late 1800s, wrote: "Another effect of the hard times through which the village passed was the removal of many cottages which had been built by the landowners for the accommodation of students of prosperous days, who were unable to procure lodging in the University Buildings. These cottages were torn down, or sold, some re-erected a mile or so away on the neighboring farms. Thus disappeared from the map 'Pandemonium,' 'Possum Quarter,' the 'Poor House,' 'Bat Hall,' the 'Crystal Palace,' and other places dear to the ante-bellum students."

Excavation

Fieldwork at the Pettigrew site was undertaken in four phases. First, the entire site area was tested with soil augers to determine the depth and structure of the underlying deposits. Next, three 5 × 5 foot test units were hand excavated by natural strata. Ten distinct stratigraphic units were eventually identified that contained artifacts from the modern era back to the late 1700s. Disturbed and recent strata over a 2,800 sq ft area were then stripped with a backhoe so that most of the archaeological effort could be directed toward sampling and documenting the more deeply buried, intact deposits. Following mechanical stripping, excavation proceeded by hand within 10 × 10 foot and 5 × 5 foot units and by natural strata. Approximately 1,600 sq ft of the area that had been stripped of topsoil was excavated by hand to subsoil, and another 900 sq ft was partially excavated. Additional units were fully excavated by hand to expose portions of the Poor House foundation that extended beyond the area of mechanical stripping (Figure 8.8).

When the Pettigrew excavation began, we expected most of the architectural remains to be associated with the fraternity house. However, we quickly discovered that the archaeological remains at the site were much more extensive. The archaeological fieldwork and archival research documented the existence of two buildings at the site: (1) the Phi Delta Theta fraternity house, which stood during the early twentieth century, and (2) a row of eight brick rooms known as the Poor House that was built and rented to students during the mid-nineteenth century. Although the Poor House is mentioned in histories of the university and Chapel Hill, its location was previously unknown.

Architectural debris associated with the Poor House was the most extensive and included window glass, cut nails, and brick rubble. Fewer artifacts could be attributed to the fraternity building, perhaps because these items were removed when the university demolished the structure in the 1930s or were removed by mechanical stripping prior to hand excavation. Items clearly associated with this structure include plumbing pipes and fixtures, electrical insulators, lightbulbs, tile, window glass, wire nails, a doorknob, and a door lock. Artifacts associated with the occupation of the Poor House and the Phi Delta Theta fraternity include whiteware, porcelain, and stoneware sherds, glassware, bottle fragments, lamp glass, personal items, and animal bones. Smaller quantities of creamware and pearlware sherds, some of which were found beneath the Poor House, likely are associated with the original occupants of Lot 11 (Figure 8.9). The town plat illustrated in Figure 8.1 shows that a structure stood at the northeast corner of this lot by about 1797. Interestingly, numerous shallow plow scars also were observed, which cut into the subsoil clay beneath the Poor House. These reflect the property's use as a garden before the Poor House was constructed in the 1830s or 1840s.

Substantial intact architectural elements for the Phi Delta Theta house and the Poor House also were found and were sufficiently complete to determine the size and placement of these structures. The fraternity house was a frame structure two and a half stories high that stood on brick piers and had a small shed attached to the west side. Its location and appearance are well documented in early nineteenth-century photographs and insurance maps (Powell 1979: 134–35). It measured approximately 32 by 36 feet, had a wraparound porch, and was heated by two interior fireplaces.

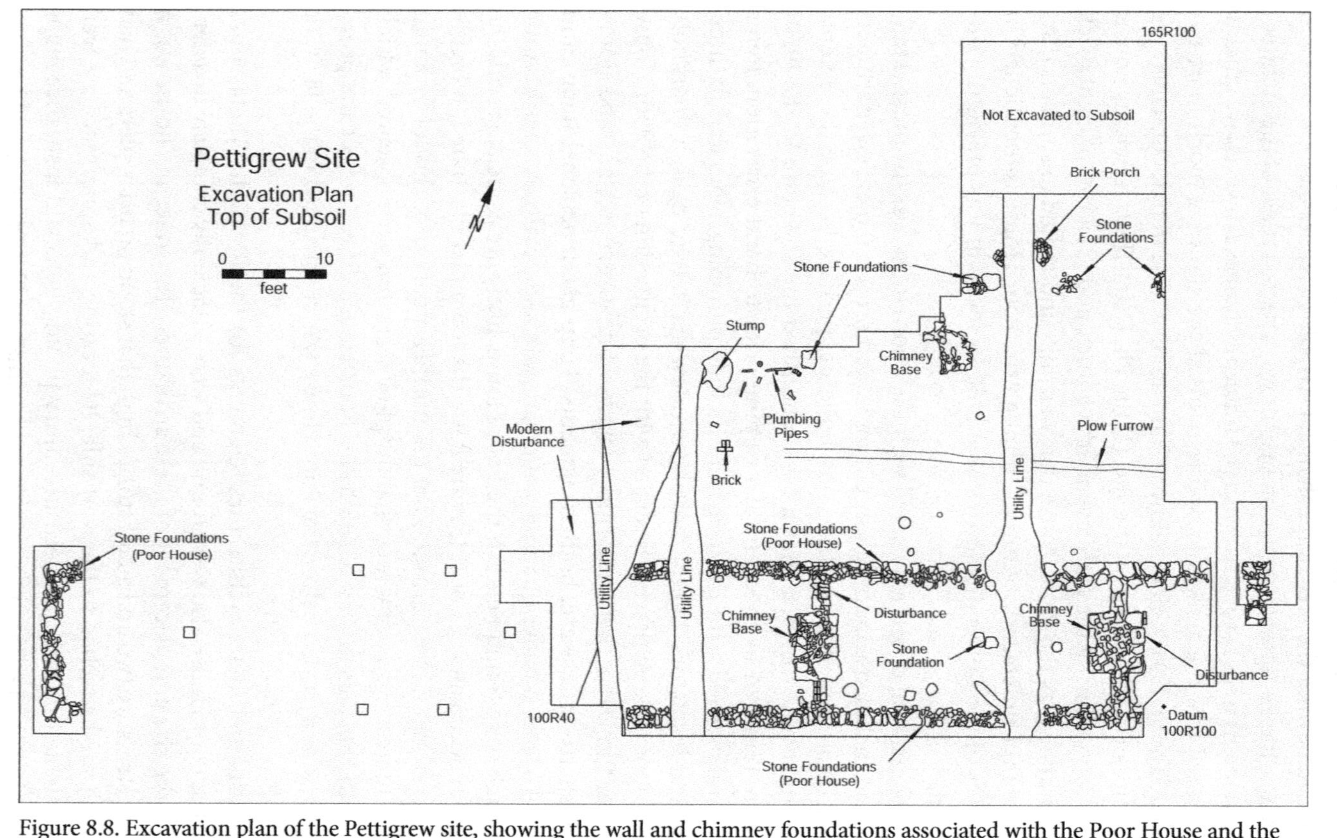

Figure 8.8. Excavation plan of the Pettigrew site, showing the wall and chimney foundations associated with the Poor House and the chimney base, foundation piers, and other remains associated with the Phi Delta Theta fraternity house.

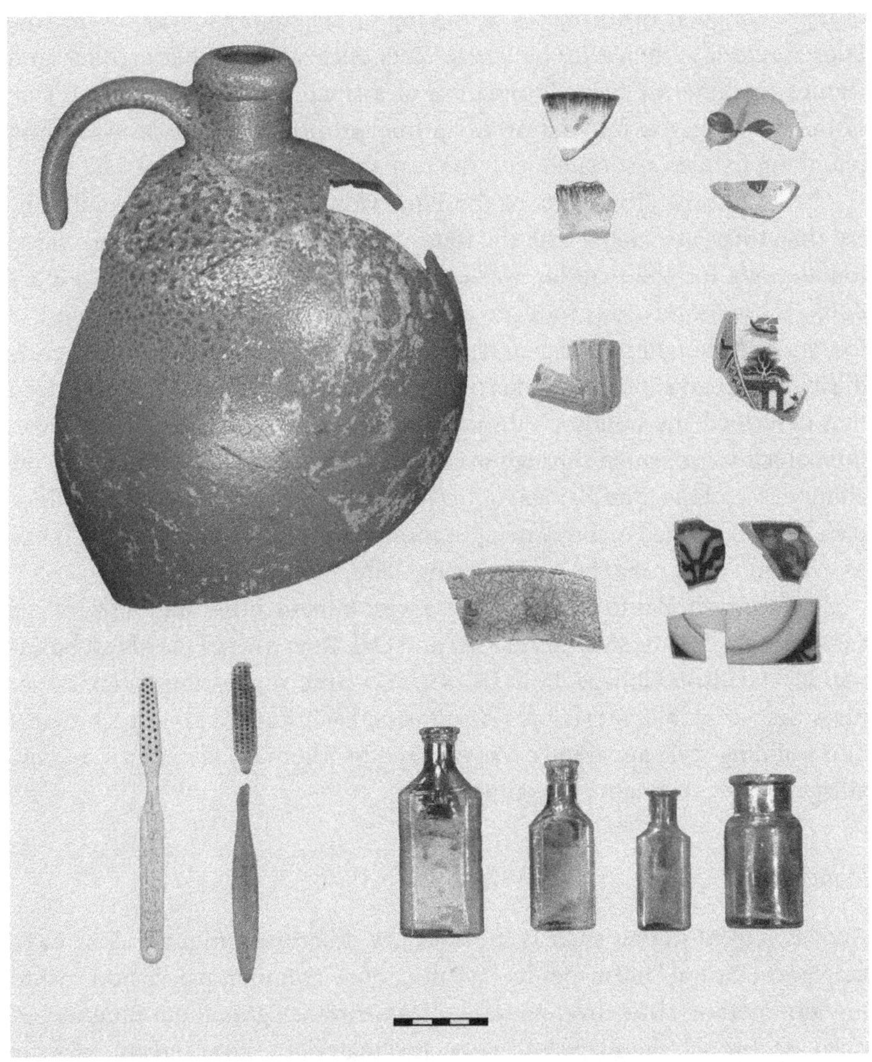

Figure 8.9. Artifacts from the Pettigrew site: (*top left*) salt-glazed stoneware jug, (*top middle*) blue shell-edged, (*top right*) polychrome hand-painted, (*row two*) locally made earthenware pipe, and chinoiserie transfer-printed pearlware sherds, which likely predate the Poor House; and (*row three*) transfer-printed whiteware sherds attributable to the Poor House occupation; and (*bottom row*) bone toothbrushes and pharmaceutical bottles associated with the Phi Delta Theta fraternity house.

The archaeological remains of the fraternity house closely match this description. Five stone foundations for brick piers were uncovered, and three other rectangular disturbances in the top of the stone foundations for the Poor House also appear to be where piers once stood. Other architectural features include the brick foundation of a small porch on the north side of the building, the foundation of an interior fireplace and chimney, and plumbing fixtures associated with the rear shed addition (Figure 8.8).

The architectural remains of the Poor House are much more substantial than those associated with the fraternity, consisting of continuous stone foundations for the exterior walls, interior walls, and chimneys (Figure 8.10). These foundations indicate a building that was 120 feet long and 16 feet wide. Although its width and eastern end were determined fairly early during the excavation, the western end was not located until the 1883 deed that described the building's dimensions was discovered. The length was then quickly confirmed through excavation. The building had four interior chimneys, and the foundations for two of these were fully exposed. The floor plan likely consisted of a row of eight rooms approximately 15 feet by 16 feet in size, with each room heated by a single fireplace.

Structures similar to the Poor House were built on other southern college campuses during the 1830s. Elm Row and Oak Row (two of the oldest buildings at Davidson College, built in 1836–37) were single-story brick structures that originally served as dormitories; each housed sixteen students. This building style apparently was inspired by Thomas Jefferson's academic village at the University of Virginia.

Conclusion

Archaeological studies such as the ones just described uniquely allow us to map past cultural landscapes by revealing once-common places now lost to modern memory. Moreover, these studies permit insights about campus and town life through the analysis of associated material culture and also provide an alternative perspective on broader social and economic conditions.

For example, the artifact assemblages from the Graham Memorial site excavation indicate both the importance of the tavern and hotel to town and gown and the day-to-day behaviors and habits of student boarders. The overall composition of the assemblages is typical of what we might expect at a nineteenth-century hotel or boardinghouse. Table glass consists primarily of thick, sturdy tumblers, and ceramic tablewares often were undecorated or minimally decorated. These items could have withstood heavy everyday

Figure 8.10. View of the excavated foundation for the Poor House at the Pettigrew site (looking west). The entire foundation extends from just beyond the bottom of the photograph to the stone wall at the very top of the photograph.

use and were inexpensive to replace. The many human teeth found at the Graham Memorial site indicate that in addition to providing daily nourishment these establishments also served other needs of the student body and community, such as dentistry. Items such as glass test tubes and pipettes, ceramic marbles, tobacco pipes, and fragments of writing slates and pencils are perhaps more indicative of student life.

Artifacts found at both sites address some of the more serious issues regarding student behavior that faced early university officials. The prevalence of wine and ale bottle fragments throughout the excavated deposits at both the Graham Memorial and Pettigrew sites lends weight to the administration's concern that off-campus public establishments such as the Tavern House and Eagle Hotel—however necessary they might have been for providing daily sustenance—were a corrupting influence on its students. These remains also suggest that (as revealed in many student diaries) the university was not always effective in controlling this behavior, even during periods when the sale of liquor on or near campus was explicitly banned.

University restrictions on weapons also appear to have been largely ignored. Students often brought their guns with them to college, whether intended for personal safety, for sport, or as a necessity to obtain food. Histories of the university indicate that in the early nineteenth century the firing of guns by students as part of public celebrations was commonplace (Battle 1907: 270). The occurrence of firearm-related artifacts (from a pistol flint and small birdshot in early deposits at Graham Memorial to bullet casings and shotgun shells in more recent contexts at both sites) suggests that guns were fairly commonplace on campus until the mid-twentieth century.

The University of North Carolina at Chapel Hill is fortunate that many of its earliest buildings are still standing, for they provide a unique character to the campus that evokes both a sense of tradition and an appreciation of the university's formative years. The present campus bears only a superficial resemblance to the campus of the late eighteenth, nineteenth, and early twentieth centuries, however, and Chapel Hill is even less a reflection of its former self. While a partial understanding of the university and town in this bygone era may be gained from diaries, contemporary histories, and a handful of turn-of-the-century photographs, institutions such as the Tavern House/Eagle Hotel and the Poor House can never be fully understood by those sources alone.

The physical remains of these and other unique sites (in terms of archaeological features, foundations, and associated artifact assemblages) provide important clues about the past and need to be preserved where possible and properly studied. As new facilities are planned and built to meet the educational demands of future generations, our continuing challenge on UNC's historic campus will be to ensure that its rich archaeological heritage is not lost.

Acknowledgments

As with most archaeological projects, the research at the Graham Memorial and Pettigrew sites benefited from the collaboration and support of several people. We are grateful to and wish to acknowledge all who contributed to the success of these excavations. Linda Carnes-McNaughton and Jane M. Eastman conducted preliminary surveys of the University of North Carolina campus in the early 1990s, which identified and led to the excavations at these two sites. They were assisted by Patricia Samford and Elizabeth Jones, who researched the university's early history as part of the Bicentennial Observance and later conducted more extensive research on the Tavern House, Eagle Hotel, Poor House, and Phi Delta Theta fraternity.

Excavations at the Graham Memorial site were undertaken by twenty-one students who participated in two consecutive archaeological field schools during the 1993–94 academic year, under the direction of Jane Eastman and Steve Davis. Funding for these investigations was provided by the UNC Bicentennial Observance Committee. Excavations at the Pettigrew site were prompted by the planned construction of a new building on the site and were funded by UNC's Office of Facilities Planning and Design. The field crew for this work consisted of five students who had just completed the 1997 UNC field school at the Jenrette site, who were directed by Thomas O. Maher and Steve Davis. Both projects also benefited from the participation of numerous volunteers.

Finally, we would like to acknowledge and thank Vin Steponaitis and Trawick Ward of the Research Laboratories of Archaeology for their support, assistance, and thoughtful advice throughout both projects.

Notes

1. In early 2007 excavations for a new steam line behind New East revealed a mid-nineteenth-century humus layer that was buried beneath almost two feet of fill. This layer contained numerous pearlware sherds, wine bottle and glass tumbler fragments, pieces of molded clay pipes, window glass, and a brass doorknob. These artifacts appear to represent refuse discarded behind Steward's House as well as debris from the destruction of this structure in the late 1840s.

9

"Post-Revolutionary Degeneracy"

Washington and Lee University's Landscape of Control

LAURA J. GALKE

In 1776 patriotic fervor was ubiquitous in the Shenandoah Valley of Virginia. It inspired Augusta Academy to change its name to Liberty Hall Academy. Nearby, this enthusiasm was shared by the townspeople of Lexington, Virginia, who named their town after the revolutionary battle of the same name in Massachusetts (McClung 2001:56). This patriotic enthusiasm apparently possessed a down side: the resistance to British authority was cited by some at the academy to have incited "post-Revolutionary degeneracy" among the students (Crenshaw 1973: 85). Despite a written code of conduct, numerous breaches occurred at this and other academies located throughout the thirteen colonies (Jackson 2000). The reaction of the academic administration to these breaches was reflected in the manipulation of the Liberty Hall Academy (later known as Washington College) landscape, which was dedicated to monitoring and controlling student behavior at all hours. These alterations in the landscape and structures of the academy were designed to "restrain vice and encourage virtue" (Whitescarver 1993: 458).

Between 1782 and the Civil War, college administrators at Liberty Hall Academy exerted greater surveillance of, and control over, student behavior through landscape, architecture, and objects. School administrators of this era expanded their authority beyond the classroom, extending their influence over what contemporary pupils would consider their personal lives (Jackson 2000: 54). Such a distinction between "public" classroom pursuits and the "personal" after-hours domain of a pupil's dormitory room developed different meanings and obligations during the 1782–1860 period. Ultimately, college students were awarded freedom from such scrutiny into their after-class lives, beginning after the mid-nineteenth century. This period was a time of negotiation and boundary experimentation, which is preserved in the landscape and archaeology of today's Washington and Lee University

(W&L). The landscape of W&L is distinctive because its landscape of control has been minimally impacted by the school's subsequent endurance and growth.

History of Washington and Lee University

Small regional academies developed during the colonial era and through the mid-nineteenth century to provide a secondary education for the American schoolboy (Hessinger 1999: 237). These private schools were administered by independent boards of trustees and offered a classical curriculum as well as instruction featuring practical skills such as agriculture, navigation, and surveying, to name a few (Bailyn 1960; Sizer 1964: 5–7). However, the low populations that characterized the rural areas in which these schools were established led to a crisis in enrollment that left most academies struggling to survive. Admission requirements were often relaxed to allow greater numbers of tuition-bearing pupils to attend (Bailyn 1960; Hessinger 1999: 238).

Augusta Academy, precursor to W&L, was founded in 1749. Notions of freedom and liberty, motivated by events such as the signing of the Declaration of Independence and the Battles of Lexington and Concord, inspired Augusta Academy to rename itself Liberty Hall Academy in 1776 (McDaniel et al. 1976). After receiving a substantial donation from George Washington, Liberty Hall Academy became Washington Academy in 1797 and Washington College in 1813 (Loth 1967: 3; McDaniel, Watson, and Moore 1979: 39; Ruffner 1890: 53–54).

Academies continued some of the educational traditions that originally developed in medieval monasteries, including the notion that members of the academy should form a secluded community of scholars with minimal contact with the outside world (Allmendinger 1971: 383; Herbst 1996: 1; Jackson 2000: 54). Consistent with this tradition, when Liberty Hall Academy moved to the Lexington, Virginia, area in 1780, the academy consciously situated itself outside the town's limits. While it was a mere half mile away, the academy's distance from town was considered essential for maintaining the cloistered environment needed both to promote learning and to avoid the town's many diversions (Ruffner 1893:5–6). In contrast, the townspeople of Lexington were anxious to have the academy located within their town limits. Despite repeated appeals from the townspeople throughout the late eighteenth century, the academy refused to relocate (Washington and Lee University 1783, 1793).

This prohibition against free interaction between academy students and the town of Lexington demonstrates the institution's early preoccupation with controlling student behavior. These concerns were well founded, as research into the lives of antebellum southern college life suggests (Geiger 2000: 10–13; Hessinger 1999; Howe 2002: 5–6; Jackson 2000; Pace 2004: 82–97; Pace and Bjornsen 2000; Wagoner 1986: 172). The rules of Liberty Hall Academy from 1783 have survived. They prohibited ball playing, card playing, swearing, lying, intoxication, and dancing (Washington and Lee University 1783). Such explicit rules and regulations were typical of academies, which detailed forbidden activities (Bailyn 1960: 38; Geiger 2000: 11). Like many institutions of the time (Jackson 2000: 53), Liberty Hall Academy stipulated a daily schedule for its students, including the appropriate time to rise in the morning, followed by prayers and then study. On a weekly basis, the rector selected a student monitor to record any transgressions by his fellow classmates (Washington and Lee University 1783).

Historical documents record numerous breaches of conduct, and archaeological discoveries provide physical evidence of behavior that was contrary to the academy's official rules. The trustees' minutes document swearing, playing cards, drinking, stealing a neighbor's beehive, and even threats by some students to burn the Liberty Hall Academy building itself (Washington and Lee University 1787). Other documented infractions by the students included fighting, name-calling, and armed threats (Washington and Lee 1794, 1795). One evening in 1795 student David Flournoy asked Sally Millar into his academy room, though she refused the invitation. He tried physically to prevent her from leaving. Testimony revealed that Flournoy had previously fought with other students, behaved offensively during dining, threatened other students, and beaten the steward. For these offenses, he was expelled (Washington and Lee 1795).

Archeological excavations on the Liberty Hall Academy campus were conducted by W&L students between 1974 and 1979. Led by John McDaniel, these investigations discovered abundant evidence for recreational games (Figure 9.1). In addition, the recovery of wine bottle glass fragments suggested that alcohol consumption occurred on the campus. The distribution of these materials was not limited to the building in which the students were housed: all of the structures associated with the Liberty Hall Academy campus contained artifacts demonstrating that official rules were violated on occasion (McDaniel et al. 1994: 141–42).

By 1793 Liberty Hall Academy had the resources to construct two structures: a Steward's House, where students would be provided meals, and a multipurpose classroom and student dormitory building (Figure 9.2). Stone

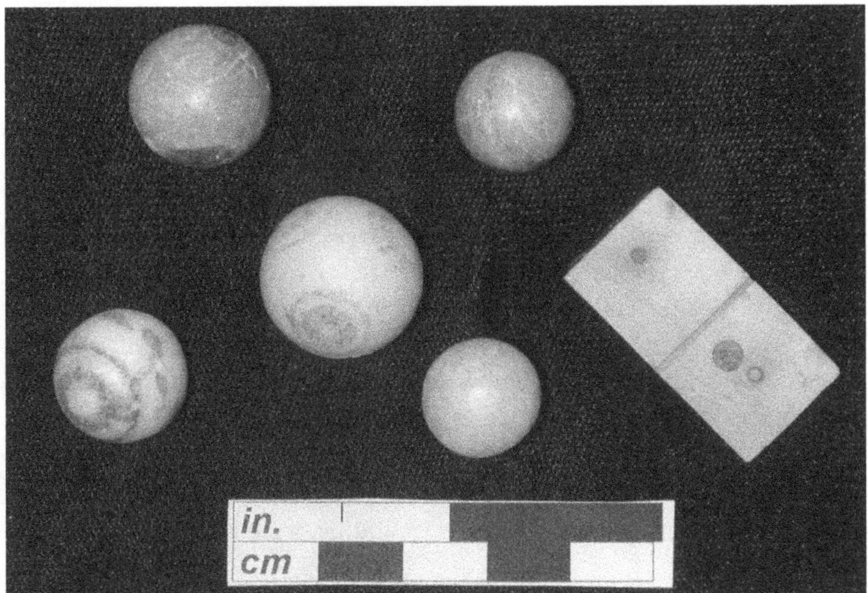

Figure 9.1. Recreational artifacts recovered from the Liberty Hall Academy Campus included marbles and this domino.

Figure 9.2. Conjectural drawing of Liberty Hall by Larry Dreschler (from Lyle and Simpson 1977: 2). (Courtesy of the Historic Lexington Foundation)

was used for the construction of the new academy buildings (Loth 1967: 2; McDaniel et al. 1994: 40). The construction of durable architecture such as this occurred in several communities throughout the eastern United States after the American Revolution (McCleary 2000:92). The first floor of the main Liberty Hall Academy building was used for classroom instruction, while the upper two floors provided living space for the students (McDaniel et al. 1994: 77, McDaniel, Watson, and Moore 1979: 23). McDaniel's archaeological investigations discovered the foundations for all of the major campus structures, which by 1803 included the main Liberty Hall Academy structure, the Steward's House, the spring house, the stable, and the Rector's House. The main academy building was the largest in size and the highest in elevation of all the buildings on the Liberty Hall Academy campus (McDaniel et al. 1994: Figure 10.3). Just ten years after it was constructed, however, an accidental fire destroyed the main academy building, which was never rebuilt.

Union Hall and Graham Hall: Multipurpose Academic Structures

> Blame not the people of Lexington, because they greatly desired the presence of the Academy in the town, whereby they might most conveniently educate their own sons, and most copiously extract money from the sons of others.
> (Ruffner 1890: 88)

During the antebellum period, colleges across the nation experienced intense competition for student enrollment. In order to meet operating expenses, admittance standards increasingly accommodated young boys who were ill prepared for the structure, responsibilities, and instruction they were to encounter in college (Allmendinger 1971: 383; Bailyn 1960: 38). The crisis was exacerbated at Washington College by the relaxation of its curriculum in the early decades of the nineteenth century. Washington College historian William Henry Ruffner described the curriculum of that time as one in which "an idle student was kept four years doing . . . what was in fact only the work of two" (Ruffner 1893: 97). It was increasingly apparent that the traditional cloistered community model of education had to yield to the realities of a student body composed of young men from a variety of educational and social backgrounds (Figure 9.3) and with virtually unlimited access to nearby towns and their diversions (Allmendinger 1971: 381–85; Geiger and Bubolz 2000: 88–89; Herbst 1996: 8).

With the main educational structure a charred ruin, Washington Academy was at a crossroads: rebuild or move the institution to a prominent ridge

Figure 9.3. Students came from a variety of backgrounds. Images by Powell, a student artist. (*Calyx* 1900: 169–75)

within the town limits. After serious deliberation, and encouragement from Lexington residents, the academy moved to this ridge in 1804. Three structures were built: two multifunctional buildings devoted to student housing and instructional space and a new Steward's House (Loth 1967: 7–11). Instilling appropriate dining etiquette was considered essential during the colonial and Early Republic periods (Jackson 2000: 60), and the presence of the Steward's House on the early Washington College landscape demonstrates an attempt to maintain its increasingly antiquated role. Shortly after establishing the Steward's House on the new campus, the steward was fired in 1807. The position remained unfilled for over a decade (Ruffner 1893: 32). It is unclear how meals for the student body were provided at this time, and it is possible that some students enjoyed meals in Lexington. In 1821 a steward was again preparing food for the academic community, but within a few years he too left; the college no longer provided food to its pupils, instead encouraging them to seek sustenance in Lexington (Ruffner 1893: 32; Jackson 2000: 60). Throughout the brief tenure of the steward on the antebellum campus, tensions with the students were common. These squabbles sometimes involved harsh words and threats, and a few evolved into physical actions (Crenshaw 1969: 98, 1973: 7–10, 12–14). Apparently, the nineteenth-century students progressively expected the freedom to dine when and where it suited them, even if that meant dining beyond the confines of the academic environment.

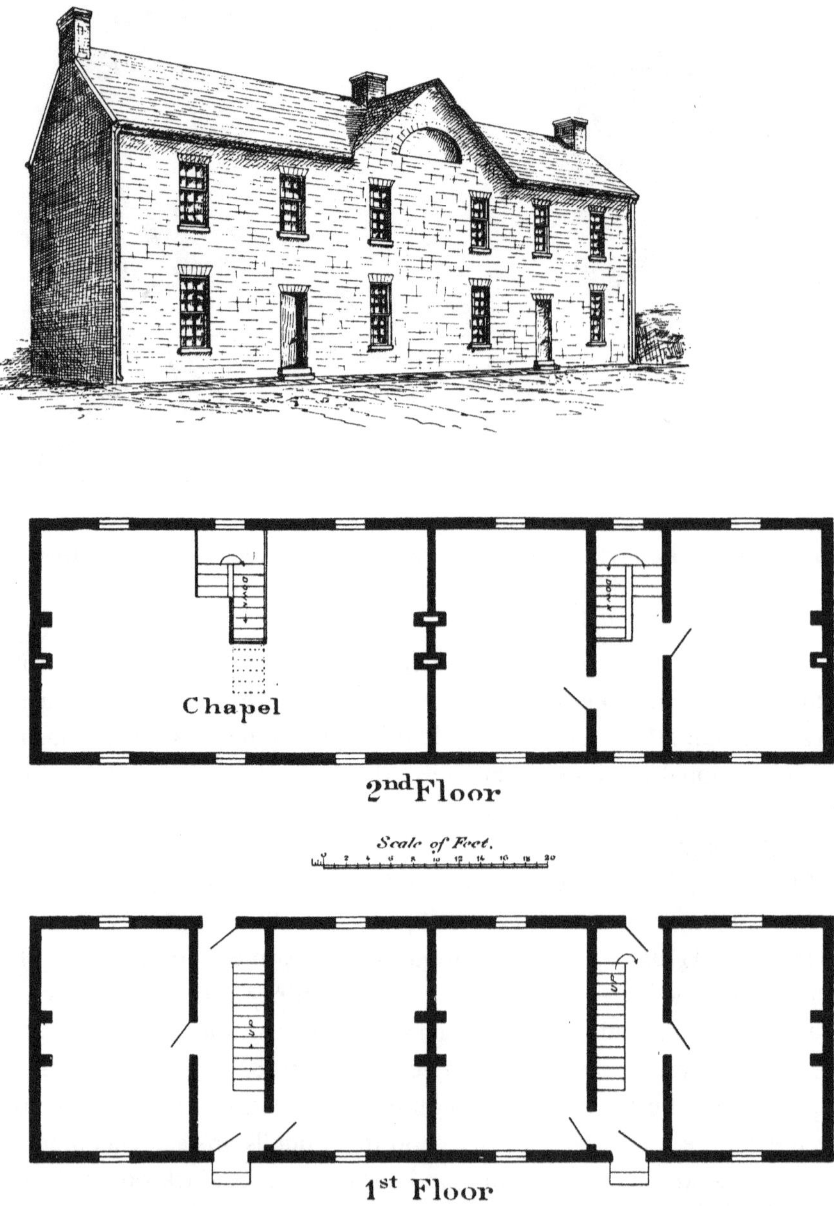

Figure 9.4. A sketch of the 1804 Graham Hall structure by David Humphreys in 1893, based upon details in historical documents. Union Hall was identical in appearance but had additional classroom space in place of Graham Hall's Chapel.

A Steward's House, with its regimented dining schedule, etiquette curriculum, and capriciously prepared menu, became obsolete on the sovereign landscape of the Early Republic.

The multifunctional, dormitory and classroom structures situated on either end of the ridge were named Graham Hall and Union Hall (Figure 9.4). While both instruction and boarding occurred within each of these structures (as was true of the former Liberty Hall Academy building), a significant alteration in the organization of these activities was implemented on the Washington College campus. Graham and Union Halls situated the students' quarters on the first floor and classrooms on the second floor, the reverse of the organization employed in the Liberty Hall Academy building. Using the second floor for teaching made the first-floor dormitory room living areas a more public throughway, which had to be accessed and crossed by faculty members regularly on their way to and from the second-floor classrooms. This was a deliberate technique designed to provide administrators and faculty with unrestricted access to the hallways just outside the student dormitory rooms, where any digressions in behavior or actions contrary to the rules of the academy could be more easily observed and corrected.

Washington College students continued to abide by written rules, including some familiar prohibitions: against playing cards, dice, bringing intoxicating beverages onto campus, and swearing (Washington and Lee University 1839). A surviving schedule indicates that a typical day began with prayers followed by study, with defined dining periods. At all other times the students were expected to remain within their rooms (Washington and Lee University 1839: 13–15). The nineteenth-century faculty members were expected to drop in on students at such times: "the faculty shall exercise a constant and parental oversight of the students; and shall frequently visit their rooms, to prompt them to diligence in their studies and attention to the college rules" (Washington and Lee University 1839: 5). Members of the faculty were encouraged to burst into student rooms in the evenings without knocking to ensure that students were occupying their personal time profitably (Crenshaw 1969: 97; Washington and Lee University 1839). One enthusiastic professor donned slippers in carrying out his duties, while another employed heavy boots in the execution of this task (Crenshaw 1969: 97).

Unless students lived in the immediate vicinity, they were required to live on campus. Students shared these rooms and were responsible for obtaining their own furniture and fuel (Ruffner 1893: 26). Meals were to be taken at the Steward's House, a policy that lasted only about three years. At that point the college began to relinquish control over the location of student meals, and

Figure 9.5. Establishments such as the Blue Hotel offered Washington College students alternative lodging and an outlet for activities discouraged on campus. (*Calyx* 1900: 158)

some students patronized town businesses (Ruffner 1893: 31–32). The traditional model of a secluded academic community was deteriorating.

Rather than remaining cloistered on campus, students preferred to avoid the 24-hour scrutiny of the faculty by boarding within the surrounding community in hotels (Figure 9.5), boardinghouses, and private homes (Allmendinger 1971: 384; Geiger 2000: 12; Geiger and Bubolz 2000: 83). Researcher David Allmendinger (1971: 385–87) argues that this breakdown of the cloistered academic seclusion contributed to "a crisis of disorder" during the early nineteenth century. This "crisis" of nineteenth-century colleges was certainly not limited to Washington College. A committee was formed in Virginia with representatives from various educational institutions requesting that the Virginia legislature provide college administrators with the power to administer oaths and subpoena witnesses in the pursuit of formal inquiries of the student body (Crenshaw 1973: 98).

Louis Marshall's Administration, 1830–34

One particular Washington College president is noteworthy because his administration added significantly to the crisis in campus life during the second quarter of the nineteenth century. Louis Marshall introduced innovative but ill-conceived educational policies in 1831 that contributed to a minor "crisis" in academics at the college (Crenshaw 1969: 47). He was not only critical of traditional teaching methods but scornful of those who adhered to them and also made it no secret that he found the qualifications of the existing college faculty suspect (Ruffner 1904: 4).

Marshall served as Washington College president between 1830 and 1834

Figure 9.6. This post-1855 photo of the Washington College Colonnade shows the brick dormitories and (flanking) faculty housing on each side.

and favored giving students great freedom. Class meetings became voluntary, the amount of time to obtain the college degree was unlimited, and classes "lasted only as long as the students wished" (Crenshaw 1969: 48; Ruffner 1904: 3). "Faculty . . . were to make themselves available to their students 'at all hours' to aid them in the preparation of their work, . . . individually or in groups as . . . [students] might determine" (Crenshaw 1969: 48). Examinations were to be administered by professors *outside* the discipline in which the student was being assessed (Ruffner 1904: 7–8).

Marshall's own classroom came complete with a bed and an easy chair (Ruffner 1904: 10), where he could be found surrounded by copious amounts of smoke, billowing from his pipe. He enjoyed being "one of the boys" and joined the students in their games and in the friendly exchange of insults (Crenshaw 1969: 48; Ruffner 1904: 10). Student conduct deteriorated and enrollment declined during Marshall's term (Ruffner 1904: 12).

Marshall's teaching methods came to an abrupt end during the summer of 1834, when he left the community without formally resigning from his position (Ruffner 1904: 12). A report that evaluated his methods was produced that same year. It denounced his scheme and further suggested that off-campus student boarding contributed to the current academic crisis (Crenshaw 1969: 52). It was in this atmosphere that the Union and Graham Hall structures were destroyed and new single-story brick dormitories were constructed in their places (Figure 9.6).

The next college president, Henry Vethake, was a more traditional administrator. Washington College returned to a more classical method of instruction. Vethake resigned in 1836, however, one year after being physically attacked by a dismissed student (Crenshaw 1969: 54; Ruffner 1904: 26–27).

1836 Dormitories

In 1830 the Trustees first considered the idea of remodeling Union Hall and Graham Hall. It was clear that they had been badly constructed and made from poorly fired bricks (Loth 1967: 27; Ruffner 1893: 8). This was a particular problem given the high visibility of these structures to the outside community. The ridge upon which Washington College was situated overlooked Lexington: it was no marginalized property but one that commanded the attention, and the scrutiny, of the townspeople below. An 1834 editorial from the local newspaper described Union and Graham Halls: "The two . . . buildings erected at the opening of the institution have crumbled or are now crumbling to ruins and are wholly useless, and have long ceased to be occupied by any who had regard either to comfort or safety" (James Reid Jordan, *Lexington Union*, September 13, 1834; quoted in Loth 1967: 33). Other editorials by Jordan indicated that some of the windows had no glass and that the interiors were filthy (*Lexington Union*, September 27, 1834; quoted in Loth 1967: 35). At the end of 1835 arrangements were made to dismantle both Graham and Union Halls and to construct a set of dormitories on their sites (Loth 1967: 39–40). Students participated in the demolition, using joists from the former buildings as battering rams (Ruffner 1893: 8). Two identical brick dormitories were constructed in 1836: structures that demonstrate obsessive efforts on the part of the college administration to facilitate control of their student occupants. In place of the local stone that had been so prominently used in the eighteenth-century Liberty Hall Academy campus structures, brick became the dominant material used on the nineteenth-century Washington College campus. Each single-story dormitory was designed to be used solely as student living quarters (Loth 1967: 41). William Henry Ruffner's inaugural address as president of Washington College in 1837 expressed his concern with college discipline, noting that when men are secluded together they "are prone to adopt vices, and neglect the decencies of life" (Ruffner 1904: 33).

No method of student control was overlooked in the design and construction of the dormitories. Other than transoms located over the doorways, windows were permitted only on the back side of the structures (Figure 9.7). This was explicitly done to prevent distractions from the front of the campus or from the town below (Loth 1967: 41; Ruffner 1904: 28–29). Each room could only be entered from the front of the structure, with no interior hallways or doors connecting the small rooms to each other. This discouraged contact between the students and made certain that whatever interaction did

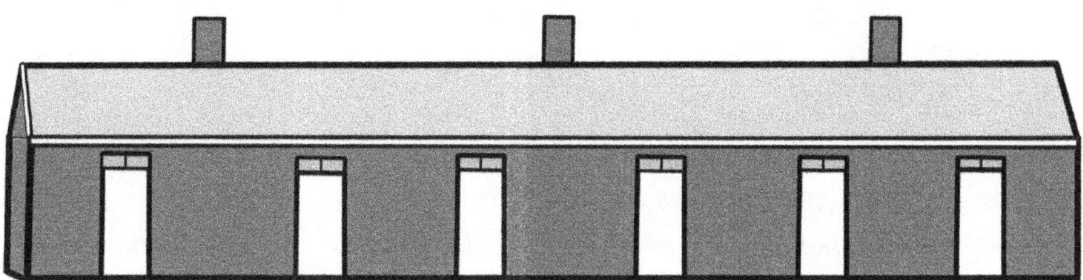

Figure 9.7. A digitized rendition of the 1836 brick dormitory, showing the transoms above the doorways and the lack of windows facing the front of the structure. (Courtesy of Bernard K. Means)

occur between the students between their dormitory rooms was potentially observable. Due to the height of the ridge and its visibility from Lexington, this arrangement created an effective method of surveillance not only by the campus faculty but also from the town below. Furthermore, the construction of faculty housing in 1842 in close proximity to the dormitories also served the benefit of "hav[ing] a restraining and improving effect on the students" (committee report quoted in Loth 1967: 47).

In plan view the dormitories consisted of a simple rectangle, thus providing "little cover for the skulking mischief-maker" (Ruffner 1904: 28–29). By eliminating corners and ells from these structures, visual monitoring of the students was made easier. Throughout their decades-long existence, these dormitories remained nameless: students colloquially referred to them as "hell" and "purgatory" (Taylor Sanders personal communication, February 9, 2005). It is no accident that such strident measures were taken after the end of Washington College president Louis Marshall's innovative administration.

Unlike the now-demolished Graham and Union Hall structures, which served as both classroom and dormitory space, these replacement structures were used solely for student housing. Academic instruction occurred in other campus buildings dedicated to that purpose. The design of these dormitories represented an explicit attempt by the administration to use these structures to manage student behavior and interaction beyond the classroom: within their own quarters.

Washington College student John Rutherford likened these dormitories to dog kennels and wrote that they were marred by "tobacco juice, mud, and water-melon-seed" (Crenshaw 1969: 97, 1973: 407). By 1842 plans were already made for their demolition, as reported in the local paper (*Lexington Gazette* July 7, 1842). Both brick dormitories remained standing and in use until 1881, however, when the southwestern dormitory was demolished to construct Newcomb Hall; in 1899 the northeastern dormitory was destroyed to build Tucker Hall.

In 2005 and again in 2007 archaeological testing was completed on the Washington College campus, where the academy was relocated in 1804 (Galke 2006; Galke and Means 2008: 2). The archaeological investigations took place on the southwestern end of the Colonnade, where "Union Hall" would have been situated. They uncovered evidence of the Union Hall academic structure and the subsequent 1836 dormitory, which occupied the same space. The Liberty Hall Academy faculty members were concerned about student discipline, even in the ideal, agrarian environment of the eighteenth-century campus. Given the reluctance with which the academy approached relocation within the modest town limits of Lexington, the archaeological excavations on the nineteenth-century campus sought to investigate the measures taken by the administration to negotiate this social and potentially distracting "urban" landscape (Galke and Means 2008: 40–45).

Archaeological excavations on the nineteenth-century Washington Academy campus were designed to reconstruct the development of academic culture at Washington and Lee University between 1804 and 1900, as the administration approached life within the town limits: a situation that those who founded the academy never intended. During this time the relationship between faculty and students altered dramatically, from a student body whose movements were dictated by a strict 24-hour routine during the eighteenth century to the modern university at the turn of the twentieth century, in which faculty members were only responsible for student behavior during the course of a specific lesson. How did such a dramatic transformation take place? The Liberty Hall Academy campus revealed abundant archaeological evidence for student leisure activities despite its ideal, cloistered surroundings. Therefore we anticipated that the more convivial academic setting of the Washington Academy campus within the town limits would result in a similar material signature: the recovery of marbles, dice, alcohol bottle fragments, and tobacco pipes in at least the same frequencies or even greater numbers than on the Liberty Hall Academy campus.

To test this expectation, excavation units were placed in areas that represented the interior (such as the subfloor) as well as in the backyard of the antebellum Union Hall classroom/dormitory structure (behind it) and its unpopular 1836 replacement, the brick dormitory (Galke and Means 2008: 11). These areas represented places where students had the greatest degree of privacy from the scrutiny of faculty, administrators, and townsfolk. Excavations on the nineteenth-century campus succeeded in documenting intact strata from as early as the initial occupation of this area by the academy, including the remains of the original 1804 builder's trench for Union Hall (Galke and Means 2008: 13–18).

A landscape characterized by intense scrutiny was revealed in the material culture, including the architectural remains and the organization of nearby academic buildings on the campus landscape. This environment reflected an antebellum academic environment that was dedicated to facilitating student surveillance and control. Surprisingly, the artifacts recovered demonstrated no evidence of games or leisure activities such as tobacco consumption. Given the plethora of marbles and tobacco pipe fragments recovered on the cloistered Liberty Hall Academy campus, the discovery of at least some evidence for a continuation of these activities or florescence of such behavior was expected, given the proximity of the nineteenth-century campus to town. The archaeological record revealed that the antebellum Washington Academy landscape was characterized by far more restrictions upon leisure activities than had been the case on the more secluded eighteenth-century Liberty Hall Academy Campus. Historical records make it clear, however, that student discipline and intoxication on the antebellum Washington College campus continued to challenge college staff and increasingly impacted the nearby townspeople (Crenshaw 1969: 97–101, 1973: 11–12). It is clear that school officials made great efforts to counter the effects of the college's urban location in its 1836 dormitory architecture and the placement of faculty housing adjacent to those dormitories in 1842. These measures enjoyed some degree of (temporary) success by the 1840s, when a temperance society was established on campus (Crenshaw 1969: 102–3).

Caution must be exercised when comparing the extensive remains recovered during the six-season investigations of Liberty Hall Academy in the 1970s to the more modest assemblage generated during the limited testing beside Newcomb Hall in 2005 (Galke 2006: 25–26; Galke and Means 2008). Fragments of pipe stems and bowls, common surrounding the main Liberty Hall Academy building (McDaniel, Russ, and Potter 1979: 90–91), were entirely absent on the Washington College campus (Galke 2006: 25; Galke and Means 2008: 40–41). The discovery of numerous marbles and a domino indicates that games, although certainly discouraged, did take place on the Liberty Hall Academy campus. Yet no evidence for games or toys was discovered on the nineteenth-century Washington College campus (Galke 2006: 25; Galke and Means 2008).

The proximity of the town to the nineteenth-century campus may have

Figure 9.8. Powell's sketch of a Washington and Lee College student and a professor. (*Calyx* 1895: 143)

encouraged college officials to be more strident in the enforcement of rules than was the case on the eighteenth-century Liberty Hall Academy campus (Figure 9.8). Lexington may have provided students with a more suitable setting for these prohibited or discouraged activities, thereby removing them from the campus landscape. Given the proclivity for fires that characterized the early history of the institution, the absence of tobacco pipes may indicate that smoking was no longer allowed on campus, though President Marshall (1830–34) was known to smoke a pipe in his classroom.

Liberty Hall Academy had a separate Steward's House structure dedicated to providing student meals. On the Washington College campus, the steward's position was eventually dropped by the late 1820s (Ruffner 1893: 32).

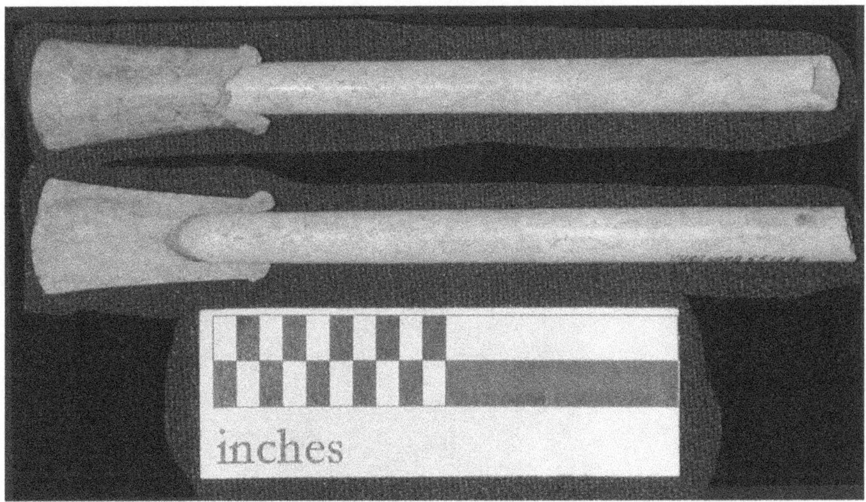

Figure 9.9. Front (*top*) and reverse (*bottom*) of a broken pointer fragment discovered during the 2005 excavations on the Washington and Lee Colonnade.

Archaeologically recovered bone from the site of the Washington College dormitories clearly shows cutlery marks. The amount and variety of ceramics recovered from these same deposits suggest that meals may actually have been prepared by students within their rooms, a fact not evident from historical documents. While students undoubtedly dined in Lexington on occasion, it seems clear from the archaeological record that some meals were prepared within the students' dorm rooms.

Material evidence for Washington College physical discipline may be inferred from one particular artifact: a pointer made of horn and bone (Figure 9.9). This object was clearly used as a pointer by professors during their lectures (Figure 9.10) and perhaps was also used for corporal punishment. Such punishment was alluded to by one Washington College student, when Professor George Junkin threatened to cane the traitorous student(s) responsible for displaying a secessionist flag over the main campus building in 1859, over a statue of George Washington himself. Servants asked to remove the flag quickly discovered that students had concealed all of the campus ladders (Crenshaw 1973: 119–20).

Conclusion

Documentary, photographic, and archaeological evidence was used to examine the evolution of one academic administration's approach for housing

Figure 9.10. Powell's image of a Washington and Lee University professor. (*Calyx* 1895: 5)

students from the late eighteenth century through the mid-nineteenth century. At Liberty Hall Academy (later Washington College) the architectural styles used for student housing over time reflect an approach that eventually placed the surveillance of pupils above aesthetics and comfort. This dedication to controlling student interaction and conduct was a response both to local factors (such as Marshall's problematic tenure as college president) and to a national transformation occurring in educational practices. This trend in academic institutions, perhaps accelerated by the democratic ideals of the American Revolution, involved modification from the traditional cloistered fellowship of students who largely sought to become ministers to a group of young men of diverse social and economic backgrounds who came to expect interaction with the surrounding community and rejected the tradition of 24-hour surveillance.

The structures used by this institution to house students between 1782 and the Civil War reveal that the development of student housing evolved from multifunctional (academic and residential) structures to single-function student dormitories. Significantly, the aesthetic design of these buildings dramatically diminished in importance, as concern over controlling student conduct became the major factor in designing student housing by 1836. Decades later these unpopular, austere, and nameless dormitories easily passed out of memory, with little comment from the community once they were finally destroyed in the late nineteenth century.

The pursuit of increased surveillance of the student body on the part of this college was discernible in the landscape, in the campus architecture, and in historical documents and was preserved in the archaeological record. These efforts met with dubious success. The historical record contains many descriptions of student pranks throughout the colonial and antebellum periods, evidence of the broader issues faced by academic institutions of the day, in which revolutionary ideals and unprepared boys entered an academic world of outdated patriarchal control and rigid discipline.

10

Beyond the Course Catalogue

Archaeological Insights into the Life of Santa Clara University

RUSSELL K. SKOWRONEK AND LINDA J. HYLKEMA

Banking to the right, the Boeing 767 speeds north up the Santa Clara Valley toward its destination, the Norman Mineta San Jose International Airport. Thirty miles south of the plane's destination it begins: the suburban sprawl associated with Silicon Valley that runs all the way from Gilroy to the Golden Gate.

Here "old" and "out of date" are defined in terms of Moore's Law: in years not decades (Malone 2002: 177). Because land is so valuable, adaptive reuse of existing structures is rarely contemplated. Instead they are usually torn down. It is not uncommon to see a single parcel pass through three incarnations in a decade (Skowronek with Thompson 2006: xviii–xix). From the birthplace of the modern computer age at what was an IBM plant to the 150–year-old adobe home of Juana Briones, a California entrepreneur, the few remaining "historic" structures more often than not are regularly demolished. Business dictates the fast pace of change in every corner of the valley.

As the airplane begins its final approach into the airport for Silicon Valley, what seems to be a timeless hundred-acre oasis of tile roofed buildings, green sports fields, and a church is visible a few blocks west of the airport: Santa Clara University.

Santa Clara College/University

> This institution is under the super-intendance [*sic*] of the Fathers of the Society of Jesus, and it is open to all, who choose to avail themselves of its advantages.
>
> Preface, *Catalogue, Santa Clara College, Academic Year 1870–71*

Santa Clara College, the forerunner of Santa Clara University, opened it doors in 1851: 225 years after Harvard was founded, 3 years after the signing of the Treaty of Guadalupe Hidalgo, 2 years after the start of the California

Gold Rush, and a year after California statehood. It is the oldest institution of higher education west of the Mississippi River. Over its century and a half of existence it has gained notoriety in its sports, its faculty, and its curriculum.

In 1949 its football team defeated the University of Kentucky (led by famed coach Paul "Bear" Bryant) in the Orange Bowl; more recently, the women's soccer team won the NCAA championship in 1999.

Its faculty boasted John Montgomery, one of the pioneers of "heavier than air" flight, who was immortalized in the 1946 film *Gallant Journey*, and Father Jerome Sixtus Ricard, S.J., the meteorologist and astronomer credited with correlating sunspot activity and weather (Hayn 2002; McKay 2002). Both men were commemorated on campus with a monument and buildings and in Washington, D.C., at the Smithsonian's Air and Space Museum on the Mall. Another faculty member, Bernard Hubbard, S.J., became known as the "Glacier Priest" in the 1930s and 1940s for his work in Alaska. Though he was trained in geology, Father Hubbard's fame is derived from the thousands of photographs and thousands of feet of films he made among the Native peoples of Alaska (Hayn 2002; McKay 2002; Scarborough 2001). A significant fraction of Hubbard's photographic collection and other material collections remain on campus, but much of the movie footage is now housed in the Smithsonian, where it may be readily accessed by researchers and Native Alaskans (Scarborough 2001).

For more than a century Santa Clara's student body was male. During World War II the university began to change. Enrollments fell as young men and many priests enlisted or were drafted (McKay 2002: 150; McKevitt 1979: 261). The Santa Clara School of Law closed due to lack of enrollment. By 1944 the regular student body numbered 91, but they were joined by 375 soldiers obtaining special training in engineering. Other classes were opened to female students for the first time (McKay 2002: 150).

In 1955 Santa Clara hired its first female professor. Shortly thereafter, in 1956, women matriculated in the law school and in nursing classes. The school of business became coeducational in 1958. Finally, in 1961 women were admitted as undergraduates for the first time. At the beginning of the twenty-first century women make up the majority of the student body.

The Santa Clara University Archaeology Research Lab

Today more than 8,000 undergraduate and graduate students are enrolled in this highly rated institution. They come because of the school's academic reputation and its pledge to provide ample courses for an individual to complete a course of study in four years. To meet this vow the university began a major "bricks and mortar" capital campaign in the 1990s that led to the construction or reconstruction of nine buildings and a parking structure in the space of a decade. Prior to this work the university had experienced several periods of expansion. The last of these ended in the 1970s, before the creation of state laws pertaining to the mitigation of cultural resources and before local historic preservationists became acutely aware of the loss of the historic fabric of the community. When the construction projects were initiated, the school for the first time faced rules regarding cultural resources and their management. The enactment of the California Environmental Quality Act (CEQA) in 1970 and the subsequent California Local Government (CLG) status obtained by the City of Santa Clara meant that some reasonable degree of mitigation is legally required during discretionary projects.

Santa Clara University is unique in many ways. The school was established and has continued to be operated by the Society of Jesus (the Jesuits). It is the only institution of higher education housed on lands and in buildings originally used as a Franciscan mission. Under its hundred-acre campus is a microcosm of California history. It includes a prehistoric cemetery (Hylkema 2007; Skowronek and Graham 2004; Skowronek and Pierce 2006), the aforementioned Spanish and Mexican era Franciscan Mission (Skowronek with Thompson 2006), former parts of the City of Santa Clara (Harris et al. 1995), and forgotten parts of the school's history. The oldest section of the school that incorporates mission-period structures is eligible for inclusion in the National Register (Caltrans 1985: 17–22).

As more archaeological features and their associated artifacts were discovered, it was clear that the university had no one to clean, inventory, or study them and, more importantly, no long-term strategy for future mitigation. Furthermore, ethical issues arose regarding the long-term disposition of these existing collections and those previously found in the 1980s during the reconstruction of the Adobe Lodge (Jenkins et al. 1998) and the Palm Drive entrance at the third mission site (Skowronek with Thompson 2006). The university had the choice of divesting the collections to an official repository (at a cost then estimated at $750,000) or supporting the creation of the SCU Archaeology Research Lab. Vice President Steve Privett, S.J., saw that such a lab facility would have great utility as a repository, place of research, locale for student learning, and aid to the Facilities department for small construction projects.

To surrender intellectual control of these materials to cultural resource management (CRM) firms begged the question regarding the purpose of the lab as a center for research and education. As a result the lab was created in 1995 and in a few short years showed such success that it was hailed "as a trailblazer in heritage resource management planning in the university setting" by the Environmental Program of the Associated Colleges of the South (1999:2).

In 2003 the university released the Environmental Impact Report (EIR) for Ten Year Capital Improvement Plan. Due to the complexity of known archaeological resources on the campus and the immense scale of future projects planned by the university, the EIR required the development of a long-term strategy for the management and mitigation of future impacts. A resulting Cultural Resources Treatment Plan for the Ten Year Capital Improvement Plan is currently the university's and the City of Santa Clara's primary archaeological planning document (Allen et al. 2003).

Today the lab serves as a coordination center for CRM firms hired to mitigate these very large projects on campus, and the assistant campus archaeologist provides project oversight and direction to those firms. Materials are washed and labeled by students in the lab, then transferred back to the CRM firms for inventory, and returned to the lab ready to be studied and researched. The assistant campus archaeologist uses these materials to teach the lab components of the Introduction to Archaeology and Historical Archaeology classes in the Anthropology Department. Students thus have a tremendous variety of prehistoric and historical materials with which to complete research projects.

Although dozens of CRM archaeologists have worked on campus over the years, the assistant campus archaeologist has remained the lone full-time representative dealing with the day-to-day operation of the lab, which involves creating exhibits, supervising student technicians during their tasks (which include initial processing and cataloguing of artifacts, creating reference collections, and researching existing collections), collections management, teaching all the Introduction to Archaeology Labs, supervising CRM archaeologists and providing direct guidance to the University Operations Department, conducting research, and giving tours for elementary schools, museum docents, and other special interest groups.

Campus Memories, Changing Landscapes, and Historical Archaeology

> The spirit must be broad, embracing everything that goes to make up college life, participating in everything when this is possible, encouraging everything from lawn tennis to the study of quarternians, from the foot-ball [*sic*] field to the editorial staff of the college paper.
>
> *The Redwood*, Santa Clara College (November 1903)

Every year Santa Clara University is invaded by its alumni. They return to "find" their favorite professor, residence, class or locker room, or pub. All alumni view the existing landscape from the vantage point of when they last saw the campus. The familiar is embraced as a touchstone of "their" past. For them these are the tangible reminders that they were there.

At Santa Clara countless members of past Bronco football squads often stagger into the Archaeology Research Lab, thinking it is still "their" Field House. The lab has been housed in the old athletic Field House (built in 1942) since 1995. The still-tiled shower room contains wooden lockers and stubbed-off pipes but little else. Now the Field House is torn down, and there is nothing left except the memories of the athletes and a plaque that greeted generations of students as they crossed the threshold into the building (Figure 10.1).

O'Connor Hall is another touchstone for those few left who return to mark their fiftieth class reunion. For them it was a residence hall (during the 1950s and earlier). Today the third floor of this edifice houses faculty offices, and many of them sport two small closets. Today they are jammed with unused books, caps, and gowns, but in their day they held the limited wardrobes of the two inhabitants of that space. In a few years refurbishment will erase the last tangible traces of this structure's history as a residence hall.

Santa Clara may be unique in that many of its faculty and administrators are graduates. Also, many of its graduates grew up in the area and have continued to reside in the region. Their memories of the campus landscape, while long-term, may be more blurred. They have witnessed the incremental loss of familiar landmarks throughout the valley. While some have lamented these losses (Garcia and Mahan 2002), others recall how bleak things could be in the past (McKay 2002: 147), and still others look toward a technology-filled future (Locatelli 2002: 189) on the historic campus.

This juxtaposition of old and new creates a nuanced accumulative landscape. It has been said: "All landscapes are 'historical,' provided that they are now—or once were—altered, inhabited, visited or interpreted by people" (Holtorf and Williams 2006: 235). Santa Clara University is just such an ac-

Figure 10.1. (*Clockwise from lower left*) door with a plaque overhead; threshold plaque; the Field House Building; demolition of the Field House, 2008. (Photos by Linda Hylkema)

cumulative landscape that has preserved (in structures and in the earth) the story of the school, from its prescribed curriculum to the lives of its students.

Since 1995 investigations conducted by the Santa Clara University Archaeology Research Lab have revealed a picture of everyday life on the historic campus that sometimes amplifies and sometimes contradicts the institutional history of the past century and a half.

Beginnings: The College Years, 1851–1912

> On March 19, 1851, Father John Nobili, with a capital of one hundred and fifty dollars and a brave heart, laid the foundation of Santa Clara College and began the great work.
>
> *Santa Clara College Prospectus*, for the year 1909–10

Santa Clara was founded directly in response to the Gold Rush. Father Michael Accolti, an Italian Jesuit writing of San Francisco in December 1849, said: "Whether it should be called a villa, a brothel, or Babylon, I am at a loss to determine," which summed up the state of affairs in northern California at the time (McKevitt 1979: 7). In 1851 there were only 21 priests to minister to more than 40,000 Roman Catholics among a population of more than 150,000 non-Indians who had arrived in the two years since the discovery of gold. These numbers included children who needed an education in a safe environment close to their families but away from the vices of the gold fields or the city of San Francisco. Lying some fifty miles to the south of the city was their answer: Santa Clara. The former Franciscan mission had been secularized fifteen years earlier and now served as a parish for a nascent community of the same name (Garcia et al. 2002). In February of that year Bishop Joseph Alemany offered the site to the Society of Jesus for a school, and Santa Clara College was born on March 19 in the "wretched" adobe hovels that were the surviving remnants of the original Franciscan mission (McKevitt 1979: 23–24, 26).

Today we think of a college as a place of learning usually associated with students who are eighteen to twenty-one years old, but their charge 150 years ago was to create a preparatory school. Within two years of its founding it had seventy-eight students between the ages of four and eighteen (McKevitt 1979: 28). This practice was consistent among other Roman Catholic institutions of the period, including Georgetown and Notre Dame. Santa Clara would award the first bachelor's degree in California in 1857.

Most of the students were boarders living far from their families. Considered to be *in loco parentis*, the original faculty members, mostly Italian-born Jesuits, were more than teachers and clergy—they were parental role models whose goal was to educate the "whole person" by living an exemplary life that would be emulated by their wards (Fitzgerald 2002). The Jesuits felt that the liberties found at other California colleges were doing a disservice to the students (Giacomini 2002: 120). At Santa Clara the students' lives were closely regulated and disciplined, as was their contact with the outside world: "August of 1888 found me matriculated at Santa Clara College—the days of

Figure 10.2. Santa Clara University course catalogues: 1870, 1885, 1900, and 1922. (Collection of Linda Hylkema)

the high fence, when we lived in a little world of our own. Everybody knew everybody; we shared each other's joys and sorrows, even the contents of a mate's trunk stored with many delicacies that were not found on the College menu" (James J. Nealon, '92, *Monthly Santa Claran*, February 1934).

They lived within their small, walled campus, where they helped prepare meals, cleaned the buildings, and had their personal mail inspected. From the earliest days of the school the use of tobacco in any form was strictly prohibited until 1876, when, with permission, smoking was allowed (Figure 10.2). Certainly, that did not preclude the use of tobacco. A student essayist writing in the *Owl* in 1872 noted that those who partook would often "seek the shade of some far-spreading tree, and there, with a cigarette in their sleeve, they 'lie low' for prefects, whose watchful eyes might detect the wreathes of smoke" (Giacomini and McKevitt 2000: 69). Alcohol was permitted, but in 1865 "intoxication" was grounds for immediate expulsion. The only variations in the prescribed schedule were monthly day visits to family.

Revealing Campus Life

> With most complete and appropriate accommodations in every department, and a full staff of professors, this institution presents uncommon advantages for the moral, mental, and physical training of young men and boys.
>
> *Descriptive Catalogue*, Santa Clara College (1885)

In the first decade of the college's existence academic life was centered on a single building known as the California Hotel. When erected in the 1820s this adobe structure was used in the waning days of the mission era as a granary. In the 1840s it was modified and used as an inn. From 1851 to 1909, when it was demolished following damage in the 1906 earthquake, it housed a dormitory, debating hall, and eight classrooms (Giacomini 2002: 122; McKevitt 1979: 44–45). In the next three decades the remaining "decrepit" mission-period adobe buildings including the church were renovated. They were joined by a swimming pool in 1856 (Giacomini 2002: 128; McKevitt 1979: 63). Other important structures soon were added that figured prominently in the school's first century. One was the Scientific Building (1864–1929), a three-story wood frame structure that housed a dormitory, dining hall, and science classrooms and labs. Another wooden structure, College Hall, became known as the "Ship" because it was rumored to have been pegged together with treenails. Over the century of its existence (1870–1962) it held a

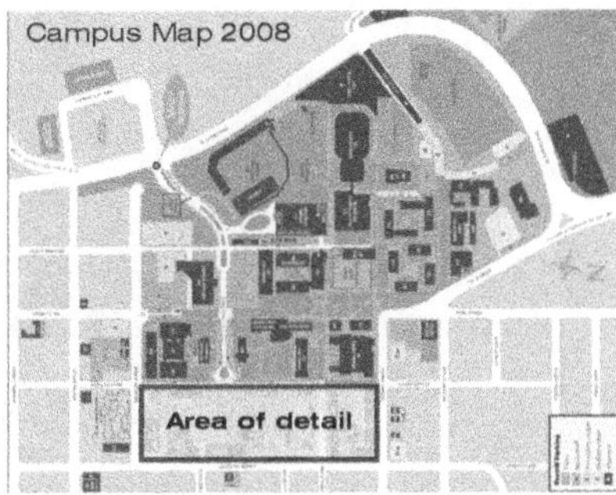

Figure 10.3. Campus map showing archaeological deposits on the Old Quad. (Drawing by Linda Hylkema)

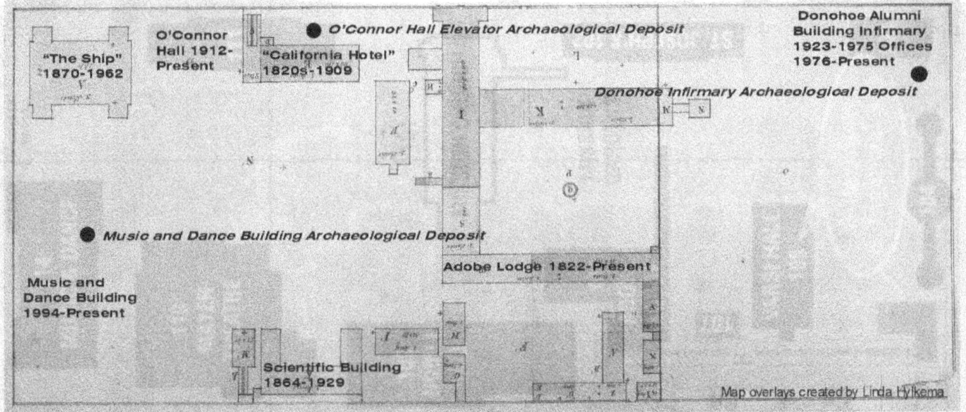

dormitory and a theater. The only brick structure constructed during this period was the two-story Commercial Building (1877–1929), which contained classrooms and related facilities (Figure 10.3).

The extensive campus renovation also effected a modernization of student life. In the process of building St. Joseph's Hall in 1911, the board fence that had once kept the students isolated from the rest of the world was taken down. Now students could leave the campus proper and even go on weekend outings. As one alumnus put it, "the new Santa Clara entered the march of progress" (Giacomini and McKevitt 2000: 108). With access to the neighborhood surroundings for the first time, students were able to purchase goods and services from local businesses and integrate themselves with the growing downtown areas of Santa Clara and San Jose. A number of these purchased products clearly were transported back to campus to be used and ultimately discarded.

During the construction of a new Music and Dance Building in 1994, vestiges of the nineteenth century were discovered. A very large historical

Figure 10.4. Artifacts from the Music and Dance Building excavation (*clockwise from upper left*): "Jules Haule & Co. Phila"; snuff bottles; stoneware bottle with lid; black and aqua glass shoe polish (?) bottles; embossed mineral water bottles; "Worlds Hair Balsam" bottle and cologne bottle; three French embossed cologne bottles; redware pipe bowl; ceramic Petri dish and crucible. (Photos by Linda Hylkema)

deposit, variably interpreted as a trash pit or privy, was encountered within the future Dance Building's footprint and excavated by the Archaeology Research Lab. The deposit was located adjacent to the former location of the Scientific Building and the Ship. The deposit contained a large amount of architectural and household debris that appeared to have been dumped in large episodes, perhaps in response to the major 1868 or 1906 earthquakes that rocked this section of California (Figure 10.4).

In addition to structural materials such as window glass, cut nails, copper sheeting, and wire, domestic artifacts were recovered that included metal keys, weighted metal candlestick bases, fragments of kerosene lamps and their associated glass chimneys, a pendulum from a wall clock, a stove leg, a stovepipe trim collar, and a pearlware chamber pot lid. Because this deposit is located in an area that would have been situated between three former buildings that housed dormitories at various times (the Scientific Building, the Ship, and the California Hotel), the presence of these domestic materials is not incongruous. In an era before electricity was common, kerosene lamps and candles would have provided the only lighting, and stoves would have been a primary heat source. Also, chamber pots would likely have been in every room.

The deposit also contained many different items that could be construed as indulgences. Dating from the 1870s, they included wine and "blob top" soda/mineral water bottles and their associated pontiled glass cordials as well as drinking tumblers. Clay tobacco pipe stems and numerous glass snuff bottles were also present.

Clearly, there was some attention to hairstyling and grooming, as the deposit also contained numerous nineteenth-century personal items. Among them were ceramic shoe polish bottles, pearlware and whiteware cosmetic (or toothpowder) pots, cologne bottles (with and without pontils), and a shaving brush. One bottle fragment was embossed with the words "for the hair and skin." The variety of colognes could easily have served as the deodorants of the period, because the dormitories only had communal washbasins and "warm baths in the winter" (Catalogue, Santa Clara College, Academic Year 1870–71).

Health care items also figured prominently in the deposit. These included many pharmacy and medicinal bottles with rough pontils and a number of unembossed and embossed patent medicine bottles. "Burnetts Cocoaine [*sic*]" was a hair tonic touted as a cure for baldness, and "St. Jakob's Oel [*sic*]" was a remedy for pain or hair loss that dated from 1881 to approximately 1900.

The location of this deposit also hints at the proximity of the old dining hall building, as well as the Scientific Building's own temporary use as a dining hall. The Montgomery Science Building served as the science building and held classrooms, and some of the artifacts from the deposit clearly reflect this. They include umbrella and master ink bottles and slate slab pieces/pencils. We also know that nineteenth-century students were taught assaying, which seems to be confirmed by the presence of lead slag and terracotta crucible-type vessels. Also present were thin and delicate glass tubes, possibly early vacuum tubes or part of an early electrical experiment. They are not complete, however, so additional research is needed to bear out this supposition (Figure 10.5).

Most puzzling are several blue, green, and red glass fragments. Most are rectangular and appear to have cut and ground edges. Were they part of a stained glass window? Or were they used in one of the early scientific instruments that the university was famous for during the nineteenth century?

Figure 10.5. Photographs of the Chemistry Lab building (*top*) and the "Letter A" room (*bottom*). (Courtesy of Santa Clara University Archives)

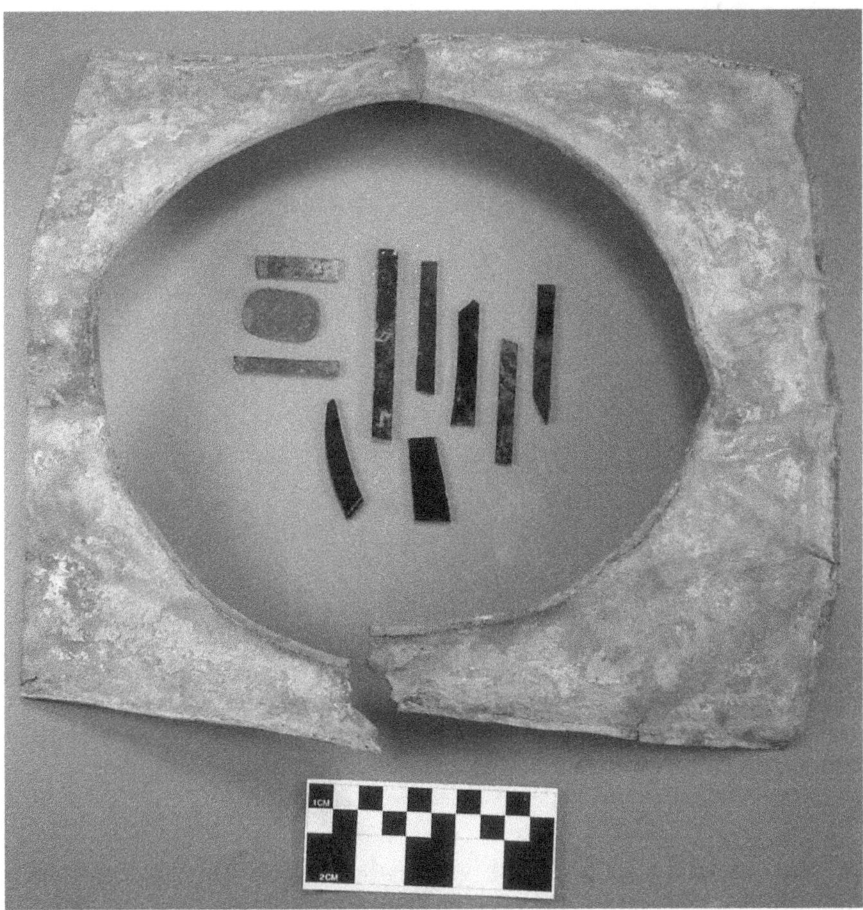

Figure 10.6. Colored glass fragments and copper "frame." (Photo by Linda Hylkema)

The answer may lie in with another artifact. Made of copper, it is a square frame with a circular opening 13.5 inches in diameter, which may represent a forerunner of theater spotlight gels (Figure 10.6). Given the location of the university's theater, the Ship, this is a parsimonious interpretation.

Another deposit, similar in size and temporal range, was discovered in 2003 during the installation of an elevator shaft in O'Connor Hall. O'Connor Hall was built in 1912, so clearly this deposit predates the building. Like the Dance Building deposit, this one also included large amounts of window glass. This deposit is more complex, however. While the majority of the materials date from 1870 to 1880, this is a multicomponent deposit. There is a thin layer of Mexican-era materials at the very bottom, including roofing tiles and flooring bricks, pearlware table ceramics, and fragments of cleaved

Figure 10.7. Artifacts from the O'Connor Building Elevator Project excavation (*clockwise from upper left*): ground glass tumblers (reused as inkwells?); "Stickwell & Co" adhesive and umbrella inks; ". . . Oil" (unreadable) with partial labels (cod liver oil?); sliced horn cores (from cattle), function unknown. (Photo by Linda Hylkema)

or hacked bone (Figure 10.7). This was overlain with artifacts that we associate with the California Hotel (Figure 10.8). Among these there are molded whiteware serving and tablewares, candlesticks, and condiment bottles.

Above these were artifacts associated with the first thirty years of the college. Once again there were items such as master and umbrella ink bottles and crucibles associated with educational activities. The deposit also contains snuff, cologne, and medicine bottles similar to those found at the Music and Dance Building. Of particular interest is the presence of several black glass bottles dating from the 1860s and 1870s. These still carried remnants of paper labels indicating that they contained "cod liver oil." Also present were bottles for "Burnett's Cocoaine [*sic*]"; J. Hostetter's Bitters; Radway's Ready Relief (circa 1870); J. C. Spencer's Fragrant Sapoine for the Teeth (circa 1880); Mexican Mustang Liniment, C. Langley Wholesale Druggist, San Francisco (circa. 1879–80); L. W. Glenn & Co. (circa 1880); and several dozen fragments of clear and aqua glass apothecary and chemical jars and bottles. There were large chunks of sulphur, which was widely used in the nineteenth century

Figure 10.8. Photographs of the California Hotel circa 1860 (*top*) and an early classroom on the second floor of the California Hotel circa 1890 (*bottom*). (Courtesy of Santa Clara University Archives)

as an antiseptic, antifungal, and keratolytic (http://www.antiquebottles.com/apothecary/glossary.html).

Large numbers of wine, soda, and snuff bottles were also present. Despite the bans on tobacco and liquor, it is clear that the students were smoking and drinking anyway. Given that the campus was walled off from the outside world, the importation of illicit items was probably made more difficult, which in turn likely made them all the more enticing.

From College to University

> Much about old Santa Clara was romantic, and, as is often the case, with romance went inconvenience. Round about the back gate had sprung up a number of buildings—the domestic offices—neither convenient nor romantic. They had come into existence as the need of the moment demanded, and to the moment's need only, did they respond. . . .
>
> These have all disappeared. They were equally inconvenient, inefficient, unsanitary and unsightly.
>
> *University of Santa Clara Diamond Jubilee Volume 1851–1926*

The first half of the twentieth century brought great physical changes to the campus in the form of many new buildings that are still in use in the twenty-first century. Some were built (or rebuilt) following catastrophic fires (1909 and 1926) and the Great San Francisco Earthquake of 1906. Others were built to serve an expanding student body as classroom and office buildings (Kenna Hall, 1924; Alumni Science, 1923; Montgomery Laboratories, 1923–71; Ricard Observatory, 1928); residence halls for students and priests on the faculty (St. Joseph Hall, 1909; O'Connor Hall, 1911; and Nobili Hall, 1930); the George Seifert Gymnasium (1923–75), constructed out of bricks recycled from the old Commercial Building; a library (Aloysius Varsi, 1930); and the Mission Church (1927).

In this same era the Donohoe Infirmary (1923) was constructed. It would serve the health-related needs of the campus until 1975, when Cowell Health Center was constructed. The impetus for building Donohoe was the great influenza epidemic of 1918, which killed two students and sickened dozens more (McKevitt 1979: 184). During the half-century of Donohoe's use-life as an infirmary, it offered 24–hour nursing, a hospital ward, and private rooms for sick and infirm Jesuits.

Today the building is used by the Alumni Association, but the soil behind the structure contains evidence of its former function. In 1995 utility work along the north and west side of the old infirmary building yielded an archaeological deposit containing large numbers of pharmaceutical containers, including vials and ampoules (Figure 10.9). These date from the 1930s to the early 1960s. Maker's marks indicate that the bottles were made by Owens-Illinois Glass Company in the 1950s to 1960s, the Anchor-Hocking Glass Company in the 1950s, and the T. C. Wheaton Glass Company. T. C. Wheaton still manufactures bottles for scientific use. Many of the vials are made of "N-51A" glass, which is a borosilicate glass made specifically for caustic chemicals. It has the highest resistance to chemical attack of any

Figure 10.9. Medicinal artifacts from the Donohoe excavation: (*left*) corked medicines and (*right*) "snap-top" ampoules. (Photo by Linda Hylkema)

known commercial available glass (http://www.kimblepharma.com/KPCatalog.pdf).

Documents from the University Archives reveal that the infirmary dispensed a plethora of potent (and now illegal) drugs to students and Jesuits to bring relief from headaches, allergies, colds, diarrhea, rashes, sore throats, aching feet, and more serious illnesses. Through the 1930s, before they were outlawed, Santa Clara dispensed opium, heroin, cocaine, and codeine to its patients (Santa Clara University Archives—Inventory of Opium, Etc., No. 8301, June 30, 1937). Records from the 1950s housed in the Santa Clara University Archives reveal that students and the Jesuit faculty were receiving allergy, tetanus, and typhoid shots, smallpox vaccinations, and injections of panmycin and penicillin. Others were given doses of common over-the-counter medicines such as aspirin, Pepto-Bismol, milk of magnesia, castor oil, and Kaopectate. A few received more potent medicines such as Phenobarbital, sodium seconal, Coricidin, Demerol, and thorazine.

Archival records indicate that most of these drugs were in tablet form. A large number of single dose ampoules with "snap-off" tops were recovered during the excavation, however, indicating that specific dosages of medicines were administered to individuals. It is quite likely that vaccines were administered from the contents of these ampoules.

World War II and Beyond

> Many of us, too, aren't really civilian yet. We dress like civilians and we look like anyone else on the campus. But still we don't think like civilians. We find it hard to take seriously some of the courses that we realize we must take. It's hard to be serious about conjugations of a verb when such a short time ago the things we learned might make a difference between life and death.
>
> Veteran Orr Kelly, '48, *Santa Clara*, January 17, 1946

The university would probably have closed during World War II due to low enrollments. Instead nearly three-quarters of the campus housed the Army Specialized Training Program. Its goal was to train artillery officers. Those who graduated were commissioned as second lieutenants in the artillery.

In the thirty years following World War II an expanding student body strained the prewar facilities. To meet these needs the university purchased surrounding neighborhoods and industries and began a period of adaptive reuse, demolition, and construction that increased the size of the campus fivefold, to its current hundred-acre size. This included the construction of residence halls, a student union, a library, an engineering building, and other classroom structures. Students who returned after the war were often married.

In the spring and summer of 1946, in conjunction with the National Housing Agency, Santa Clara University met the veterans' housing needs at the locations where Buck Shaw Stadium, Ryan Field, the Malley Fitness and Recreation Building, and the Leavey Center are located today (Figure 10.10). Known as Project CAL-V-4454, University Village (known variably as Veterans' Housing or Veterans' Village) was created with a complex of some thirty-four 20– × 20–foot military surplus Butler Huts. Relocated from the Point Montara Anti-Aircraft Training Center (also known as Radar Station J-80 at Point Montara) on the Pacific coast, the structures were originally meant to house up to a dozen men. These prefabricated buildings were subdivided to accommodate two families (McKay 2002: 152). Veterans' Village was torn down seventeen years later, in July 1963.

Beyond a handful of photographs (Figure 10.11) no tangible remains of this brief period were known until 1998, when construction activities associated with the Pat Malley Fitness Center uncovered a number of mid-twentieth-century materials associated with the Veterans' Village. The variety and scope of the materials discovered differed from the Dance Building and O'Connor Hall deposits because they clearly reflect the addition of women and children to the residential units (Figure 10.12). Unlike the ceramics in

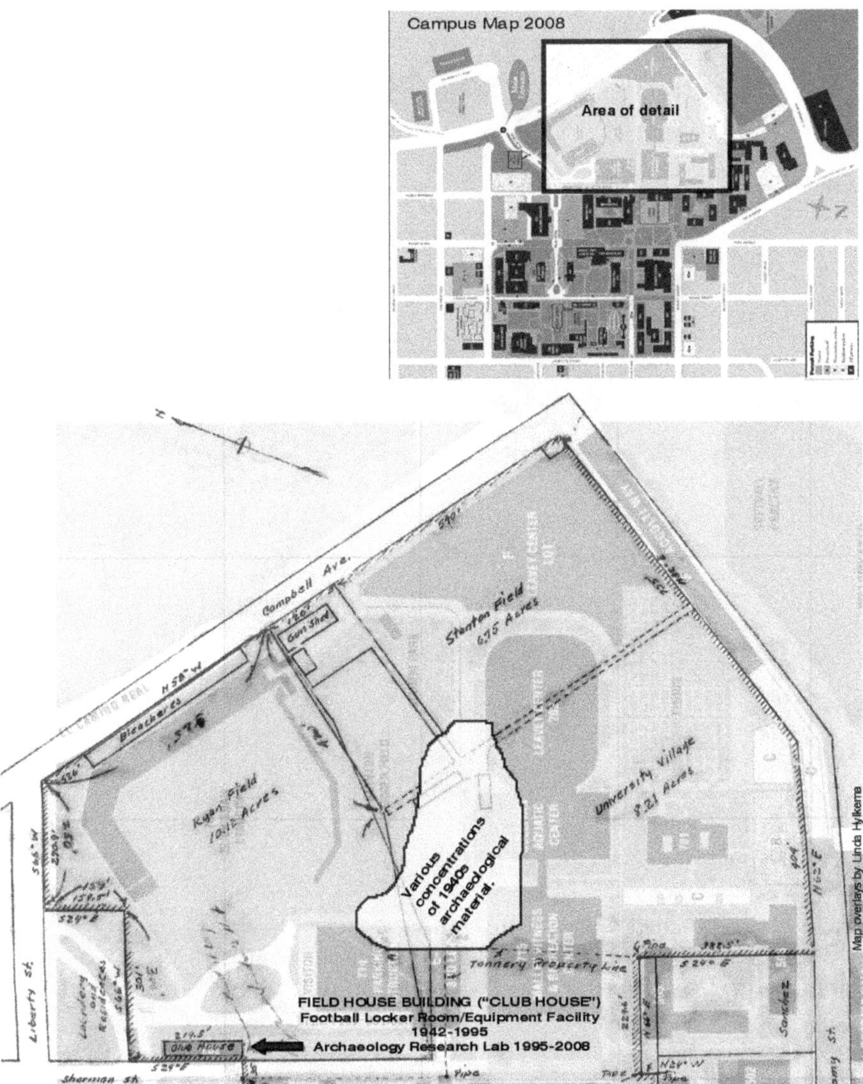

Figure 10.10. Map showing the location of University Village. (Drawing by Linda Hylkema)

the earlier nineteenth-century deposits, the Veterans' Village examples were often more decorative than utilitarian. These included a decal-ware plate, yellow ceramic teapot, decorative majolica leaves from a dish or figurine, and a decorative majolica peach and leaf cluster handle from a covered dish as well as orange, pink, and yellow glazed Bauer-Fiesta pottery, flowerpots, and carnival glass. All of these bespeak a feminine touch in the household.

Figure 10.11. (*Top*) Photograph of University/Veterans' Village; (*bottom*) Reserve Officers' Training Corps (ROTC) infantry unit on the parade grounds. (Courtesy of Santa Clara University Archives)

Other household and utilitarian objects were also present, including a butter pat dish made by the Syracuse China Company with a date stamp of July 1936, whiteware fragments (some molded), and a brown crockery lid. Food service and kitchen items consist of Fire-King green glass, Depression glass, stemware, bone-handled cutlery, drinking glass tumblers, glass tubes for percolator coffeepots, a coffee percolator filter base and drain with a chain (circa 1936), a salt shaker, a tea strainer, and spoons.

We can almost imagine a housewife on a sunny morning fixing coffee and seeing her student-husband off to class. Perhaps he rode his bicycle, which

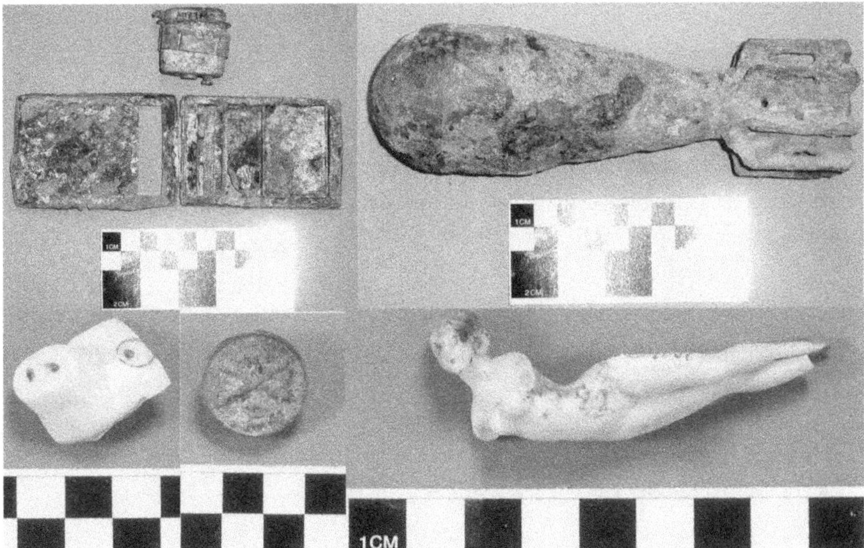

Figure 10.12. Artifacts from the University/Veterans' Village excavations (*clockwise from top left*): Zippo lighter and lady's compact; "dummy" or practice mortar; ceramic female figurine; army infantry enlisted man's collar disk; ceramic pig snout.

he lubricated with 3-in-One Oil (the precursor to WD-40), made originally for use on bicycles. Its name, given by the inventor George W. Cole of New Jersey, derives from the product's triple ability to "clean, lubricate and protect." Or maybe he slicked his hair back with Wildroot Hair Tonic. Cosmetic creams, lipstick tubes and compacts, and glass marbles indicate that families were definitely living there. A broken ceramic pig snout may even represent a piggy bank.

The consumption of alcoholic beverages continued. In addition to generic wine and beer bottles, a Petri Wine Company bottle dating from 1948–49 was found. Soft drinks such as Coke, Hires Root Beer, Nehi Soda, and Circle "A" Sparkling Beverage were also enjoyed by the residents of Veterans' Village.

Although these objects represent everyday families trying to get on with their lives, two objects in particular serve as reminders of the war that preceded those halcyon postwar college days. The noted historian Peter Brown once spoke of the "inverse magnitude" between the tiny bone shard relics of martyred saints and the huge holy power ascribed to them by medieval Catholics (in Starn 2004: 197) That such innocuous objects can be ascribed such importance is an amazing concept. A few items at Santa Clara bear a similar connotation. We have recovered an enlisted man's Type III bronze collar disk bearing crossed cannons with a "2" (indicating the second artillery regiment) and an M69 practice mortar round. Without the presence of these two objects, the Veterans' Village deposits would look much like any other domestic household trash. The collar disk and mortar are poignant reminders that the world war did not just occur "over there" and did not just involve other people.

An Education beyond the Books: The Significance of Archaeology at Santa Clara

> I'd rather be wrong in an interesting way, than be right and boring.
> James Deetz, circa 1981 (in Praetzellis 1998)

The time of transition between high school and the "real world"—that fledgling period fraught with the changes and challenges of adulthood while still tied to the apron string—marks the magical phase of life we call college. It is the period when most students live away from home for the first time yet are still almost completely dependent upon their parents for support. It is usually the time when the concept of personal freedom first becomes reality—not as much as they would like, but enough to whet their appetite for more and entice them to do things they could not get away with at home. It is the time to try new things, to experiment with vice or simply with frivolous things not allowed at home. In almost every case, there is no going back. It is a time marked with learning, but not just about what is taught. Often what is experienced outside the classroom is the best teacher. Life is about limits, expectations, permissions, and exceptions to the rules.

Today anonymous student surveys reveal that prohibited activities are common in university residence halls. This includes seemingly innocuous things as cooking as well as ingestion of alcohol, tobacco, and controlled substances. People regularly illegally download music and films and engage in consensual sex. While many of these proscribed behaviors can leave potentially recoverable material remains (such as pots and hot plates, cigarette butts and ashtrays, liquor bottles, roach clips and bongs, or condoms, condom wrappers, diaphragms, or pill packages), they seem to leave no evidence when the trash from these buildings is surveyed. When students are asked how this can be, most respond with a nod and a wink that they have ways of disposing of such incriminating evidence. This should give pause not only to campus administrators but also to archaeologists seeking to document campus behavior.

Archaeology is good at revealing those secrets. The ground at Santa Clara University has yielded a wealth of information on the ways of education in the nineteenth century, the lives of the male students and their Jesuit faculty, and ultimately the lives of returning veterans and their families. The expectations meant to guide the students in their education are dictated by the university catalogues, rulebooks, and historical papers and are well documented through archival and library resources. In addition to documents and oral history, however, the artifacts provide another and often different perspective. Sometimes they tell the truth about what really went on. Smoking, dipping snuff, drinking, and general mischief during the early years at Santa Clara occurred despite the written bans on such behavior. Even walls could not keep the students inside. Prohibited materials from the outside world often made their way in.

As times changed, so did behavior. World War II brought on new challenges and responsibilities both for the university, which struggled to stay open while the majority of its student body was overseas, and for the students, who struggled to regain some semblance of their old lives after they returned.

Individuals often leave their mark on the landscape in ways not revealed through traditional archaeology. People like to be remembered, but how? Personal trash is ephemeral. Carving initials on a tree, table, or desktop or writing in fresh concrete may result in fines or expulsion. But people still purposely leave their mark and so make a lasting personal statement that they were part of the university's history. At Santa Clara in addition to detritus we have found numerous examples of that very collegiate experience. Graffiti in the form of names etched onto various surfaces have been discovered (Figure 10.13). The Archaeology Research Lab is fortunate enough to have a glass cabinet front with the names and dates of the freshman and junior chemistry classes from 1914–15 etched on it. It had been salvaged during the demolition of the building in the 1920s and recycled as a garage window in the city of Santa Clara. When that building was being torn down, the family returned the window. During the 1980 renovation of the oldest building on campus (the Adobe Lodge) a seventy-five-year-old inscription written on wall plaster by a former student was found. It simply reads: "Charles R. Plank—October 11, 1905." And inside a dorm room closet is the message "to all those I leave behind, my memory will live with you . . . Mack Daddy Player, '90." His real name underneath is unreadable.

Figure 10.13. Examples of student graffiti (*clockwise from upper right*): dorm room closet "autograph" circa 1990; 1905 wall writing; etched glass cabinet windows, circa 1912, from the Montgomery Science Building.

As the University of Arizona's long-term Garbage Project has demonstrated, the archaeological record can both complement and contradict the documentary record and in so doing create for the discerning a more nuanced and complete picture that goes beyond the "ideal" to the "real" story of the past (Rathje and Murphy 1992). At Santa Clara University the efforts of the Archaeology Research Lab are rewriting campus history while training the archaeologists of tomorrow.

Acknowledgments

We are indebted to the following students (some of them served as archaeology technicians at the Santa Clara University Archaeology Research Lab), whose studies of Santa Clara's history and insights into its material culture made this a better chapter: Catherine Aldinolfi, Julia Canavese, Nicholas Fussell, Kelly Greenwalt, Melissa Johnson, Eric Loewe, Michael O'Sullivan, Olivia Sorrell, and Paige Wilson. We also wish to thank SCU archivist Anne McMahon and archives specialist Sheila Conway, SCU campus historian Gerald McKevitt, S.J., and George Giacomini, Jr., in the Department of History for their guidance and insights into the history of the campus. We also gratefully acknowledge the historian for the City of Santa Clara, Lorie Garcia, for always graciously sharing her knowledge. We wish to thank the more than a thousand students from Santa Clara University, San Jose State University, and Stanford University who have labored to reveal the Santa Clara story over the past dozen years. Thank you also to Shirley Hammond, our friend and a former nurse who is quite familiar with the use and administration of medication and recognized the ampoules and medicine bottles. We want to give special recognition to Joe Sugg, vice president of university operations, for his ongoing support of the CRM program. Finally, we would like to thank the President's Office, the Provost's Office, the College of Arts and Sciences, and our colleagues in the Departments of Anthropology and Sociology, without whose support this story would never have been told.

11

Love, Let, and Life

An Archaeology of Tennis at the College of William and Mary

DONALD SADLER

On a crisp fall day in 1941, she stepped out onto the clay. Bending down to make sure her laces were fixed tight, she gripped the newly taped handle of the racket, eager to test it against her opponent across the net. Her teammates applauded her with their usual verve, offering sharp female yells of encouragement. There were boys to root for her as well, though soon enough most of their cheers would be silenced, as unforeseen events led them to their life's great calling. Plans were being hatched in the Pacific, and very soon America would lose its naive innocence, becoming forever changed. The war would alter her own life too, though she did not think of that now; she thought only of victory as her sneakers kicked up the dirt off the sun-baked red clay of the tennis court. The dust danced through the air, past the chain-link fence at her back and right, and out and on toward the dormitories and classroom buildings on the grounds of the College of William and Mary. Dorothea Kissam played tennis. She was the tallest of the twenty-three girls on the women's team that year and also the only one with long, flowing blonde hair, helping her to stand out and be noticed. Sixty-two years later, she was.

When breaking ground during archaeological work on the second oldest college in America, expectations are higher than revealing the fact that girls played tennis here. The College of William and Mary began in 1693 and followed only Harvard University as the country's first seat of higher learning. Modern-day William and Mary is consistently ranked as one of America's finest public small colleges, and the modest but growing student body is ripe with some of the brightest youth today's preparatory schools can produce. The increasing number of incoming students requires that William and Mary adapt over time and expand upon its quaint colonial roots. Unfortunately for some, expansion meant the need for a new dormitory on the spot of one of the most popular green areas on campus, the Martha Barksdale Athletic Field. The field was named after the innovator of women's athletics at the college, who taught and played over a dozen sports. Used for multiple activities for both genders, Barksdale Field was also a great spot to hang out, catch some sun, study for that demanding class, or just people watch. The oncoming dormitory was seen as an evil, and as archaeologists we were unfairly viewed as the harbingers of that field-threatening wickedness. Tools were tampered with, site markers taken up, test units refilled by environmental saboteurs—all in an effort to delay or prevent construction. One particular brand of protest saw slogans burned into the lawn, such as "Save Our Field" and "Go Home," making for worrisome digging to say the least.

The crew hoped that the uncomfortable environment would be offset by the discovery of wonderful things. The earlier Phase I survey (Monroe and Lewes, 2004) on Barksdale Field had revealed a scattering of eighteenth- and nineteenth-century structural and domestic artifacts. Given the location of the project area along a historic road between Williamsburg and Jamestown, research questions were directed at the possibility of locating individual farmsteads of the middling sorts. Also, troops of various wars had marched across these fields and camped here or nearby, possibly leaving some trace of their passing. Students and common folk of varied lives had walked this ground within the colonial capital of Virginia since the late seventeenth century. Though earlier maps of the area revealed no structures throughout time, we hoped that the archaeological effort would produce some long-lost foundation or colonial household away from the bustle of the main streets of Williamsburg. Thirty-one test units and eight test trenches later, we found out that Dorothea Kissam played tennis.

Expecting Thomas Jefferson's lost pocket watch and instead getting net holders and concrete fence posts can be a little exasperating. Despite finding hundreds of scattered artifacts from the eighteenth and nineteenth centuries, the team began to come to grips with the fact that the only features discovered were associated with the twentieth-century campus. Once all these modern features were related with one another and mapped out, however, they began to correlate into an interesting revelation. Checking twentieth-century maps of the area revealed a tennis court being constructed at the site in 1929. After realizing that our "modern" features were actually parts of a seventy-five-year-old athletic arena, and with the absence of anything else of archaeological interest, we turned our attention to the archaeology of tennis.

Suppressing grins while pondering if we were pioneers in this archaeological endeavor, we simply told ourselves that they were paying us to tell them what was here, and so we would.

Features 1–3 of the Tennis Court

The following features are various parts of the tennis court complex discovered in the archaeological investigations at Barksdale Field. The detailed analysis of each component of the courts reveals the complexity of tennis court construction and provides insight into the early use of the women's athletic field. According to the United States Tennis Court and Track Builders Association (USTCTBA) guidelines, a tennis court should be sited to minimize the need for players to look into the sun. The guidelines also state that courts in the southern United States are often oriented according to either the spring or fall equinox and that collegiate facilities courts should be oriented west of north for the months of April and May to minimize conflict with the afternoon sun, since most play would be during that time of year. Other structures and features on the site as well as vehicle and pedestrian traffic are also factors in determining the orientation of the courts. According to the guidelines, all courts should be oriented in relation to true north, not magnetic north (USTCTBA 2004). The archaeologically revealed courts on Barksdale Field seemed to fit these specifications.

Feature 1

Prior to machine stripping at the site, a number of test units were opened. In some of the units the team found red clay that at the time was deemed to be subsoil. Upon stripping the site and exposing the entirety of the area, the red clay became isolated in certain areas. Once we knew we were on the trail of a 1929 tennis court, our research led us to investigate the evolution of tennis court construction in the field.

At the turn of the twentieth century the College of William and Mary officially embraced the sport of tennis. Courts were established at successive locations as the institution grew rapidly from circa 1900 to circa 1930. Where they were situated became a predictor of where building construction would subsequently occur, as in the case of Barksdale Field.

As early as 1904 tennis courts existed on the William and Mary campus in the field behind the Wren Building. A structure south of the Wren Building was built in 1901 to serve as a gymnasium, making it sensible to locate the tennis courts nearby. During the 1920s the structure was converted into a classroom and was named the Citizenship Building. At this time the tennis courts would have represented the western edge of campus. By 1920 the courts had been moved away from the Wren building, in the area now known as the Sunken Garden. The next tennis courts stood at the site of Monroe Hall prior to the start of its construction in April 1923. The courts then were moved to the site of Blow Gymnasium before it was underway in September 1923. The courts were relocated to the site of Washington Hall prior to its construction in March 1928 (Lambert 1958: 36). Aerial photographs confirm this, showing the courts located on the site that would become Washington Hall in 1924. In 1929 the courts were moved to the location of the women's athletic field, currently Barksdale Field (Figure 11.1). There they remained until 1956, when the field was used for construction material in building Phi Beta Kappa Memorial Hall. So we learned that from 1929 through 1956 courts had existed at the spot of our archaeological investigation, which caused us to look harder at that compact red clay.

The red clay used for the courts may have been periodically replaced: clay is a porous surface material consisting of natural clay or processed clay that has been mixed, crushed, screened, and blended with sand and silt and is therefore susceptible to weather conditions. The red clay of Feature 1 was 0.3 feet thick and was mapped in profile along part of the northern wall of one of the machine-stripped sections. In another excavated section archaeologists were able to get a clear view of the edge of the red clay court, connecting it with several concrete and clay fence posthole remains, which represented the back northwestern section of the fenced-in courts (Figure 11.2).

The USTCTBA has very detailed guidelines for the construction of modern clay tennis courts. It is fair to assume that similar building guidelines existed during the William and Mary courts construction in 1929 and during their periodic upkeep. According to these guidelines, a compacted subbase needed to exist beneath the court. Where the natural soil at the bottom of the subbase course was stable, as evidenced by stability under construction equipment, hand auger, or other exploration, base course material could be placed on this soil. A base course of crushed stone or gravel would be installed over the subbase. The thickness of the base course could vary to meet local soil and climatic conditions but was not less than 3 inches after compaction. The surface of the base course, after compaction, was smooth and even. A surface course of natural clay or processed clay was applied over the finished base course to a compacted thickness of no less than 3 inches for natural clay or 2 inches for blended material (USTCTBA 2004).

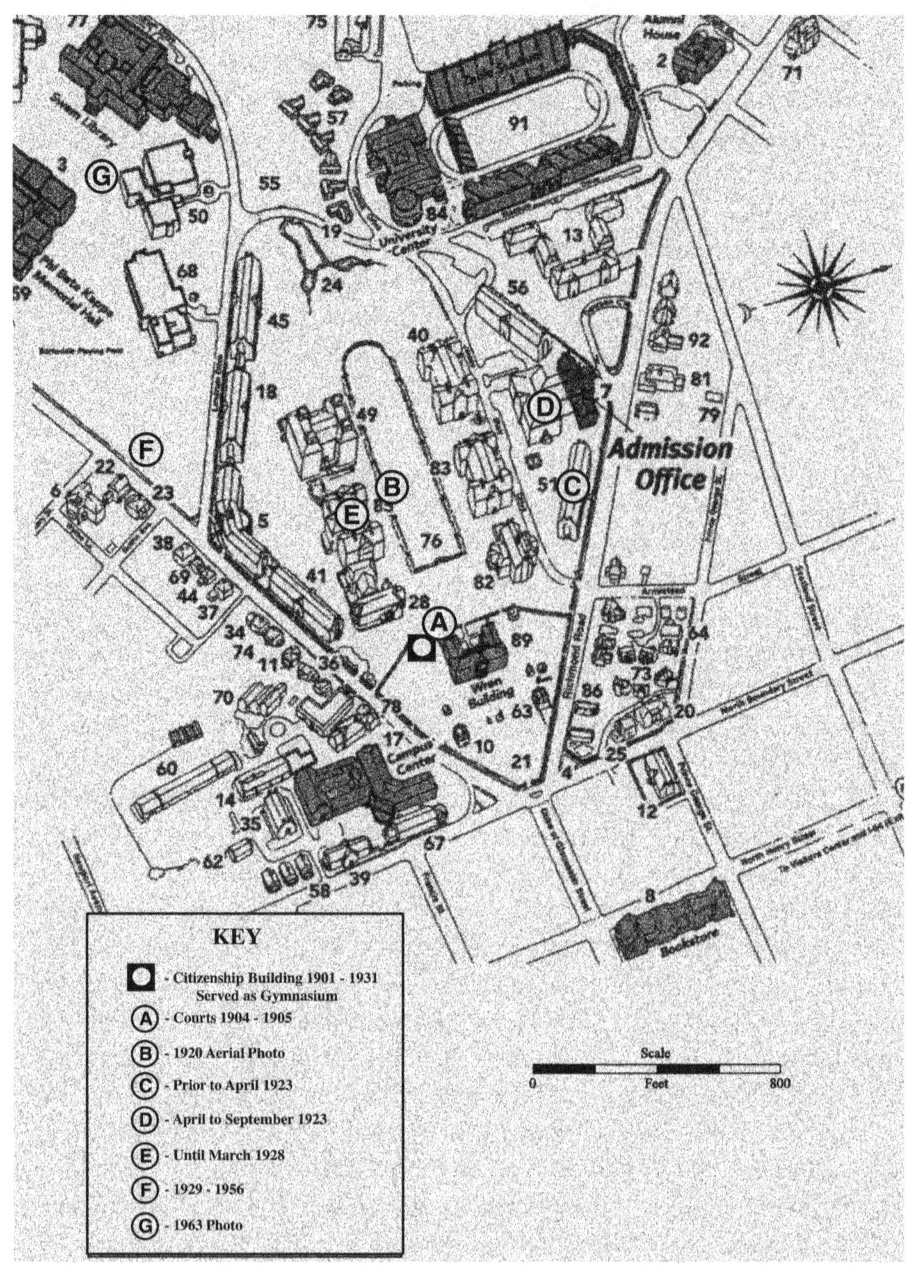

Figure 11.1. Tennis court evolution at William and Mary.

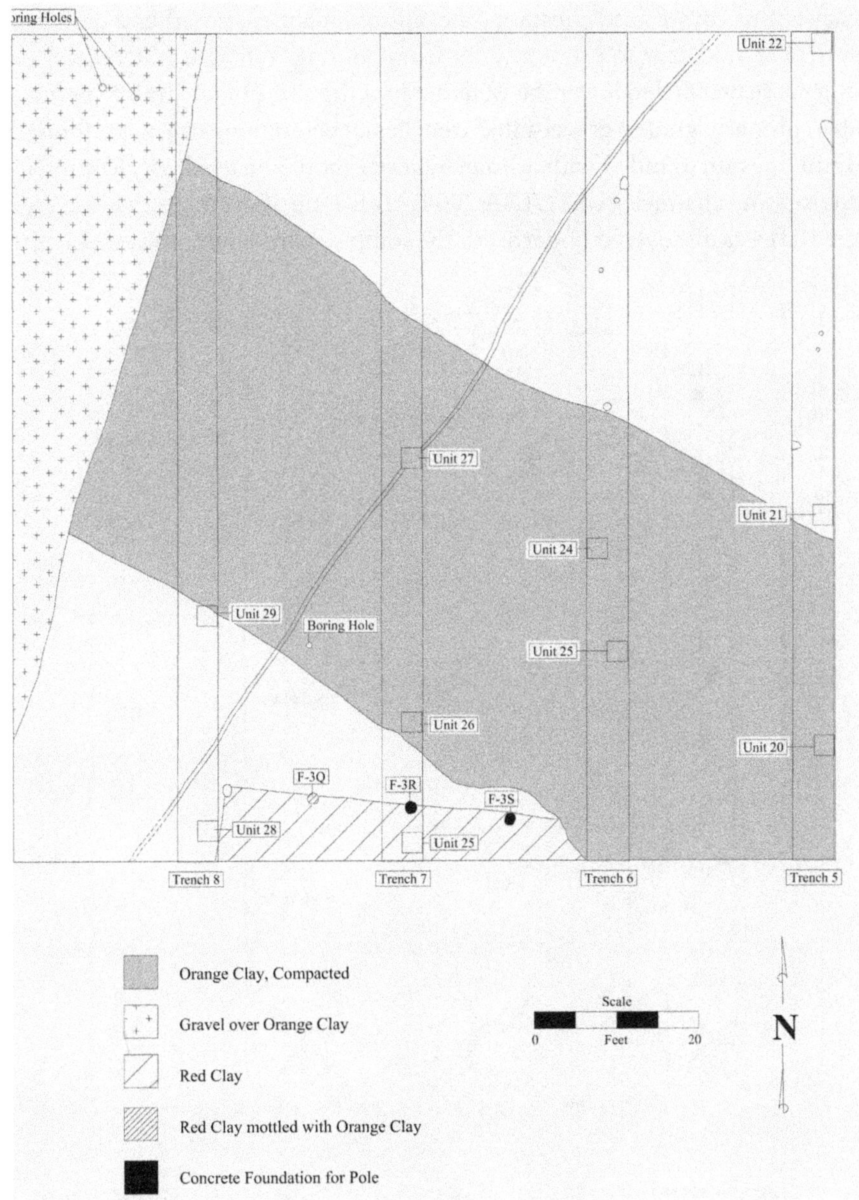

Figure 11.2. The northwestern section of the tennis court.

Feature 2

Clay tennis courts need constant watering and maintenance; thus a drainage system should exist to prevent water from pooling. Where it is necessary or otherwise decided to lower the water table at the site, French drains (permeable, properly graded gravel-filled trenches), geo-composites, or perforated drain lines surrounded with a stone material should be used, discharging to appropriate channels (USTCTBA 2004). This type of drainage system (Figure 11.3) was discovered underneath the southwestern court, presumably the

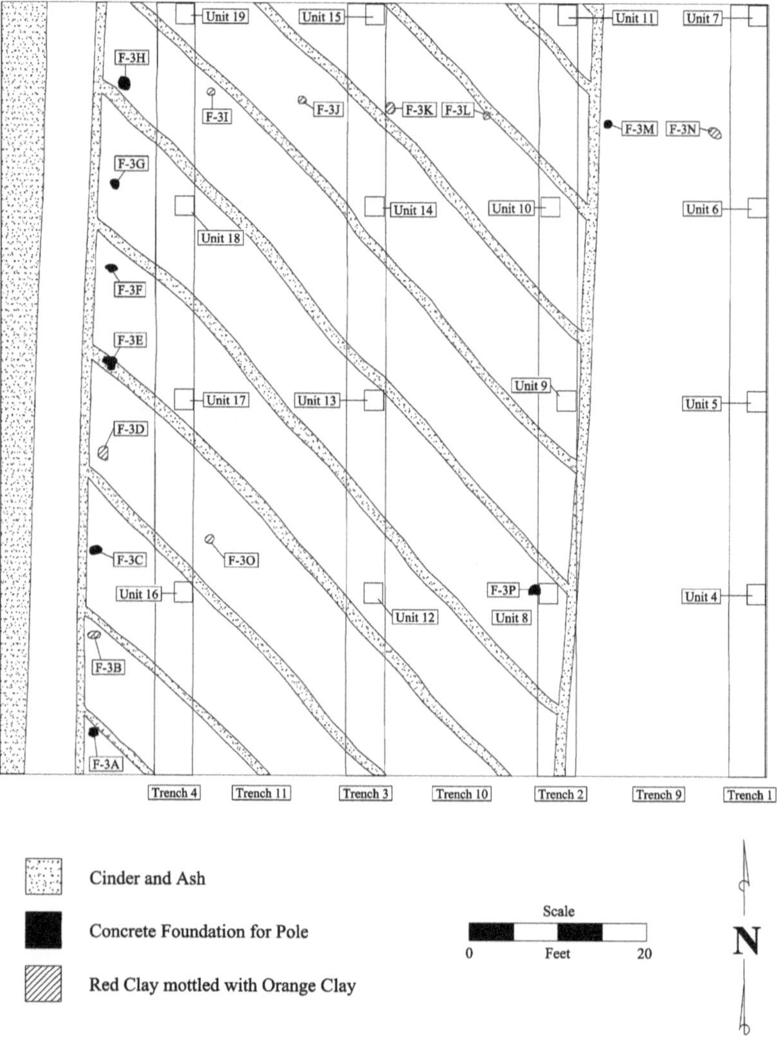

Figure 11.3. A French drain beneath the tennis court.

Figure 11.4. A French drainage pipe with cinder fill.

lowest part of the playing area. The main stoneware pipes that ran northeast/southwest across the excavated section were designated Feature 2A. These pipes were found on the eastern and western sides of the court. Feature 2B was a series of terra-cotta pipes that connected the two main stoneware pipes (Figure 11.4). Eleven parallel terra-cotta pipes were discovered, and the distances between them ranged from 10 feet to 15 feet. The stoneware pipe was .07 foot thick, while the terra-cotta pipe was .05 foot thick. Both were surrounded by a matrix of crushed cinder and ash, possibly from the nearby power plant in use at the time.

Feature 3

Feature 3 was the designation for a series of fence post remains that enclosed the tennis court area. Nineteen such post remains were discovered; ten of these still retained the concrete base and the remnants of the metal pole (Figure 11.5), while the rest were clay posthole stains. The majority (sixteen) of the fence post remains were located within the excavated section, including the evidence of a divider fence that ran east/west across the section. The fence pole remains were evenly spaced, 12 feet apart, suggesting that the concrete and clay posts were all part of one fence structure. It appears that either some concrete bases were removed when the courts were demolished or

Figure 11.5. An excavated concrete fence post base.

the fence originally had irregular concrete bases interspersed with postholes simply sunk into the orange clay.

According to the archaeological evidence cited above as well as oral history and aerial photographs, the tennis court system at Barksdale Field consisted of four fenced-in courts, constructed in a rectangular complex. The distance from a fence post found in the excavation (which represents the back north fence of the courts) to a center divide fence post is 120 feet. This corresponds with the current standards for tennis court construction set by the USTCTBA guidelines (USTCTBA 2004). Seven post remains ran north/south and probably represent 84 feet of a fence assumed to be 120 feet long. Using the same corner post, a series of seven posts ran east/west across the excavated section, giving the 60 feet needed for a baseline and suggesting that the fence continued to enclose a neighboring court. Where courts are constructed within the confines of a common enclosure, the distance between side lines should be not less than 12 feet, so that could add another fence post and suggest that five more lie east of our excavation. Two postholes were discovered within the court area and inside the fence line spaced at 42 feet apart. At first archaeologists considered them to be part of the south wall of the fence line, but the measurements did not correspond. Playing a hunch, we visited an existing tennis court at the college and measured the distance between the net holders. The distance matched that of our mystery postholes, and after double-checking with the USTCTBA guidelines we confidently labeled these two posts as net holders.

The purpose of fencing around a tennis court is obviously to keep most of the balls within the court during play. Chain-link fencing is most commonly used for this purpose. The fencing area is required across the back of the court (backstop) and along each sideline from the corner 20–40 feet up the sidelines (sidestop). The area up to 40 feet on either side of the net can be left open, or shorter fencing may be used (USTCTBA 2004). This side fencing is clearly visible in a photograph in the College of William and Mary archives taken in the early 1940s (Figure 11.6), extending around 36 feet along the eastern side of the court then stopping. This photograph also seems to show a back fence line south of the court and apparently another fenced-in court in the background, thus revealing two separate fenced-in courts. This information does not match the findings of the archaeological work, which shows one single divider fence separating the four courts. Photographs from the college archives dating to earlier decades show the fence line matching the findings of the archaeological work. Apparently the courts went through evolving phases throughout the decades. As I sorted through the old sepia-

Figure 11.6. The red clay court and fence line (with smokestack in background). (Courtesy of Martha Barksdale Papers, Special Collections Research Center, Earl Gregg Swann Library, College of William and Mary)

tinged photographs of yesteryear's tennis teams, it dawned on me that we could do a bit of ethnographic research and find someone who had played on these courts, to confirm the placement and movement of the courts through time.

The College of William and Mary's archives were then located off campus, so a day was spent away from the dirt and eco-terrorism of the field in the climate-controlled rooms of precious papers and photographs from the history of the college and beyond. Going through the Martha Barksdale Papers, I pulled a folder out labeled simply "Women's Tennis" and began to experience the rarity of being able to see what we had discovered in the ground as it once was. The materials showed the fence posts, the net holders, and even the smokestack in the background to suggest where the cinder for the French drain had come from. And there were the faces. My teachers at William and Mary had long teased me for my romantic stance on archaeology. Perhaps it was the poet in me, but I had always been one to glamorize the past, to see in it the ability to express the stories and thoughts of people long since gone and to make these people of the past live again. In its own unique way, archaeology could rescue them from obscurity, whether they were kings,

Figure 11.7. Dorothea Kissam (*top row, second from the left*) and the William and Mary Tennis Team of 1942. (Courtesy of Martha Barksdale Papers, Special Collections Research Center, Earl Gregg Swann Library, College of William and Mary)

colonists, Native Americans, or, well, tennis players. So it was in that climate-controlled room, with pictures splayed out before me, that I first laid eyes on Dorothea Kissam.

She stood tall and elegant and spoke to me from the picture, telling me of autumn days when her world was filled with possibility (Figure 11.7). There were earlier pictures of tennis players, with long dresses down to their ankles in the 1930s, gradually getting higher as time moved on and styles took on the mindset of the country, wilder and free. But Dorothea stood out in 1941, and again in 1942, and I knew she had to be the one I contacted.

At some point my research at Barksdale Field (and therefore this chapter) stopped being about archaeology and started being about the human element. For what reason do we dig? We aim to find out how the people in our research lived, how they thought. We utilize the material in the ground in order to tell us about their life and our own. So I found Dorothea Kissam, suppressing my fears about even looking in the first place, the possibility that I would find out that this beautiful young woman in these old photographs had left this world. While uncovering a long forgotten piece of ceramic it is easier to realize that the person who ate off that plate or drank from that mug is no longer here. To my relief, I discovered Dorothea Kissam, alive and well.

Switching hats from archaeologist to ethnographer, I tried to come up with interesting interview questions for my key actor in this tennis drama. In this situation (since we already had an accurate understanding of the historical facts) a retrospective interview would provide useful information about this individual witness to the history of the dig. The worldview of individuals may be expressed through the way in which they emphasize their values and histories (Fetterman 1998: 40). It was my hope that these principles would emerge in my interview with Dorothea Kissam, along with any details about the tennis courts that she could provide. Dorothea is a somewhat private person, so the interview process had to be undertaken through an intermediary representative of the Kissam family. Denied the ability to hear her voice and emotion, relate my own, and use that connection to formulate a link to the past and the present, I instead satisfied myself with the results.

Dorothea Kissam left the College of William and Mary's tennis courts behind after her sophomore year. The war was on: with wounded men coming home, she felt the call of Columbia's School of Nursing, from which she graduated in 1946. She served proudly as a nurse for forty-three years, retiring in 1990. She then became a tour guide to the Emily Dickinson home in Amherst, Massachusetts, where she discovered and was moved by the words of the also very private Dickinson. In 2004, at the time of our excavation, she was retiring from this position.

Dorothea admitted being "intrigued" by an archaeologist's interest in her tennis-playing days, and it must have made her smile to think that some sixty-two years later someone would "unearth" her actions on the clay. She remembered Martha Barksdale as the athletic director at the time and said the courts were the best she had ever played on, which gave us some insight into the quality of their construction. She described herself as a "good" player but not the best on the team and talked of her opponents from schools like Manhattanville, Hunter, Swarthmore, Notre Dame, and Farmville State Teachers College. Dossi, as friends call her now, continued to play tennis "for fun" until knee replacement surgery only a few years ago forced her to give up the game. In folders in the college archives, in the photograph in this chapter, and in my mind now forever young, she plays on.

Life on a college campus offers a myriad of daily activities. Proper archaeological research joined with ethnographic opportunities offers insight into the daily lives of the students. Athletics, and in this example specifically women's athletics, are a very large contributor to the overall campus environment. As athletics began to increase in popularity in the late nineteenth and early twentieth centuries, their impact in the archaeological record also increased. The ways in which students enjoy either casual or competitive recreation may help reveal how they eventually see themselves or interact with others.

III

Architecture, Space, and Identity

How Constructed Landscapes Reflect Institutional Goals

Of all the disciplines in social science, archaeology is perhaps the most visible. Perhaps because of the romance of field exploration or because of its ability to reveal "hidden" information about the past, archaeology holds great fascination for the public. Consequently, when we carry out excavations on campus to investigate what is literally our own past, people pay attention. But campus archaeology is more than a public show. It involves the archaeologist with a larger community, including academics, students, administrators, and the public, all of whom share an interest in the work and its results. The following three chapters explore the nature of public archaeology in the campus community. In this context not only is our work carried out publicly, but its results are intended for the multiple audiences who are stakeholders in its results. In three instances the authors discuss how campus archaeology has addressed the needs and concerns of those invested in its results and how archaeology has become an integral part of planning and public outreach as well as education.

12

Digging in the Golden Bear's Den

Archaeology at the University of California, Berkeley, in Three Voices

LAURIE A. WILKIE, KIMBERLY E. CHRISTENSEN, AND MICHAEL A. WAY

Laurie: Archaeology under the Big C

It's a rainy winter day in Berkeley, and I'm staring into a muddy pipe trench, surrounded by an anxious crew of construction workers. I really don't want to jump into the trench. I was comfortably sitting in my not-so-warm but definitely dry office when the phone call came. I left my office quickly, donning a hard hat but forgetting my jacket. The heavy mist that passes as northern California rain is slowly soaking my clothing, and I don't want to get my feet wet as well. I sigh and slowly climb down the makeshift ladder and descend into the muddy hole. Based on previous experiences, a visit from the archaeologist isn't official until someone—me—gets dirty. The construction workers, now drinking coffee and nicely bundled in rain gear, all peer in after me and watch as I pull out a tape measure and make some quick sketches and take depth measurements.

"Yes," I declare as authoritatively as I can. "You do seem to have found part of the foundation of the original philosophy building. Quite substantial, isn't it?" I climb out and check the back-dirt for any obvious artifacts. There are none (there never are: the foundations have usually been sheared off below the original surface years ago). The crew members are silent. They watch as I quickly jot down some notes and try to focus my camera in the rain.

"So," the crew chief asks hesitantly, "what do we have to do now?" I hear the dread in his voice. Everyone in construction seems to believe that no good can come of finding archaeological remains.

I shrug. "Well, now we know that this is here, and if there is ever any large-scale development of this part of campus, we'll need to do some excavations beforehand. For now, though, you've only uncovered a small portion of a very large building. You can finish up what you're doing." He looks surprised and relieved. I continue: "If everyone in the planning office does what they are supposed to do, archaeology should not stop construction on campus. We should be working together, and coming out when you find things during small projects like this helps us plan for the future."

Most of the time campus archaeology isn't very glamorous. One brick foundation looks very much like another. Yet each time I go look at an exposed foundation and do not hinder small-scale trenching projects like pipe replacements, I'm making it more likely that I'll be involved if and when something important is uncovered. I hope that it also increases the likelihood that the university will incorporate archaeology during the planning process for campus projects. Yes, there are environmental laws that mandate archaeology on state lands and on development projects that involve state and federal funds. But, as I've learned over the years, the University of California system is good at playing the development game to the detriment of all kinds of cultural resources, be they architectural or archaeological. I have also learned that there are no sticks big enough that I could wield (unless, perhaps, Native American burials were found) that could force the university to do anything it didn't want to do. So, using my position as a faculty member, over the last twelve years I've taken the strategy of offering carrots to the stubborn mule of campus bureaucracy to encourage its participation in the management of archaeological resources.

Along the way, I have found that campus archaeology has a powerful pedagogical role to play in archaeological education and have developed a keen research interest in themes that characterize the social, political, and intellectual history of the campus. In the process, undergraduate and graduate students at the university have become involved in different aspects of campus archaeology; two of them offer their experiences of campus archaeology in these pages. Kim is a doctoral student in the Department of Anthropology who is using one of the campus archaeological sites in her dissertation work. Mike is an undergraduate anthropology major from the class of 2007, who has experienced campus archaeology as a field school and laboratory student and as a lab worker. Together, we hope to introduce the wonderful potential of campus archaeology and, we hope, encourage other archaeologists to dig in academic backyards.

Laurie: Planning and Pedagogy

My involvement in campus archaeology was accidental. My first semester at Berkeley (fall 1995) coincided with the expansion of the University's Law School library. Bulldozing commenced behind my office. The Archaeological Research Facility (ARF), where my office is located, was built as a fraternity house in 1910. As I watched the bulldozers remove a parking lot, I idly wondered what would happen if they hit any archaeological remains.

The following day, after returning from class, I was approached by a staff member of ARF, who informed me that he had spotted construction workers filling buckets with bottles, which they hid when approached. We marched out, confronted the workers, and got phone numbers of bosses and campus contacts. Several of us made irate phone calls until bulldozing was stopped and we were allowed access to the site. As the new historical archaeologist on campus, I was "elected" leader of the effort.

The deposit, which I later learned was a backfilled swimming pool built by the fraternity (don't ask), was nearly completely destroyed. We collected all the artifacts, excavated a small unit in the remnants of the pit's sidewall, and profiled what we could. I was left with hundreds of whole bottles (mainly liquor) and hundreds of sherds of ceramics and other artifacts. The prohibition site received a great deal of media attention (Wilkie 2001), but frankly I was not particularly interested in taking on this project at that time—I had tenure to work for, and the numerous jokes I was receiving about being a "fratologist" convinced me that there was little *gravitas* to be gained from this project. Still, the materials were great for teaching, so in the spring of 1996 I offered a lab course. I divided different sets of materials from the site among the students, who also undertook archival and oral histories of the site. I found it to be an easy course to run—archival materials were widely available on campus and the students were enthusiastic to research "their" own history. As members of the university's student population, the undergraduates were uniquely situated as stakeholders in the project. They felt empowered to be conducting truly original research on the materials. The experience convinced me of the site's research potential and that campus archaeology could have a powerful role in the classroom.

In 2000 the ARF was scheduled for retrofitting. As part of the project, the interior plank floor of the atrium was to be removed. Documentary research demonstrated that this was an open courtyard during the fraternity's occupation of the structure and that remnants of the original 1876 fraternity house could be preserved there. Working with the retrofit committee and

Capital Projects, I convinced the university that archaeology should take place in the atrium and that it could be done as part of an archaeological field school. The field school enrolled thirty students, many of whom (due to family, work, or financial circumstances) would not have been able to attend a remote field school. We were able to work around the retrofit schedule of the construction crew and recovered significant archaeological information that would have been lost had I not interfered in the planning process.

Based on the success of the 2000 project, Capital Projects approached me about coordinating another field school for summer 2003, this time at the future site of the new East Asian Library. The area to be impacted had once been the site of the university's 1870s astronomical observatory and an 1890s glass conservatory (Wilkie and Kozakavich 2005). This time the university's Capital Projects significantly funded the project, underwriting the vast majority of the field school's cost and the costs of graduate and undergraduate student labor during report preparation. Based on the report, the university agreed to fund another field school in 2005, to serve as the mitigation phase of the project. Clearly, the situation is not ideal from a management perspective, and no doubt local CRM firms have reason to be displeased when academics undercut their livelihoods. I could be seen as an enabler who is allowing the university to escape its obligations. I have thought through these issues; and while I am not comfortable with some of the political and economic implications of my involvement in campus archaeology, I also realize that this is not a simple case of stealing work that could be done by other archaeologists—if I was not involved in these projects, the sites would be lost. As I write, there are other projects on campus that have underconsidered impacts on archaeological resources. Maybe in another twelve years the situation will be different.

Combined, these three field campus schools employed fifteen graduate students and twelve undergraduates and enrolled over a hundred students. The 2003 field school also attracted the positive attention of the university's vice chancellor, who voiced his pleasure to several project directors at Capital Projects. It has been made clear to me on a few occasions that the administration's goodwill has gotten me to the table in development meetings.

While I will let my co-authors speak more to the educational benefits of campus archaeology, let me share a few concluding thoughts on how this archaeology feeds into the classroom. Our anthropology department's Introduction to Archaeology course now regularly features a tour of sites that have been studied on campus. This was instituted by my colleague Kent Lightfoot, as a way of illustrating to students that archaeology is and can be anywhere.

It also emphasizes the dynamic nature of the archaeological record as ever changing and developing due to natural and human processes. Doing research on campus allows students, whether as part of a formal field school, laboratory class, apprenticeship, or senior thesis, to follow the process of conducting research from the stage of data collection to interpretation and synthesis. The highly public nature of campus research instills in them a sense of archaeologists' obligations to make their studies accessible to a wide range of community groups.

Kim: Pedagogy

In addition to research experience encapsulated within course offerings and formal archaeological field schools, we have been able to work with a preexisting university program, the Undergraduate Research Apprenticeship Program (URAP), in order to offer students research experience in campus archaeology. The URAP allows faculty members to post a listing of research projects for which they want undergraduate student involvement during the academic year, and students then apply to the projects that interest them. Students receive academic credit for their involvement based on the hours of work per week, which are negotiated between faculty and students in a learning contract that details responsibilities and expectations for the research relationship.

The URAP has proven indispensable for campus archaeological research. Excavations at the on-campus site that I am currently directing, the May and Warren Cheney House, have been undertaken entirely with the assistance of URAP students (in partnership with Laurie), student volunteers, and several graduate students. The house, built in 1885 and owned by the Cheneys until 1939, is slated to be removed as part of the Southeast Campus development plan, so our excavations seek to uncover information regarding the family's daily lives before the site is destroyed by development. The site's on-campus location—immediately adjacent to the Archaeological Research Facility, no less—has allowed us to conduct excavations throughout the academic year on weekdays with URAP students. This has permitted us to work in concert with the Office of Capital Projects' timeline for development, while offering students archaeological field, laboratory, and archival research experience equivalent to that of a formal field school, without the extra cost or intensive time commitment that they typically require. Moreover, as this site is deeply entangled with university history, students typically have a strong sense of identification with the site's past occupants; as Laurie mentioned above, this kind of archaeology is effectively an archaeology of student life, and current students are in a unique position as stakeholders.

For a graduate student, pursuing archaeological research on campus has decided benefits. Running excavations several days each week has enabled me to keep up my digging chops, while gaining valuable experience in teaching and supervising students. Moreover, it allows me to build teaching and public outreach into the very core of my dissertation research.

The May and Warren Cheney House's location on campus has also allowed the project and site to function as a sort of learning laboratory. In addition to the research efforts of the undergraduate students involved through the URAP, various graduate and undergraduate student projects have emerged from the overall excavation and research project. These efforts include macrobotanical and soil chemical analyses, an X-Ray Fluorescence Spectrometry (XRF) study of porcelain recovered from the site, and the use of the site for conducting lessons on 3–D laser scanning of the standing structures. As a result, the Cheney House site is situated at the nexus of research efforts by a number of graduate and undergraduate students due to its campus location and research potential. In terms of pedagogy, the site has proved invaluable for hands-on research experience for a number of students. Although the site's usefulness in terms of a learning laboratory is fleeting (because the site will be developed by the university), we are putting it to good use within the time that we have; all of the studies conducted will ultimately inform our interpretation of the site.

This approach to pedagogy, like Laurie's course-related original historical research, conforms to Jean Lave and Etienne Wenger's concept of legitimate peripheral participation. In this analytic model of learning based on refining notions of apprenticeship, Lave and Wenger (1991: 37) argue that learning itself is a part of social practice in general rather than a simple, unidirectional process of internalization. Participants who engage in the social practice of a community of practice thus eventually progress toward "identities of mastery" in learning. At the core of this is the availability of and "access to practice as resource for learning, rather than to instruction," as well as to perceived legitimacy of practice. In this understanding of learning, participation in practice is the very condition required for effective learning (Lave and Wenger 1991: 85, 93).

Archaeological research on campus fits this mode of learning by enabling both graduate and undergraduate students to participate in a community of practice—composed of university-affiliated archaeologists—and contribute original research to the communal learning effort. Rather than employing a "banking" approach to education (Freire 2000) or forcing students to complete assignments that are little more than busy work, this allows students to contribute meaningfully to ongoing research practices and projects and thereby shape their very form and outcomes. As a result, students renegotiate the social relations they are enmeshed in through the process of research and gradually increase their knowledgeability and participation within the wider community of practice, changing from newcomers to old-timers in the process. Likewise, as a graduate student, participating as a field school instructor provides experience that later comes into play when we head up our own projects. For instance, our first inkling regarding the research potential of the Cheney House came about as the result of a student research project from Laurie's historiographic methods course taught in the spring of 2005. This particular student paper, on the history of what we now know as the Cheney House, created the impetus for the currently ongoing archaeological research project at the site. My own experience as a graduate student instructor for the University Conservatory field school functioned as a kind of legitimate peripheral participation in the overall project and helped prepare me for "graduating" to the next level of mastery: directing my own research project. In sum, campus archaeology has proven invaluable for various pedagogical purposes at the graduate and undergraduate levels.

Mike: Oranges, Undergraduates, and Campus Archaeology

If archaeology is like eating an orange, then excavations are the equivalent of peeling off the skin; peeling an orange does not satisfy hunger any more than excavating answers questions about archaeology. The acts of chewing the orange and extracting nutrients from its fresh pulpy core are comparable to analysis and interpretation, respectively. Attending a campus field school provides students with the opportunity to process, analyze, and interpret the data that they collected from the ground. This is beneficial for the sake of continuity and because it gives undergraduates a taste of what archaeology really is. On campus digs we don't just peel the orange; we eat it and digest it too.

Fieldwork is invaluable to students considering archaeology as their area of emphasis, but the prospect of going to a far-away field school can be daunting for many students. Financial constraints, familial commitments, interference with other classes, and lack of time are some of the major reasons why distant field schools are not practical for university students. I am an example of a student who was constrained by familial commitment but received more archaeological experience than I had thought possible by participating in a campus dig.

I took my introductory archaeology class in the spring a few years ago, and the professor kept us up to date on what digs were being offered this summer. I was convinced that archaeology was something I wanted to try, so I kept an ear out for field schools that were right for me. But the only field schools that summer were to be in Greece, Turkey, and Japan. I did have the option of field schools outside of my university, but I wanted to go to one affiliated with my school so I could get to know my fellow undergraduates, graduate students, and professors, because I would potentially be working with them for the next two years. On a sunny spring day in a dark lecture hall, the announcement I had been waiting for finally came: a dig was to take place on campus over the summer, an excavation of Berkeley's conservatory, then buried beneath a parking lot that needed to be removed to make way for a new library.

I knew immediately that this field school was for me. Berkeley is about thirty miles from the home where I grew up with my family. My mother had multiple sclerosis, a degenerative nerve disease that limited her physical capacities. I would be able to go home at least one day every weekend to spend time with her and to give my father a break; and I was always on call during the week, in the occasional case that my help was needed before my father returned home from work. A field school on campus would allow me to maintain my commitment to my family and to experience archaeology the way it was meant to be experienced—down and dirty!

Beyond the benefit of being close to home and saving a lot of money, campus archaeology provides students with an opportunity to see a project through all phases of the archaeological process. Excavation is crucial to archaeology but is not the entire process, even though many people associate archaeology with "digging stuff up."

When the campus excavation ended, the undergraduates had opportunities to clean and catalogue the artifacts, which I did. A follow-up class was offered in the fall that allowed us to analyze and interpret the artifacts. Hundreds of terra-cotta potsherds later, I realized why it was so important to see the archaeological process the entire way through. Though the flowerpot analysis was tedious, when I finished I could speak with a new and profound sense of authority about what I had done.

Authority is a major reason why campus digs are important. By allowing students to engage with the material throughout the process, they are able to find their feet and their voice. When I first began analyzing materials, I was hard on myself, often wondering what in the world gave me authority to say anything about anything. After finishing the flowerpot analysis, I realized that I had authority on the matter because I had seen these materials through all parts of the process.

In addition to developing authority, campus digs invest students with a sense of ownership and pride and make archaeology relevant to their daily lives. Undergraduates study other undergraduates, their predecessors, and the history of the institution that they now call their own. It is an amazing thing to think that the last people to handle those flowerpots were undergraduates, standing where I knelt to excavate almost a century ago. All sorts of nostalgia come with campus digs: figuring out that it is worthwhile to study students in the past can empower students today to feel that their archaeological work is important and they are important themselves, both as stewards of the past and as people who will become part of the past as well.

Campus digs are significant because they allow students to experience all steps of archaeology—and even afford them the opportunity to be published. In the end, these digs and the following laboratory work are integral in helping undergraduates decide whether they want to pursue archaeology or not. It is hard to make that decision based on a lecture-based course or even on a month-long dig. When students are introduced to the process of archaeology, they become well rounded and confident in their knowledge of the discipline and receive training that they would miss at a remote field school. A prolonged engagement with the process of archaeology makes campus digs invaluable to budding archaeologists. In addition to saving money, being close to home, and delving into the lives of our academic ancestors, students can also shower every day after fieldwork and sleep in their own beds.

Laurie: Researching the Not-So-Ancient Greeks and Other Manly University Men

The University of California was settled on a plot of land in Berkeley as the first land-grant institution of the great state of California. It has sat on the edge of Strawberry Creek since 1873, when the first commencement was held on the site. Before that, the creek and surrounding slopes were home to local Ohlone groups, though many of their archaeological traces had been wiped from much of the campus through nonstop development projects.

The university always fancied itself as progressive and modern. The administration has never been fond of maintaining old buildings when it could have new ones instead. The effort to be modern, up-to-date, cutting edge, and socially, politically, and economically relevant has been a theme running through the history of the campus. Thus the university becomes a laboratory where the issues, ideas, and controversies of society are played out in miniature. The University of California, in no small way, was a primary force behind the development of ongoing mining and petroleum industries in the state. Many of the advancements in horticulture and soil science that allowed for the development of the state's massive agricultural industries were fashioned at the university and its associated agricultural stations. Presidents (with the notable exception of number 43) were regular visitors and speakers. The University of California, Berkeley, may not have been the center of the world, but it was always at the center of something.

Of particular interest to me has been the university's role in shifting gender ideologies from the late nineteenth century to the present. In 1871 the Regents realized that they had forgotten to declare the university to be a single-sex one and proclaimed it a co-ed institution after realizing that several women had already enrolled. Only the University of Michigan became a co-ed institution earlier. While women started out at the university in small numbers, by 1900 their enrollment numbers were almost equal to those of men. This is not to say that co-education was embraced by all. Administrators, faculty, and students all expressed clear opinions on whether they supported co-education or not, and the history of the campus is filled with examples of gender politics at play (Nerad 1999).

A number of the campus sites where I have worked have shed light on gender relations. Science was seen as a clearly white, masculine realm, just as progress was seen as intrinsically male. The Conservatory, a Victorian glass house designed to house agricultural experiments, is an example of male scientists' raising horticulture to a science, with all the implications for modern practice that marks. Artifacts testify to careful temperature control of buildings, mixing of plant-specific fertilizers, and the clean look of standardized pot sizes. The absurdity (for the men working in the structure) that a place of scientific research was housed in a Victorian monstrosity ultimately doomed the building to demolition.

A more obviously gendered archaeological site is the fraternity site that I described earlier. The fraternity represented a homosocial space in an increasingly mixed-sex campus. In the fraternity, men used ritualized activities like dining from ceramics emblazoned with the fraternal crest, beer consumption, and strictly hierarchical house organization to create a communal privilege: white, masculine identity (Wilkie 1998, 2006). Much of my previous work, outside of the campus grounds, has focused on the experiences of

African American men and women living in circumstances that threatened to rob them of their dignity and humanity. The campus research allows me to continue to explore my interests in race and gender, but in a way that examines how privilege and white patriarchy came to be naturalized and, ultimately, contested. Instead of being an obscure line of research, archaeologies of universities are very compelling and yield insights for any historical archaeologists. Universities are social, economic, political, and cultural centers. Research conducted at universities impacts all levels of society. For instance, Eugene Hilgard's soil science experiments directly contributed to the development of California's agricultural economy. Universities are centers of progressive and youth-based social, political, and cultural movements. They exist not only as microcosms of greater society but also as places where society is actively and consciously created and re-created. Given this, historical archaeology's failure to engage in explicit study of universities to any large degree is strange.

Kim: Research

My research at the May and Warren Cheney House also focuses on gender relations within the university setting as well as the ingrained social practice of reform in household settings. As mentioned earlier, the house was built in 1885 and was home to the Cheney family until May Cheney sold it to the university in 1939. May and Warren were both early graduates of the university (classes of 1883 and 1878, respectively) and were both products of the hotly contested practice of co-education. Warren owned a real estate and insurance company and wrote pieces for *Overland Monthly* and *Sunset Magazine* in addition to several published nonfiction books, poetry, and novels. May owned and managed a teaching placement service in San Francisco for about a decade, which placed teaching graduates in public school positions in the state. Beginning in 1898 and continuing for forty years, May worked as appointments secretary for the university, certifying and placing Cal graduates in teaching positions throughout the state. As 80 percent of female students at the university sought to become teachers (Nerad 1999: 36), May Cheney's efforts to standardize teaching certifications and placements had a profound effect on the professionalization and elevation in status of a predominantly female occupation. Moreover, she was intimately involved in efforts to improve the training and social experiences of female students. May was an honorary charter member of the Prytanean Society, an honor society for female Cal students formed in 1902. She urged students to form a campus chapter of the College Equal Suffrage League and helped in the push for the creation of a School of Domestic Science at the university in order to open up more professional employment opportunities for women. As vice president of the California chapter of the Association of Collegiate Alumnae (precursor to the American Association of University Women), she was connected to a nationwide network of college-educated women seeking to improve social and employment conditions for female students and graduates.

The Cheney house itself, a neighbor to the fraternity house studied by Laurie, functioned both as the family home where their four sons were raised and as an informal salon of sorts for writers, artists, and progressives. Luminaries such as Mary Hunter Austin, Frank Lloyd Wright, and Jack London were friends of the family and visitors to the home. May was listed as one of the "well-known local women" who acted as vice presidents of an equal suffrage rally held at the local high school two nights before the 1911 vote that extended suffrage to California women, and the family car was used in the Berkeley equal suffrage auto parade that took place the following day (Hester Harland papers, Bancroft Library).

Thus we have gained a good sense of the family's social and political involvements from the documentary record, although the family's day-to-day life has proved more elusive. Archaeological study of the yard areas surrounding the house, in contrast, provides a window onto the daily practices of the household and can illuminate how such social and political practices were wrapped up in daily life. This research puts the lie to the often-assumed enactment of gendered "separate spheres" during this period, which dictated the strict separation of masculine and feminine domains (with the household functioning as the feminine, apolitical half). It also shows how the gender debate over co-education played out within the university setting and how some women sought to work within the system to create more socially recognized opportunities for women to advance within academia and in outside employment.

Laurie: Many Campus Publics

I began my research as part of the post–African Burial Ground generation of scholars who realized that we could not direct our research from the comfort and isolation of the ivory tower but that our work had implications for broader descendant communities. While most of these disciplinary discourses (for example, LaRoche and Blakey 1997) focused upon including the concerns and ideas of minority communities, engagement with the fraternity research led me to realize that archaeologists were still considering our descendant communities too narrowly. Interviews with alumni and representatives of the Zeta Psi's National Chapter forced me to realize that privileged white men can be stakeholders as well, even if political correctness can lead archaeologists to discount their concerns (Wilkie 2001). The "public" and the "engaged community" or "descendant community" for the sites we have studied on campus are quite broad.

In excavating the Student's Observatory, graduate student Stacy Kozakavich and I (Wilkie and Kozakavich 2005) found that even though this structure was nearly completely demolished in the 1970s members of the current astronomy department still have a sense of strong and enduring connection to the memory of this place. They were eager both to share information about the community's history in this space and to complain about the university's overly enthusiastic demolition of the 1870s structure, although the observatory had been rendered scientifically obsolete by both its technology and the encroaching city lights that obscured its astronomical views.

Other sites engender different responses from those we might perceive to be natural communities of interest. The conservatory site was of interest to the broader campus community because of the impressiveness of the architectural remains that had been so completely hidden by a parking lot. The excavations were also near main pedestrian thruways on campus, drawing onlookers who otherwise might not visit an archaeological site. Many who visited felt a sense of investment based on their affiliation with Berkeley as a student, faculty person, or staff member. The visiting Regents of the University of California drove by the site on a faux cable car and enthusiastically waved at us; we were apparently pointed out to them by Berkeley administrators as an example of how undergraduate education and research could be blended on campus. Goodwill from this project directly led to our ability to work at the Cheney house. The conservatory project also engendered hostility from some segments of the population. Residents of nearby Haviland Hall resented the premature loss of their parking, the cordoned-off walkways, and the streams of dirty students (who always wiped their feet) traveling to the water fountains and restrooms. Several residents of this building determinedly marched through the site, past barriers, every day refusing to "see" the excavations they were stomping through. The Berkeley Historical Society, concerned about the environmental impacts of the East Asian Library that was to be built on the site, invited me to present information on the site and came for a site tour organized and run by the field school students.

Public archaeology is a vital component of all our campus projects. It is important for as much of the public as possible to be aware of the archaeology and why it is being conducted. We use site tours, newspapers, and other local media to communicate our findings and goals to as many people as possible, then let these audiences determine what their particular engagement with the site is. The University of California has been nervous about this aspect of our research and, frankly, in many cases would prefer us to do our work quietly and discreetly. This has not been a great strategy on their part. Rumors always circulate that the university has found skeletons and has hidden them away. Rapidly covered foundations inspire speculation and mistrust. If nothing else, we are advocating for the university to be transparent in its compliance with the environmental process and, we hope, to train its employees to take their obligations more seriously.

Mike: Explaining Why We Don't Find Dinosaurs

On-campus digs allow undergraduates, graduate students, and professors to climb down out of the ivory tower and into the terra firma surrounding it. The land around Berkeley's ivory tower is a potpourri of people from all walks of life, and campus excavations attract the same varied crowd. Community members, faculty, school groups, and construction workers were among the many visitors to our sites, providing us with an excellent opportunity to practice public archaeology.

Public archaeology is a great way to get people interested in local history, to help them understand archaeology as a discipline and a science, and to bridge the gap between academics and the general public. Excavations always attract curious onlookers who ask what we are finding; they are impressed when we show them even small finds, usually admitting with chagrin that they did not know there was anything here of historical importance. Beyond that, we curtail and hope to eliminate the phrase that makes an archaeologist's blood boil: "Are you looking for dinosaurs?" The irritation can be compounded when the well-intended visitor breaks into a long story about an acquaintance who went on a dig looking for raptors in Utah. As archaeologists we must take this as a cry for increasing public awareness of archaeology and should take advantage of our ability to excavate on campus, a place where (with rare exception) paleontologists cannot dig. The advantage of academic and public relations is that members of the public have an opportunity to become interested in archaeology, which could lead to support for further archaeological ventures. It also helps archaeologists synthesize what they know about the site, preparing them for the grueling papers and presentations that are sure to follow. Finally, it brings the academics and the community together in a setting that allows comfortable personal encounters that would otherwise never happen. Public archaeology is a public service: it has the potential to stimulate critical thinking, it can bolster interest in local sites and preservation of antiquities, and it allows the public to appreciate the discipline as a whole.

The archaeologists, be they first-year students or professors, have the opportunity to brush up on their public relations and to take ownership of the site. Offering site tours, holding public presentation nights, and chatting with people who pop in allow the archaeologists to take ownership of their site, infinitely renewing their sense of purpose and fortifying their agency and authority as experts on the site. It is important to remember to be a friendly expert, and public archaeology on campus offers us the opportunity to be social beings as well as scientists or undergraduates. Public archaeology on campus keeps us in touch with our public roots—as social scientists who study people—and provides the potential for improved community relations and increased interactions.

Kim: Public Outreach/Public Archaeology

Campus archaeology is ideally situated for the enactment of public outreach and public-oriented archaeology, in keeping with the theme of the site as a learning laboratory introduced earlier. In its most basic terms, conducting archaeological research on campus is inherently public in that it engages the interest of the campus community by its very visibility. Due to this expectation, outreach has been built into the Cheney House Project from its inception. In addition to engaging the questions of passersby when we are working on site, we have erected an interpretive sign at the site that provides basic background information on the site history and our research there. Judging by the number of people who stop to read the sign when we are excavating, its presence has helped raise considerable awareness regarding the site's history, our research interests, and future plans for the site's use by the university.

We also have a project weblog and online photo pool, both set up by graduate student Colleen Morgan. These web applications include student contributions and extend our project presence beyond our time physically on site and aid in our efforts to spread the word about the project. Colleen has also filmed on site and conducted informal interviews with the excavation team, which will be cut into a short film about the project.

In addition to these passive onsite outreach efforts, we have partnered with the ARF's Archaeology Outreach Program and held site open houses on homecoming weekend and Cal Day, the annual university-wide open house held in April. We have also hosted visits from local elementary school classes. These visits include using simulation "dig kits" in the ARF, site tours, screening soil and mapping test units on site, and a grab bag of other hands-on activities. Through these outreach efforts, we hope to show members of the public how archaeologists do what we do, why, and what might be gained from our research. While no formal survey of public attitudes toward the Cheney House Project has been undertaken, it is apparent from anecdotal evidence that most visitors are surprised by the site's rich history—which some have been walking past on campus for years—and express disappointment that it will eventually be destroyed by university development. By making the project approachable by the public we have in fact gained new information regarding the university-era use of the property. One day several months into our excavations, an emeritus chemistry professor, who for weeks had been a frequent passerby while we were working on the site, stopped and related how he remembered that the Cheney House was used as housing for graduate students by the university in the 1940s. We had not been previously aware of this use of the property, although it could potentially have a profound influence on our interpretations of the archaeological materials recovered at the site.

Finally, we hope that building public outreach into the Cheney House Project from the outset has modeled "best practice" guidelines for the undergraduate students involved in the project. With an increasing emphasis within the archaeological discipline on the necessity of reaching out to a variety of stakeholders, involving students in the practice of disseminating archaeological techniques and knowledge to the public—however construed—is crucial for the continued effort to create a less insular, less hegemonic, and less imperialistic archaeology. In sum, the Cheney House site's physical on-campus location has enabled us to build public outreach into the project from the outset, through opening the site to the public regularly and partnering with the existing ARF Archaeology Outreach Program.

Laurie: Conclusion

Doing the archaeology of a college campus and its past research endeavors and communities is an example of doing archaeology in the mirror. The three of us have very different communities on campus that we engage with and have different lifelong commitments to the campus. I see myself here for a long time, and campus archaeology makes me wonder about my place in this institution's history. For instance, when we found a letter that May Cheney had written to President Benjamin Ide Wheeler, urging him to hire a female faculty person in 1902, I had an emotional reaction—I saw my hiring ninety-three years later as an outcome of May's and other women's activism. Kim and Mike have different yet just as important and transformative engagements. Our subject positions shape how we relate to the materials we study and what benefits we take from the experiences. What should be clear from our little dialogic exercise, however, is that there are many benefits (for students, faculty, the campus community, and the public) from stepping outside our offices and labs and taking a trowel to the quad.

This work is more than an act of intellectual vanity, however. As discussed above, the campus projects have served a number of stake-holding communities. Hundreds of local schoolchildren have visited the campus excavations both on organized field trips and through the university's annual public day, Cal Day. Undergraduates who would not have the opportunity to participate in archaeological field schools otherwise have learned not just archaeological techniques but an appreciation for how archaeology can contribute to our understanding of the recent pasts.

Public days and lectures on site have brought the broader community of the city of Berkeley to the sites. Local preservation groups have been educated on how archaeological resources can be used as part of the argument for preserving historical structures. Other faculty persons on campus regularly use evidence drawn from the excavations in introductory archaeology courses, exposing literally thousands of students to this part of campus history. Women's Studies students from Cal and Mills College have been drawn into working at the Cheney House, thrilled to be undercovering—literally—the forgotten history of an early campus feminist. Alumni of Zeta Psi fraternity have used the archaeology of their chapter house to draw together multiple generations of their community and renew their commitment to the currently active students. We hope that the high profile and goodwill generated by these projects are slowly awakening UC's Capital Projects to the importance of mitigating the loss of archaeological resources.

13

More Than Bricks and Mortar

A Story of Community Archaeology

JODIE A. O'GORMAN

Michigan State University

"Remember your past. Connect with the present. Engage with our Future." The Michigan State University (MSU) administration put forth this tripartite invitation to participate in the 2005 Sesquicentennial Anniversary through a variety of symposia, exhibits, parades, and other events. Knowing the power of archaeology to address cultural connections between the past, present, and future, and realizing the importance of answering opportunity when it knocks, several archaeologists in the Department of Anthropology proposed a public archaeology project as part of the celebration.[1] The institution's first dormitory, called Saints' Rest by early students after a popular devotional of the time, seemed the perfect focus for exploring early campus history.

Our goals were to educate our academic community about archaeology and address preservation and research priorities while helping the community strengthen its sense of heritage. One of my interests in the project, given the nature of the sesquicentennial celebration, was how we might use and contribute to the developing specialization of community archaeology. At the heart of all community archaeology projects lies the recognition that "communities have a sense of their own past and they want to be part of the decision-making process regarding their own heritage development" (Shackel 2004: 2). Our challenge was to help the community develop a sense of heritage linking what began as a bold, innovative experiment in education for the common man (Widder 2005) with a modern research institution that is one of the most successful land-grant universities in the nation. I present a summary of the many ways in which this project was used in heritage building and to educate our community about archaeology. Through the interactions with archaeological research, members of our community came to see the archaeological remains of Saints' Rest as more than just a buried pile of bricks and mortar; they found value and meaning in material remains of the past. The examples presented here also provide the context from which we gained a unique perspective as archaeologists embedded in a community. In the conclusion I offer a number of insights for community archaeology in general.

Community Archaeology and Saints' Rest

Community archaeology is a form of public archaeology and shares some concerns with indigenous archaeology, reflexive archaeology, and efforts to decolonize archaeology (Hodder 2003; Marshall 2002; McGimsey 1972; Moser et al. 2002; Sandlin and Bey 2006; Smith and Wobst 2005; Watkins 2000). What sets community archaeology apart from other public archaeology is that the community retains partial control of all aspects of the project, from planning stages through curation and postfieldwork activities. This was certainly the case with the Saints' Rest project, as archaeologists shared control of various aspects of the project (for example, extent of excavation, publicity, classroom outreach projects) with key community groups. I define the community for this project very broadly as students, alumni, administration, faculty, staff, and members of the local area who feel a connection with the school. These groups include various subgroups, each with different concerns and interests in the creation and celebration of academic heritage.

Sharing control in community archaeology requires developing more interpersonal relationships and working with many more members of the community than in most traditional archaeology. In the Saints' Rest project archaeologists worked primarily with administration and student stakeholders, but other groups contributed and weighed in on matters, as discussed below. Community archaeology also requires a much different and broader range of skills than any single archaeologist possesses. In addition to having traditional field skills, archaeologists may collaborate with local organizations, provide field and museum training, interview community members, and develop tourism (Moser et al. 2002). Doing this kind of archaeology within the archaeologists' own community requires similar investment and relationship-building, but being embedded has distinct advantages. At Saints' Rest these advantages included insights into stakeholder group membership and some of their concerns and dynamics, knowledge of existing community resources to enhance the project's effectiveness, and the community's recognition that the archaeologists are themselves a stakeholder group within the community.

This kind of archaeology has given little consideration to nontraditional communities and instead has addressed the needs of residentially and/or ethnically defined communities. One issue that will need to be addressed with nontraditional communities is whether they are communities at all. Is the college campus a community? And if so, who are its members? Generally, community can be defined based on traditional notions of spatially and temporally distinct aggregations of people (such as a specific rural or urban community), but we can also conceive of community by focusing on identity, agency, and social boundaries (Anderson 1987; Sen 2002; Zimmerman 2005). Our academic community is defined by a combination of these—some members live in the area for a time, the different groups have many kinds of interactions, and we share certain values and linkages to the institution. Descent within the academic community is remarkable, as it is reckoned by a mix of historical, cultural, and symbolic factors (Singleton and Orser 2003). Students and alumni are part of a long descent line originating with the occupants of the first dormitory. Likewise, the administration, faculty, and staff are part of a tradition also beginning at the inception of the college.

In the Saints' Rest project, stakeholders are members of the community with an interest in creation and celebration of its heritage. Our alums form a diasporic group (Singleton and Orser 2003). Unlike most traditional diasporic groups, our stakeholders share a "homeland" experience then become part of the diaspora. For the academic community to remain viable and successful, both the local and the diasporic student/alumni groups need to be engaged in heritage building and understand its symbols and ideology. At Saints' Rest we included many different types of events and media to reach these diverse groups.

Universities tend to be very good at building a sense of tradition and allegiance to the institution; increasingly, their financial well-being depends on it. Heritage has an important role to play in the identity of a university community and in strengthening that sense of tradition and allegiance. Heritage is not simply something that exists in any community but is created by its members. It may be shaped and displayed by those in power, but heritage can have multiple meanings for different stakeholders; archaeologists may work with any or all of these groups (diZerega Wall et al. 2004; Mullins 2004; Shackel 2004). Students, administrators, and archaeologists at Saints' Rest experienced firsthand how heritage is negotiated and shaped by our interactions with each other and the ways in which we imbue the material past with meaning. In this way, archaeologists served the community in a manner that goes beyond traditional excavation and interpretation.

As a relatively new approach, community archaeology raises some questions about the role of archaeology and the archaeologist working within a community. One of the issues is the integration of scientific research with the community's needs. It has been suggested that community archaeologists will need to forego their own research questions at least some of the time (Marshall 2002). Unlike public archaeology in general, community archaeology attempts to reduce the risk of imposing our own sense of importance on the site and alienating the community. Others may value the material culture of the past and the heritage they wish to create in ways that differ from our own scientific value system (Matthews 2004; Waterton 2005). In the following sections, the role of archaeologists and their attendant ethical concerns are explored through the window of Saints' Rest.

Saints' Rest Foundation: Understanding and Engaging Stakeholders

As members of our community, Saints' Rest archaeologists enjoyed insights into stakeholder needs and how we might mesh those needs with good archaeological practices. We found that archaeologists have an important role in helping the community initially envision what archaeology might have to offer, in addressing misconceptions, and in clarifying what such a project will require.

From the start, discussions among archaeologists, students, and administrators about the possibility of excavating Saints' Rest made it clear that stakeholders had different interests and concerns. The archaeologists were concerned about preservation issues, and our exploratory research questions developed out of our interaction with the archival record and historic accounts of the institution's history (Kuhn 1955; Widder 2005).[2] We were also focused on the field school as an educational experience and on educating the rest of the community about archaeology in general. Students seemed particularly interested in learning about early student life and seeing artifacts belonging to earlier students. However, having the opportunity to learn field techniques was of central concern. This focus on hands-on learning was also valued by the higher administration, archaeologists, the larger student body, and the faculty. Many stakeholders shared a concern with preservation of heritage resources, but this meant different things to various stakeholders.

Initially, finding common ground with stakeholder groups that were fo-

Figure 13.1. The top of the foundation wall lay just a few inches below the sidewalk and marker seen in this photo at the far end of the wall. (Courtesy of the Michigan State University Department of Anthropology)

cused on upkeep and development of the modern campus was most challenging. Although the higher administration and others were interested in knowing what archaeological resources existed, they were also concerned about resources such as trees, walkways, and the parklike atmosphere of the campus "sacred space" (Stanford and Dewhurst 2002). Although it was not voiced, there may have been some reluctance about doing archaeology and setting a precedent that could mean slowing construction projects on campus. In her interviews with stakeholders, Heather Mustonen (2007) found an element of skepticism that any archaeological remains existed. From this perspective, disturbance of green space, the possibility of damaging valuable trees, inconvenience, and safety issues made an archaeological project less than attractive.

Some concern for preservation focused on artifacts with tangential connections to Saints' Rest, such as the cement marker set into the sidewalk in the early twentieth century, which reads "N.E. CORNER SAINTS' REST BUILT 1856 BURNED DEC 9 1876." Generations of students walked over this unassuming marker, and for some it became part of campus folklore. A representative of one of the alumni groups contacted us early in the project to voice concerns about removal of the plaque, which remains in place today. The plaque itself represented a tradition with meaning to be shared with descendant students. Most stakeholders had not considered, however, that remains of the building and its contents might be right below their feet (Figure 13.1). It was the archeologists' role to help these groups envision what might lie beneath the surface and what symbolic and research-related value it might have.

Archival work was integral to the project from the start, as we incorporated different levels of document use while introducing students to critical reading of such resources (for example, Noël Hume 1969; Orser 2004; Schuyler 1988). Initial work in the archives produced inventories and personal accounts of life in the dormitory, but no blueprints were found. A handful of photographs and various descriptions gave clues to the building's size and function. The daunting list of problems due to substandard construction that was compiled shortly after the building was complete piqued the interest of administrators and students. These data also helped us to illustrate the kinds of information that archaeology might provide about the dormitory.

Armed with historical information on the size and location of the dormitory, faculty and graduate students were able to probe from the cement sidewalk marker and roughly delineate the boundaries of the dormitory. Thankfully, the marker actually was at the northeast corner of the ruin. For the administrative stakeholder groups, this information helped address their concerns centering on understanding what we might actually find and perhaps, from their perspective, helped justify the use of valuable labor and other resources. We also worked very closely with these groups to address their safety concerns and limit damage to the landscape.

Building on this foundation and incorporating informal discussions with students, alums, and administrators, we put forth a proposal to use historical archaeology as a unique mechanism through which the campus community could engage with the past in a meaningful and powerful way. In the end, I think our proposal was acceptable to the university administration and funded for three reasons. First, the project had value as a way to highlight the kind of hands-on, active learning that was unique to MSU's beginnings and is central to our approach today. Second, it was a unique, timely, and appropriate contribution to the Sesquicentennial Anniversary. Third, the Department of Anthropology and its chair had established a relationship of trust with the administration through a history of delivering on its promises.

Saints' Rest Bricks and Mortar: Connections to the Past

Unpacking my favorite yellow toolbox and demonstrating at leisure the proper usage of the plumb-bob, trowel, folding rule, Munsell Chart, and other tools is one of my favorite first day of field school rituals. Saints' Rest was quite a different experience. Here our first day was marked with an opening ceremony (complete with podium and electronics!) largely organized by our Office of University Relations. The media were in attendance, recording speeches and interviewing our anxious students on their first day. MSU president Lou Anna K. Simon, dean of the College of Social Sciences Marietta Baba, and Department of Anthropology chair Lynne Goldstein ceremonially broke ground. Their participation in the program along with students firmly placed the archaeology of Saints' Rest in the public domain and sent the message that this was a project by and for the community. It began a dialogue with the broader campus community through media outlets and University Relations webpages that would last throughout the fieldwork phase of the project. And eventually I did unpack my toolbox.

After this opening event, stakeholders interfaced with the Saints' Rest project through many formal and informal avenues. These can only be briefly summarized here (they are discussed at length in Mustonen 2007). At these events and interactions material culture became a focal point of connection with the past. In postexcavation interviews, the ability of archaeology to provide tangible connections to the past was one of the most frequently cited observations about the project (Mustonen 2007). At the same time, material culture also occasioned stakeholder interactions and discourse about the past through which a sense of heritage emerged.

Formal avenues of interaction targeted toward both local and diasporic groups were facilitated by web-based and other media, courses, open houses, and other events. University Relations and the College of Social Science constructed and updated a website that provided excellent prolonged exposure (Figure 13.2). The site included video footage, photographs, event information, and links to the Sesquicentennial website and departmental information (http://special.newsroom.msu.edu/digMSU/).[3] A two-day open house at the end of the field school brought hundreds of visitors to the site. Students and archaeology faculty put together exhibits of artifacts and archival information, led tours, and engaged in a multitude of conversations about the dormitory, archaeology, and early student life (Figure 13.3).

Community members frequently told us that the excavation should be kept open indefinitely. After explaining the logistical and preservation-re-

Figure 13.2. Working with University Relations photographers. (Courtesy of the Michigan State University Department of Anthropology)

Figure 13.3. Artifact displays, excavation tours, and select archival resources mounted on the security fence provided many opportunities for interaction. (Courtesy of the Michigan State University Department of Anthropology)

lated reasons why this would not be a good idea, we then talked about ways in which others would be able to see and hear about the excavation. We also extended our plans for interaction opportunities. At the request of President Simon, two additional open houses were held after the close of the field season. Select excavation units were protected and security fencing was left in place to preserve the site for viewing during convocation events early in the fall semester. The final open house occurred during tailgating hours for the first home football game of the season.

Public classes, formal lectures, and lab volunteering opportunities were also offered. A women's club, high schools, and an engineering club were among the many interested groups in the greater Lansing community that requested presentations. A two-week high school field experience through the MSU Museum ran concurrently with the field school, as did a teachers' workshop. The local chapter of the Michigan Archaeology Society hosted two evenings of lab work and enjoyed a workshop on preservation. A short continuing education class also attracted members of the broader community.

Located within a busy area of campus, the field school provided ample opportunity for informal encounters, and we engaged with members of the campus community on a daily basis. Many visited regularly, including President Simon, faculty, staff, and students. This prolonged and ongoing informal forum for interaction was as important as the scheduled events discussed above, if not more so. Display cases of recently found artifacts and project information were always available on site, and students and faculty alike interacted with individuals and groups. A number of closer relationships developed, bringing a broad range of interests and expertise together in the excavation. For example, identification of most of our wood architectural features and artifacts was done by Frank Telewski, professor of plant biology, who made regular visits to the site and advised us on stabilization techniques. Historians and art historians provided insightful historical context. Others proposed experimental collaborations in data recovery and botanical research. University and local community firefighters contributed to our understanding of the fire that had destroyed the building (Quates et al. 2006). The university mason helped us understand construction and removed a segment of the foundation for future exhibit purposes. University photographers and other media specialists aided in recording and disseminating information to a broad audience.

While many individuals found their own connection to Saints' Rest, the community archaeologist can also help make the past relevant for others

(Bowser 2001; Shackel 2004). In an academic community that originally admitted only white males, we worked to find ways to connect our heritage to the modern and very diverse community. Although a course of study for women fully integrating them into the institution would not be formalized until 1896 (Widder 2005), women were able to take courses in 1876 and even lived in the Saints' Rest dormitory: "ladies were admitted last March into a few rooms of the hall in the floor across from the family of the steward . . . 10 ladies have been in attendance studying botany, trigonometry, surveying, bookkeeping, French and horticulture" (T. C. Abbott to Baldwin, December 11, 1876, Box 861, Folder 26, TCAP/MSUAHC). This was juxtaposed with another reality for women in the nineteenth century.

> 2 girls are employed to do the whole of the washing, ironing & soap making. 2 women are in the kitchen as cooks. 1 woman in the same place for general work such as the clearing of dishes and the preparation of vegetables. 2 girls have charge of the dining room. 1 girl has charge of all the chamber work. 1 girl is employed to keep the halls, cellar washrooms, stairs clean and also does the washing of the coarse towels needed in the dressing and washing room, and also makes the candles used in the building. (R. F. Johnstone to J. M. Gregory, October 27, 1859, Box 1141, Folder 66, MKC/MSUAHC)

While many found the changing status of women at the university an interesting part of our heritage, this also stimulated conversation about the changing nature of behavior and the archaeological record (see Lewis, this volume). When we gave impromptu tours or talked with hundreds of stakeholders at the open houses, dynamic aspects of the past such as these were presented along with the archaeological record. As we guided visitors through the layout of the basement, women who worked in the basement kitchen, made the soap and candles, and otherwise ensured that the boardinghouse ran smoothly were made visible. Through discussions of occupants and the changing status of women of the time, visitors realized that inkwells as well as hairpins found in the excavation could have belonged to women (Figure 13.4). Bricks and mortar became not simply demarcations of walls and hallways but the remnants of a common heritage where real people, much like themselves, had lived, worked, and studied (Figure 13.5).

Today's larger Lansing area community regularly deals with student behavior and made connections between past and present campus life. Our posting of early institutional rules along with the archaeological record led

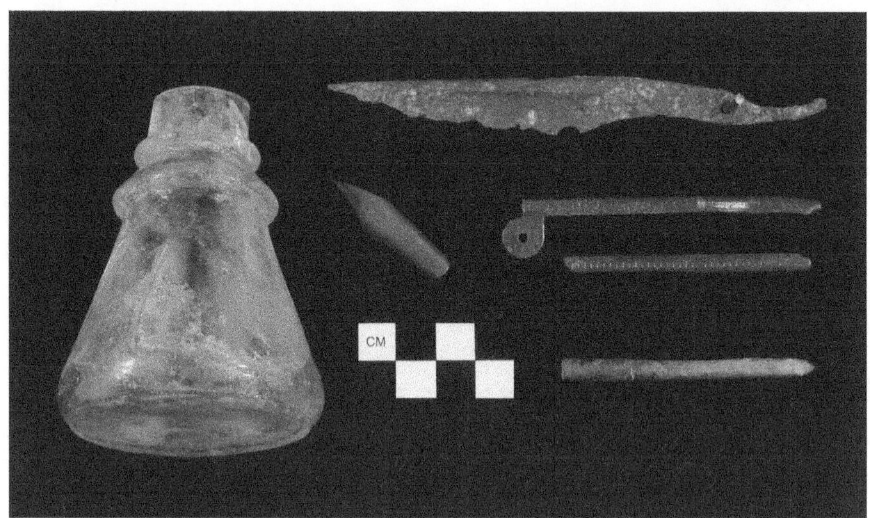

Figure 13.4. Inkwells, pen nibs, and other writing implements were common at Saints' Rest; (*top right*) scissors and (*middle right*) a compass were also recovered. (Courtesy of the Michigan State University Department of Anthropology)

Figure 13.5. A section of a basement wall dividing the raised central hallway (the photo board sits upon a cast iron stove) and rooms. (Courtesy of the Michigan State University Department of Anthropology)

to the common observance that "students will be students" and that breaking the rules was nothing new. Nineteenth-century institutional rules included attendance, prohibitions on "spirituous or intoxicating liquors . . . use of tobacco and other narcotics . . . obscene or profane language . . . games of chance, firearms," and calls for "upright and gentlemanly deportment" (M/RSPI 1858). We recovered evidence for most of these prohibited items in the archaeological record, and the rest were documented in archival sources. At the same time, the more positive tradition of physical labor and a passion for learning shared by present students and their ancestors was also highlighted.

The excavation provided an opportunity to illustrate the various uses of historical documents in archaeology, and the written record stimulated discussion about the broader social context of our heritage. As excavations proceeded, as a way to contextualize their archaeological findings, we had graduate teaching assistants select passages from archival material to read to the students each morning before work began. Sometimes these passages related to particular areas in the dormitory or activities that took place there. At other times archival sources reflected concerns and opinions on a variety of broad topics, such as the Civil War, Charles Darwin's newly published ideas about natural selection, and the role of scientific method and goals of popular education. Through these readings and discussion, students were actively creating a past with which they and other community members could connect.

Sometimes the linkages between what happened in the past and the present were easily made. As students excavated jumbled masses of cast iron stoves and stovepipe, we were also reading accounts of early students tending those same stoves and cutting wood for fuel (Figure 13.6). Connecting with ancestral groups is enhanced by recovery of personal items, such as a toothbrush and other toiletry items (Figure 13.7). For others, a segment of brick hallway or the massiveness of the foundation wall gives substance to the past.

Sometimes connections to the past were more symbolically laden and were negotiated among stakeholder groups. Around 1860 a petition signed by thirty-one students was submitted to the faculty, asking that they not be discriminated against with a coffee and tea tax (Students to faculty, circa 1859–60, Box 862, Folder 3, LRFP). While our students could relate to the original petitioners' caffeine habits and "chemical and physiological laws" related to their use and draw on age-old student vs. faculty/administration

Figure 13.6. Stove parts, bricks, and other artifacts were jumbled in the rubble layer. The darker ash zone on top of the basement floor can be seen to the right. (Courtesy of the Michigan State University Department of Anthropology)

Figure 13.7. Toiletry and other personal items. (Courtesy of the Michigan State University Department of Anthropology)

sentiments, this account also served as inspiration for negotiation of the past.

Among the many things a community learns as it does archaeology is that the material things that link us to the past may have different meanings for stakeholders. These meanings can form as archaeology occurs. In our case, bricks and mortar literally become more than bricks and mortar through community archaeology.

As the excavation proceeded and our piles of bricks grew, so did our worries about what we would do with these artifacts. Bricks that were recovered within the rubble layers were obviously from the building but were of little scientific value. We archaeologists talked at great length about what to do with these artifacts. Curation of all the brick in our repository space was out of the question. But were we obliged to curate them? If we collected a representative sample (there were several kinds of bricks) could we rebury the rest? How would other members of the community perceive discarding the bricks? Would the administration want to sell them? Although we could not curate them, their sale would violate the anticommercialization ethic. None of the archaeologists were particularly comfortable with any of these options. Seeking help from the professional community, Goldstein explained our situation to a number of archaeologists with experience in dealing with these issues. The nationally prominent historical archaeologists and others who focus on archaeological ethics agreed unanimously—the bricks must not be sold but could be given to donors as gifts. While this might have been the end of discussions on some projects, our community focus meant that this perspective was only one among several.

Interestingly, many of the students had another viewpoint that other stakeholders (including the archaeologists) had not considered. The field school students felt they had a sweat equity investment in those bricks—the bricks and mortar had become a symbol of their dedication and hard work. They found the idea of using the bricks to benefit some unknown aspect of the university completely unacceptable.

Drawing upon their ancestor's petition approach, the field school students crafted a letter to President Simon. The students essentially wanted two things. First, they wanted the donations to benefit archaeology and specifically undergraduate field experiences in archaeology. Second, they wanted a monument for Saints' Rest, something that would tell others about the past and their role in bringing it to light for the community.

At this juncture it is important to refocus on the role of the archaeologist in intracommunity negotiations of cultural material This story has a happy ending because of the role of the archaeologist as steward of the past. This includes not only educating others about the possibilities of what lies beneath the ground but also sharing our ethical and other concerns so that they can be good stewards of the past. Both the students and the administration needed the expertise of archaeologists. Stakeholders needed to understand the ethical principles regarding what should and should not happen with the bricks. They also needed to understand issues of preservation. For example, at one point the students wanted a monument constructed of the old bricks and needed the archaeologists to explain that their physical condition would make that a poor choice. Likewise, the administration understood the broader ethical issues of selling the bricks once Goldstein made clear our concerns.

Another influential factor in the ultimate disposition of the bricks was the students' wishes expressed in their letter. Throughout the excavation President Simon regularly visited the site and interacted with the students. She saw firsthand their passion for archaeology and was impressed with how seriously they took their role in uncovering the campus heritage. And so, when the students voiced concern about the bricks, President Simon listened.

Several very positive outcomes resulted from the brick debate. President Simon personally recognized the efforts of students and faculty at the close of the project with a letter along with a small plaque. She also told each student and faculty member to select a brick to keep. Significantly, the administration also recognized the heritage symbolism of the bricks, which are now in storage awaiting further use in fund-raising campaigns. Rather than waiting for future donation-related funds, President Simon allocated a generous annual sum for support of undergraduate field experiences. A two-sided permanent monument has also been placed at the site, and the field school students contributed to the content (Figure 13.8).

In any archaeology project, and particularly in community archaeology, making the findings of fieldwork relevant and accessible to the community is a necessity. In addition to the monument, we cultivated continued involvement of the community and incorporation of new stakeholders, focusing on exhibition and continuing research and preservation. To this end, the university supported a sequence of classes culminating in an online museum exhibit. The first course allowed us to do much-needed conservation work to stabilize metal and other artifacts. Professional conservators instructed and worked with students continuing the practical hands-on learning aspect of the project. At the same time, students also conducted extensive archival investigations centered on the following themes that they helped to

Figure 13.8. Two sides of the historical marker. The "Saints' Rest Excavation" side explains that the site was excavated by MSU archaeology students in 2005, talks about the use of archival information, and summarizes the artifacts and building remains. The "Saints' Rest" side identifies the significance of this building and College Hall and discusses the modest beginnings of the college, when students slept two to a bed. (Courtesy of the Michigan State University Department of Anthropology)

define: construction, work, women, architecture, the fire, health and illness, classroom, furnishings and contents of the dormitory, student backgrounds, surrounding community, food, and social activities. The second course was designed to build upon the field, lab, archival, and conservation work to create the online exhibit.

To date, the final collaborative piece of the Saints' Rest project is the online exhibit developed by the second postexcavation class. Students in this course included several who had been involved in the excavation and/or the archival and conservation course but also students new to the Saints' Rest project. Students learned about different aspects of the project and were provided with comments and insights from earlier students. Working together, they defined and developed three main topics, which became the main sections of the website: Learn about Archaeology, Discover Student Life, and Explore Campus (http://anthropology.msu.edu/saints_rest_gallery/index.html).

Saints' Rest Windows: Archaeological and Other Insights

As defined by Paul Shackel (2004: 10), "Heritage is based on a shared value system that people have about culture and their past. Heritage is what each one of us individually or collectively wishes to preserve and pass on to the next generation." Through the Saints' Rest project it was possible to guide our university community on an exploration of our past. By interacting with the archaeological record, stakeholders began to form ideas and negotiate meaning about what parts of our culture and its material remains we value. From an archaeologist's perspective we were successful at heritage building as well as in research and preservation realms. In addition to the chapter by Lewis in this volume and Mustonen's thesis, we now curate a well-documented collection from an important period for our institution and the nation (encompassing the Civil War). We successfully demonstrated the nature of archaeological remains related to our institutional history and the need for further archaeology on campus.[4]

To gauge whether the community views the project as a success, we can turn to Mustonen's (2007) postexcavation interviews, media accounts, and other observations. Three common themes identified by Mustonen's interviewees as positive aspects of the project included making history tangible, hands-on learning, and firsthand exposure to archaeological research. We have on file twenty-five newspaper and other popular print articles published about the excavation, reflecting many of the same positive outcomes. Themes identified in the articles include topics connected to heritage such as links to the past, early student lifeways, and preservation. These topics appeared in 80 percent of the articles. The educational value of the project in student training, typically emphasizing the real-life and hands-on experience of the field school, was included in 24 percent of the articles. The public is interested in the practice of archaeology; 52 percent of the articles discussed details of how archaeology is done. The project earned a State of Michigan Governor's Award for Preservation, which also speaks to the success of the project from the public's perspective.

For those contemplating the archaeology of academia, Saints' Rest provides an excellent example of how useful a community archaeology approach may be. In our case, the community focus was key to gaining permission to conduct any archaeology on campus. Community archaeology enabled us to achieve our research and preservation agenda while educating the community about archaeology. A community approach gave us insight into the different ways people think about the past and its material record and allowed us to witness the development of a sense of heritage among those who participated.

From the perspective of Saints' Rest, several observations regarding the role of the archaeologist may benefit the developing field of community archaeology. Work in nontraditional communities is a worthwhile endeavor. It may provide unique insights into the ways communities value the past and use the material record in heritage building. I found the archaeologists' role as negotiators, educators, and archaeological advocates most vital to doing this kind of archaeology. Communities will need guidance regarding the archaeological record—its nature, potential, interpretation, and care. It is our responsibility to "enlist public support for the stewardship of the archaeological record . . . explain and promote the use of archaeological methods and techniques in understanding human behavior and culture . . . [and] communicate archaeological interpretations of the past" (SAA Committee on Ethics 2007). Our commitment to the community does not excuse us from ensuring that the destructive excavation we do is based on sound archaeological research and practice. If we can teach the value of scientific study and preservation of the archaeological record while helping the community members meet their own needs we will have participated not only in good community archaeology but in good archaeology.

Notes

1. Lynne Goldstein, Department of Anthropology chair, along with faculty members Kenneth Lewis, William Lovis, and Jodie O'Gorman initiated the Saints' Rest project. O'Gorman and Lewis instructed the field school, and O'Gorman taught the subsequent courses. Lewis and graduate student Heather Mustonen directed the inventory-related lab work.

2. The research and preservation agenda for the Saints' Rest project included: (1) an examination of architectural and other organizational and aesthetic aspects of the building itself (as no blueprints or interior photographs survive); (2) documentation of material culture from a tight temporal span that included the Civil War; and (3) documentation of the changing function of the boarding hall and archaeological interpretation of such buildings (Mustonen 2007; Lewis, this volume).

3. The Council for the Advance and Support of Education awarded the MSU University Relations staff the 2006 Circle of Excellence Silver Medal for a Year Long Special Event for their efforts on the Saints' Rest project.

4. Three years after the Saints' Rest project, we have a Campus Archaeology Program funded through the Graduate School and the Office of Planning and Budget. We are now notified of all planned construction and remodeling projects. A graduate student serves as the campus archaeologist, and we have developed an undergraduate internship program.

14

The Campus as Cultural Landscape

Archaeology and the Formation of Collegiate Identity

LAURA JONES

Collegiate identity is strongly connected to places—student residences, libraries, athletic facilities, theaters—where students spend their time and have memorable experiences. Archaeological field schools on college campuses, like community archaeology projects elsewhere, should also create a lasting memory of place for students at the site of the excavation (Bardavio et al. 2004). Campus field experiences should build a deeper connection to the entire campus as a cultural landscape, shaped over time by the actions and intentions of a variety of stakeholders, including the students themselves. Moving from an intensive exploration of a highly local site to the broader patterns of the campus landscape, students' learning from the field school should then carry forward and outward as they move on in their lives and careers (Peters 1997: 80–81). The goal is to create an experience that creates a sense of social identity and responsibility connected to the campus, of course, but also to the conservation of cultural landscapes and heritage sites everywhere.

This chapter is a reflection of my own experiences teaching archaeological field methods more than a dozen times, first as a graduate teaching and research assistant (1985–91) and later as campus archaeologist at Stanford University (1994 to present). When invited to teach the course again in 2008 after a six-year hiatus, I realized that it was time for me to reexamine the form and content of my teaching in this foundational course in our program. This chapter presents a new approach to the special teaching opportunity presented by field school excavations on a college campus. The approach brings together strands from recent writing on the teaching of archaeology, the revival of liberal education, and cultural geographies.

I began by asking myself three questions. First, who am I teaching? And as a corollary question: what do they already know? Students have a wide range of personal and academic experiences to connect to the class project. Activating these connections is a key strategy in integrative learning. Second, what do they learn in the field methods class? Students in archaeological field methods fall into two basic groups: archaeology (or anthropology) majors and students from other majors who just want to have the experience of participating in a dig. Relatively few of my students—including the archaeology and anthropology majors—go on to professional careers in archaeology. I reviewed the course lists, and of the more than three hundred students I've had in field methods courses perhaps a dozen are practicing professionals in archaeology today.

Our field methods course at Stanford has always been focused on providing a first experience in field excavation that prepares students—primarily our majors—to take advantage of a host of opportunities to dig at major sites in the United States and abroad. Some authors note the "weeding" effect of field excavation in helping students decide not to pursue archaeology as a career: the reality of fieldwork rarely lives up to its romantic reputation. Certainly it is easier for all involved if students discover that they don't enjoy excavation before they arrive on the overseas site for the long summer field season. The nonarchaeology majors were of interest as potential recruits (not that I recall many of them changing majors)—and they performed precisely the same activities—but the focus of the pedagogy was on developing archaeologists. This pattern of high attention to a relatively small proportion of the participating students is also reported by other authors (Perry 2004).

In the next section I review the literature describing the field school experience in preparing archaeologists, before turning to the larger issue of the place of archaeological fieldwork in undergraduate liberal education. Here I refocus my attention on those students who choose to follow paths other than archaeology. What do they learn in the campus field school? I can do more to help them create connections between archaeology and other disciplines, making the field school a more memorable and meaningful experience.

Archaeology for Archaeologists

The teaching of archaeology generally has become much more than the teaching of culture history, as it moves toward a view of teaching as "the emancipation of the archaeological imagination to be mobilized to encourage critical thinking as much as to gain greater understandings of the human past" (Conkey and Tringham 1996: 247). The Society for American Archaeology's MATRIX (Making Archaeology Teaching Relevant in the XXIth Century) project, sponsored by the National Science Foundation, specifies seven curriculum reform principles for the teaching of archaeology:

> (1) Foster stewardship by making explicit the proposition that archaeological resources are nonrenewable and finite; (2) Foster understanding that archaeological remains are endowed with meaning, and that archaeologists are not the sole proprietors or arbitrators of that meaning because there are diverse interests in the past that archaeologists study. Archaeologists, therefore, share their knowledge with many diverse audiences and engage these audiences in defining the meaning and direction of their projects; (3) Recognize diverse interests in the past; (4) Promote awareness of the social relevance of archaeological data and its interpretations; (5) Infuse the curriculum with professional ethics and values that frame archaeological practice; (6) Develop fundamental liberal arts skills in written and oral communication and computer literacy; and (7) Develop fundamental disciplinary skills in fieldwork and laboratory analysis and promote effective learning via the incorporation of problem solving, either through case studies or internships. (Bender 2000)

In recent years, following the trend toward greater reflexivity, archaeologists have turned their scholarly attention to the archaeological field excavation as a subject for inquiry. Some have focused on the excavation as a special environment for student and adult learning, ideally suited to the application of collaborative, problem-based, constructivist theories of learning (Perry 2004; Sandlin and Bey 2006). The field excavation experience is described as an intense intellectual and social apprenticeship, a process that supports the transformative experience of becoming an archaeologist (Perry 2004). From these accounts it is clear that for those who continue in archaeology the first field excavation experience is a formative one. Other researchers have examined the field excavation site ethnographically and identified subtle patterns in excavation practices that teach lessons about hierarchy and gender in the archaeological profession as well as more practical skills (Gero 1996). Clearly, students are learning social practices as well as archaeological skills and local history in field school classes.

In a response to the SAA's call for curriculum reform, and its own interests in raising standards in the field, the Register of Professional Archaeologists

(RPA) developed a certification program for field schools that address the seven SAA curriculum principles and meet other specific guidelines. The first guideline concerns the purpose of field schools:

> The primary objective of an academic field school must be the training of students. Thus, the field school should provide the initial field experiences required as the first step in her/his development as a professional archeologist (in accordance with RPA standards). Other goals (such as employment, contract work, or salvage of threatened resources) must be secondary to the goals of student training and education. (RPA n.d.: 2)

The basic skills of mapping, sampling, excavating, and recording continue to be important in their view, but there are pressures to add more advanced content as well:

> This is how most our students continue to be introduced to archaeology and I believe it is an appropriate and essential experience. No matter how long you've been in archaeology you will remember coming face to face with the archaeological record for the first time. I also believe, however, that as a profession we can enhance these early archaeological experiences for our students. Today's field school needs to represent today's archaeology, instilling knowledge of new cultural properties regulations, international antiquities laws, increasing the inclusion of descendant aboriginal populations in our research, and applying the many recent technological advances in the realms of remote sensing, preservation, and computerization of many field tasks. (RPA n.d.)

Archaeologists in Europe and Australia are also calling for reform in the content of field school experiences, echoing the concern regarding the gap between the field school experience and professional practice standards expected upon graduation (Bender 2000; Colley 2004; Nassaney 2004). The common thread is a concern for understanding what preparation is necessary to enter the profession: how many hours of field and lab work, or years of experience, or graduate degrees and certificates and what counts as evidence for mastery of the complex legal, ethical, and social dimensions of archaeological practice.

Despite repeated calls for standardization of data recovery methods and movements to "register" or "certify" professional archaeologists, a uniform set of procedures and criteria has not been widely adopted. This reflects in part the gap between academic archaeologists and archaeologists in public or private practice. It also reflects the tremendous diversity of highly local contexts in which we practice. As a teacher, I believe that archaeologists should have a strong ethical grounding and deep understanding of the basic principles of scientific excavation, including the value of using standard techniques to increase comparability among data sets. But it would be a disservice to my students if they learned the inflexible notion that there is only one right way to collect data in the field—especially as they report to me that as soon as they join another excavation project they encounter variations in practice.[1]

Even if we question the call for teaching uniform standards of data collection, there is a legitimate concern that we go beyond data collection to introduce students to the full cycle of archaeological research—from proposal to publication. Further, we are asked to acquaint students with the wider context of the archaeological project: stakeholders that may include diverse local community groups, landowners, government officials, property developers, construction companies, tourism promoters, and collectors as well as the dizzying variety of regulatory processes at the local, state, national, and international levels.[2] Viewed from within the constraints of a ten-week academic quarter, this seems to imply less time for learning and practicing field methods. I will return to this problem in a moment, as I believe that one pedagogical approach may address both the challenge of providing comprehensive professional training to archaeologists and the desire to provide better liberal education to the larger group of my students who choose other paths.

Archaeology for Liberal Education

Archaeological courses at many colleges fulfill "general education" requirements designed to ensure that undergraduates receive a well-rounded education. A growing theme in the undergraduate curriculum is the revival of the notion of "liberal education" as the holistic formation of intellectual habits of mind that transcend disciplinary lines—such as critical thinking, rhetorical fluency, and creativity—along with moral formation as a responsible citizen (Schneider 2004). The key pedagogy for liberal education is "integrative learning," where students draw together the threads of their experiences in college courses, at work, and in their communities. Integrative learning is a strategy to build connections between the abstract and the concrete, between theory and practice, synthesizing knowledge across domains and bridging from understanding to application (Walker et al. 2008). A number of colleges have approached the reform of their entire undergraduate curriculum from the perspective of fostering integrative learning in service of liberal education (Huber et al. 2007).

These goals closely mirror the curriculum reform principles promoted by the Society of American Archaeology, as outlined above. A further description of the pedagogy of integrative learning is helpful: "Many familiar pedagogies can serve the goal of integrative learning. Indeed, just about any format that allows groups of students to turn their attention to common problems, issues, themes or tasks—the seminar for example—can prompt integrative learning, if the topic is of sufficient scope and interest to be elucidated by insights from different disciplines and perspectives" (Huber et al. 2007: 4).

Archaeological field schools are well suited to encourage integrative learning. To be effective as a teacher in promoting integrative learning in my archaeological field methods course, however, requires that I make an intentional effort: "first, designing courses with integrative learning in mind, and second, asking questions and gathering evidence about the specific challenges and dilemmas that students are facing as they develop their capacities as integrative learners" (Huber et al. 2007: 4). This kind of teaching takes place in a "changing world where disciplinary and curricular isolation are neither feasible nor desirable" (Huber et al. 2007: 4).

An Integrative Approach to Teaching Archaeological Field Methods

The integrative learning approach applies easily to nearly any field school site: archaeological research is an excellent site for integrative learning, as the process of excavation draws on skills and knowledge from a number of prior experiences. These include the basic knowledge of mathematics necessary to lay out an excavation grid, describe the volume of irregular solids, and understand sampling strategies and basic statistics. Students apply principles of scientific reasoning drawn from basic science classes, and previous coursework in history or prehistory is extremely useful. The students' ability to connect these general skills and knowledge to the specific case of the field excavation reinforces their understanding of both the general knowledge—mathematics, science, history—and the discipline of archaeology. This kind of integrative learning can and should take place on every field excavation. The pedagogical shift is to make the integrative goal explicit: encourage students to identify connections and explore them critically both informally in discussions in the field and lab and reflectively in writing their field journals.

The special case of local excavations, however, allows for more ambitious attempts at integrative thinking. The proximity of content specialists working on the campus as colleagues (engineers, geologists, architects, biologists, and others) provides opportunities for integrating multiple disciplines in the real-time teaching and interpretation of archaeological findings. In our field school that excavated the rubble-filled foundations of Leland and Jane Stanford's Palo Alto home (which collapsed in the 1906 earthquake), colleagues in engineering, architecture, ethnobotany, materials conservation, and history were able to visit the field site and the laboratory, working side by side with our students and demonstrating the process of multidisciplinary problem-solving and interpretation that is central to understanding complex archaeological deposits (Jones et al. 1996; Reese et al. 2006). Moreover, this offered the opportunity to make data analysis and interpretation on this multiyear project more visible to undergraduate students during the field class, giving them a glimpse into the later stages of archaeological investigation as results are prepared for publication.

We have had similar success in our prehistoric site field schools with bringing specialists from biology, geology, and osteology, as well local Native Americans, to the field school and laboratory to work alongside our students. The proximity of the field site to the campus and the surrounding urban region makes this easy for everyone.

The students themselves can also be a source of diverse prior knowledge and experience. The local field school draws students and volunteers from a broader spectrum of interests than our field projects that require long-distance travel. In my field schools at Stanford we have had undergraduate majors in human biology, anthropology, engineering, mathematics, history, feminist studies, and so forth working side by side with volunteers or adult education students with professional careers in law, medicine, chemistry, real estate, teaching, engineering, architecture, and other fields. They may all be novice excavators, but an integrative pedagogy will connect their prior learning (talents and experience) to the complex problems of archaeological investigation. This should make for better archaeology, as well as more meaningful learning.

The proximity of the campus (and the possibility that students may be taking other courses at the same time as the field school) offers an opportunity for teachers to reinforce the power of integrative thinking. Some campuses offer programs that explicitly create connections for students by linking courses and course content, not just as prerequisites but as parts of a more complex, multidimensional whole. In our archaeology curriculum at Stanford we offer a number of "methods" courses taught in the classroom and the laboratory and a wide variety of field research opportunities around the world. Each class or excavation, however, is led by a different instructor. Our students are greatly assisted in integrating their learning across these experiences if we act intentionally to build connections between these experiences within our archaeology program.[3]

Surprisingly, it can be easier to design courses that create connections across disciplines. In our upcoming field school we will be investigating the ruin of a massive neoclassical men's gymnasium that collapsed in the 1906 earthquake and left not only an archaeological ruin but a lasting set of historical controversies: were poor design or shoddy construction materials responsible for the catastrophic structural failure of the building? Did decisions made by university co-founder Jane Stanford contribute to the catastrophe? The design of the gymnasium itself raises a host of topics about concepts of health, fitness, gender, and the body in the early years of American higher education. The site is linked to a campus construction project (a new performing arts center) and thus provides opportunities to teach the complexities of land-use decision-making as well.

In past years we have brought in specialists during the excavation on an ad hoc, opportunistic basis. If we had a special find that called for expert treatment, or a serendipitous occasion called a colleague to the campus, then our students had the opportunity to observe this firsthand. Rarely was it designed into the course. This year we are co-designing the course with colleagues from Civil and Environmental Engineering. This will greatly improve our understanding of the structural faults of the building and its behavior in the earthquake. It is also an opportunity for both engineering and archaeology students to learn from different approaches to mapping and digital reconstruction technologies.

To do justice to the broad range of possible topics for investigation we plan to organize the students into topic-based teams. Each team will generate research questions and propose methods to collect data relevant to those questions; these are expected to include archival methods as well as field excavation techniques. Following Margaret Conkey and Ruth Tringham's suggestions on a "feminist pedagogy in archaeology" (Conkey and Tringham 1996), we will rely on the students to teach themselves and each other through preparation of their research questions, proposals for investigation, and presentation of their results at the end of the course. Colleagues in engineering, gender studies, history, and law will also serve as "coaches" (in Conkey and Tringham's terms) for the student research teams.

This pedagogical approach preserves the strengths of our traditional field methods course: authentic sites, substantial time spent in excavation and laboratory analysis, a focus on teamwork, and substantial participation by local community members. The new format, however, requires greater intellectual initiative from our students, more reading and writing, and perhaps less time spent with a trowel in hand pushing lumps of clay through the screen. The teaching experiment is to see whether the students can achieve competence and confidence as archaeological investigators as we increase time spent in research design and interpretation and decrease time in the field and laboratory.[4]

The multidisciplinary, integrative learning approach to archaeological methods is easier to implement on campus than at remote sites. It is also easier to experiment with student-generated research designs when the university is the landowner/client to whom we are accountable for the results. The shift to a model that maximizes student learning (over approaches that privilege data collection based on a research design developed by the instructor) is one of the key insights that drove my rethinking of the course design based on wider trends in higher education reform. The second strand is the connection of the archaeological excavation to the campus as a cultural landscape and the power of this connection to foster deeper student commitment to the goals of the course and to the stewardship of heritage resources beyond the campus. The pedagogical expression of this idea is described in the next section.

The Campus as Cultural Landscape

In my role as campus archaeologist, I work every day with planners, architects, landscape architects, engineers, construction companies, and campus maintenance workers who create and sustain the cultural landscape of the campus. They work in a vocabulary of affinities, axes, connections, hierarchies of public and private, memory and rootedness. They are currently engaged in consciously re-creating the campus, based on the view that interaction across traditional disciplinary boundaries is the future of higher education. Furthermore, they believe that the quality of face-to-face interaction and the campus physical environment are the keys to sustaining the campus as an intellectual community in the face of rapidly evolving opportunities in the digital world. The cultural geography of the campus is shifting as the disciplinary borders are deliberately blurred by new, mixed-use facilities. New buildings have more social space and fewer walls, which subtly promotes the practices of collaboration. More and better on-campus housing and expanded recreational and social facilities are also part of this deliberate strategy to sustain the campus as a physical community.

In contrast to the sometimes utopian rhetoric of planners and designers, the literature on place in anthropology and archaeology is more concerned with expressions of power, agency, and resistance:

> The idea that space is made meaningful is, of course, a familiar one for anthropologists; indeed, there is hardly an older or better established anthropological truth. East or west, inside or outside, left or right, mound or floodplain—from at least the time of Durkheim anthropologists have known that the experience of space is always socially constructed. The more urgent task would seem to be to politicize this uncontestable observation. With meaning-making understood as a practice, how are spatial meanings established? Who has the power to make places of spaces? Who contests this? What is at stake? (Gupta and Ferguson 1997: 40)

The campus cultural landscape is thus more than the shell of the designers' vision. It reflects complex hierarchies of seniority and patronage that swirl around the faculty, administration, donors and funders, alumni and students, neighbors and politicians. Nearly every campus has at least one contested space: a meadow, grove, garden, or historic building whose preservation fuels a community movement. Space is a fiercely protected commodity, creating a conservatism that resists the designers' vision of flexible use, collaboration, and transformation.

These are some of the conversations about the campus as a place that I witness among design professionals and academic colleagues. But how do my students experience the campus as a place? Do they notice patterns of hierarchy and inequality in the distribution of space? I think they do, in the context of their own social experiences. For example, at Stanford the undergraduate students have developed an elaborate taxonomy of student residential spaces, which are assigned in an annual lottery known as the Draw. Each residence, whether large dorm or small "row" house, has either adopted an official theme (Maison Française, Muwekma-Ta-Ruk, the Enchanted Broccoli Forest . . .) or been attributed an unofficial dominant character in the cultural geography of the undergraduate experience at Stanford. Articles in the student newspaper (bemoaning the authors' residential assignments) explicitly connect residence and social identity.

Faculty and staff actively compete for desirable office and lab space, which they may occupy and "control" for decades; students are randomly assigned housing in a process they recognize as entirely outside of their control. (Once they are assigned, they often expend enormous effort customizing the space they will occupy for nine months.) As an archaeologist I would expect, based on the differences in occupational patterns, that the student view of the campus landscape will be quite different from mine. The issue of power raised by Gupta and Ferguson is clearly central in these differences.[5]

Our undergraduates also experience the campus as a setting for elaborate social games like Assassin and scavenger hunts.[6] They search for entrances to our century-old network of steam tunnels and the vast interconnected attics of the Main Quad. Some of them are enterprising enough to seek out historical documents in their quests and devise elaborate ruses to get access to information and locked doors. There are pedagogical opportunities in these customs: I refuse to cooperate with the Assassin game, but I have devised more than one scavenger hunt and mystery contest for my students over the years, designed to increase their awareness and experience of the campus.

My students and their approaches to learning are changing, the campus landscape is evolving, and the discipline of archaeology has certainly been transformed over the course of my career. I cannot continue to teach field methods in the same way I learned them twenty-five years ago, however formative that experience was for me. I want to find new ways to use student curiosity, competitiveness, and need for control over their environment to improve learning in my archaeological field school. There are risks to yielding control to students, but I believe they will rise to responsibility. What will I learn as I engage the campus landscape through the eyes of my students? I expect to be frustrated, surprised, and amazed in my experiment with student leadership in the archaeological field school.

The archaeology of college campuses presents special opportunities for archaeologists as educators to create an experience that reinforces student awareness of belonging to a place and time that has depth, history, and human agency embedded within it. I believe we can adapt the field school to integrate multiple disciplines, generate surprising new research questions, and provide a more memorable experience for all our students. This is a special type of community archaeology: one that recognizes our common connection to the campus as a cultural landscape.

Afterword

As this chapter goes to press, I have completed one-quarter of this new approach to teaching archaeological field methods. Some of my goals were not met: for example, the multidisciplinary approach proved difficult to deliver. We had many visitors to the site representing a variety of disciplines, but no real intellectual collaboration on either the research or the teaching emerged as a result. Other strategies worked very well: the focus on research design and student-initiated research problems did produce evidence of integrative reasoning and, I believe, a deeper understanding of the intellectual challenges of archaeological interpretation. As I plan for another field methods course on the same site this year I expect to make further progress toward a truly multidisciplinary, integrative approach to archaeological field methods.

Notes

1. There are, for example, a small number of differences between how archaeologists at the University of California at Berkeley excavate and how we here at Stanford prefer to treat the same problems. For example, they leave "balks" between adjacent excavation units to preserve four complete soil profiles as they excavate. We view this as a strange and questionable practice—stranding potential data in these unstable forms and creating artificial barriers to the recording of horizontal patterning and features. Fortunately our view of professional standards is flexible enough that this does not appear to be a barrier to student mobility between our programs.

2. Michael Nassaney's account of service learning through archaeological field excavations in western Michigan focuses on the problem of multiple points of view in stakeholder communities. This is a particularly complex example of exposing students to the ethical dimensions of public archaeology. See Nassaney 2004.

3. Some departments have more intensive collaboration on course design than is customary at Stanford, where instructors have nearly absolute control over the content of their courses; the habits of interdependence, compromise, and co-construction may take some time to develop within our highly individualistic community.

4. Under our traditional teaching model, they spent about eighty hours in the field excavating and about thirty hours in the lab over the ten-week quarter. Under the new approach, the excavation time will drop to fifty hours.

5. It comes as a shock to faculty members, however, to learn that despite their place of privilege in the academic hierarchy they can be moved around the campus over their strenuously voiced objections. Here we see the power of the design vision and its view of the communal good over the interests of individuals—and perhaps other dimensions of hierarchy as well.

6. Assassin is a game in which players are assigned "targets"—other players—to "kill," using mock weapons such as Nerf Darts. One key principle is that players do not know the identity of their assassin until the "hit" takes place. The game is widespread on college campuses. A Massachusetts Institute of Technology master's thesis on the subject is available at http://cms.mit.edu/research/theses/Philip2003.pdf (accessed November 15, 2008).

15

Hail to Thee, O Alma Mater

Considering the Archaeology of Academia

RUSSELL K. SKOWRONEK

Knowledge Is Good

Motto of Faber College (*National Lampoon's Animal House*, 1978)

Education and America

Fewer than twenty years after the Pilgrims established "Plimouth [*sic*]," private elementary and higher education was born in Massachusetts at the Boston Latin School in 1635 and Harvard in 1636. Less than a decade later the first genuinely public tax-supported schools were opened in Rehoboth in 1643 and Dedham in 1644. At that time half of the male populace of London and one-third of their rural neighbors were literate (Cohen 1974: 17). During the remaining 140 years of British rule eight more colleges (Table 15.1) and hundreds of public and parochial town schools were established throughout the colonies. After the American Revolution education figured prominently in the nascent United States. Even before the ratification of the Constitution the Northwest Ordinance specifically reserved a sixteenth of a township's section to support education in the form of public elementary education. There students would learn the basic skills of reading, writing, and arithmetic (Figure 15.1). Secondary school education for children aged twelve to eighteen was created by the end of the nineteenth century to address more advanced intellectual and vocational needs.

During the first half of the nineteenth century the United States experienced a college building boom: more than two hundred degree-granting institutions were established by churches and state governments. While higher education in the colonial and early federal period was largely reserved for elite males, these new colleges opened their doors to a wider economic spec-

Table 15.1. Colleges in colonial America

Date Founded	Original Name	Modern Name	Public or Private
1636	Harvard	Harvard	Private
1698	William & Mary	William & Mary	Public
1701	Collegiate School	Yale	Private
1740	University of Pennsylvania	University of Pennsylvania	Private
1746	College of New Jersey	Princeton	Private
1754	King's College	Columbia University	Private
1764	College of Rhode Island	Brown University	Private
1766	Queen's College	Rutgers	Public
1769	Dartmouth	Dartmouth	Private

Figure 15.1. A century of continuity in elementary education creates discernible patterns in the archaeological record. With few changes in clothing, the 1928 eighth-grade school room in Chicago, Illinois, of Dorothy Trevor and Walter Graham in 1928 (*top*); Helen Wyszpolski Skowronek's first-grade class in rural Silt, Colorado, circa 1966 (*middle*); and the sixth-grade classroom of Allison Smith in Edinburg, Texas, in 2008 (*bottom*) demonstrate consistency in American education from the era of the Civil War to the present. (Courtesy of Dennis M. and Margaret A. Graham; Helen Wyszpolski Skowronek; and E. Olga Skowronek)

Figure 15.2. The traditional gowns of these graduates from North Carolina State in 1940 (*left*) and from New York University in 1942 (*right*) are "timeless" aspects of the world of academe. (Courtesy of Lester John Skowronek and Helen Wyszpolski Skowronek)

trum of the free white male and female populace. In 1862 the federal government became directly involved in higher education with the passage of the Morrill Act, whereby states received profits from sales of federal lands for the creation of "land-grant" schools where agricultural, mechanical, and military sciences and the liberal arts were taught.

By the turn of the twentieth century education as we currently construe it was taking shape. In addition to the three traditional professions of medicine, law, and theology, modern universities began conferring the doctor of philosophy degree within the context of a number of other graduate programs (Figure 15.2). During the 1920s and 1930s enrollments increased in tandem with the growing popularity of intercollegiate athletics. This was the era of Knute Rockne, Prohibition, and Rudy Vallee singing "Betty Co-Ed." The new media of motion pictures and radio created a "shared" collegian culture in America. In this era Santa Clara had a number of All Americans on its football teams. When they played rival St. Mary's College the games were held not in Santa Clara or Moraga but in Kezar Stadium in San Francisco in front of a crowd of 60,000 (McKay 2002: 147). While the documentary record includes these activities, it does not recall those of their contemporary, "Suitcase Sullivan." Sullivan was an entrepreneur dealing in alcohol during Prohibition. According to one oral history I heard, he would leave a suitcase filled with "booze" at the base of the cross in front of the Mission Church while retrieving a matching empty one. Such is the unwritten history of this campus and many others. It is a story, though, that can leave a material legacy.

Perhaps the defining moment in collegiate education came at the end of World War II with the passage in 1944 of the Serviceman's Readjustment Act or G.I. Bill. This financial aid program enabled an unprecedented number of veterans to attend college. According to the Federal Public Housing Authority, of some 1,300 schools thought to have attracted these returnees, 75 percent lacked sufficient housing for them. The result was a coast-to-coast creation of "Veterans' Villages," usually constructed of military surplus prefabricated structures. Just as the war had been a defining moment for the men and women of the Greatest Generation, these apartments, classrooms, and labs became the defining moment for the young civilian families of the era. And it was this generation that shaped the last half of the twentieth century.

Given America's broad, shared experience with education, we might consider how it has shaped the perception of schools.

Forming Campus Memories

Every year it is the same: thousands graduate and become alumni, and a few months later thousands more matriculate and become freshman collegians. A handful of the graduates will remain on the campus or in the nearby area. Most, however, will pass through the school and either never return or return only as part of a planned reunion far in the future. For those who join their alumni association, the connection to their alma mater will be limited to quarterly alumni magazines that will probably end up in the pile with the other unread periodicals that inundate our lives. Their only other contact will be in the form of seemingly incessant telephone calls from current students and sometimes faculty members shilling for money on behalf of the school. For these alumni the campus becomes frozen in their memories.

Class reunions are sobering for everyone. Returning alumni might feel the same as they did in their salad years, but a quick check in the mirror tells the real story: they are balding or gray-haired, paunchy or fat, wearing glasses and hearing aids or using canes or wheelchairs. Viagra, hair transplants, plastic surgery, and personal trainers will not change the fact that they have aged and are not the same people they were years before. Still, they come to search the campus for some tangible evidence of their past. If they are fortunate, a vaguely familiar face of a now aged classmate or a decrepit professor will be juxtaposed against a building or other place that will transport them back to their student days. Far too often they are disappointed. Professors have died or retired and moved away. Classmates may not attend or may no longer "connect" as they did or imagined they did so very long ago.

That leaves the built landscape as their touchstone to the past, and that too may be disappointing. Often the college campuses are seen as monolithic and largely unchanging. Of course, that is not true. For example, over the past century and a half Santa Clara University has grown from less than ten acres in size to more than one hundred. Over the course of that expansion the school has destroyed many surrounding "watering holes," restaurants, and neighborhoods and even busy thoroughfares. Landscaped commons now lie where students in the 1930s once caught streetcars to nearby San Jose or others in the 1980s dodged thousands of cars to reach the campus library and class rooms and the school's football stadium. Some may literally have left their mark on a closet door or wall or had it officially emblazoned on an engraved window or plaque, but it is all seemingly ephemeral. Buildings, often in use for over a century, may repeatedly be reused adaptively by other departments and then demolished. For all the hard work of alumni associations, most returnees leave feeling morose and wondering if they were ever that young and why they came.

Faculty members might seem to have a better recollection of campus life than the students do, but even that is not true. Their lives are largely dictated by where they can park. As creatures of habit they move between their office, a handful of classrooms, the library, and perhaps a few other locations on campus. If they are asked about particular aspects of the campus with which they had no contact, their knowledge of it is usually very limited. For them, the students and jokes never really change—just as their lectures do not. If they stay long enough they might have two or even three generations of a family pass through their classroom. When they leave or die they will be forgotten by the students and most of the faculty within a few years.

Most administrators also have short shelf-lives. They may be planning for the future of an institution, but they are also looking to their future. Some perhaps see their legacy as "bricks and mortar" presidents who build the next iteration of a university, but others view it as the last step to retirement or as a stepping stone to a better job at a more prestigious university. Because they do not teach and are usually not engaged in active research, their campus world is even more tightly constricted to their office, the grounds, and meetings with the trustees and donors in ceremonial venues. Even if they are alumni, they are paid to look to the future and often see the past as dead and gone and a hindrance to their plans for the campus.

But a campus is more than these perspectives. As Laura Jones points out in her chapter on Stanford University, space is socially constructed. "The campus cultural landscape is thus more than the shell of the designers' vision. It reflects complex hierarchies of seniority and patronage that swirl around the faculty, administration, donors and funders, alumni and students, neighbors and politicians."

The reality is that a common ground can exist between memories of the past and the future. This common ground can benefit students, institutions, and the larger community. It can serve as a focus for scholarly research and undergraduate education while celebrating the past. The nexus for this is archaeology and public history.

Memories, Landscape, and Archaeology

> Americans often turn to the past to explain current social conditions, to comfort themselves, to build self-esteem, and to create cultural pride. What aspects of the past are remembered and how they are remembered and interpreted are important issues that allow us to see how public memory develops. Memories can serve individual or collective needs and can validate the holders' version of the past.
>
> (Shackel 2001: 655)

Our knowledge of landscape is shaped by oral histories and traditional institutional histories, but those "memories" are shaped by personal values, worldviews, and time. What is important to one generation may be forgotten or relegated to a footnote by the next. How schools and colleges situate themselves on the landscape may not simply reflect functional needs but may also be indicative of larger ideals. In a recent discussion of the interplay between landscapes and memories Cornelius Holtorf and Howard Williams (2006: 254) cautioned that "archaeologists cannot fully consider the complex significance and meanings of landscape to past people without considering the memories" of those who inhabited that landscape. As we turn to the research presented in this volume on the archaeology of academia we can see how the archaeological record can at times contradict institutional history while confirming oral histories.

The work of Lewis at Saints' Rest on the Michigan State University campus predicted what materials would have been part of the systemic world of this isolated Victorian agricultural college and the form their deposition would have taken when the structure burned. As he points out, when artifacts are considered within their larger behavioral milieu, their context and patterning can reveal information that is not otherwise available in the documentary record. Schurr at Notre Dame and South at South Carolina provide a detailed methodological approach that served them well in their study of the Log Chapel and Old College.

We also learn from these contributions how buildings were sited and how schools were used as places for social change. The work on rural schools focused on how preventative sanitation efforts were put in place to avoid epidemic diseases. At other campuses we see how institutional histories may not indicate that buildings were initially sited elsewhere. In some cases archaeology reveals where structures were and recaptures long-lost segments of a school's history. Whether it is the story of Dorothea Kissam and her life on the tennis courts of William and Mary, the fraternity brothers of the University of California, or the lives of the post–World War II occupants of Santa Clara's Veterans' Village, the very specific stories of these people are part of the texture of a school's history and also point toward social identity.

Institutional histories are largely mute on the subject of day-to-day living in the classroom and in the dormitory. From anatomy specimens to the assaying of ore samples, a picture of the detritus of classroom life in past centuries is coming into focus. Familiar items such as pencils, ink and glue containers, slates, chemistry and biology labware (Figure 15.3), and even theater-related artifacts bring the memories of these lost landscapes back to a new generation. The very fact that these artifacts from sites across the country show great similarity speaks not only to the issue of mass production but also to the relative economic position of students.

The archaeology of academia lends insights into the foodways, personal hygiene, and health of yesterday's students. We can see that toothbrushes, combs, and hair tonic and patent and prescription medicines have been a common part of dormitory life for centuries. Dietary evidence, be it ceramics, condiment jars, or faunal remains, indicates a consistency with the larger culture of their respective eras. This is also the case for the issue of tobacco and alcohol.

Figure 15.3. New York University Class of 1942 biology-chemistry graduate Helen Wyszpolski used her education during and after World War II for malaria research at Welfare Island, New York; for chemical soil analysis at North Carolina State University; and for hematology analysis at Memorial Sloan-Kettering Cancer Center in New York. The material culture associated with biochemical research remained largely unchanged for most of the late nineteenth and twentieth centuries. (Courtesy of Helen Wyszpolski Skowronek)

Today, when the front page of a school papers announces: "Alcohol illnesses double this year—12 students hospitalized, 246 citations so far in fall—university is concerned with students' reckless use of alcohol" (O'Connor 2006: 1, 4) and when students report witnessing other prohibited behaviors, the chapters bring us a perspective on the behavior of largely unsupervised students. Even in settings where prohibitions against gambling, the use of tobacco products, or the consumption of alcohol were reportedly often zealously enforced (such as at Harvard, Washington and Lee, South Carolina, and Santa Clara) we find evidence of such activities.

Finally, a common theme runs through all of the chapters, regarding the largely unrealized potential of campus-focused archaeology in the life of an academic institution, its students, its faculty, its alumni, and the larger community. The contributors to this volume clearly represent success stories in their ability to have conducted their research, but the question should remain for them and those who follow: could there be more?

Recognizing Scholarship in the Archaeology of Academia

Anthropology, the most scientific of the humanities and the most humanistic of the sciences, is the study of humankind in its broadest sense. As a field of study it was born in the last third of the nineteenth century, just as America's educational system was taking on its current configuration. Within the larger discipline, educational anthropologists have focused their research on how people learn in various cultures, while their colleagues in archaeology have rarely conducted their research in their own backyards; instead they have focused on more exotic locales for their investigations.

Many of the contributors to this volume commented on the value of on-campus research sites for teaching students the nuances of archaeology. From research design to analysis and reporting, students can participate in the entire endeavor. Alumni, it is pointed out, may be drawn into projects as providers of oral history or as donors. And, of course, archaeology is of interest to the larger community. Today's grade-school pupils are tomorrow's matriculated students.

But there is a reality to contemplate when we consider how rare this kind of research is in the United States. Often in-house research and other projects with an applied dimension are less valued on college campuses (Nassaney 2004). Perhaps it is because colleagues might view them as officially sanctioned and therefore above reproach, except at promotion time. Others may believe that going into the field in exotic international places or at least sites remote from the campus constitutes genuine research. If peer-reviewed publications are considered to be the coin of the realm for promotion, what is the value of in-house reports? Beginning in graduate school we are urged to "do the right thing" and complete our reports before publishing on a project's findings. Yet promotion reviewers often hold such publications in disdain. This collegial discrimination can be further compounded by administrators who are concerned about what might be found that could delay construction projects or prove to be an embarrassment to their institutions. This unfortunate tendency can often result in denials of tenure and promotion and thus should be recognized and proactively countered with explicitly worded letters in individual personnel files.

Heritage Resource Management—An Untapped Resource

Late in 1999 thirty-three presidents, provosts, deans, physical plant managers, faculty members, and students representing Centenary College, Centre

College, Millsaps College, Berry College, Furman University, the University of Richmond, the University of the South, and Washington and Lee University met with archaeologists from the National Park Service and Santa Clara University to consider the place of heritage resources in the environmental stewardship, educational, and operational programs of the Associated Colleges of the South (see the appendix). They concluded that such resources existed on each of their campuses and that they could enrich their respective educational programs through experiential learning. It was recognized that these were unique, fragile, and nonrenewable resources and that they contributed to the distinctive character of each institution. The group noted that a commitment and action toward preservation of such heritage resources by administrators, directors, faculty, and students could have significant, long-term, and broad positive effects. Nine recommendations were outlined for the member institutions of the Associated Colleges of the South. These ranged from creating Heritage Resource Management Programs and inventorying their respective resources to getting students, law enforcement, and members of the local community involved. One specifically suggested that the institutions follow the National Register of Historic Places process for identifying and registering their resources.

It was a unique meeting, filled with such promise that one might have imagined the participants singing "Kumbaya" as they headed off to their respective campuses. But all was not well. Within weeks of the meeting the environmental administrator for the Associated Colleges of the South, who championed the meeting and the concept of heritage resource management, had been terminated, and the recommendations were largely forgotten. At the colleges and universities it was business as usual. Rather than acting as a consortium to herald a new way of considering their campuses, they left it to individuals, be they concerned faculty or administrators, to salvage what time and nonexistent resources would allow.

As the contributors to this book illustrate, the archaeology of academia is not new. For decades both faculty and cultural resource management archaeologists have endeavored to reveal and salvage the ephemeral traces of these educational institutions and their surrounding community. Often they have been one step ahead of the bulldozers. When I started at Santa Clara it was not unusual for me to be called out of class when bones of an unknown species or other significant features were encountered.

In 1995 Santa Clara University established an Archaeology Research Lab to coordinate campus-focused research, provide oversight for cultural resources, support teaching efforts, and curate artifacts and supporting doc-

Figure 15.4. Historical interpretation on college campuses can include simple photo-enhanced wayside exhibits or the marking of the outline of the historic structure, which is easily maintained by groundskeepers. These not only are terrific alumni donation opportunities but provide passive educational opportunities that celebrate the traditions of an institution. (Santa Clara University campus photo by Russell K. Skowronek)

umentation generated during campus construction and research projects. Additionally, Archaeology Research Lab staff members have lent their expertise to the City of Santa Clara and hosted the county archaeology society and dozens of visiting speakers. They have provided tours and lectures to docents, visiting dignitaries, new faculty, and students. Their energies have created a brochure for a "Walking Tour" of the campus, produced a number of wayside exhibits that celebrate the history of the campus (Figure 15.4), and established an occasional publication series that has printed the work of faculty, students, and a variety of off-campus scholars (Figures 15.5). The Archaeology Research Lab has worked closely with the Santa Clara University Archives and faculty from environmental studies, history, and modern languages. They see the entire campus as a classroom where wayside exhibits provide passive education to students, faculty, visitors, and alumni. They also offer opportunities for donors who wish to leave a legacy, while enhancing the image of the university as a place where education occurs throughout the campus.

The Saints' Rest project of 2005 proved to be a watershed event for archaeology at Michigan State University. Its results helped the university realize

Figure 15.5. Campus-focused studies produce not only research reports but also publications that are of interest to other scholars, alumni, and members of the community. Since 1994 Santa Clara University has supported such a series (the Research Manuscript Series on the Cultural and Natural History of Santa Clara and *Telling the Santa Clara Story: Sesquicentennial Voices*). (Photo by Russell K. Skowronek)

the need to include archaeology in its development and construction plans. Archaeologists have now become one of the regular and routinely informed parties on all planned projects and are involved early in the planning process. Significantly, the university has also begun to recognize that the work we do needs to be funded. As part of a program in graduate student development, the dean of the Graduate School has agreed to pay the salary of one or more graduate students to serve in the capacity of campus archaeologist for up to two years, so that students can get on-the-job training working with the campus bureaucracy under the supervision of faculty. In addition, the dean has offered to fund several special projects that focus on aspects of campus archaeology and provide more limited practical training experience for student archaeologists. The prerequisites for applying for these positions include graduate status in anthropology, archaeological training, and completion of the department's Professionalism in Anthropology course.

Clearly, a growing part of academe is coming to appreciate what archaeology can reveal about the past of their institutions. Many of the chapters in this volume discuss the importance of using the campus as a classroom for education of students and to mitigate the adverse effects of construction. The explicit mission of these institutions is to teach, to do research, and to be engaged in public service. As a result of those efforts they have been able to tell new stories about life on their campuses.

When we can link the educational process, research, alumni and community involvement, legal compliance, and the celebration of tradition in a single project it makes sense to support it. Yet, for all the benefits of heritage management of resources within the world of academe, it is amazing how few schools actively embrace the concept and are engaged in making it a reality. This may simply be a reflection of transient administrators who are unable to recognize that learning does not only take place in campus classrooms and professors who see such endeavors as a lesser form of "applied" research with little scholarly merit.

Campuses are natural laboratories where archaeologists can practice what they preach under the watchful eyes of, and in collaboration with, students, colleagues, administrators, alumni, and various community groups. Archaeological preservation programs in conjunction with interdisciplinary programs should be an active part of an institution's heritage stewardship endeavors. As the chapters in this book demonstrate, it is through archaeology that teaching, learning, research, and service can be integrated while preserving and interpreting the heritage of the academy.

Richard Waldbauer of the National Park Service summed up the significance of campus heritage stewardship programs in the following way (personal communication to Skowronek and Lewis, April 9, 2008):

> First, the archaeology of academia provides irreplaceable evidence about growth and change not only of significant institutions but of all human history preserved within the lands that schools, colleges, and universities own or control. This means that they must be good stewards of and responsible for a broad set of cultural heritage as well as their own institutional pasts. The consequences of failure to do so are both tragic and irretrievable. Second, few opportunities for simultaneous success in both educational and research goals can be achieved so resoundingly as in the archaeology of academia. The entire landhold-

ings are prime laboratories to test, operate, and analyze creative approaches to education and research. Indeed many schools were given their lands expressly for those purposes. Most often, successes in these two areas will be interdisciplinary because archaeology lends itself easily to cooperative effort and varied kinds of communication. Third, colleges and universities are frequently the longest lived institutions in their communities. They are centerpieces within their social contexts. That different publics respond enthusiastically to campus archaeological projects is no accident. Community identity is at stake. When the archaeology of academia is done well, it is perforce a socially responsible act.

In an age when discussions focused on ethics are a common part of campus life these words ring true. The time has come for schools who talk the talk to walk the walk: it is the responsible and ethical thing to do.

More than thirty years after conducting work on the University of South Carolina campus Stanley South, one of the founding fathers of historical archaeology, expressed his frustration with the lack of action on the part of campus administrators and their reluctance to support the preservation of "the authentic character of the past for generations still to come." Undeterred by their foibles, he continues to advocate that campus archaeology programs be "established on campuses nationwide in the future. When and if that ever happens, the value of conducting on-campus research to address the cultural resources waiting to be archaeologically discovered will be demonstrated as each new dig is undertaken." Let us hope that this volume will help speed the date when South's hope becomes a reality.

The bell is ringing. Class is dismissed!

Appendix

Heritage Resources Management in the College and University Environment

I. Preamble: Associated Colleges of the South, Environmental Program, *Heritage Resource Management in the College and University Environment*, Sewanee, November 11–14, 1999

We are 33 presidents, provosts, deans, student conference interns, students, business managers, faculty members, physical plant managers, campus operations managers, archivists, librarians, and staff of the Associated Colleges of the South (ACS), representing Centenary College, Centre College, Furman University, Millsaps College, The University of Richmond, The University of the South, and Washington and Lee University. We invited and urged presidents, administrators, faculty, and students of all ACS member institutions to participate. Also participating at our invitation were President Scott Colley and Dean of Mathematics and Natural Sciences Bruce Conn of Berry College, which has a land base of 44 square miles; Richard Waldbauer of the National Park Service, Office of Departmental Consulting Archaeologist; and Russell Skowronek, University Archaeologist at Santa Clara University.

In what may have been the first effort of its kind in the nation, we met in 40 hours of intensive work sessions between Thursday evening, November 11, and Sunday morning, November 14, to consider the place of heritage (archaeological and historical) resources in the environmental stewardship, educational, and operational programs of our ACS institutions. We engaged in five progressive policy discussions and debates; presentations of case studies from ACS schools, other universities, and the National Park Service; intensive field sessions; and an excellent series of exhibits, GIS demonstrations, and poster sessions. We also benefited from an extensive topical web site and suite of electronic pre-conference homework that was prepared by the University of the South, and we recommend this to your attention.

We completed our work convinced of the value of uniform, special stewardship efforts by our institutions, which are uniquely positioned, and responsible, to identify, evaluate, protect, preserve, educate, and share with regard to heritage resources. These resources exist on each of our campuses; they contribute to the distinctive character of each institution; like books in our libraries, they contain unique information on the human past and our interaction with the natural environment; they are fragile and non-renewable; and they can vastly enrich our educational programs with experiential learning.

In a college or university, perhaps better than anywhere else, a commitment and action toward preservation of the institution's resources by directors, administrators, faculty, and a core of students can have significant, long term, and broad positive effects. Such an institution, committed to the understanding and preservation of its heritage resources, can:

—serve as a permanent steward of important samples of the record of the past,
—teach by example the value of such preservation efforts,
—influence in this way an entire student body, not just the students specialized in a single discipline or enrolled in the courses in this field,
—extend these positive effects over generations of students through sustained commitment, and
—disseminate the effects widely in the persons of environmentally sensitive graduates in all walks of life in communities throughout the country—people who can make a real difference in their own communities on issues of identifying, understanding, preserving, and interpreting important samples of the record of human adaptation to the environment since time immemorial.

We participated in a remarkable learning and sharing experience, and we came away energized to learn what evidence of the human legacy lies beneath our feet and before our eyes at each ACS school, how each of us can make a contribution that will last, and how the immense human journey can be made more meaningful for all. It appears that as one important outcome of the conference, Berry College (Rome, GA), one of the largest and most diverse campuses in the U.S., will rapidly embark on a heritage resource inventory and management program.

The inspiration for our conference came from Major McCollough, David Michaels, and the Joseph Johnson Preservation Archaeology Program at the University of the South (Sewanee), where heritage resource inventory, evaluation, research, preservation, experiential learning, and policy making efforts are being built in a model program on the 15 square mile Cumberland Plateau campus. Among institutions of higher learning in the U.S., Sewanee is clearly one of the most richly endowed with comprehensive evidence of the human past. And in sharing its resources and its vision, Sewanee has inspired us all.

In the conference, Richard Waldbauer of the National Park Service provided us with a national perspective on the importance of our efforts. John McDaniel shared his experience with the archaeological program he founded twenty-seven years ago at Washington and Lee University. Dean Elizabeth Perkins of Centre College reported on the exciting interdisciplinary Sinking Spring project, in which archaeological, historical, and other scientific fields of knowledge are employed, and students, faculty, administration, and physical plant are involved, in the study of a spring in the center of the college campus that is a metaphor for the life of the school and the community of Danville, Kentucky. And Russell Skowronek of Santa Clara University, who is a trailblazer in heritage resource management planning in the university setting, shared his experience with the opportunities and challenges of planning at the only American institution of higher learning to occupy the site of a Spanish Colonial mission.

The document that follows summarizes the results of our deliberations and our recommendations for heritage resource management program development throughout the ACS. This is a living, evolving document, but in its initial form we hope it will inspire and guide all ACS schools to begin or intensify their efforts in heritage resource management, and to establish lively interaction among our students, faculties, and administrations in this area of learning and stewardship.

We hope that each ACS school will consider and adopt our recommendations, and that each institution will discuss this document with Robert Whyte of ACS and other interested persons working toward the management of our heritage resources in the college and university environment.

II. Recommendations from the Associated Colleges of the South Environmental Program *Conference on Heritage Resource Management in the College and University Environment*, held at the University of the South, Sewanee, November 11–14, 1999.

RECOMMENDATION 1. That each ACS institution develop and implement a Heritage resource Management Program.

RECOMMENDATION 2. That the building of an inventory of heritage resources be the first step in the development of the management program.

An inventory will identify and describe the several types of resources, both archaeological and historical, which are owned by the institution. The condition of each resource should be included in the inventory.

An adequate inventory must be on-going. The institution should make a commitment to building the inventory and maintaining it into the future by recording additions, deletions, modifications, and changes in the condition of a particular resource.

Attention should be paid to the form of the information so that it will be useful to all who need it: trustees, administrators, faculty members, construction engineers, architects, and campus planners. Even the work of a backhoe operator in laying a new underground network of pipes should be informed by the information in this inventory.

The organizing and storing of the information in the inventory should use the best information technology available. The use of GIS technology is recommended.

The inventory should pay attention to a larger context. It should definitely employ the existing state format for recording basic, initial inventory information on prehistoric and historic resources.

The evaluation of historical and archaeological resources is essential for effective management of these resources. Thus the development of the inventory should include the additional step of evaluation, using the institution's adopted criteria of significance. The significant historic and archeological resources should be clearly identified.

As the identification and evaluation of the significant historical and archaeological resources proceed, the institution should develop and implement effective means for protection and preservation of these resources.

The inventory should be used as a most important tool in the planning phase of projects involving construction and campus development.

There should be student participation in accomplishing the inventory; the inventory effort provides excellent projects for laboratory work in certain courses in the college's curriculum.

The development of the inventory should involve and use available external resources.

In planning for the inventory, the institution should develop a policy that establishes guidelines for determining appropriate limitations on the access to the information which is contained in the inventory.

RECOMMENDATION 3. That the college or university develop its own position on the issue of formal designation in the National Register of Historic Places (NRHP) of its significant heritage resources.

Some considerations in using the NRHP process for identifying and registering an institution's significant resources are these:

Using the well-developed and comprehensive evaluation system of the NRHP can be a valuable tool for doing the evaluation and prioritizing which are needed for proper management and planning of the institution's campus.

With the assumption that the technical aspects of evaluation are being done by faculty members and students in an educational setting, the NRHP provides the best model for the heritage study process and therefore will contribute to the education of the students.

There will be public relations value in having an institution's prized heritage resources given the distinction of being listed in the National Register.

The NRHP designation contributes standard information to a national resource that is used to improve understanding of history and prehistory in the locality, region, and nation.

It makes the institution eligible for federal grants for preservation projects under the National Historic Preservation Act. (Examples of projects include developing an inventory, stabilization, maintenance, and repair of sites.)

NRHP designation may offer some protection to an institution's resources in relation to the planning and projects of local, state, or federal government that might have an effect on these resources.

The National Register clearly states as a matter of policy that it does not limit or restrict the rights of property owners to use, develop, or sell their historic properties; nor does it require that historic properties be maintained, repaired, restored; nor does it require that historic properties be open to the public.

Some considerations which might argue against using NRHP designation:

The step of evaluation and prioritization of heritage resources must be done. Using the NRHP process is only one way of accomplishing this. An institution can take the NRHP process as a model and develop an institutional program for designating its own premier sites. In this way, the institution can develop a more focused process because it will be describing its own particular place and history.

The process of placing a site on the National Register of Historic Places generally involves a step in which the institution deals with an agency of the state government. There are variations among states in how these matters are handled. The actual practice of the state agency through which NRHP designation is handled should be considered by an institution in making the decision of whether or not to use the NRHP process.

While it is true that NRHP designation does not legally limit a private owner in how the property is to be used, it is also true that NRHP designation will raise public knowledge and sensitivity regarding cultural heritage issues. The perception that the NRHP "gives a voice" to constituencies opposing institutional objectives may require effective public education efforts.

RECOMMENDATION 4. That students should be an integral part of the Heritage Resource Management Program.

Because the primary mission of the ACS colleges and universities is the education of undergraduates, the development and implementation of the heritage resource management program should connect with the curriculum of the college or university in as many ways as possible.

The archaeological and historical resources owned by the institution should be laboratories for learning by its students.

Projects that identify and preserve heritage resources can very appropriately be included within an institution's program for service learning.

The traditions of the ACS colleges and universities include the concern for teaching our students the value of an environmental and stewardship ethic. This goal for our students should be an intentional aspect of the development of a management plan for heritage resources. Projects grounded in or related to the heritage resource management program can provide opportunities for hands-on learning related to courses which are interdisciplinary in nature.

If the college or university has an environmental studies program in its curriculum, the educational opportunities that are available through the heritage resource management program should be related to the environmental studies program.

Working visits to projects at other ACS schools, interaction with other college and university programs, field schools, and short-term visits to off-campus sites should be considered as ways to integrate the heritage resource management program with the program of education being offered to the college's undergraduate students.

RECOMMENDATION 5. That the college or university should seek outside partners in the development of its Heritage Resource Management Program.

Possible partners include:

Agencies of the Federal government (the National Park Service and others which have an interest in historic or prehistoric resources in the region in which the college or university is located).

Agencies of state government (including the State Historic Preservation Office), which have responsibility for heritage resources.

Other colleges and universities, particularly those that already have strongly developed management programs for heritage resources.

The programs of the ACS that are related to environmental issues.

Private organizations that have an interest in the stewardship of archaeological and historical resources.

Members of the public who might volunteer or otherwise participate in projects.

RECOMMENDATION 6. That each institution develop an appropriate organizational structure to direct the Heritage Resource Management Program as a permanent activity.

The organization and administration of the Heritage Resource Management Program will vary with the governance and decision making process of member institutions.

Each institution should vest responsibility for the Heritage Resource Management Program in an appropriate committee, organization, or individual, and a committee or other organ should be formed to provide for input from governance, administration, academic interests, students, physical plant, law enforcement, and others and to provide information to these interests on how the program is to be managed. Heritage resource management issues should be addressed and resolved at the earliest possible stage of planning for activities that could affect archaeological or historical resources.

The committee or organ should periodically make recommendations to assure that heritage resource management practices are consistent with the institution's master plan.

The committee or organ should have the responsibility of informing the public of its work and sponsoring occasions when members of the various constituencies of the college and university can express their views on issues related to cultural heritage management.

The work of the committee or organ should always be taken into consideration in formulation of institutional master plan objectives.

The management of heritage resources by the institution will be done always in compliance with appropriate laws and regulations and with adherence to the professional standards of those such as archaeologists, historians, and architects who are actively engaged in the process of management.

RECOMMENDATION 7. That the administration establish a contact who will be responsible to act as a liaison between heritage resources managers and the appropriate law enforcement agency.

Looting, vandalism and other unauthorized impacts threaten nonrenewable heritage resources. Laws and ordinances, which may apply, include criminal trespass, theft of property, interstate trafficking, and state and county statutes regarding the protection of human remains.

Effective enforcement programs require consultation among heritage resource managers, law enforcement officials, and attorneys who will work together to build a plan for investigation and prosecution of violations.

RECOMMENDATION 8. That the institutions provide the resources (financial, staff, technical, and information) to establish and support a heritage resource management program.

It is further recognized that heritage resource management should be an integral component of any college or university environmental studies program, and reflected in the curriculum and staffing.

Funding sources may be internal or external. Internal funds may come directly from the institution(s) and include:

—Cooperative funding across departments (e.g., joint appointments)
—Institutional funds that recognize savings from cost-avoidance programs
—Student activity funds
—ACS collaborative funding from such efforts as the environmental initiative and the technology and library programs
—Student participation in projects that are linked to the education, which the students are receiving.

External funds may come from:

—Development Office through fundraising activities (focusing on the campus and its unique cultural heritage to celebrate the past and enhance the distinctiveness of the institution)
—Alumni gifts and endowments
—National Historic Preservation Act historic preservation grants awarded through the State Historic Preservation Office
—Research and program development grants in archaeology, history, and historic preservation from such sources and NSF, NEH, National Trust for Historic Preservation, and private foundations
—Grants (for students, programs, and operating expenses)
—Volunteers
—Partnerships (e.g., with federal, state, and local agencies, groups, and institutions with specific interests in heritage resource management)
—Contract work (to include overhead to the college or university)
—Sales of publications

The college or university administration should recognize that while the development of an effective and useful program for heritage resource management will carry a cost in dollars, there will be several off-setting benefits, which will tend to balance the cost of such a program.

RECOMMENDATION 9. That the Associated Colleges of the South share this Heritage Resource Management initiative with other colleges, universities, and consortia, and encourage its wider adoption in American higher education.

References Cited

Allen, Rebecca, Tom Garlinghouse, Jennifer Farquhar, Clinton Blount, Leslie Fryman, and Dana McGowan. 2003. Santa Clara University Cultural Resources Treatment Plan for the Ten Year Capital Plan. Report prepared for Santa Clara University Operations Department (August).

Allmendinger, David F., Jr. 1971. New England Students and the Revolution in Higher Education, 1800–1900. *History of Education Quarterly* 11(4): 381–89.

Amherst Record. 1877. Agricultural College Commencement. June 20, p. 4.

Anderson, Benedict. 1987. *Imagined Communities: Reflections on the Origin and Spread of Nationalism*. London: Verso.

Anonymous. 1895. *A Brief History of the University of Notre Dame du Lac, Indiana, from 1842 to 1892*. Prepared for the Golden Jubilee. Chicago: Werner Company.

Ascher, Robert. 1974. How to Build a Time Capsule. *Journal of Popular Culture* 8: 241–53.

Associated Colleges of the South. 1999. Preamble and Recommendations. Conference on Heritage Resources Management in the College and University Environment. November 11–14, University of the South, Sewanee, Tennessee.

Bailey, Liberty H. 1911. *The Country Life Movement*. New York: Macmillan Company.

Bailyn, Bernard. 1960. *Education in the Forming of American Society*. Chapel Hill: University of North Carolina Press.

Ball, James M. 1928. *The Sack-'em-up Men: An Account of the Rise and Fall of the Modern Resurrectionists*. London: Oliver and Boyd.

Baram, Uzi. 1989. "Boys, Be Ambitious": Landscape Manipulation in Nineteenth Century Western Massachusetts. M.A. thesis, Department of Anthropology, University of Massachusetts, Amherst.

Bardavio, Antoni, Cristina Gatell, and Paloma Gonzalez-Marcen. 2004. Is Archaeology What Matters? Creating a Sense of Local Identity among Teenagers in Catalonia. *World Archaeology* 36(2): 261–74.

Barksdale, Martha. 1941–42. *Tennis Team c. 1941–42*. College of William and Mary Archives. Martha Barksdale Papers. Archives account number 1985.54, Box 3. Williamsburg, Virginia.

———. 1942–43. *Tennis Team c. 1942–43*. College of William and Mary Archives. Martha Barksdale Papers. Archives account number 1985.54, Box 3. Williamsburg, Virginia.

Barron, Hal S. 1997. *Mixed Harvest: The Second Great Transformation in the Rural North, 1870–1930*. Chapel Hill: University of North Carolina Press.

Batchelder, Samuel F. 1921. The Singular Story of Holden Chapel. *Harvard Alumni Bulletin*, February 3.

———. 1924. *Bits of Harvard History*. Cambridge, Mass.: Harvard University Press.

Bateman, Newton, and Paul Selby, editors. 1914. *Historical Encyclopedia of Illinois and History of Grundy County*. Chicago: Munsell Publishing Company.

Battle, Kemp P. 1907. *History of the University of North Carolina, Volume I*. Raleigh, N.C.: Edwards and Broughton.

———. 1912. *History of the University of North Carolina, Volume II*. Raleigh, N.C.: Edwards and Broughton.

Beal, W. J. 1915. *History of the Michigan Agricultural College and Biographical Sketches of Trustees and Professors*. East Lansing: Michigan Agricultural College.

Bender, Susan J. 2000. A Proposal to Guide Curricular Reform for the Twenty-first Century. In *Teaching Archaeology in the Twenty-first Century*, edited by Susan J. Bender and George S. Smith, pp. 31–38. Washington, D.C.: Society for American Archaeology. http://www.indiana.edu/~arch/saa/matrix/principles.html (accessed September 20, 2007).

Berger, Joseph B., and Maria Vita Calkins. 2002. Higher Education in the United States. In *Encyclopedia of Education*, pp. 1034–45. 2nd ed. 8 vols. New York: Macmillan.

Bergesen, Albert. 1987. Oh, Well. *Atlantic* (July): 16–18.

Bidwell, Percy Wells, and John I. Falconer. 1941. *History of Agriculture in the Northern United States, 1620–1860*. Washington, D.C.: Carnegie Institute of Washington, 1925; reprint, New York: Peter Smith.

Binford, Lewis R. 1978. Dimensional Analysis of Behavior and Site Structure: Learning from an Eskimo Hunting Stand. *American Antiquity* 43: 330–61.

———. 1981. Behavioral Archaeology and the "Pompeii Premise." *Journal of Anthropological Research* 37: 195–208.

———. 2005. Contemplation of the Hidden Issues Suggested by the Word "Historical." In *In Praise of the Poet Archaeologist: Papers in Honor of Stanley South and His Five Decades of Historical Archaeology*, edited by Linda F. Carnes-McNaughton and Carl Steen, 24–29. Publications in South Carolina Archaeology, No. 1. Columbia: Council of South Carolina Professional Archaeologists.

Biographical Publishing Company. 1900. *Genealogical and Biographical Record of Will County*. Chicago: Biographical Publishing Company.

Bird, M. Catherine. 2007. Public Education, Rural Schools, and Reform. In *Phase III Data Recovery of the Lower Ridge School Site (11–Wi-2807) Jackson Township, Will County, Illinois* by Carrie Koster-Horan, Rochelle Lurie, and M. Catherine Bird. Cultural Resource Management Report No. 1321. Marengo, Ill.: Midwest Archaeological Research Services, Inc.

Bishop, Levi. 1877. Recollections. *Michigan Pioneer and Historical Collections* 1: 511–17.

Bledstein, Burton J. 1976. *Culture of Professionalism: The Middle Class and the Development of Higher Education in America*. New York: W. W. Norton and Company.

Boles, Frank. 1998. One-Room Schools: Michigan's Educational Legacy. Web exhibit hosted by the Clarke Historical Library, Central Michigan University.

Bowker, William H. 1907. The Old Guard and the Faculty of Four. *MAC: College and Alumni News*. Amherst, Mass.: Carpenter and Morehouse Press.

Bowser, Gillian. 2001. National Park Service Community Report. http://www.nps.gov/community/community_report.htm. (accessed May 9, 2007).

Branstner, M. C. 1989. Ceramics and Table Glass. In *Excavations at the Trombley House (20By70): A Settlement Period House Site in Bay City, Michigan*, edited by E. J. Prahl. *Michigan Archaeologist* 35: 153–70.

Bright, Arthur A., Jr. 1949. *The Electric-Lamp Industry: Technological Change and Economic Development from 1800 to 1947*. New York: Macmillan Company.

Brown, Virginia Sparr. 1981. *Grundy County Illinois Landmarks: A Guide to Places of Interest in Aux Sable, Erienna, Goose Lake, Nettle Creek, Saratoga, Wauponsee, and Morris Townships*. N.p.: Grundy County Historical Society.

Bryan, John Morrill. 1976. *An Architectural History of the South Carolina College 1801–1855*. Columbia: University of South Carolina Press.

Caltrans. 1985. Final Environmental Impact Report/Statement State Route 82 in the Vicinity of the University of Santa Clara, Widening and Realignment between State Route 880 and Scott Boulevard in the Cities of Santa Clara and San Jose in the County of Santa Clara. Section 4(f) Evaluation on the Murguia Mission Site. California Department of Transportation, District 4, San Francisco and U.S. Department of Transportation, Federal Highway Administration.

Calyx. 1895. Vol. 1. Published by the Students of Washington and Lee University, Lexington, Virginia. Cleveland, Ohio: Press of J. B. Savage.

———. 1900. Vol. 5. Published by the Students of Washington and Lee University, Lexington, Virginia. Roanoke, Va.: Stone Press.

Camp, Helen B. 1975. *Archaeological Excavations at Pemaquid, Maine, 1965–1974*. Augusta: Maine State Museum.

Carnes, Mark C., and Clyde Griffen, eds. 1990. *Meanings for Manhood: Constructions of Masculinity in Victorian America*. Chicago: University of Chicago Press.

Carnes-McNaughton, Linda F. 1991. Summary of Research Notes for Bicentennial Archaeology Project. MS on file, Research Laboratories of Archaeology, University of North Carolina, Chapel Hill.

Carpenter, Edward, and Charles F. Morehouse. 1896. *A History of the Town of Amherst*. Amherst, Mass.: Carpenter and Morehouse Press.

Cary, Harold W. 1962. *The University of Massachusetts: A History of One Hundred Years*. Amherst: University of Massachusetts Press.

Castille, George, Cinda Baldwin, and Carl Steen. 1986. *An Archaeological Survey of Alkaline Glazed Stoneware Pottery Kiln Sites in the Old Edgefield District of South Carolina*. Columbia: McKissick Museum and the South Carolina Institute of Archaeology and Anthropology, University of South Carolina.

Cecil, Andrea. 2001. 100–Year-Old Time Capsule Opened in Detroit. *Kalamazoo Gazette*, January 2, p. D6.

Chronicle of Higher Education. 1993. Time Capsule Eludes U. of Montana. August 4, p. A5.

Clark, Christopher. 1979. Household Economy, Market Exchange and the Rise of Capitalism in the Connecticut Valley, 1800–1860. *Journal of Social History* 13 (1979): 169–89.

———. 1990. *The Roots of Rural Capitalism: Western Massachusetts, 1780–1860*. Ithaca: Cornell University Press.

Cochrane, Willard W. 1979. *The Development of American Agriculture: An Historical Analysis*. Minneapolis: University of Minnesota Press.

Cohen, Lawrence A. 1974. *American Education: The Colonial Experience, 1607–1783*. New York: Harper and Row, Publishers.

Collard, Elizabeth. 1987. *Nineteenth-Century Pottery and Porcelain in Canada*. Kingston: McGill-Queens University Press.

Colley, Sarah. 2004. University-Based Archaeology Teaching and Learning and Professionalism in Australia. *World Archaeology* 36(2): 189–202.

Collins, Chris. 1996. Time Wasn't on the Side of Buried Capsule. *Recorder* (Greenfield, Mass.), October 23, p. 3.

Colonial Society of Massachusetts (CSM). 1925. *Harvard College Records*. Vols. 15, 16. Boston, Mass.: Colonial Society of Massachusetts.

Commonwealth of Massachusetts. 1863. Commonwealth of Massachusetts Statutes, Chapter 220, Act of 1863, An Act to Incorporate the Trustees of the Massachusetts Agricultural College, April 29, 1863, 1–2, Record Group 1/29–Legislation. Special Collections and Archives, W.E.B. DuBois Library, University of Massachusetts, Amherst.

Conkey, Margaret W., and Ruth E. Tringham. 1996. Cultivating Thinking/Challenging Authority: Some Experiments in Feminist Pedagogy in Archaeology. In *Gender and Archaeology*, edited by Rita P. Wright, pp. 224–50. Philadelphia: University of Pennsylvania Press.

Connor, R.D.W. 1953. *Documentary History of the University of North Carolina, 1776–1799*. 2 vols. Chapel Hill: University of North Carolina Press.

Cook, John Williston. 1912. *Educational History of Illinois: Growth and Progress in Educational Affairs of the State from the Earliest Day to the Present*. Chicago: Henry O. Shephard Company.

Copeland, Robert. 1982. *Blue and White Transfer Printed Pottery*. Shire Album 97. Bucks, UK: Shire Publications.

Crenshaw, Ollinger. 1969. *General Lee's College: The Rise and Growth of Washington and Lee University*. New York: Random House.

———. 1973. General Lee's College: The Rise and Growth of Washington and Lee University. Typed manuscript.

Dalsin, Jerry. 2003. *Land & Water* 4 (July): 1–3.

Danhof, Clarence H. 1969. *Change in Agriculture: The Northern United States, 1820–1870*. Cambridge, Mass.: Harvard University Press.

Dart, Sarah. 1897. Early Lansing. *Michigan Pioneer and Historical Collections* 28: 172–79.

Davenport, Charles B. 1911. *Heredity in Relation to Eugenics*. New York: Holt and Company.

Davis, James E. 1998. *Frontier Illinois*. Indianapolis: Indiana University Press.

diZerega Wall, Diana, Nan Rothschild, Cynthia Copeland, and Herbert Seignoret. 2004. The Seneca Village Project: Working with Modern Communities in Creating the Past. In *Places in Mind: Public Archaeology as Applied Anthropology*, edited by Paul A. Shackel and Erve J. Chambers, 101–17. New York: Routledge.

Doctorow, E. L. 1985. *World's Fair*. New York: Random House.

Dovilliers, Edwin J. 1986. *A Columbia Reader, 1786–1986*. Columbia: University of South Carolina, Institute for Southern Studies, South Caroliniana Library.

Downey, A. J. 2002. An Evaluation of CAD Mapping at the Old College and Log Chapel Site. Manuscript on file. Notre Dame, Ind.: Archaeology Laboratory, Department of Anthropology, University of Notre Dame.

Drucker, Leslie, Ronald Anthony, Susan Jackson, Susan Krantz, and Carl Steen. 1984. *An Archaeological Study of the Little River Buffalo Creek Special Land Disposal Tract*. Columbia: Carolina Archaeological Services.

Edmund, Larry. 1973. Archaeologists Solve Horseshoe Mystery. *Gamecock*, July 19, 1.

Edward G. Grainger Papers (EGGP/MSUAHC). 1858–60. UA 10.3.144. Michigan State University Archives and Historical Collections, East Lansing.

Elliot, Marc. 1991. Profs to Plan Furlough Protests. *Massachusetts Daily Collegian*, April 10, p. 1.

Ellis, Neenah. 2005. *One-Room Schools Holding on in Rural America*. Story posted on National Public Radio website. http://www.npr.org/templates/story/story.php?storyId=5064420 (accessed August 18, 2008).

Engs, Ruth Clifford. 2000. *Clean Living Movements: American Cycles of Health Reform*. Westport, Conn.: Praeger.

Farrington, Leslie Joseph. 1967. Development of Public School Administration in the Public Schools of Will County, Illinois, as Shown in a Comparison of Three Selected Years, 1877, 1920, and 1965. Ph.D. dissertation. Department of Education, Northern Illinois University.

Fetterman, David M. 1998. *Ethnography: Step by Step*. 2nd ed. Thousand Oaks, Calif.: Sage Publications.

Fischer, David Hackett. 1989. *Albion's Seed: Four British Folkways in America*. New York: Oxford University Press.

Fitzgerald, Paul J., S.J. 2002. Santa Clara University and the Jesuit Tradition of Education. In *Telling the Santa Clara Story: Sesquicentennial Voices*, edited by Russell K. Skowronek, pp. 105–18. Santa Clara: City of Santa Clara and Santa Clara University.

Foght, Harold Waldstein. 1910. *The American Rural School: Its Characteristics, Its Future, and Its Problems*. New York: Macmillan Company.

Freehling, William. 1965. *Prelude to Civil War: The Nullification Controversy in South Carolina 1816–1832*. New York: Harper and Row.

Freire, Paulo. 2000. *Pedagogy of the Oppressed* (1970). New York: Continuum Publishing.

Fuller, Wayne E. 1982. *The Old Country School.* Chicago: University of Chicago Press.

Galke, Laura J. 2006. Constructing Discipline, Deconstructing Ideology: The Archaeology and History of Washington and Lee's Antebellum Dormitories. *Journal of Middle Atlantic Archaeology* 22: 19–29.

Galke, Laura J., and Bernard K. Means. 2008. Final Report on the Phase II Archaeological Test Excavations of the Union Hall Site, 44RB489B. Lexington. Report on file, Special Collections, Leyburn Library, Washington and Lee University.

Garcia, Lorie, George Giacomini, and Geof Goodfellow. 2002. *A Place of Promise: The City of Santa Clara 1852–2002.* Santa Clara: City of Santa Clara.

Garcia, Lorie, and Patricia Mahan. 2002. Ground Zero for Silicon Valley—The Last Fifty Years: A Personal Perspective. In *Telling the Santa Clara Story: Sesquicentennial Voices*, edited by Russell K. Skowronek, pp. 162–67. Santa Clara: City of Santa Clara and Santa Clara University.

Garnet and Black. 1899. South Carolina College Yearbook.

Gates, Paul W. 1960. *The Farmer's Age: Agriculture, 1815–1860, Vol. 3: The Economic History of the United States.* New York: Holt, Rinehart and Winston.

Gates, William C., Jr., and Dana E. Ormerod. 1982. *The East Liverpool, Ohio, Pottery District: Identification of Manufacturers and Marks. Historical Archaeology* 16 (1–2).

Geiger, Roger L. 2000. Introduction: New Themes in the History of Nineteenth-Century Colleges. In *The American College in the Nineteenth Century*, edited by Roger Geiger, pp. 1–36. Nashville: Vanderbilt University Press.

Geiger, Roger L., and Julie Ann Bubolz. 2000. College as It Was in the Mid-Nineteenth Century. In *The American College in the Nineteenth Century*, edited by Roger Geiger, pp. 80–90. Nashville: Vanderbilt University Press.

Gero, Joan M. 1996. Archaeological Field Practice and Gendered Encounters. In *Gender and Archaeology*, edited by Rita P. Wright, pp. 251–80. Philadelphia: University of Pennsylvania Press.

Gerry, John. 1988. The Old Stoughton Hall Site: An Archaeological view of Eighteenth Century Harvard. Unpublished research project, School of Extension Studies, Harvard University.

Giacomini, George F., Jr. 2002. A Very Happy Group: Nineteenth Century Student Life at Santa Clara. In *Telling the Santa Clara Story: Sesquicentennial Voices*, edited by Russell K. Skowronek, pp. 119–32. Santa Clara: City of Santa Clara and Santa Clara University.

Giacomini, George F., Jr., and Gerald McKevitt, S.J. 2000. *Serving the Intellect, Touching the Heart: A Portrait of Santa Clara University, 1851–2001.* Santa Clara: Santa Clara University.

Godden, Geoffrey. 1954. *Encyclopedia of British Pottery and Porcelain Marks.* New York: Crown Publishers.

Goodrich, Enos. 1886. Locating the State Capitol at Lansing. *Michigan Pioneer and Historical Collections* 8: 121–30.

Gorman, Frederick R. 1984. A Proposal to Conduct Harvard's 1984 Archaeological Field School in Harvard Yard. MS on file, Peabody Museum, Cambridge, Massachusetts.

Grabar, Robert. 1991. Jobs Axed: UMass Cuts 56. *Daily Hampshire Gazette*, August 7, p. 1.

Graffam, Gray. 1981. *Final Report, Phase III, Red Line Extension, Northwest: Excavation of the Olmstead-Goffe House Site at Wadsworth Gate*. Cambridge, Mass.: Institute for Conservation Archaeology, Peabody Museum, Harvard University.

———. 1982. The Use of Pattern in Student Material Culture: A Preliminary Report from Harvard Yard. *North American Archaeologist* 3(3): 207–24.

Gray, A. 1916. The Teacher's Home. *Elementary School Journal* 17(3): 201–8.

Gray, Lewis Cecil. 1958. *History of Agriculture in the Southern United States to 1860*. Washington, D.C.: Carnegie Institute of Washington, 1933; reprint, Gloucester, Mass.: Peter Smith.

Green, Edwin L. 1916. *A History of the University of South Carolina*. Columbia: State Company.

Gritt, Henry. 1955 Changing Chapel. *Harvard Crimson*, March 15, http://www.thecrimson.com/article.aspx?ref=488670 (accessed May 29, 2009).

Gupta, Akhil, and James Ferguson. 1997. Beyond "Culture": Space, Identity and the Politics of Difference. In *Culture, Power, Place: Explorations in Critical Anthropology*, edited by Akhil Gupta and James Ferguson, pp. 33–51. Durham, N.C.: Duke University Press.

Harrington, Thomas F. 1906. *The Harvard Medical School: A History, Narrative, and Documentary*. New York: Lewis Publishing Company.

Harris, Samantha, Jennifer Geddes, Kate Hahn, Diane Chonette, and Russell Skowronek. 1995. *The Eberhard Privy: Archaeological and Historical Insights into Santa Clara History*. Research Manuscript Series on the Cultural and Natural History of Santa Clara, No. 7. Santa Clara: Santa Clara University.

Hayn, Carl H., S.J. 2002. Early History of Science at Santa Clara. In *Telling the Santa Clara Story: Sesquicentennial Voices*, edited by Russell K. Skowronek, pp. 134–42. Santa Clara: City of Santa Clara and Santa Clara University.

Henderson, Archibald. 1949. *The Campus of the First State University*. Chapel Hill: University of North Carolina Press.

Hennig, Helen Kohn. 1936. *Columbia, Capital City of South Carolina: 1786–1936*. Columbia: Columbia Sesquicentennial Commission.

Herbst, Jurgen. 1996. *The Once and Future School: Three Hundred and Fifty Years of American Secondary Education*. New York: Routledge.

Hessinger, Rodney. 1999. "The Most Powerful Instrument of College Discipline": Student Disorder and the Growth of Meritocracy in the College of the Early Republic. *History of Education Quarterly* 39(3): 237–62.

Hibbard, Benjamin Horace. 1924. *A History of the Public Land Policies*. Madison: University of Wisconsin Press.

Hobsbawm, Eric, and Terence Ranger, eds. 1983. *The Invention of Tradition*. Cambridge: Cambridge University Press.

Hodder, Ian. 2003. Archaeological Reflexivity and the "Local" Voice. *Anthropological Quarterly* 76(1): 55–69.

Hoffman, Urias John. 1908. *The One-Room Country Schools in Illinois*. Circular No. 28. Springfield, Ill.: Department of Public Instruction.

Hoffman, Urias John, and W. S. Booth. 1912. *The One-Room Country Schools and Village Schools*. Circular No. 65. Springfield, Ill.: Department of Public Instruction.

Hollis, Daniel Walker. 1951. *University of South Carolina South Carolina College*. Vol. 1. Columbia: University of South Carolina Press.

———. 1968. *U.S.C. Guide: The Historic Horseshoe—The Old University Campus* (brochure). Columbia: South Caroliniana Library, University of South Carolina.

———. 1982. *Remembering the Days: An Illustrated History of the University of South Carolina*. Columbia: Institute for Southern Studies, University of South Carolina/R. L. Bryan Company.

Holtorf, Cornelius, and Howard Williams. 2006. Landscapes and Memories. In *The Cambridge Companion to Historical Archaeology*, edited by Dan Hicks and Mary C. Beaudry, pp. 235–54. Cambridge: Cambridge University Press.

Howe, Daniel Walker. 2002. Church, State, and Education in the Young American Republic. *Journal of the Early Republic* 22(1): 1–24.

Huber, Mary T., Pat Hutchings, Richard Gale, Ross Miller, and Molly Breen. 2007. Leading Initiatives for Integrative Learning. *Liberal Education* 93(2) (Spring).

Hylkema, Linda J. 2007. Native American Remains at Santa Clara University: A Summary of Findings. Paper presented at the Society for California Archaeology 41st Annual Meeting, March 22–25, San Jose, California.

Illinois Secretary of State. 1827. *Session Laws of Illinois, 1826–1827*. Springfield: State of Illinois.

Illinois State Board of Education (ISBOE). 2004. Illinois Education Timeline. Document on file with the ISBOE.

Jackson, Leon. 2000. The Rights of Man and the Rites of Youth: Fraternity and Riot at Eighteenth-Century Harvard. In *The American College in the Nineteenth Century*, edited by Roger Geiger, pp. 46–79. Nashville: Vanderbilt University Press.

Jameson, John H., Jr., editor. 1997. *Presenting Archaeology to the Public: Digging for Truths*. Walnut Creek, Calif.: AltaMira Press.

Jenkins, Isabel R., B. Mark Lynch, and Russell K. Skowronek. 1998. The Adobe Lodge: A Review of Archaeological Excavation and Historical Background (1981.1). Report on file. Santa Clara University Archaeology Research Lab, Santa Clara University, Santa Clara, California.

Johnson, Richard B., M. Catherine Bird, and Carrie Koster-Horan. 2003. *Results of a Phase I Archaeological Reconnaissance Survey of 1,400 Acres of Land in Jackson*

Township, Illinois. Cultural Resource Management Report No. 1192. Marengo, Ill.: Midwest Archaeological Research Services, Inc.

Jones, Elizabeth A., Patricia M. Samford, R. P. Stephen Davis, Jr., and Melissa A. Salvanish. 1998. *Archaeological Investigations at the Pettigrew Site on the University of North Carolina Campus, Chapel Hill, North Carolina*. Research Report No. 20. Chapel Hill: Research Laboratories of Archaeology, University of North Carolina.

Jones, Laura, Elena Reese, and John Rick. 1996. "Is It Not 'Haunted Ground'?": Architectural, Archival and Archaeological Investigations of the Stanford Family's Palo Alto Home. *Sandstone and Tile* 20(1): 31–44.

Jones, Lewis. 1971. *South Carolina: A Synoptic History for Laymen*. Orangeburg, S.C.: Sandlapper Press.

Jones, Thomas B., and Olaf F. Larson. 1975. A National Survey on Country Life in America: The Unpublished Data from the Roosevelt Commission on Country Life (1908). Paper presented at the annual meeting of the Rural Sociological Society.

Joseph R. Williams Papers (JRWP/MSUAHC). 1827–67. UA 2.1.1. Michigan State University Archives and Historical Collections, East Lansing.

Kaestle, Carl F. 1983. *Pillars of the Republic: Common Schools and American Society, 1780–1860*. New York: Hill and Wang.

Kern, A. R. 2004. Evaluation of Iron Conservation Techniques. Manuscript on file. Notre Dame, Ind.: Archaeology Laboratory, Department of Anthropology, University of Notre Dame.

King, Dianne. 1996. From the Casket: Words of Wisdom and Hope from a Century Ago Offer Inspiration and Examples for Today. *Chicago Tribune*, March 10, section 13, p. 1.

King, Thomas F. 2003. *Places That Count: Traditional Cultural Properties in Cultural Resources Management*. Walnut Creek, Calif.: AltaMira Press.

Kirkendall, Richard S. 1986. The Agricultural Colleges: between Tradition and Modernization. *Agricultural History* 60(2): 3–21.

Klimm, L. E. 1933. The Relation between Certain Population Changes and the Physical Environment in Hampden, Hampshire, and Franklin Counties, Massachusetts, 1790–1925. Ph.D. dissertation, University of Pennsylvania, Philadelphia.

Koster-Horan, Carrie. 2002. *Phase II Testing at the Tamarack School (11–Wi-2487), Wheatland Township, Will County, Illinois*. Cultural Resource Management Report No. 1113. Marengo, Ill.: Midwest Archaeological Research Services, Inc.

———. 2003. *Phase II Archaeological Testing at the Meade School (11–Gr-257) in Aux Sable Township, Grundy County, Illinois*. Cultural Resource Management Report No. 1191. Marengo, Ill.: Midwest Archaeological Research Services, Inc.

———. 2004. *Phase II Testing of Site 11–Wi-2807 (Lower Ridge School), Jackson Township, Will County, Illinois*. Cultural Resource Management Report No. 1245. Marengo, Ill.: Midwest Archaeological Research Services, Inc.

Koster-Horan, Carrie, Rochelle Lurie, and M. Catherine Bird. 2007. *Results of a Phase III Data Recovery of the Lower Ridge School Site (11–Wi-2807), Jackson Township,*

Will County, Illinois. Cultural Resource Management Report No. 1321. Marengo, Ill.: Midwest Archaeological Research Services, Inc.

Kottak, Conrad P. 1987. *Cultural Anthropology*. 4th ed. New York: Random House.

Kuhn, Madison. 1955. *Michigan State: The First Hundred Years, 1855–1955*. East Lansing: Michigan State University Press.

Kulik, Gary, Roger Parks, and Theodore Z. Penn. 1982. Introduction. In *The New England Mill Village, 1790–1860*, edited by Gary Kulik, Roger Parks, and Theodore Z. Penn, pp. xxii–xxxv. Cambridge, Mass: MIT Press.

Lambert, Jay Wilfred. 1958. Buildings and Grounds—Tennis Courts. Oral History Collection. On file, University Archives, College of William and Mary, Williamsburg, Virginia.

Lansing Republican. 1876. Fire at the Agricultural College, Old Boarding Hall Destroyed, December 12.

Larkin, Jack. 1988. Massachusetts Enters the Marketplace, 1790–1860. In *A Guide to the History of Massachusetts*, edited by Martin Kaufman, John W. Ifkovic, and Joseph Carvalho III, pp. 69–82. New York: Greenwood Press.

LaRoche, Cheryl, and Michael Blakey. 1997. Seizing Intellectual Power: The Dialogue at the New York African Burial Ground. *Historical Archaeology* 31: 84–106.

Lave, Jean, and Etienne Wenger. 1991. *Situated Learning: Legitimate Peripheral Participation*. Cambridge: Cambridge University Press.

Legg, James, and S. Smith. 1989. *The Best Ever Occupied . . .* Research Manuscript Series No. 209. Columbia: University of South Carolina, South Carolina Institute of Archaeology and Anthropology.

Leone, Mark. 1981. Archaeology's Relationship to the Present and the Past. In *Modern Material Culture: The Archaeology of Us*, edited by Richard A. Gould and Michael B. Schiffer, pp. 5–14. New York: Academic Press.

Leuchtenburg, William E. 1963. *Franklin D. Roosevelt and the New Deal*. New York: Harper and Row.

Lewis, Kenneth E. 2002. *West to Far Michigan: Settling the Lower Peninsula, 1815–1860*. East Lansing: Michigan State University Press.

———. 2004. Mapping Antebellum Euro-American Settlement Spread in Southern Lower Michigan. *Michigan Historical Review* 30(2): 105–34.

———. 2006. *Camden: Historical Archaeology in the South Carolina Backcountry*. Belmont, Calif.: Thomson Wadsworth.

Lewis, Kenneth, and Helen Haskell. 1978. *The Middleton Place Privy*. Research Manuscript Series No. 104. Popular Series 1. Columbia: University of South Carolina, South Carolina Institute of Archaeology and Anthropology.

Lewis Ransom Fiske Papers (LRFP). 1859–63. UA 2.1.2, Michigan State University Archives and Historical Collections, East Lansing.

Lexington Gazette (Lexington, Virginia). 1842. Washington College. July 7.

Lincoln, Abraham. 1832. Letter. *Sangamon Journal*, March 15.

Link, Arthur S. 1954. *Woodrow Wilson and the Progressive Era, 1910–1917*. New York: Harper and Row.

Lipe, William D. 2002. Public Benefits of Archaeological Research. In *Public Benefits of Archaeology*, edited by Barbara J. Little, pp. 20–28. Gainesville: University of Florida Press.

Lishman, F. J. G. 1951. Rural School Sanitation with Special Reference to Chemical Toilets. *Public Health*. 64(8): 147–51.

Little, Barbara J. 2002. Archaeology as a Shared Vision. In *Public Benefits of Archaeology*, edited by Barbara J. Little, 3–19. Gainesville: University Press of Florida.

Little, W. L. 1960. *Staffordshire Blue*. London: B. A. Batsford Ltd.

Locatelli, Paul, S.J. 2002. Santa Clara University: 2025. In *Telling the Santa Clara Story: Sesquicentennial Voices*, edited by Russell K. Skowronek, pp. 180–90. Santa Clara: City of Santa Clara and Santa Clara University.

Lonergan, Jonelle M. 1999. Arsenic Found in Holden Chapel Excavation Site. *Harvard Crimson*, July 16, *http://www.thecrimson.com/article.aspx?ref=97238* (accessed May 29, 2009).

Loring, George B. 1870. The Farmer and the College. In *Seventeenth Annual Report of the Massachusetts Board of Agriculture, with an Appendix Containing Reports of Delegates Appointed to Visit the County Exhibitions, and Also Returns of the Finances Agricultural Societies for 1869*. Boston: Wright and Potter, State Printers.

Loth, Calder Conrad. 1967. The Ante Bellum Architecture of Washington and Lee University. Master's thesis, University of Virginia, Charlottesville.

Lowenthal, David. 1985. *The Past Is a Foreign Country*. Cambridge: Cambridge University Press.

Lyle, Royster, Jr., and Pamela H. Simpson. 1977. *The Architecture of Historic Lexington*. Published for the Historic Lexington Foundation. Charlottesville: University Press of Virginia.

Madison Kuhn Collection (MKC/MSUAHC). 1827–1966. UA 17.107. Michigan State University Archives and Historical Collections, East Lansing.

Malone, Michael S. 2002. The Mission Bell's Toll. In *Telling the Santa Clara Story: Sesquicentennial Voices*, edited by Russell K. Skowronek, pp. 170–79. Santa Clara: City of Santa Clara and Santa Clara University.

Marshall, Yvonne. 2002. What Is Community Archaeology? *World Archaeology* 34(2): 211–19.

Massachusetts Agricultural College (MAC). 1877. Programme of Exercises at the Planting of the Class Tree by the Class of '78, Massachusetts Agricultural College, June 19, 1877, at 4 p.m. Special Collections and Archives, W.E.B. DuBois Library, University of Massachusetts, Amherst.

———. 1878a. *Class of Seventy-eight, Its Oration, Poem, Prophecies, History, Etc., as Delivered at Class Supper, Parker House, Boston, June 21, 1878*. Amherst, Mass.: Transcript Job Office.

———. 1878b. Secretary's Record, Class of 1878. Record Group 50/6. Special Collections and Archives, W.E.B. DuBois Library, University of Massachusetts, Amherst.

Matile, Roger. 2005. The Post Offices That Are No Longer There. *Oswego Ledger-Sentinel*, January 27.

Matthews, Christopher N. 2004. Public Significance and Imagined Archaeologists: Authoring Pasts in Context. *International Journal of Historical Archaeology* 8(1): 1–25.

Maue, August. 1928. *History of Will County, Illinois*. Indianapolis, Ind.: Historical Publishing Company.

Maxcy, Spencer J. 1979. The Teacherage in American Rural Education. *Journal of General Education* 30(4): 267–74.

May, Lee. 1991. Lost Time Capsules: When History Gets Mislaid. *Los Angeles Times*, July 22, section A.

Mays, Patricia J. 1997. On Eve of Millennium, Time Capsule Fever. *Kalamazoo Gazette*, June 15.

McCleary, Ann E. 2000. Forging a Regional Identity: Development of Rural Vernacular Architecture in the Central Shenandoah Valley, 1790–1850. In *After the Backcountry: Rural Life in the Great Valley of Virginia, 1800–1900*, edited by Kenneth E. Koons and Warren R. Hofstra. Knoxville: University of Tennessee Press.

McClung, Anne Drake. 2001. *Among these Ancient Mountains: The Story of Rockbridge County, Virginia*. Hong Kong: Alone Mill Publishing.

McDaniel, John M., David Moore, Charles Watson, Gary Funkhouser, and Ellis Coleman. 1976. An Eighteenth-Century Academic Institution: A New Archaeological Focus. Paper presented at the Southern Anthropological Society Meeting, Atlanta, Georgia.

McDaniel, John M., Kurt C. Russ, and Parker B. Potter. 1979. A Description and Analysis of Tobacco Pipes Excavated at Liberty Hall. *Quarterly Bulletin Archeological Society of Virginia* 34(2): 83–92.

———. 1994. *An Archaeological and Historical Assessment of the Liberty Hall Academy Complex, 1782–1803*. James G. Leyburn Papers in Anthropology, Vol. 2. Lexington, Va.: Liberty Hall Press.

McDaniel, John M., Charles N. Watson, and David T. Moore. 1979. *Liberty Hall Academy: The Early History of the Institutions Which Evolved into Washington and Lee University*. Lexington, Va.: Liberty Hall Press.

McGimsey, Charles. 1972. *Public Archaeology*. New York: Seminar Press.

McKay, Leonard. 2002. The Great Depression and World War II: Recollections of Santa Clara University. In *Telling the Santa Clara Story: Sesquicentennial Voices*, edited by Russell K. Skowronek, pp. 143–54. Santa Clara: City of Santa Clara and Santa Clara University.

McKevitt, Gerald, S.J. 1979. *The University of Santa Clara: A History, 1851–1977*. Stanford, Calif.: Stanford University Press.

Meriwether, Colyer. 1889. *History of Higher Education in South Carolina with a Sketch of the Free School System*. Bureau of Education Circular of Information No. 3, 1888. Washington, D.C.: Government Printing Office.

Merriman, Nick, editor. 2004. *Public Archaeology*. London: Routledge.

Meyer, Douglas K. 2000. *Making the Heartland Quilt: A Geographical History of Settlement and Migration in Early-Nineteenth-Century Illinois*. Carbondale: Southern Illinois University Press.

Michie, James L. 1990. *Richmond Hill Plantation 1810–1868: Discovery of Antebellum Life on a Waccamaw Rice Plantation*. Spartanburg, S.C.: Reprint Company.

Michigan. Acts of the Legislature (MAL/A). 1850–55. Acts. Lansing: Hosmer and Kerr.

Michigan. Annual Report of the Superintendent of Public Instruction (M/RSPI). 1858. Lansing: Homer and Kerr.

Michigan. Superintendent of Public Instruction (M/SPI). 1858. *Reports for the Years 1855, '56, '57*. Lansing: Homer and Kerr.

———. 1877. *Fortieth Annual Report for the Year 1876*. Lansing: W. S. George and Company.

Michigan Agricultural College. 1857. *First Annual Catalogue*. Michigan State University Archives and History Collections.

———. 1876. *Twentieth Annual Catalogue*. Lansing, Mich.: W. S. George and Company.

———. 1878. *Twenty-second Annual Catalogue*. Lansing, Mich.: W. S. George and Company.

Michigan Railroad Commission. 1919. *Aids, Gifts, Grants, and Donations to Railroads, Including Outline of Development and Successions in Titles to Railroads in Michigan*, by Edmund A. Calkins. Lansing: Wynkoop Hallenbeck Crawford.

Michigan State University. 2007. Saints' Rest: Early Campus Life at Michigan State University. http://special.news.msu.edu/digMSU/ (accessed May 29, 2009).

Miller, George. 1990. A Revised Set of CC Index Values for Classification and Scaling of English Ceramics from 1787 to 1880. *Historical Archaeology* 25: 1–29.

Miller, George, and Robert Hunter. 1990. English Shell Edged Earthenware: Alias Leeds Ware, Alias Feather Edge. In *35th Annual International Wedgwood Seminar*, 107–36.

Monroe, Elizabeth J., and David W. Lewes. 2004. Archaeological Survey of the Proposed Barksdale Dormitory Site, College of William and Mary, Williamsburg, Virginia. Prepared for the Facilities Planning, Design, and Construction Department, College of William and Mary, Williamsburg, Virginia.

Morison, Samuel Eliot. 1935. *The Founding of Harvard College*. Cambridge, Mass.: Harvard University Press.

———. 1936a. *Harvard College in the Seventeenth Century*. 2 vols. Cambridge, Mass.: Harvard University Press.

———. 1936b. *Three Centuries of Harvard*. Cambridge, Mass.: Harvard University Press

Moser, Stephanie, Darren Glazier, James E. Phillips, Lamya Nasser el Nemr, Mohammed Saleh Mousa, Rascha Nasr Aiesh, Susan Richardson, Andrew Conner, and Michael Seymour. 2002. Transforming Archaeology through Practice: Strategies for Collaborative Archaeology and the Community Archaeology Project at Quseir, Egypt. *World Archaeology* 34(2): 220–48.

Mullins, Paul R. 2004. African-American Heritage in a Multicultural Community: An Archaeology of Race, Culture, and Consumption. In *Places in Mind: Public Archaeology as Applied Anthropology*, edited by Paul A. Shackel and Erve J. Chambers, pp. 57–69. New York: Routledge.

Mustonen, Heather. 2007. Public Archaeology and Community Engagement at Michigan State University: The Saints' Rest Archaeological Project. Master's thesis, Department of Anthropology, Michigan State University.

Nassaney, Michael. 2004. Implementing Community Service Learning through Archaeological Practice. *Michigan Journal of Community Service Learning* 10(3): 89–99.

Nassaney, Michael S., and Marjorie Abel. 1993. The Political and Social Contexts of Cutlery Production in the Connecticut Valley. *Dialectical Anthropology* 18: 247–89.

Nassaney, Michael S., Uzi Baram, James C. Garman, and Michael F. Milewski. 1996. Guns and Roses: Ritualism, Time Capsules, and the Massachusetts Agricultural College. *Old-Time New England* 74(262): 59–80.

Nassaney, Michael S., Alan H. McArdle, and Peter Stott. 1989. *An Archaeological Locational Survey, Site Evaluation, and Data Recovery at the Russell-Harrington Cutlery Site, Turners Falls, Massachusetts.* University of Massachusetts Archaeological Services Report No. 68. Boston: Massachusetts Historical Commission, Office of the Secretary of State.

Naumer, Walter W. 1985. School District Organization in Illinois. Report on file at the Illinois State Board of Education; Table 1 on file with Catherine Bird.

Neff, Mary. 1995. *Preserving the Family Farm: Women, Community, and the Foundations of Agribusiness in the Midwest, 1900–1940.* Baltimore: Johns Hopkins University Press.

Nelson, Lee Nail. 1968. Chronology as an Aid to Dating Old Buildings. *History News* 24 (11): 1–12. American Association for State and Local History, Leaflet 48.

Nerad, Maresi. 1999. *The Academic Kitchen: A Social History of Gender Stratification at the University of California, Berkeley.* Albany: State University of New York Press.

Neth, Mary. 1995. *Preserving the Family Farm: Women, Community, and the Foundations of Agribusiness in the Midwest 1900–1940.* Baltimore: Johns Hopkins University Press.

New York Times. 1991. A Time Capsule Helps Archivists to Look Back. Campus Life section, July 14.

Noël Hume, Ivor. 1969. *Historical Archaeology.* New York: Alfred A. Knopf.

———. 1970. *A Guide to Artifacts of Colonial America.* New York: Alfred A. Knopf.

O'Connor, Megan. 2006. Alcohol Illnesses Double This Year. *Santa Clara* 86(7) (November 2): 1, 4.

Orser, Charles E., Jr. 2004. *Historical Archaeology.* Upper Saddle River, N.J.: Prentice Hall.

Orser, Charles, and A. Nekola J. Roarak. 1982. *Exploring the Rustic Life: Multidisciplinary Research at Millwood Plantation*. Chicago: Mid-American Research Center, Loyola University of Chicago.

Outlaw, Alain C., Mary Clemons, Timothy Morgan, and Donald Sadler. 2005. Phase II Archaeological Investigations: Barksdale Field, the College of William and Mary, Williamsburg, Virginia. Prepared for Facilities Management, College of William and Mary, Williamsburg, Virginia.

Pabst, Margaret R. 1940–41. *Agricultural Trends in the Connecticut Valley Region of Massachusetts, 1800–1900*. Smith College Studies in History 26, 1–4. Northampton, Mass.: Department of History, Smith College.

Pace, Robert F. 2004. *Halls of Honor: College Men in the Old South*. Baton Rouge: Louisiana State University Press.

Pace, Robert F., and Christopher A. Bjornsen. 2000. Adolescent Honor and College Student Behavior in the Old South. *Southern Cultures* 6(3) (Fall): 9–28.

Parascandola, John L. 1998. *A Historical Guide to the U.S. Government*. Edited by G. T. Kurian. New York: Oxford University Press.

Paynter, Robert. 1982. *Models of Spatial Inequality*. New York: Academic Press.

Pendery, Steven R. 1984. *Final Report, Phase III, Chelsea-Water Streets Connector Project, Charlestown, Massachusetts: Excavations at the Wapping Street and Maudlin Street Archaeological Districts*. Cambridge, Mass.: Institute for Conservation Archaeology, Peabody Museum, Harvard University.

———. 1987. Symbols of Community: Status Differences and the Archaeological Record in Charlestown, Massachusetts, 1630–1760. Ph.D. dissertation, Department of Anthropology, Harvard University.

Penn State University (PSU). n.d. *Diversified Products* 1(13): 344–62. Penn State University (PSU) Digital Bookshelf.

Perry, Jennifer E. 2004. Authentic Learning in Field Schools: Preparing Future Members of the Archaeological Community. *World Archaeology* 36(2): 236–60.

Peters, John D. 1997. Seeing Bifocally: Media, Place, Culture. In *Culture, Power, Place: Explorations in Critical Anthropology*, edited by Akhil Gupta and James Ferguson, pp. 75–92. Durham: Duke University Press.

Plainfield Enterprise. 1911. Thomas King obituary, November 16.

Potter, Parker B., Jr. 1994. *Public Archaeology in Annapolis: A Critical Approach to History in Maryland's Ancient City*. Washington, D.C.: Smithsonian Institution Press.

Powell, William S. 1979. *The First State University: A Pictorial History of the University of North Carolina*. Chapel Hill: University of North Carolina Press.

Praetzellis, Adrian. 1998. Introduction: Why Every Archaeologist Should Tell Stories Once in a While. In *Archaeologists as Storytellers*. *Historical Archaeology* 32(1): 1–3.

Praetzellis, Mary, Adrian Praetzellis, and Marley R. Brown III. 1989. What Happened to the Silent Majority? Research Strategies for Studying Dominant Group Material Culture in Late Nineteenth-Century California. In *Documentary Archaeology in the New World*, edited by Mary C. Beaudry, pp. 192–202. Cambridge: Cambridge University Press.

Pratt, Kendra. 1990. Fall Cuts Severely Damage UMass. *Massachusetts Daily Collegian*, September 28.

Pulliam, John. 1967. Changing Attitudes toward Free Public Schools in Illinois, 1825–1860. *History of Education Quarterly* 7(2): 191–208.

Quates, E. W. Duane, Robert Pratt, Lynne Goldstein, Kenneth E. Lewis, and Heather Mustonen. 2006. The Saints' Rest Fire: Archaeology and Fire Investigation. Poster presented at the 71st Annual Meeting of the Society for American Archaeology, San Juan, Puerto Rico.

Rand, Frank Prentice. 1933. *Yesterdays at Massachusetts State College, 1863–1933*. Amherst: Associate Alumni of the Massachusetts State College.

Rapeer, Louis W. 1920. *The Consolidated School*. New York: Charles Scribner's Sons.

Rathje, William, and Cullen Murphy. 1992. *Rubbish! The Archaeology of Garbage*. New York: Harper Collins Publishers.

Reese, Elena, John Holson, and Kevin Bartoy. 2006. *Historic Archaeological Investigations at the Stanford Mansion, Leland Stanford, Jr. Mausoleum and CA-SCL-623/H on the Stanford Campus, Stanford, California*. Berkeley: Pacific Legacy.

Register of Professional Archaeologists (RPA). n.d. *Guidelines and Standards for Archaeological Field Schools*. http://www.rpanet.org/associations/8360/files/field_school_guidelines.pdf (accessed May 29, 2009).

Rosenkrantz, Barbara. 1972. *Public Health and the State: Changing Views in Massachusetts*. Cambridge, Mass.: Harvard University Press.

Rozek, Dan. 2004. Time Running Out for Last 1-Room School. *Chicago Sun-Times*, January 19.

Rubczynski, Withold. 1986. *Home: A Short History of the Idea*. New York: Viking Penguin.

Ruffner, William Henry. 1890. *Early History of Washington College, Now Washington and Lee University*. Washington and Lee University Historical Papers, No. 1. Baltimore: John Murphy and Company.

———. 1893. *The History of Washington College, Now Washington and Lee University during the First Half of the Nineteenth Century*. Washington and Lee University Historical Papers, No. 4. Baltimore: John Murphy and Company.

———. 1904. *The History of Washington College, Now Washington and Lee University during the First Half of the Nineteenth Century*. Washington and Lee University Historical Papers, No. 6. Baltimore: John Murphy and Company.

Samford, Patricia M., and R. P. Stephen Davis, Jr. n.d. The Eagle Hotel: A Report on Archaeological Investigations during the University of North Carolina's Bicentennial Celebration. MS on file, Research Laboratories of Archaeology, University of North Carolina at Chapel Hill.

Sandlin, Jennifer A., and George J. Bey III. 2006. Trowels, Trenches and Transformation: A Case Study of Archaeologists Learning a More Critical Practice of Archaeology. *Journal of Social Archaeology* 6(2): 255–75.

Santa Clara University Archives. 1937. Inventory of Opium, Etc. Dated June 30.

———. 1947. Letters and associated plans from President Gianera, S.J., and the Federal Public Housing Authority, regarding project CAL-V-4454.

———. 1954–62. Donohoe Infirmary Log.

Scarborough, Caprice Murry. 2001. *The Legacy of the "Glacier Priest": Bernard R. Hubbard, S.J.* Research Manuscript Series on the Cultural and Natural History of Santa Clara, No. 10. Santa Clara, Calif.: Santa Clara University.

Schiffer, Michael B. 1976. *Behavioral Archaeology*. New York: Academic Press.

———. 1977. Toward a Unified Science of the Cultural Past. In *Research Strategies in Historical Archaeology*, edited by Stanley South, pp. 13–50. New York: Academic Press.

———. 1985. Is There a "Pompeii Premise" on Archaeology? *Journal of Anthropological Research* 44: 18–41.

Schirtzinger, E. 1991. By the Sweat of Their Brow. Department of Anthropology, University of Notre Dame. Manuscript on file, Archaeology Laboratory, University of Notre Dame.

Schivelbusch, Wolfgang. 1988. *Disenchanted Night: The Industrialization of Light in the Nineteenth Century*. Berkeley: University of California Press.

Schlereth, T. J. 1976. *The University of Notre Dame: A Portrait of Its History and Campus*. Notre Dame, Ind.: University of Notre Dame Press.

Schneider, Carol. 2004. Changing Practices in Liberal Education: What Future Faculty Need to Know. *Peer Review* 6(3): 4–7.

Schuyler, Robert L. 1988. Archaeological Remains, Documents, and Anthropology: A Call for a New Culture History. *Historical Archaeology* 22: 36–42.

Scott, Douglas D., Richard A. Fox, Jr., Melissa A. Connor, and Dick Harmon. 1989. *Archaeological Perspectives on the Battle of the Little Bighorn*. Norman: University of Oklahoma Press.

Sen, Swadhin. 2002. Community Boundary, Secularized Religion and Imagined Past in Bangladesh: Archaeology and Historiography of Unequal Encounter. *World Archaeology* 34(2): 346–62.

Sexton, Rachel. 2000. Holden Chapel: An Archaeological Window into Harvard's Medical History. A.B. thesis, Department of Anthropology, Harvard University.

Shackel, Paul A. 2001. Public Memory and the Search for Power in American Historical Archaeology. *American Anthropologist* 103(3): 655–70.

———. 2004. Working with Communities: Heritage Development and Applied Archaeology. In *Places in Mind: Public Archaeology as Applied Anthropology*, edited by Paul A. Shackel and Erve J. Chambers, pp. 1–16. New York: Routledge.

Singleton, Theresa A., and Charles E. Orser Jr. 2003. Descendant Communities: Linking People in the Present to the Past. In *Ethical Issues in Archaeology*, edited by Larry J. Zimmerman, Karen D. Vitelli, and Julie Hollowell-Zimmer, 143–52. Walnut Creek, Calif.: AltaMira Press.

Sizer, Theodore R. 1964. The Academies: An Interpretation. In *The Age of the*

Academies, edited by Theodore R. Sizer, pp. 1–48. New York: Bureau of Publications, Columbia University.

Skowronek, Russell K., editor. 2002. *Telling the Santa Clara Story: Sesquicentennial Voices*. Santa Clara, Calif.: City of Santa Clara and Santa Clara University.

Skowronek, Russell K., and Margaret A. Graham, editors. 2004. *Discovering Santa Clara University's Prehistoric Past: CA-SCl-755*. Research Manuscript Series on the Cultural and Natural History of Santa Clara, No. 12. Santa Clara, Calif.: Santa Clara University.

Skowronek, Russell K., and Lorna C. Pierce, editors. 2006. *Revealing Santa Clara University's Prehistoric Past: CA-SCl-7559–Evidence from the Arts and Sciences Building Project*. Research Manuscript Series on the Cultural and Natural History of Santa Clara, No. 15. Santa Clara, Calif.: Santa Clara University.

Skowronek, Russell K., with Elizabeth Thompson. 2006. *Situating Mission Santa Clara de Asís: 1776–1851, Documentary and Material Evidence of Life on the Alta California Frontier*. Berkeley: Academy of American Franciscan History.

Smith, Claire, and H. Martin Wobst. 2005. *Indigenous Archaeologies: Decolonizing Theory and Practice*. New York: Routledge.

Society for American Archaeology (SAA). Committee on Ethics. 2007. Principles of Archaeological Ethics. http://www.saa.org/ABOUTSAA/COMMITTEES/ethics/principles.html (accessed May 22, 2007).

South, Stanley. 1967. The Paca House, Annapolis, Maryland: A Historical Archaeology Study. Contract Archaeology, Inc. Unpublished report on file at the University of South Carolina, South Carolina Institute of Archaeology and Anthropology, Columbia.

———. 1973a. Exploratory Archeology Project on the Campus of the University of South Carolina. MS, South Carolina Institute of Archaeology and Anthropology, Columbia.

———. 1973b. *Palmetto Parapets: Exploratory Archeology at Fort Moultrie, South Carolina 38CH50*. Anthropological Studies, No. 1. Columbia: University of South Carolina, South Carolina Institute of Archaeology and Anthropology.

———. 1977. *Method and Theory in Historical Archaeology*. New York: Academic Press.

———. 1979. Historic Site Content, Structure, and Function. *American Antiquity* 44: 213–37.

———. 1997. *Archaeology at Santa Elena: Doorway to the Past*. Popular Series 2. Columbia: University of South Carolina Institute of Archaeology and Anthropology.

———. 2005. *An Archaeological Evolution*. New York: Springer Science and Business Media, Inc.

———. 2008. *Colonial Brunswick: Archaeology of a British Colonial Town*. Raleigh: Historical Publications Section, North Carolina Office of Archives and History. Department of Cultural Resources (in press).

South, Stanley, and Carl Steen. 1992. *Archaeology on the Horseshoe at the University of*

South Carolina. Research Manuscript Series 215. Columbia: South Carolina Institute of Archaeology and Anthropology, University of South Carolina.

South Carolina. 1991. *The South Carolina Legislative Manual*. Columbia: State of South Carolina.

Stanford, Linda O., and C. Kurt Dewhurst. 2002. *MSU Campus: Buildings, Places, Spaces*. East Lansing: Michigan State University Press.

Starn, Orin. 2004. *Ishi's Brain: In Search of America's Last "Wild" Indian*. New York: W. W. Norton and Company.

Steen, Carl. 1989. The Intercolonial Trade of Domestic Earthenware and the Growth of an American Social Identity. M.A. thesis, College of William and Mary, Williamsburg, Virginia.

———. 1991. Excavations on the Bassett Hall Woods Golf Course Tract. Colonial Williamsburg Foundation, Williamsburg, Virginia.

Stubbs, John D. 1992a. Salvage Archaeology in Harvard Yard, Summer 1992. MS on file, Peabody Museum, Harvard University.

———. 1992b. Underground Harvard: The Archaeology of College Life. Ph.D. dissertation, Department of Anthropology, Harvard University.

Sutliff, J. 1992. The Old College Site: An Analysis of Ceramic Material. Manuscript on file. Notre Dame, Ind.: Archaeology Laboratory, Department of Anthropology, University of Notre Dame.

Taber, Martha Van Hoesen. 1955. *A History of the Cutlery Industry in the Connecticut Valley*. Smith College Studies in History 41. Northampton, Mass.: Department of History, Smith College.

Tepper, Steven J. 1998. *The Chronicles of the Bicentennial Observance of the University of North Carolina at Chapel Hill*. Chapel Hill: University of North Carolina.

Theophilus Capen Abbot Papers (TCAP/MSUAHC). 1848–93. UA 2.1.3. Michigan State University Archives and Historical Collections, East Lansing. http://www.rpanet.org/members/field_school_guidelines.pdf (accessed September 18, 2007).

Thorbahn, Peter, and Stephen Mrozowski. 1979. Ecological Dynamics and Rural New England Historical Sites. In *Ecological Anthropology of the Connecticut Valley*, edited by Robert Paynter, pp. 129–40. University of Massachusetts, Department of Anthropology Research Reports No. 18. Amherst: University of Massachusetts.

Towner, Donald. 1978. *Creamware*. New York: Faber and Faber.

Tozer, Steven E., Paul C. Violas, and Guy Senese. 1998. *School and Society: Historical and Contemporary Perspectives*. Boston: McGraw-Hill.

True, Rodney H. 1925. The Early Development of Agricultural Societies in the United States. *Annual Report of the American Historical Association for the Year 1920*: 293–306.

Tyack, David, Thomas James, and Aaron Benavot. 1987. *Law and the Shaping of Public Education*. Madison: University of Wisconsin Press.

United States Bureau of Census. 1870. *Population, 1870*. Washington, D.C.: U.S. Government Printing Office.

United States Tennis Court and Track Builders Association (USTCTBA). 2004. *Tennis Courts: A Construction and Maintenance Manual.* Ellicott, Md.: United States Tennis Court and Track Builders Association Guidelines.

Vickers, James. 1985. *Chapel Hill: An Illustrated History.* Chapel Hill, N.C.: Barclay Publishers.

Wagoner, Jennings L. 1986. Honor and Dishonor at Mr. Jefferson's University: The Antebellum Years. *History of Education Quarterly* 26(2): 155–79.

Walker, George, Chris M. Golde, Laura Jones, Andrea Conklin Bueschel, and Pat Hutchings. 2008. *The Formation of Scholars: Rethinking Doctoral Education for the Twenty-first Century.* San Francisco: Jossey-Bass.

Wallace, David D. 1951. *South Carolina: A Short History.* Columbia: University of South Carolina Press.

Warren, Edward. 1860. *The Life of John Collins Warren, M.D.: Compiled Chiefly from His Autobiography and Journals.* Boston: Ticknor and Fields.

Warren, George M. 1922. *Sewage and Sewerage of Farm Homes.* Washington, D.C.: United States Department of Agriculture.

Washington and Lee University. 1783. Board of Trustees' Records, January 30.

———. 1787. Board of Trustees' Records, February 1.

———. 1793. Board of Trustees' Records, June 10.

———. 1794. Board of Trustees' Records, April 2.

———. 1795. Board of Trustees' Records, March 30.

———. 1839. *Laws and Regulations of Washington College at Lexington, Virginia.* Richmond: Printed by P. D. Bernard.

Waterton, Emma. 2005. Whose Sense of Place? Reconciling Archaeological Perspectives with Community Values: Cultural Landscapes in England. *International Journal of Heritage Studies* 11(4): 309–25.

Watkins, Joe. 2000. *Indigenous Archaeology.* Walnut Creek, Calif.: AltaMira Press.

Whitescarver, Keith. 1993. Creating Citizens for the Republic: Education in Georgia, 1776–1810. *Journal of the Early Republic* 13(4): 455–79.

Widder, Keith R. 2005. *Michigan Agricultural College: The Evolution of a Land-Grant Philosophy, 1855–1925.* East Lansing: Michigan State University Press.

Wilkie, Laurie A. 1998. The Other Gender: The Archaeology of an Early 20th Century Fraternity. *Proceedings of the Society for California Archaeology* 11: 7–11.

———. 2001. Black Sharecroppers and White Frat Boys: Living Communities and the Construction of Their Archaeological Pasts. In *The Archaeology of the Contemporary Past,* edited by Victor Buchli and Gavin Lucas, pp. 108–18. London: Routledge.

———. 2006. Documentary Archaeology. In *The Cambridge Companion to Historical Archaeology,* edited by Dan Hicks and Mary Beaudry, pp. 13–33. Cambridge: Cambridge University Press.

Wilkie, Laurie A., and Stacy Kozakavich. 2005. Going Underground at Cal: 2003 On-Campus Excavations at the University of California, Berkeley. *Proceedings of the Society for California Archaeology* 18: 30–38.

Wilson, Jeff. 1999. Town Tries to Locate Missing Time Capsule. *Kalamazoo Gazette*, November 25.

Winslow, C. 1945. Changing Challenges of Public Health. *American Journal of Public Health and the Nation's Health* 35(3): 191–98.

Winstanley, Derek, Nani G. Bhowmik, Stanley A. Chagnon, and Mark E. Peden. 2002. History of the Illinois State Water Survey. In *Proceedings and Invited Papers for the ASCE 150th Anniversary (1852–2002), November 3–7, 2002, Washington, D.C.*, edited by J. R. Rogers and Frederich, pp. 121–32. Reston, Va.: ASCE.

Wiss, Janney, Elstner Associates, Inc. 2000. Rural Historic Structural Survey of Wheatland, Plainfield, and Lockport Townships, Will County, Illinois. Report on file with the Will County Land Use Department and the Will County Historic Preservation Commission.

Woman's Christian Temperance Union (WCTU). 1888. Petition of the Woman's Christian Temperance Union for the Protection of Women to Congress, May 1888, HR50A-H13.5, Box 147. Records of the House of Representatives. Washington, D.C.: National Archives and Records Administration.

Zimmerman, Larry J. 2005. First, Be Humble: Working with Indigenous Peoples and Other Descendant Communities. In *Indigenous Archaeologies: Decolonizing Theory and Practice*, edited by Claire Smith and H. Martin Wobst, pp. 301–14. New York: Routledge.

Contributors

Uzi Baram is associate professor of anthropology at New College of Florida, where he teaches a wide range of archaeology and cultural anthropology courses. His research interests include collaboration in public archaeology, race and ethnicity, and the intersection of archaeology and heritage tourism.

M. Catherine Bird (Ph.D., RPA), a principal investigator and corporate officer with Midwest Archaeological Research Services, Inc., of Marengo, Illinois, has research interests that include Langford Tradition Mississippian settlement, culture contact situations, archival and genealogical research, the nineteenth-century rural economy, and grave furniture.

Patricia Capone is associate curator, Peabody Museum of Archaeology and Ethnology, Harvard University, and lecturer, Department of Anthropology, Harvard University. With historic archaeology fieldwork in colonial New England and the American Southwest and museum implementation of the Native American Graves Protection and Repatriation Act, she has worked toward collaborative approaches to reflecting on shared pasts and toward a collective future through research, education, and public interpretation.

Kimberly E. Christensen is a candidate in the doctoral program in anthropology at the University of California, Berkeley. Her research focuses on historical archaeology, reform movements, activism, the household, public archaeology, and community research collaboration.

R. P. Stephen Davis Jr. is adjunct professor of anthropology and associate director of the Research Laboratories of Archaeology at the University of North Carolina at Chapel Hill. Although his primary research interest is the impact of European colonization on Native Americans of the southeastern United States, as a UNC alumnus he has a deep interest in the university's history and has conducted numerous archaeological excavations on campus.

Laura J. Galke is the small-finds artifact analyst at the George Washington Foundation in Fredericksburg. Her research interests focus upon analysis and interpretation of the material culture of subaltern groups and cultures in contact within the Middle Atlantic region. She has published on the material culture correlates of African American spiritual traditions and of European and Native American contact.

James C. Garman is associate professor and chair of the Department of Cultural and Historic Preservation at Salve Regina University. His research interests include the material culture of death, social inequality, and the lives of merchants in eighteenth-century Newport, Rhode Island.

Christina J. Hodge is senior curatorial assistant at the Peabody Museum of Archaeology and Ethnology, Harvard University. She is an archaeologist specializing in historic New England and the British Atlantic.

Linda J. Hylkema, assistant campus archaeologist at Santa Clara University, manages the Archaeology Research Lab and functions as the university's cultural resource manager. She has twenty-four years of experience in California and the Great Basin, specializing in the Late Holocene period in the California Coastal Ranges, historic mining along the eastern Sierra Nevada and in Nevada, and the Spanish Colonial period in central California.

Melissa Johnson, who received a B.S. in anthropology and B.A. in history from Santa Clara University, is the projects assistant at Tremaine & Associates, Inc., a CRM firm in West Sacramento, California.

Elizabeth A. Jones is an adjunct faculty member in the Department of Anthropology and a research associate at the Research Laboratories of Archaeology, both at the University of North Carolina at Chapel Hill. Her research interests include nineteenth-century gender roles and family relations, with a focus on farming families and related land use, both in the United States and in Burgundy, France.

Laura Jones, director of Heritage Services and university archaeologist at Stanford University, oversees preservation and evaluation of several hundred archaeological sites and historic buildings on the Stanford campus. Her early work was in museum studies, particularly focused on women and traditional craft production in California and the South Pacific. Between 2002 and 2007 she was also senior scholar at the Carnegie Foundation for the Advancement of Teaching, located on the Stanford campus, where she coauthored *The Formation of Scholars: Doctoral Education for the Twenty-first Century* (2008).

Carrie Koster's research interests include the archaeology of one-room schoolhouses, historic farmsteads, and historic cemeteries. She was a member of the McHenry County Historic Preservation Commission from 2000 to 2005, serving as its chair in 2005.

Kenneth E. Lewis, professor emeritus of anthropology at Michigan State University, is author of *The American Frontier: An Archaeological Study of Settlement Pattern and Process; West to Far Michigan: Settling the Lower Peninsula, 1815-1860; Camden: Historical Archaeology in the South Carolina Backcountry;* and the forthcoming *The Backcountry Venture: Tradition, Capital, and Circumstance in the Rise of Camden and the Transition of the Wateree Valley.*

Diana D. Loren is associate curator at the Peabody Museum of Archaeology and Ethnology, Harvard University. She is a North American archaeologist specializing in the early historic Eastern Woodlands, particularly glass beads and other artifacts relating to dress.

Rochelle Lurie is president of Midwest Archaeological Research Services, Inc., and serves as principal investigator for most of its archaeological projects. Her areas of interest and expertise include Archaic and Mississippian subsistence and settlement patterns and lithic analysis. Although she was trained as a prehistoric archaeologist, three years of classwork in American history have made her particularly sensitive to the need for providing a solid historic context to aid in interpreting historic archaeological sites.

Michael F. Milewski senior archives assistant at Special Collections and University Archives, W.E.B. Du Bois Library, University of Massachusetts–Amherst. Since 1981 he has been collecting, preserving, and making available to the general public the history of the University of Massachusetts.

Michael S. Nassaney is professor of anthropology at Western Michigan University, Kalamazoo. His current research interests include colonialism, the fur trade, the materiality of identity, and archaeological pedagogy.

Jodie A. O'Gorman is associate professor of anthropology at Michigan State University, where she also serves as assistant curator for Great Lakes archaeology for the MSU Museum. Her primary research interests center on communities of the late precontact and early European contact periods in the midcontinent and public archaeology. O'Gorman's work with public archaeology and the departmental field school led to involvement in mid-nineteenth-century archaeology on the campus of MSU at the Saints' Rest Projects.

Donald Sadler is employed at Archaeological and Cultural Solutions, Inc., in Williamsburg, Virginia, as the field director of archaeology, specializing in seventeenth- and eighteenth-century historical sites.

Patricia M. Samford is director of the Maryland Archaeological Conservation Laboratory at Jefferson Patterson Park and Museum in St. Leonard, Maryland formerly a staff archaeologist for the Colonial Williamsburg Foundation. Her research interests are the archaeology of free and enslaved African Americans in the American South and eighteenth- and nineteenth-century ceramics.

Mark R. Schurr is associate professor and chair of the Department of Anthropology at the University of Notre Dame. His field research focuses on the archaeology of eastern North America, especially the Southeast and the Lower Great Lakes region. An important part of his fieldwork includes the application and development of geophysical survey techniques.

Lou Anna K. Simon became the first female president of Michigan State University in 2005. For a dozen years prior to her appointment as president she served as provost and vice president for academic affairs and formerly was a member of the MSU faculty and assistant director of the Office of Institutional Research.

Russell K. Skowronek, Associate Dean for the School of Interdisciplinary Programs and Community Engagement, College of Liberal Arts, is professor of anthropology and history, and the founding Director of the Community Historical Archaeology Project with Schools Program at the University of Texas Rio Grande Valley. Skowronek is co-author of *Ceramic Production in Early Hispanic California; Craft, Economy and Trade on the Frontier of New Spain;* and *HMS* Fowey *Lost and Found: Being the Discovery, Excavation, and Identification of a British Man-of-War Lost off the Cape of Florida in 1748;* and the co-editor of *Pieces of Eight: More Archaeology of Piracy,* and X *Marks the Spot: The Archaeology of Piracy.*

Stanley South, an internationally known historical archaeologist, is best known for his book *Method and Theory in Historical Archaeology* (1977). He has worked for four decades as a research professor at the University of South Carolina's Institute of Archaeology and Anthropology, during which time he published 240 articles and book chapters and more than a dozen books. He was awarded an honorary H.H.D. from the University of South Carolina in 1997 and received the Order of the Palmetto from the State of South Carolina and the Old North State Award from the State of North Carolina. His autobiography, *An Archaeological Evolution*, was published in 2005.

John D. Stubbs is a research associate of the Peabody Museum of Archaeology and Ethnology at Harvard University. A former curatorial associate at the Peabody and member of the Department of Anthropology, he is now a counselor and teacher at the Paideia School in Atlanta.

Michael A. Way is an alumnus of the University of California, Berkeley, where he received the 2007 Kroeber Prize for Outstanding Senior Honor Thesis in anthropology. He manages the Expedition program, an archaeology-based after-school collaboration between UC–Berkeley and Roosevelt Middle School in Oakland.

Laurie A. Wilkie is professor of anthropology and director of the Archaeological Research Facility at the University of California, Berkeley. She is the author of *Creating Freedom* (2000), *The Archaeology of Mothering* (2003), and *Sampling Many Pots* (UPF, 2005).

Index

Page numbers in *italics* indicate illustrations.

www.ingramcontent.com/pod-product-compliance
Lightning Source LLC
Chambersburg PA
CBHW020821270326
41928CB00006B/399

* 9 7 8 0 8 1 3 0 6 2 1 6 7 *